Pariahs, Partners, Predators:
German-Soviet Relations, 1922-1941

Pariahs, Partners, Predators:
German-Soviet Relations, 1922-1941

Aleksandr M. Nekrich

Edited and translated by Gregory L. Freeze

With a foreword by Adam B. Ulam

Columbia University Press
New York

Columbia University Press
Publishers Since 1893
New York   Chichester, West Sussex
Copyright (c) 1997 Columbia University Press
All rights reserved

Library of Congress Cataloging-in-Publication Data
Nekrich, A. M. (Aleksandr Moiseevich)
    Pariahs, partners, predators : German–Soviet relations, 1922–1941
/ Aleksandr M. Nekrich : translated by Gregory L. Freeze.
        p.   cm.
    Includes bibliographical references and index.
    ISBN 0–231–10676–9 (alk. paper)
    1. Germany—Foreign relations—Soviet Union. 2. Soviet Union—
Foreign relations—Germany. 3. e-gx r-ur.   I. Title.
DD120.S65N45   1997
327.43047'09'042—dc21   96–29605
                                                                    CIP

Casebound editions of Columbia University Press books are printed on
permanent and durable acid-free paper.

Printed in the United States of America

c 10 9 8 7 6 5 4 3 2 1

Contents

Foreword

Adam B. Ulam

Aleksandr Nekrich completed this book shortly before his death. A well-known historian in the Soviet Union, he incurred the Communist authorities' disapproval following the publication of his *June 22, 1941* (Moscow, 1965). The book illustrated vividly Stalin's culpability for the Soviet Union's unpreparedness for the German inaction, and hence his responsibility for the Red Army's catastrophic defeats during the first phase of the war. Generally accepted by historians in the West and, after the fall of Communism in Russia, Nekrich's thesis was taboo in Brezhnev's USSR.

Subjected to chicaneries by the regime, and virtually prohibited from publishing, the author emigrated to the United States in 1976. Shortly after his arrival here, he joined the staff of the Russian Research Center of Harvard University. In 1987 Nekrich was granted the rare distinction of being appointed a Senior Research Fellow of the University.

His scholarly activity in America was extensive and many sided. He wrote a great number of learned articles and several books. Two of the latter deserve special mention. *The Punished Peoples* (1981) was a dramatic description of Stalin's deportation of entire ethnic groups within the USSR on the pretext of their alleged collaboration with Germany during World War II. *Utopia in Power* (1986), written with Michel Heller, was a history of the Soviet Union, probably unparalleled in its grasp of the factors affecting the development of Soviet political culture. Both works were translated into several foreign languages and met with the critical acclaim of the scholarly community.

With perestroika and glasnost Nekrich's works could be read and were praised in his native country. As this is being written, a number of Russian historians are preparing a collection of essays which will be published as homage to their erstwhile colleague and friend. The present book occupied Nekrich's last years, and he thought of it as the culmination of his life's work. No doubt the reader may find some of the author's conclusions contentious. But no one, I believe, will question the writer's scrupulous and imaginative scholarship in dealing with a complex subject.

Stricken by a deadly ailment, a type of multiple sclerosis, Aleksandr Moiseyevich Nekrich died in Cambridge, Massachusetts on August 31, 1993.

Adam B. Ulam
Cambridge, Mass.
July 1996

Abbreviations

ADAP   *Akten zur deutschen auswärtigen Politik*
AVP   Arkiv vneshnei politiki Rossiiskoi Federatsii
DGFP   *Documents of German Foreign Policy*
FRUS   *Foreign Relations of the United States, Diplomatic Papers*
GARF   Gosudarstvennyi arkhiv Rossiiskoi Federatsii
GEFU   Gesellschaft für die Förderung gewerblichen
                Unternehmen
KRO   Kontr-razvedyvatel'nyi otdel (Counter-intelligence
                Division)
NKVD   People's Commissairate of International Affairs
OGPU (GPU)   United State Political Administration
RGAE   Rossiiskii gosudarstvennyi arkhiv ekonomiki
RGASA   Rossiiskii gosudarstvennyi arkhiv sovetskoi armii
RTsKhIDNI   Rossiiskii tsendr dlia khraneniia i izucheniia dokumen-
                tov noveishei istorii

Archival Notation

f.   fond (Collection)
op.   opis' (register)
d.   delo (file)
l., ll.   list, listy, (folio, folios)
ob.   oborot (verso)

Introduction

Geneiral interest in Soviet-German relations between the two world wars, while strong in the postwar period, sharply declined in the 1970s and 1980s. Of late, however, interest in this topic, and especially in the origins of the German attack on the USSR in 1941, has revived. Although the revival was partly evoked by the fiftieth anniversary of the attack, of greater importance was the movement for national independence in the Baltic states, which quite naturally took a keen interest in the secret clauses of the German-Soviet pacts that preceded their annexation by the USSR in 1940. The question of the authenticity of these documents even appeared on the agenda of the supreme legislative organs of the Soviet Union; it also became the subject of numerous books and articles, accompanied by a gush of documentary publications. This subject has long been treated, indeed quite exhaustively, in the West; only recently have the most fundamental sources become generally available to professional historians and a concerned public in the former USSR.

These new documents and analysis had a dramatic impact on the educated Russian public. As is well known, when Soviet historiography had to deal with ideologically sensitive problems, it either omitted essential facts or distorted them beyond recognition. It also dismissed foreign sources as either dubious or outright fabrications.

Nor was Soviet historiography any kinder to foreign historians, especially those who dared to criticize a particular Soviet policy or action; obedient Soviet historians castigated such works as bourgeois lies and their authors as mere agents of foreign intelligence services.[1] The regime was, of course, even less ceremonious in dealing with critical historians of its own—subjecting them to deportation (as in the 1920s), purge and liquidation (under Stalin), or censure, ostracism, and exile (after Stalin's death in 1953).

All this is especially pertinent to anything that has to do with World War II or its prehistory. The reason is quite simple: apart from the victorious war against Germany in 1941–1945, Soviet history had few glorious achievements. To impugn any part of this holy myth was tantamount to sacrilege. But a scholarly reconsideration of Stalinist mythology is essential if Russia is to achieve genuine reform; an objective knowledge about Russia's past is a precondition to a true understanding of its present. That is why a reexamination of Soviet history became a primary objective of reformers who laid the foundations for the perestroika that commenced in the mid-1980s.

The desire to reconsider Soviet history, however, is not entirely new, especially with respect to the subject of this book. Shortly after Stalin's death in 1953, amidst the "de-Stalinization" campaign of Nikita S. Khrushchev, some professional historians did offer some critical assessments of the "Great Fatherland War" of 1941–1945 and what preceded it. Indeed, by the late 1950s, this new critical historiography had begun to raise questions about Stalin's actions, although still very tentatively. Apart from a full abolition of the "cult of the personality," an important new incentive to this revisionism was the rehabilitation of Stalin's victims, especially the generals and officers of the Red Army. Only then were Soviet historians prepared to speak definitively and boldly.

It was precisely in this atmosphere that I succeeded in publishing *June 22, 1941*, a study of the prehistory of the German invasion. The book had a remarkable history of its own.[2] Published in 1965, the book quickly became a bestseller and the object of persecution by the new Brezhnev regime. It has since been translated into many foreign languages, including English. But the new "line" of the Brezhnev regime crudely and brutally blocked further research, at least of a scholarly quality. Instead, it demanded that Soviet historians pay homage to the old sanctities and deal harshly with those who did not. The "years of stagnation" not only undermined the economy but also historical research.

Thus it remained until perestroika. Initially at least, Gorbachev approached these historical questions with great circumspection. After all, he wanted to preserve the prestige of the Communist Party that had elevated him to the post of general-secretary. For Gorbachev and his ideologists, it was important to sustain some semblance of continuity in power, as well as the unity of people and party with respect to goals and actions. In this case, that meant re-affirmation of the idea that the party and people had, together, achieved "the liberation of the world from the fascist plague."[3] It was for this purpose that a new party journal, *Izvestiia TsK KPSS* [News of the Central Committee of the Communist Party of the Soviet Union], began to publish selections from documents in the archives of the party, the State Defense Committee, and files of prominent figures like Stalin and Molotov. However, these publica-tions really sought only to answer two questions: (1) whether Soviet leaders knew about German plans for an attack; and, (2) whether the country, party, and army were prepared to repulse the Germans.[4] But the first question (about the Kremlin's knowledge) had been definitively resolved long ago—in the late 1950s and early 1960s, when historical journals and memoir literature provided massive and incontrovertible proof that Stalin and his cohorts had received timely and reliable information about the impending attack.[5] The new documents add nothing to this picture.

As to the second question (regarding the Soviet Union's military preparedness), however, the new documents do significantly supple-ment our earlier knowledge. It required, however, so momentous a change as the overthrow of communist rule and liquidation of the Communist Party before access could be granted and serious histori-cal inquiry made possible. The new archival authorities (renamed Roskomarkhiv, Russian Committee on Archives) liberalized and standardized rules for access and utilization of archival materials. Historians have since been able to reconsider the question of inter-war policy and war preparedness, and the archives have launched their own publications—such as the new journal, *Istoricheskii arkhiv.*

The fall of communism and opening of the archives did not, of course, automatically put an end to controversies: Soviet-German relations between the wars is still the subject of ideological debate. That was especially evident during the Soviet parliamentary debates

of 1989–1990, when the deputies turned from contemporary questions to the issue of a secret Soviet-German agreement and how
that should be assessed. It was indeed not until 1993 that Russia officially published the secret agreements of 1939, the very existence of
which had previously—at all levels of the state, at all stages in its
postwar history—been passionately denied.

The publication of Viktor Suvorov's book *Icebreaker* in 1990
ignited a debate entirely new in the Soviet Union, even if long discussed in the West: was the Soviet Union planning a preemptive
strike against Germany?[6] That accusation, admittedly, derives from
a highly dubious source—Adolf Hitler, who cited this intention as
justification for his invasion of the USSR on June 22, 1941. Although these revelations are far from complete, they have encouraged me to return to a subject that has long been my main interest,
and that I can now illuminate with the help of these new materials.
In addition to the newly released materials in the Russian Federation, I have drawn upon archival sources around the world—especially in Germany (Freiburg, Koblenz, Bonn)—and of course the
complex of printed sources at our disposal.

Cambridge, Massachusetts
May 1993

Pariahs, Partners, Predators:
German-Soviet Relations, 1922-1941

I

Revanchists and Revolutionaries

This chapter will examine the first phase of German and Soviet collaboration, from the Rapallo Treaty to the German decision in 1932–33 to end the military cooperation. It demonstrates the mutual interests and mutual suspicions that made partners of the two pariahs, while creating tensions and difficulties. Although the military cooperation had a clear advantage for the German side, enabling the Weimar Republic to flout the Versailles Treaty limits on its military armaments, it is also important to see what the cooperation yielded the Soviet partner. Attention will also be given to the domestic implications of the cooperation, especially the problem of ethnic Germans and the role of the Soviet secret police in monitoring the presence of German officers, businessmen, and industrialists.

Early Collaboration

The November Revolution of 1918 in Germany—together with a series of subsequent events in Germany and Soviet Russia—paved the way for the two powers to cooperate throughout the entire "interwar" era, defined here as not only the period of the Weimar Republic (1918–1933), but also that of Adolf Hitler's Third Reich up to the invasion of the USSR (1933–1941). These relations, to be

sure, developed under extremely complex—and contradictory—circumstances. On the one hand, the Soviet Union was repeatedly trying to realize its doctrine of world revolution (leading to recurrent
attempts to exploit the relatively radical attitude of the working
class, sometimes to its own advantage). At the same time, it was collaborating with the very state the workers were seeking to topple, for
Moscow also was pursuing a policy of military cooperation and support for those elements in German society opposed to the Versailles
Treaty. Soviet relations also developed under the strong influence
of the Polish question: the status and territorial shape of Poland
remained a central issue for both the USSR and interwar Germany.

German and Soviet military leaders had already established direct
contact in 1920, during the Polish-Soviet War. Curiously, one key
mediator was Enver Pasha.[1] On August 26, 1920 Pasha sent a letter
to General Hans von Seeckt, who was then head of the land forces of
the Reichswehr.[2] Indeed, in 1920 Pasha came to Russia owing to the
initiative of Seeckt as well as the active support of the future German military attaché in Moscow, Ernst Köstring.[3] According to
Pasha, the Soviets proposed that the Germans supply intelligence
about the Polish army and also sell military weapons, thereby easing
the plight of the Red Army on the Polish front. But the proposal was
fraught with such great risk and unforeseeable consequences that
Seeckt declined to make a commitment.[4] Nevertheless, he judged
Poland a potential adversary and therefore endeavored to strengthen
ties to Moscow as the natural and—conceivably—only ally against
the Poles. Seeckt shared completely the views of Count von der
Holz, who had predicted in 1919 that the Bolsheviks would lose a
war against the Poles.[5] The reverses in the Soviet-Polish War, in
fact, only reinforced the likelihood that Russia would seek collaboration with Germany against a common adversary.

Initial contacts, however, were also made on a semi-official government level. Thus the RSFSR opened two offices to represent its
interests before official German authorities—one in Revel (Tallin),
the other in Berlin.[6] At the latter site Viktor Kopp, an extremely
talented Soviet diplomat, established his office on Unter den Lin-
den, No. 11.[7] The "cover" for this operation was the ostensible
function of representing the RSFSR on the question of prisoners-of-
war (Soviet military personnel interned by the Germans during the
Red Army's retreat from Poland). However, Kopp's task was to
secure the return not only of the military people but also civilians.

Finally, Kopp was also to seek ways to achieve a general improvement in relations with Germany in political, diplomatic, economic, military, and other spheres.

The Germans' attitude was quite reserved, however. The idea of "an Eastern orientation" (i.e., banking on a policy that aimed to cultivate close ties with Soviet Russia) had been quite strong during the Red Army's initial success on the Polish front. But, as Kopp informed Georgii V. Chicherin (the People's Commissar for Foreign Affairs), German interest "greatly receded after the Red Army's reverses on the Polish front and the opening of peace negotiations with Poland."[8] According to Kopp, right-wing nationalist circles in Germany had originally linked the "eastern orientation" with "dreams of military alliance with Russia against France," but now perceive nothing but "retreat along the entire front." They are now swearing off "national bolshevism" like the "very devil himself."[9] Kopp reported that "bourgeois-democratic circles" show a tendency to cooperate with England as the surest means to resist French pressure. And there were even some positive signs of a new relationship between Germany and France. Under these complex political and psychological conditions, Germany's hostility toward Poland constituted a major obstacle to cooperation with the victors.

German policy toward the new Soviet regime therefore remained highly contradictory. Germany ignored the French decision to grant diplomatic recognition to P. N. Wrangel's white forces as the legitimate government of Russia, instead according de facto recognition to the Bolshevik government in Moscow as the existing authority in Russia. It declined, however, to grant formal diplomatic recognition. The resumption of normal relations was impossible for a whole series of reasons: the subversive activities of the Comintern on German territory, outstanding problems connected with the 1918 murder of the German ambassador Wilhelm von Mirbach, and—most important—the Politburo's "categorical rejection of any kind of compromise." Kopp emphasized that German public opinion firmly rejected the Soviet posture on von Mirbach, and that even Soviet officials assigned to work on German relations found it an unnecessary obstacle to the normalization of bilateral relations. The latter included Maksim M. Litvinov and an official in the Cheka identified as Brodovskii).[10] Amidst the Soviet-Polish War, Germany did take some measures to assist Moscow against its foes, impounding vessels in the Kiel Canal found to be laden with military arms and bound for

Poland.[11] In September 1920 Kopp wrote that the chances of Germany siding with Poland were remote, mainly because of the intense hostility toward Poles among Germans close to the Polish border. He noted further that the Germans praised the "model behavior" of Red Army units in the Corridor. Whereas "petty-bourgeois circles" are gripped by a "panicky fear" of Bolshevism, the population in Germany's eastern areas believe that "better Bolsheviks than Poles!"[12] Kopp warned that in the event of a second invasion of the corridor, it would be dangerous to change the policy of respecting the rights of Germans. The warning proved superfluous, however, since the Soviet Union had already lost the war and had no prospect of a further intrusion in the area.

Kopp's letter to Chicherin admonished Moscow not to imagine a scenario whereby "revolutionary workers" would seize power in Germany. Rather, he insisted, it was essential to maintain friendly relations with the existing government in Berlin and to avoid repeating the Brest episode. In Kopp's view, fallacious analogies with Brest caused Chicherin to fear good relations with the German government on the grounds that it might alienate the German workers.[13] Moscow was indeed still laboring under the impression created by the bold action of German workers in quelling the Kapp Putsch in 1920 and by their role in the uprising in central Germany in March 1921. The situation was no longer the same; according to Kopp, the workers would now regard the resumption of diplomatic relations between Soviet Russia and Germany as a victory, not as "our renunciation" of the revolutionary path. Kopp therefore urged Moscow to follow a practical, businesslike policy. This meant that Moscow must put a prompt end to the Mirbach affair (essential if diplomatic relations were to be resumed) and establish a communications line across Lithuania before spring (so that bad weather would not impede the delivery of military and other manufactured goods from Germany).[14]

Kopp warned that statements by leading officials in the Comintern also had an extremely harmful effect on Soviet-German relations. Thus in November 1920 Kopp complained of a sharp deterioration in relations with Germany for two to three weeks after the "Party Congress" in Halle, where G. Zinoviev and A. Lozovskii had made inflammatory statements.[15] As a result, he warned, the majority now favored a complete severance of ties with the Soviet Union. Thus the "few people" with whom Kopp had contacts in the

German Foreign Ministry (including the chief adviser on Russian affairs, Malzan) had no influence over policymaking.[16] But in the autumn of 1920 Moscow still hoped that the German working class would come to the aid of revolutionary Russia and therefore take steps to resolve the Mirbach matter. Although Kopp tried to settle current issues, he constantly found himself confronted by new problems. One was Moscow's visa policy: at the very time Moscow categorically denied entry visas to German specialists, Berlin was being inundated by representatives from various Soviet agencies. As Kopp pointed out to Chicherin, "the disproportion is becoming quite obvious."[17] Equally offensive to the Germans were recurrent episodes where Soviet officials attempted to deceive German authorities; evidently, their old underground habits now shaped the "new" habits of the Comintern. One embarrassing incident involved a diplomatic courier named Leandrov, who attempted to enter Germany from Revel using a falsified Austrian passport, even though there was no need for the deception. Kopp insisted that Soviet officials observe international norms.[18]

At the same time, Kopp did what he could to influence German opinion, warning that a deterioration in relations might cause the Soviet Union to cancel orders from German firms. Indeed, many German leaders regarded Soviet Russia as potentially an important market for their country's manufactured goods and also as a source of badly needed raw materials. Kopp also favored strong economic relations and urged Moscow to strengthen its financial ties to Germany.[19] That objective also impelled him to propose that the intermediate commercial center in Tallin be closed, not only because it was economically disadvantageous, but also because it obstructed the development of normal economic relations with Germany.[20] Two powerful German groups—Stinnes and Krupp—were particularly active in seeking to participate in the restoration and development of the economy in Soviet Russia. The competition between the two firms also had an effect on the position of high-ranking Soviet officials. According to Kopp, Stinnes enjoyed the support of Boris S. Stomoniakov,[21] who in turn had the backing of Leonid B. Krasin.[22] Kopp, however, supported the Krupp concern, which in fact did eventually establish very close economic ties with Soviet Russia.[23]

Under the cover of a commercial agreement signed in May 1921, the two sides also initiated contacts in the military-industrial sphere.

The exchange of war prisoners also provided a propitious opportunity for these new contacts. German naval transports were used for the exchange, and a captain in the German navy negotiated an agreement on the reconstruction of port facilities in Petrograd.[24] But that was the extent of cooperation in naval matters, for the Russians simply had nothing of interest for the German side. Only in 1939, after naval engagements at sea left the Germans in need of a base for refueling and repairs, did the German navy renew its interest in cooperation with the Soviet side.[25]

The two countries had far stronger mutual interests in the sphere of military industry. For its part, Russia wanted technical assistance to reconstruct and to develop its industry, especially those branches capable of producing military goods. Germany needed a secret and secure location where it could prepare to rearm itself and thus circumvent the prohibitions mandated by the Versailles Treaty. Specifically, the Soviet Union offered a place to manufacture military goods like artillery shells and grenades that the treaty had specifically banned.

It was Viktor Kopp's secret mission to establish military contacts with Germany and to arrange cooperation in military production. Acting on Moscow's instructions, he maintained secret ties with the Reichswehr and personally with General von Seeckt, Captain Niedermayer, and others. In a letter of December 1920 Kopp complained to Chicherin that his ties with von Seeckt had become known to high German circles, provoking "considerable consternation" among certain high-ranking officials in the German government. Kopp suspected that the secret had been leaked in Moscow or perhaps that his telegram code had been broken. He asked that all future correspondence refer to von Seeckt as "Siebert" and von Niedermayer as "Naiman."[26]

In March 1921 Kopp informed Moscow of a marked improvement in the German government's attitude toward Soviet Russia. For the latter, it was vital that the Entente not be able to use Germany as a weapon against Russia. The first test came during the Kronstadt rebellion: the German government demonstrated its good faith by staying completely out of the affair. Meanwhile, the relations with Krupp and other German firms continued to develop quite satisfactorily. Then Parvus—whom the Bolsheviks derided as a renegade Social Democrat—appeared on the scene. In the name of a consortium of textile-factory owners in Saxony, Parvus proposed a broad plan to organize barter with Russian villages and to provide Petrograd with cheap German coal. Kopp endorsed the proposal. The Reichswehr, for its part, wanted to establish military installations on Soviet territory to train personnel and test equipment in three key areas: military aviation, tanks, and the production of poison gases. The idea of military collaboration with the Bolsheviks not only obtained the approval of General von Seeckt (the intellectual and, at one point, formal head of the Reichswehr), but also led to rather prompt bureaucratic realization—in the form of the "Fischer Group," which was formed in early 1921.

The culmination came the following year: the two sides signed the Rapallo Treaty in April 1922. The agreement formally established diplomatic relations, thus helping both sides to break out of their diplomatic isolation. For its part, Russia opened wide its doors for German manufactured goods in exchange for raw materials and agricultural products.

To be sure, military collaboration with an imperialist state, even a defeated one, was somewhat contradictory to the orthodox principles of the Bolsheviks, but that did not cause much discomfort. Certainly Trotsky (chief advocate of the theory of world revolution) and Lenin (its actual leader) were untroubled.[27] Indeed, the Bolsheviks—including Lenin—were anything but overscrupulous even when they were dealing with Imperial Germany.[28] The Soviets later regarded Germany as a possible ally in the event of conflict with the Entente.

The Soviet military command, in contrast to its German counterpart, did not show any independent initiative in its relations with Germany. On the Soviet side all the decisions were taken by Lenin and, after he fell ill, by the Politburo. Similarly, in Germany negotiations on military ties with Russia could not be resolved solely by the Reichswehr; in the final analysis they were decided by President Friedrich Ebert[29] and Chancellor Karl Wirth,[30] later by other official leaders of the government. For example, Chancellor Wirth formally gave his approval for a meeting between General von Seeckt and Karl Radek (in Berlin in February 1922).[31]

The behavior of the Soviet side reflected, indeed markedly so, the ideology and often quite surrealistic imagination of its leadership, which was still capable of believing that a socialist revolution in Germany was imminent. The abortive communist uprising in 1923, however, temporarily put an end to such fantasies, although such notions still percolated among functionaries of the Comintern, including its chief expert in German affairs, Karl Radek. The latter, incidentally, had aroused the suspicion of Feliks Dzerzhinskii (head of the Cheka).Dzerzhinskii thought Radek might have leaked information about the situation in the Soviet leadership to the German embassy.[32]

Negotiations in 1921–1923

Lenin's primary strategic goal was to break out of diplomatic isolation, and he therefore approved the military negotiations with the Germans. Following Kopp's report from Berlin, the exchange of delegations was continued in Moscow. The Soviet side, at various times, was represented by L. Krasin (People's Commissar of Foreign Trade), Kopp, and Pavel Lebedev (chief of staff of the Red Army); the Germans sent Major (later Colonel) Oskar Ritter von Niedermayer (the "Naiman" in Kopp's talks in Berlin) and Colonel (later General) von Hasse. Although not officially a participant, General von Seeckt would play a significant behind-the-scenes role in the negotiations.

In 1922 Count Ulrich Brockdorf-Rantzau was appointed to serve as the German ambassador in Moscow. In 1917 he had been Germany's envoy to Copenhagen, where he assisted in arranging Lenin's return to Russia. According to his personal assistant for Russian affairs, Andor Hencke (later a high-ranking official in the Ministry of Foreign Affairs), Brockdorf-Rantzau had assisted in the repatriation of the Bolsheviks not because he sympathized with communism, but because he "hoped to shatter the enemy coalition by promoting the revolutionary movement in Russia."[33] Brockdorf-Rantzau, who had been a member of the German delegation at the Paris Peace Conference, took a position that General von Seeckt thoroughly detested. The importance of the ambassador's role in Moscow was reflected in the fact that Brockdorf-Rantzau was in direct communication with Chancellor Wirth and could also write personally to President Ebert. The ambassador summarized his program in a memorandum on Russian policy, dated July 8, 1922. It argued that the principal objective should not be to create a German-Russian coalition against the victorious powers, but to seek together ways to escape from their current status as international pariahs.[34]

As we shall see, the differences between General von Seeckt and Brockdorf-Rantzau were eventually resolved, and the Germans then posted a military delegation to Moscow. Headed by General von Hasse, the delegation included Major Fritz Tschunke (a former adjutant under Seeckt), Captain Fischer (also a Seeckt adjutant), and also a representative of German industrial circles. The conversations with Hasse in Moscow in 1922 were conducted under conditions of the utmost secrecy. The members of the German delegation came under pseudonyms and stayed in a state residency for special guests, not in an ordinary hotel.[35] The discussions focused on German assistance for providing the Red Army with modern arms. For the Germans, such cooperation would provide the opportunity to evade the Versailles Treaty's limits on German armaments,[36] to conduct secret tests of the new weapons on Soviet soil, and to open facilities to train new officers. The two sides also discussed the possibility of sending Soviet officers to study in German military schools. Finally, the negotiations also considered the possibility of preparing joint strategies in the event of war with Poland.

The Polish question became a prominent element in negotiations between the two sides. Thus, when Radek came to Berlin in February 1922 to hold talks with a Seeckt aide, they discussed military cooperation between the two general staffs in general and the Polish issue in particular. Radek, who asked if Germany was prepared to support Russia in the event of a resumption of hostilities against Poland, had no trouble finding sympathetic ears in high circles, including Chancellor Wirth.[37] On the eve of the Rapallo Treaty, Wirth sought to have it include a special military agreement. The chancellor, who favored the liquidation of Poland, was in full agreement with General von Seeckt on this point. The general's view was no less unequivocal: "Poland's existence is intolerable and incompatible with the survival of Germany. It must disappear; and it shall disappear—through its own internal weakness and through Russia, with our assistance."[38] Seeckt assumed that Poland's existence was even more intolerable for Russia than for Germany.[39]

But there were also some significant obstacles to military cooperation between the two governments. One was the vested interests of different state agencies. On the Soviet side, it required the Politburo to resolve such differences—most notably, between the GPU (successor to the Cheka)[40] and the People's Commissariat for Foreign Affairs—sometimes after heated debate. Whereas the latter

looked favorably upon diverse ties with Germany, the GPU and its
successors, as we shall see, regarded the operation with the deepest
skepticism and distrust.

There were problems on the German side as well. Although the
Reichswehr was extremely influential and united on this issue, it had
to deal with opposition from some civilian quarters. Thus, although
Chancellor Wirth favored cooperation with the Soviet Union, President Ebert was firmly opposed. The German ambassador in Moscow,
Brokdorf-Rantzau, shared Ebert's view and in principle was against
permitting the German military to act autonomously and make their
own policy in Soviet Russia. His goal was quite different: collaboration with Russia should serve to strengthen Germany's position with
respect to the West, especially France. The ambassador therefore
attached the greatest importance to political and economic ties and
feared any intervention of the military in foreign affairs. Rantzau was
especially irritated that Hasse had given his Russian partners a written memorandum of intent, without receiving a similar document in
return. It bears noting that his vexation preceded Hasse's arrival, for
Rantzau and Seeckt had a long-standing enmity. Their sharp difference of opinion about priorities in German political and economic
interests dated back to the Versailles Peace Treaty, when Seeckt infu-
riated Rantzau with accusations that the latter had sacrificed the
honor of the German nation. Relations became so strained that
Rantzau informed the chancellor of his intention to resign from his
post in Moscow. It required the personal intervention of President
Ebert to bring the two together and to reconcile their differences. As
a result, the Reichswehr renounced any claim to conduct its own
policy in Moscow and agreed to consult the ambassador, who could
count on Ebert's opposition to a military agreement.

Despite the reconciliation, relations between Rantzau and von
Seeckt remained tense. Hence Rantzau urgently requested that
Chicherin arrange a meeting with Trotsky as head of the military
commissariat[41] so that he could form his own impression on just how
seriously the Russian side considered the establishment of military
cooperation. On the basis of Rantzau's comments, Hencke claims
that Chicherin did not want to set a precedent by establishing direct
contacts between the German ambassador and a member of the
Politburo (and head of the Soviet military); he wanted all such contacts to go through his own commissariat, as the ministry responsible

for all foreign relations. The importunate Rantzau insisted, however, and eventually had his way: Chicherin arranged a meeting between Trotsky and the ambassador at the latter's official residence (with Trotsky taking special precautions to assure secrecy). Rantzau then heard directly from a Politburo member himself that the Soviet leadership did indeed want long-term military cooperation with Germany.[42] It was all the more important to hear this come from the lips of the very same man who had been the chief ideologue for "world revolution." For his part, Rantzau made no attempt to conceal his own view that priority should be given instead to developing political and economic relations.

The words were, in fact, soon becoming deeds. When Arkadii Rozengol'ts (a member of the Revolutionary Military Council) was sent to Berlin on a return visit in the summer of 1923, he attempted to obtain a subsidy of 50 million gold marks to assist in the construction of military industrial plants.[43] The new chancellor, Wilhelm Cuno, managed to persuade his colleagues to give the requested assistance, notwithstanding the difficulties in Germany's financial situation. In return the Soviet side agreed to military cooperation, namely: to open a German school for pilot training on Soviet territory, to provide a testing and training site for tanks, and to cooperate on the development and testing of poison gases. Soviet officers were given the opportunity to study at the military academy of the German general staff and to participate in military exercises.

As for the preparation of joint strategic plans in the event of war with Poland, Hencke claims that this issue was not given serious consideration—either at this time or later.[44] Indeed, in 1923 the prospects of war with Poland had become quite remote. Furthermore, in the wake of the collapse of passive resistance to France in the Ruhr, Germany was simply in no condition to participate in joint military action against Poland. Hencke cites the following remark by Karl Radek about the Polish issue: "For a mere measly 50 million marks we were not about to take on such far-reaching and dangerous obligations."[45] Moreover, Radek—in accordance with Comintern policy—was far more interested in exploiting social tensions in Germany, even to the point of fomenting armed insurrection. The Soviet military attaché, in fact, became personally embroiled by giving arms and money to his German comrades. The arms were even stored in the buildings of the Soviet diplomatic mission. Moscow made a flaccid attempt to dissociate itself from the affair; Trotsky, who had issued inflammatory statements in support of a communist uprising in Germany, publicly announced that his remarks represented only his personal opinion, not the official views of the Soviet government.

Although the uprising was a failure, it taught the Germans a lesson: the new government, with Gustav Stresemann as foreign minister, reoriented its focus from the Soviet Union to the West. The result was the Locarno Pact, signed on December 1, 1925, which guaranteed German borders in the West and demilitarized the Rhineland. Significantly, the Locarno Pact did not guarantee Germany's eastern borders; the Soviet Union consequently regarded this agreement as a transparent attempt by the Western powers to divert German expansion eastward, i.e., against the USSR.[46]

Even before the Locarno Pact had been signed, however, Germany warned Moscow that good relations between the two countries would be possible only if the Soviet side ceased meddling in Germany's internal affairs and stopped fomenting unrest through various communist organizations. If this condition were not met, warned Germany, military cooperation was out of the question. The Germans also demanded the immediate recall of the military attaché implicated in the earlier incident. When Rantzau informed Chicherin of this decision, he also left no doubt that he would resign as ambassador if he did not receive a satisfactory answer. Chicherin responded to these demands at the Trotsky-Rantzau meeting. Replying to the reprimand about "incendiary" speeches (which Rantzau deemed incompatible with the existing relations between the Soviet and German armies and as a source of particular alarm in Germany), Trotsky declared:

> What do you want? If Stresemann himself declares in the Reichstag that his cabinet is the last bourgeois government in Germany, we communists must draw the conclusion that the mass of the German people want a change of systems. If the bourgeois regime proves itself sufficiently strong to remain at the rudder, I would gladly want to work together with it.[47]

As a result of the conversations in Berlin and Moscow, the Soviet Union and Germany commenced a military collaboration that would last until 1934, one year after Hitler's accession to power.

Military Cooperation and the OGPU

The German organization responsible for the cooperation with Soviet Russia was known under the acronym of GEFU—die Gesellschaft zur Förderung gewerblicher Unternehmungen (Society for the Advancement of Commercial Enterprises). This organization evoked considerable distrust and skepticism from the OGPU, the Soviet secret police. According to a report from its Counter-intelligence Office (*Kontrrazvedyvatel'nyi otdel*, or KRO), GEFU functions as "a special military and military-industrial group to handle for Germany large-scale military orders in Russia, while simultaneously reconstructing the military industry of the USSR."[48] This organization represented the interests of the German military administration and the Reichswehr. Its head was Major Tschunke—the former adjutant of the Reichswehr's head, General Seeckt. Formally, Tschunke was responsible for coordinating the activities and interests of various German representatives and organizations in Moscow. However, on the basis of the interception of German correspondence,[49] the KRO concluded that GEFU also engaged in espionage and provided Berlin with concrete information about military and political conditions in Soviet Russia.[50] According to the OGPU, German engineers who worked at Soviet plants under the agreement for military cooperation filed very detailed reports about the condition of the plants and the specific sections where they worked.[51] In addition, the OGPU accused the Germans of sending to Berlin sketches, blueprints, and other documents.

Among the various German concerns holding a concession in the USSR, an enterprise called "Mologoles" deserves particular attention. It had the contract to finish construction of the Mga–Rybinsk railway line and to exploit the adjacent forests. According to the Economic Office of the OGPU, investors in the concession included the former chancellor, Wirth, and also a leader of the Democratic Party (Dr. Hugo Haase). The Stinnes firm also participated in the enterprise. The OGPU drew a horrifying picture of the concession, which allegedly failed to fulfill its obligations, bribed local authorities, and exploited "the workers and peasants." Our own people warned the OGPU, were redirecting their dissatisfaction from foreign concern to the Soviet state. The OGPU also drew an unflattering portrait of Soviet citizens who had participated in negotiations with the concession and subsequently went to work for the Germans. The OGPU accused them of concealing the fact that the concession was taking "valuable sections of forest suitable for aviation—almost the only such in the Soviet Union." The OGPU further claimed that the Germans, not satisfied with exploiting the concession, had accepted orders for timber from Soviet enterprises and expanded its operations to the Ukraine and North Caucasus. However, the OGPU refrained from drawing any general conclusions, admitting that it did not have information about the political ramifications in terms of foreign policy.[52]

After Rapallo

During the two years that followed the Rapallo agreement the Soviet Union improved its international status, with formal diplomatic recognition accorded by all the major Western states (with the exception of the United States). Nevertheless, the USSR continued to have its closest ties with Germany and assiduously implemented the agreement for military cooperation. The Reichswehr created a special unit—"Sondergruppe R"—in charge of its relations with Soviet Russia. Special inspectorates of the General Staff also prepared the plans to open its three military sites in Russia: the school for military pilots in Lipetsk (designed by the Inspectorate for Aviation), the test site for poison gases at Vol'sk-Tomka (prepared by the Artillery Inspectorate), and the tank school and military camp in Kazan' (under the responsibility of the Transport Inspectorate).[53]

In November 1923 the Reichswehr sent Colonel von der Lieth-Thomsen (a famous aviator in World War I) to Moscow. He subsequently became a key figure, if not the dominant spirit, in the German air force. At this point, his main objective was of course to circumvent the Versailles Treaty, which specifically prohibited Germany from having an air force at all. His initial task in Moscow was to establish a secret military administration, which he himself was to head. He was assisted by Major Oskar von Niedermayer, who later succeeded Lieth-Thomsen as the head of the organization.[54] Called the "Moscow Center" (Zentrale Moskau, abbreviated "Z.Mo."), the unit administered all three German military operations in the USSR. Niedermayer, because of his position, also maintained contacts with the command of the Red Army and with the OGPU.[55] This military administration also worked closely with the

German ambassador, Brockdorf-Rantzau. In effect, Lieth-Thomsen served as Germany's military attaché, although the position was not formally reestablished until early 1933.[56]

But military cooperation was only one dimension of German-Soviet relations at the time. Others included Moscow's attempt to recruit German specialists to come and work in Soviet industry. Given the desperate economic situation in Germany itself, German specialists could be hired for quite modest sums. A report by Dzerzhinskii on the prospects of attracting German specialists, discussed at a Politburo meeting of August 9, 1923, clearly encouraged the employment of German specialists. Moreover, the Politburo sought to expand substantially its foreign trade. Specifically, the Politburo annulled an earlier decision to reduce imports by 30 to 40 million rubles and specifically resolved to increase imports in the military industrial sector (for raw materials and equipment needed for military purposes). Point 4 of its resolution acknowledged the need to obtain "imports from Germany," and another article prohibited the export of goods that would increase the military potential of countries that might act against the USSR. The latter article referred implicitly to England, France, and Poland. The Politburo's decision, it should be noted, was taken at a time when the Soviet Union still considered a German revolution as a real possibility.[57]

Nevertheless, there was also some skepticism on the Soviet side about the utility of military cooperation for the USSR itself. That attitude pervaded a letter from Iosif Unshlikht (deputy chairman of the Revolutionary-Military Council), who oversaw Soviet-German military relations, and wrote to Stalin at the end of December in 1926. He argued that the main idea of cooperation was to exploit foreign capital in order to raise the Soviet "defense capabilities" (in party jargon equivalent to military potential, offensive as well as defensive). As far as the Germans were concerned, their main objective was "to have a completely secret base for illegal armaments."[58] In general, Unshlikht was pessimistic about the prospects for military cooperation. He proposed that, in the future, the Soviet objective be to master the Germans' tactical and operational experience in World War I as well as the technical and tactical innovations developed by the Reichswehr. But Unshlikht's position was a minority viewpoint, especially the following year, amidst the famous "war scare" of 1927, which reaffirmed the importance of the German ties in the face of a presumed attack by the Western powers.

Soviet military intelligence, in particular, stressed the need to avert "an irreversible switch" of Germany to the enemy camp and the resolution of territorial issues between Germany and Poland.[59] Two years later Soviet military intelligence was still of the opinion that the cooperation with Germany must be continued.[60] However, military cooperation was also endangered by public revelations in the West.[61] Shortly after von Seeckt's retirement in September 1926, Social-Democratic members of the Reichstag demanded an investigation of the relations between the Reichswehr and paramilitary nationalist organizations. In the course of the heated debates it was revealed that the Reichswehr had received deliveries of 300,000 shells that had been manufactured in the USSR. On December 3, 1926 *The Manchester Guardian*, a liberal English newspaper, published an exposé that not only confirmed the delivery of shells, but also disclosed the secret cooperation between the Reichswehr and the Red Army.[62] The organ of the German Social Democrats, *Vorwärts*, reprinted the article in German. As a result, the Reichswehr and the German concerns that had participated in the clandestine operation were subjected to intense criticism in the Reichstag by a prominent Social-Democrat, Philipp Scheidemann. In retribution the Soviet press routinely referred to Scheidemann as "Social-Traitor" and "Social-Fascist." Nikolai Krestinskii, chief of the Soviet diplomatic mission in Berlin, met with Gustav Stresemann in early 1927, informed him of Moscow's deep concern over the revelations, and requested that the German government deny the reports. Stresemann, however, was reluctant to comply.

In any event, the incident impelled both sides to discuss the prospects for Soviet-German military cooperation. From the Reichswehr's point of view, the cooperation with Soviet Russia offered unique opportunities—for example, the testing and production of poison gases, or the construction and testing of Junkers. Their development in the Soviet Union could form the basis for an accelerated expansion and development in Germany itself. Nevertheless, it was essential to avoid any complications in relations with England and France over this matter. After all, the essence of Stresemann's foreign policy was to remove obstacles to restoring Germany's role in Europe through an orientation toward the West. For example, negotiations to give the Soviet Union credits were held up because of Germany's appeal in Geneva to alleviate the burden of reparations. Berlin believed that to offer credits to the Soviet Union

"can seriously injure Germany's position in the impending, final
regulation of the reparations question."[63]

The intensity of German-Soviet economic ties is reflected in the
constant increase in the size of the staff at the Soviet trade mission
in Berlin. Thus in 1930 a resolution of the Politburo increased the
staff by one hundred persons. Just the previous May, there had been
yet another downturn in Soviet-German relations, provoked when
high-ranking Soviet officials had voiced support for the German
Communist Party, as well as for demonstrations and counter-demon-
strations in Berlin, Moscow, and Leningrad. But now the Soviet
government, which was seeking to make a radical transformation of
its whole economy, was desperately eager to obtain sizeable credits
and technical assistance from Germany. That is why it now assumed
such a conciliatory position. B. Stomoniakov, the official at the
commissariat of foreign affairs responsible for Germany, tried to persuade Herbert von Dirksen that "given such a great difference in our
political and economic systems a certain number of conflicts, incidents and disputes between the two states are absolutely unavoidable." But the point was not to exaggerate the significance of such
problems: "One must maintain a certain philosophical equanimity
with respect to these things, which are an inescapable part of
Soviet-German friendship. . . . We must not allow ourselves to go
astray and lose perspective."[64]

The Soviet fears of losing the military cooperation were not well-
grounded: the German side, including President Paul von Hindenburg, remained deeply committed to the collaboration at least until
Hitler's accession to power. When Köstring was appointed in 1931
to represent the Reichswehr in its ties with the Red Army (the post
of military attaché would not be established until two years later),
Hindenburg gave him the following instruction: "Maintain good
relations with the Red Army!" Hindenburg then added that "I
would like to give it to the Poles, but the time has not yet come
for that."[65]

The military collaboration between Germany and the Soviet
Union took sundry forms, but despite claims to the contrary officers
of the Reichswehr did not directly participate in the training of Red
Army military personnel. Nor did officers of the Red Army train
soldiers of the Reichswehr. Köstring categorically denies such
claims, which were widespread at the time.[66] Nevertheless, the
Soviet side was keenly interested in learning from the Reichswehr

and having its critical assessment of the condition of the Red Army. Köstring, for example, received many invitations to visit Soviet military units and noted a striking reluctance to take decisions for fear of responsibility.[67]

Petr Ivanovich Baranov, who headed the Soviet air force from 1924 to 1931, was particularly enthusiastic about collaborating with German aviation. He had two main organizations in mind: the training school for military pilots in Lipetsk (Voronezh oblast) and the plant for the production of Junkers in Fili (in the environs of Moscow). Baranov periodically—and with great pleasure—visited the school for German military pilots in Lipetsk. Ordinarily, his visits were timed to coincide with the end of the course and testing of the pilots. The school made careful preparations for Baranov's arrival, with a full and elaborate program, prepared with the participation of the Soviet liaison, an officer permanently assigned to Lipetsk. The latter, however, proved a rather proud man and given to quarreling with the head of the German school; it fell to Baranov to smooth over their relations.[68] Baranov would arrive by train, accompanied by several high-ranking people from his own staff. During a visit to celebrate the school's third anniversary (in late September, 1929), Baranov was not sparing in his praise of the school. He declared that it had the best of everything needed for war: airplanes, motors, weapons, and photographic and radio equipment. He claimed that the Lipetsk school combined sophisticated German technology in aviation with the experience of the Soviet air force in the field of tactics and practice. It was therefore a laboratory and experimental field for German aviation technology, providing a firm basis for "Russian-German association." Again and again Baranov emphasized the importance of cooperation between Germany (whose "magnificent successes in the domain of aviation technology are well-known") and the Soviet Union (which, "with determination and consistency, is strengthening its air force").[69]

Obviously, Baranov's statements were not the casual comments of an exuberant individual, but reflected official policy: speeches on such occasions were not left to the whim of individual officers or officials. As Iakov Alksnis (deputy head of the Soviet air force) informed a representative of the Reichswehr, the commissar of the armed forces, Klim Voroshilov, firmly believed in the desirability of further collaboration with Germany. Indeed, by January 1930 there was talk of having Soviet specialists develop weapons for the German airplanes, since the Germans ("because of their very limited opportunities") cannot do it themselves. At issue were a large-calibre machine gun and canons, which would enable warplanes to fight at greater distances. Alksnis also suggested the creation of joint offices in Russia that would engage in aviation design. The German side expressed interest in the idea.[70] A high-ranking Soviet official from military administration and a specialist in aircraft weaponry discussed details for organizing cooperative work in Germany itself. It was to involve representatives from the Soviet air force, whose duties would include visits to aircraft plants and test sites. One of the German participants in the talks promised that the Soviet visitors would be shown both the aircraft plants and the airfields for testing, but emphasized the enormous difficulties due to "the secrecy caused by the foreign-policy situation."[71]

Meanwhile, the Reichswehr also conducted periodic inspections of its military bases on Soviet territory. Major-General Werner von Blomberg, the Reichswehr's chief-of-staff and later minister of defense, visited the Soviet Union in 1928 along with six other officers of the Reichswehr. As Blomberg explained, the objective was to visit German military sites, to establish personal contacts with leading military authorities, and to study the Red Army. He visited the tank school in Kazan, an installation for testing poison gas near Vol'sk-Tomka, the pilot-training school at Lipetsk. The German delegation also inspected a Soviet military camp near Voronezh and observed air maneuvers near Gomel and exercises of the Ukrainian military district in the Kiev area. Von Blomberg came away with a very favorable impression of the cooperation with the Red Army, which he claimed served predominantly German, but also Soviet, interests:

> There can be no doubt about their great significance for our armament. From the perspective of military defense, it is vitally necessary to exploit these to the maximum. That the Russians have given us the opportunity to run these undertakings usefully is extraordinarily important for us. Their own interest in them is considerable, although the advantage from these operations falls predominantly on the German side.[72]

Von Blomberg's report also underscored the exceptional cordiality and hospitality of his Soviet colleagues; Voroshilov had indeed given strict orders to comply with his guests' wishes and placed a special railway car at their disposal.[73] To judge from the documents, the relations between the Red Army and the Reichswehr were rather warm during the term that Lieutenant-General Wilhelm Groener was minister of the Reichswehr (1928–1932).[74]

The reports by General Hans Halm are also exceedingly important. Between the summer of 1927 and January 1930, Halm had many opportunities to observe the status of military training in the Red Army. The detailed reports to his superiors in Berlin (running to 345 folio-sized pages) were intercepted and copied by OGPU agents, and this Soviet copy is now preserved in the Red Army archives in Moscow.[75] In 1927 Halm noted that negotiations about his visit in the USSR were conducted "in a spirit of mutual assistance." In autumn 1929 he reported a dinner speech by the head of the Soviet air force academy, R. P. Eideman, who (in the presence of I. P. Uborevich) spoke warmly of Soviet-German military cooperation. The following year Halm visited the 24th Saratov-Ul'ianov infantry division; its commander, Dannenberg, had been on military assignment in Germany the previous year—which perhaps served as the pretext for the visit. On this occasion Halm noted some weaknesses in Soviet military training; among the most important was the poor preparation of troops and officers for offensive action.[76]

During this 1930 trip Halm evidently had instructions to study the political mood among military personnel. The curiosity of the Reichswehr was understandable: collectivization was in full swing, the party congress had just been held, and Stalin's article ("Dizziness from Success") had given the signal to slow down the campaign against the village. The overwhelming majority of the soldiers and NCOs, and probably some of the middle-level officer corps, had themselves come from the peasantry and thus could be expected to have strong ties to the village and its interests. Nevertheless, Halm discerned no signs of unrest. On the contrary, in his opinion the relations between officers and soldiers appeared to be "harmonious and comradely," creating the "impression of complete security and satisfaction." Halm also noted that, in contrast to the civilian population, the soldiers of the Red Army were provided with ample food and tobacco. He further noted that political propaganda among Soviet troops seemed to be highly effective. In particular, the difficulties that the "imperialist states" experience because of the current economic crisis, the high rates of unemployment in the West, and the success of the revolutionary movement in Asia provided excellent material for Soviet political instructors, who could thereby offset the difficult conditions prevailing in the Soviet Union itself. According to Halm, the leitmotif in Soviet political indoctrination was the claim that the interests of the army and party are absolutely identical. It must be noted, however, that Halm's assessment of the political mood was superficial; to have a well-informed judgment, Halm would have needed far more information than conversations with Red Army personnel who had been carefully coached in their answers.[77]

Indeed, the mood in the army was quite different from that reported by Halm. Indicative of the actual sentiment in military ranks is a report, submitted on June 1, 1929, to the chairman of the Revolutionary-Military Council, Voroshilov. Its author was an adjutant in the 1st Battalion of the 296th Infantry Regiment of the 99th Infantry Division. The document itself deserves to be called "the document of the epoch" and to be quoted in full:

> I consider it my duty to report on distortions in the party line, especially [as set by] the July plenum of the Central Committee, with respect to grain requisition. Local authorities in Shevchenko Okrug (Gorodishchensk raion) have perpetrated the following. At village meetings of the peasantry, they issue resolutions for the surrender of "surpluses," without indicating the amounts due from each peasant. But in the minutes of the meeting, they insert a specific quantity of poods from each peasant—based on figures previously prepared by communist activists and a representative of the district military commissariat (Raionnyi voennyi komissariat). The majority of peasants, however, simply are in no condition to comply because of the bad harvest of 1928 and because some peasant households have shifted to sowing intensive crops (e.g., sugar beets and the like). If a peasant does not deliver the prescribed poods of grain, the commission compiles an inventory of everything he owns and within three days sells it all off. When they conduct searches, they take every last ounce of grain, even baked bread, and do not leave the family a crust for food. Personal property is sold at a tenth of its real value; the aim is to cover the deficit in undelivered grain, which is valued at 7 rubles per pood. If a peasant tries to resist and refuses to give his last store of grain, if he loses his temper and says something, he is immediately arrested and accused of making threats, of counter-revolutionary acts, etc. For days on end these peasants are held under arrest without charges or investigation. The village is filled with wailing, weep-

ing and screams. Women hanged themselves in Pskov; some in des-
peration attempt to burn their property, to suffocate their children.
Most say that "this is a provocation and we shall not give in to it;
they are plundering us—well let them feed us, let the government go
ahead and seize the land and property. We are in the land of the soviets, not on Mars or the Devil knows where." The press ignores all
this and, when you try to obtain orders for the confiscation of property, you get this answer: "Go out there and demand, but there are no
orders from higher bodies." The poor and middling village has 0.38
dessiatines per inhabitant. Having informed the Revolutionary Military Council of all this, I ask that this be brought to the attention of
the Central Executive Committee of the USSR and that a commission be sent to investigate and to explain to the peasants the purpose
of grain requisition and to calm them down.

[Signed:] S. *Fediai*, Village of Khlystunovok, Gorodishchensk Raion,
Shevchenko Okrug (Ukraine).[78]

It takes very little imagination to suggest that Fediai's life after this
appeal to the Military-Revolutionary Council was less than idyllic,
for he had written to Voroshilov—one of those who sanctioned the
campaign to destroy the peasantry.

Apart from the military training and political mood, the German
observers paid close attention to the technical preparation of the
Red Army and, especially, its air force. Very interesting in this
respect is a curious archival document revealing the Germans'
rather contradictory, but generally negative evaluation of Soviet
aviation. Above all, they noted that most of the equipment was
imported: the photographic section used German equipment, and
even the weapons relied on foreign machine guns. Only in a few
areas had the Soviets produced weapons of their own. Among the
aircraft shown the Germans was, to their surprise, a plane made
entirely of metal; it was manufactured at a plant called TsAGI. This
led a German observer (Wilberg) to conclude that the Russians had
begun to manufacture metallic aircraft. Together with Baranov, he
witnessed a test flight of the craft: it flew for 15 minutes and at an
altitude of 30 meters. Wilberg regarded it as noteworthy that the
Russians had been able to construct the plane with their resources
and on their own.[79] Another document (from 1926) reported that
the Soviet air force had fifteen large airplanes (model K-30), which
had been built at the Junkers plant in Sweden, shipped in sections

to Russia, and assembled at a Junkers plant in Fili (near Moscow). Altogether, the Soviet Union spent 1.75 million rubles for the aircraft—a considerable sum at the time.[80] Wilberg was also shown Red Army testing grounds for toxic substances near the railway station at Podosiniki.

Participants in the "Fiebig" group also provide interesting information on the German impressions of the Red Army. The group had contact with the school for radio operators in Moscow, a flight school for pilots and navigators in Leningrad, the air force academies in Smolensk and Vitebsk, and the school for aviation bombing in Serpukhov.[81] They pointed out that instruction at the air force academies was based on experience acquired during the civil war and hence outmoded for a future conflict that would be conducted under very different conditions.[82]

Because of language barriers, Germans who studied at the Air Force Academy encountered serious difficulties in dealing with the Russian students. But that was not the only problem. The entire way of life was alien to them, especially the conditions generated by Soviet ideology. Russians are extremely cautious toward foreigners, for example, which prevents much personal contact; it was extremely difficult to surmount this barrier. The Soviets had their own problems—such as the difficulty of pronouncing the names of their fellow students from abroad. Authorities therefore decided to give each of the German students a Russian name; the aim, of course, was not to facilitate contacts, but to ensure the secrecy of identity for the foreign students.[83]

Whereas that kind of problem was easily resolved, far more ticklish was the Soviet suspicion that the Germans were concealing their latest achievements in aviation technology. Thus Alksnis (deputy head of the Soviet air force) expressed his dissatisfaction that pilots at the Lipetsk school did not have the latest improvements in German aviation—from the K-47 fighter to new weaponry, radio, photography, and support equipment. Soviet aviation was particularly interested in instruments that would enable flight during foggy or cloudy weather. The Germans made excuses which did not, of course, satisfy their Soviet partners. Voroshilov expressed this disgruntlement during a meeting in Moscow with General von Hammerstein. The latter replied: "Yes, indeed, the work is progressing very slowly, but there are great difficulties. One should not forget, however, that Germany is forbidden to have its own air force, and hence the available means are limited. Moreover, the parliamentary system imposes its own limits; one has to keep the cooperation [with the USSR] a secret."

Von Hammerstein nevertheless promised to show the newest developments to the head of the Soviet air force on his next visit to Germany. Moreover, the pilot school in Lipetsk made plans to use the new German warplane Albatross-78 in its training schedule for 1931.[84]

Apart from the benefits from military cooperation, the Soviet Union actively sought to obtain assistance for Soviet industry (including the military sector) from foreign and, especially, German firms. According to classified Soviet documents, by 1931 its military plants (excluding aviation) had eleven contracts with foreign firms: nine provided technical assistance and two involved cooperation with foreign designers to develop new models for a tank and an anti-aircraft gun. Of particular importance was a contract between the Krupp concern and the State Association of Metallurgical Plants, signed on June 17, 1929.[85] Krupp provided technical assistance to some of the largest enterprises in the Soviet Union—Barrikad, Zlatoustovskii, Krasnyi Putilovets, Krasnoe Sormovo, and Elektrostal'. This contract led to a significant improvement in steel casting in open-hearth furnaces (including those needed for the military production of carbide and specialized steel) and the heat treatment of barrels in artillery systems. As a classified document confirms: "Previously, the defective production had been massive, because the steel did not meet the technical specifications set by the Artillery Directorate." Improvements were also made in the forging of mine containers and crankshafts. As one might expect, the Soviet plants often were not ready for the Krupp people; a vast amount of time was lost before various organizational problems could be resolved. The firm Rhein-Metall set up the production of new artillery systems in the plants of a Sovet weapons conglomerate, Oruzhob"edinenie. The German concern Walter performed work on the boring process for small-calibre rifles, three-lined military rifles, and machine-gun barrels. The method Walter proposed would complete the boring in a few minutes—rather than the hour previously required. The firm Folmer designed a halftrack tank. The German designer Otto Schmitts offered Soviet military plants the design and blueprints for a 37-millimeter twin anti-aircraft gun.

The firm Girsch contracted with the Patruboob"edinenie (the conglomerate for pipe manufacturing) to design and construct a shop
for rolling and cladding at the Tula Weapons Plant. These are only
a few examples of the direct participation by German firms in the
construction and improvement of Soviet military production.
French firms also contributed to the strengthening of Soviet military-industrial potential, especially in chemicals.[86]

The Military-Chemical Directorate of the Red Army exhibited
a certain impatience about receiving technical assistance from the
Germans. In a memorandum addressed to the chief of technical
services for the land forces, the service demanded "a shift from the
level of 'conversations' about technical assistance to the real
involvement of foreign companies." From the list of possible forms
of assistance it is clear that the service was interested in defense
measures in event of chemical warfare as well as offensive chemical weapons (in particular, equipment for a mustard-gas plant from
the firms of Goldschmitt and von Stolzenberg). The Directorate
demanded the allocation of specific sums in 1931 for "both defensive and war gases."[87]

Military Cooperation and Political Tensions

Soviet-German relations developed in the 1920s amidst periodic
complications, which were often provoked by bureaucratic self-
interest and conflict. These included, for example, the political
attack on the Soviet trade mission in May 1924; as part of the
Soviet diplomatic mission, it enjoyed the right of extraterritoriality
and therefore immunity from such invasions.[88] Another disturbing
incident was the Skoblevsky affair, involving a German communist
who tried to assassinate General von Seeckt and received a death
sentence for the crime. Problems also followed the publication of an
article in *Krasnaia zvezda* (the organ of the political branch in the
Leningrad Military District), reporting that the German government had given huge sums to assist industrialists in the Ruhr. The
article ended with these words: "Such stories can transpire only
where a handful of tyrants dominate; such oppressors should be
overthrown. And that is the cause led by the glorious party of German communists."[89] This article was nothing short of an overt call
to overthrow the government of a friendly state. Responding to a
protest from the German ambassador Rantzau, Chicherin sent a let-

ter to Frunze (commissar of defense), supporting the German complaint. The letter closed as follows: "Can you not indicate to me how, through what means, it will be possible to avert in the future the appearance of such inconvenient displays of candor on the pages of an organ in the military branch?"[90] There were also diplomatic complications due to the arrests of German citizens by the OGPU in Moscow and elsewhere. In all these incidents the Soviet state was intensely concerned to see that the military cooperation with Germany not be made public.

Diplomatic problems also erupted in the late 1920s over the case of Max Hölz (1889–1933). A German communist who had engineered the uprising in central Germany in 1921, he had been convicted of murder and sentenced to life imprisonment. Given an amnesty in 1928, he came to the Soviet Union where he was received like a revolutionary hero. When the Soviet government awarded him "the Order of the Red Banner" in 1929, the German government took offense: to award a medal to a convicted criminal was scarcely an act consistent with the friendly relations existing between the USSR and Germany. Ambassador Rantzau put the question in terms of principle: is it possible to have secret military cooperation with a government which not only received a political criminal (who had been convicted of a real attempt to overthrow the existing order), but even expressed openly its approval of what he had done? Rantzau therefore recommended a vigorous démarche in Moscow and in Berlin (toward the Soviet mission head, Krestinskii).

Although Germany eventually decided not to use the incident as a pretext to change its relationship with the USSR, the affair did have a lasting effect. The main reason for this self-restraint was the fear that it might raise the question of military cooperation with the USSR, and that this in turn could lead to a serious aggravation of the internal political situation—which the German government wished to avoid at all costs. Nevertheless, Rantzau lodged a vigorous protest with Chicherin, who, however, knew that the ambassador did not enjoy the support of his home government in the matter. But Rantzau's threat to resign put the German government in a difficult position; it finally gave him permission to tell Moscow that Berlin took this provocation quite seriously and that its military cooperation with Russia was now at risk. Although the Soviets took a more conciliatory position in the following months, the affair put an end to the confidential relations between Rantzau and Chicherin.

The contradictory Soviet policy that so astonished and irritated Rantzau was the product of several factors. One was the rather pragmatic attitude of the Soviet leadership toward the advantages from its cooperation with Germany. That was apparent, for example, in Voroshilov's candid remarks in September 1929 to General Kurt Freiherr von Hammerstein-Equord (Chief of Army Command) when the latter visited the German tank school at Kazan': "We have different interests in collaborative work. The Reichswehr wants to have a base to test its new tank design, to train its tank specialists, and to study the tactics and properties of tanks. But we are also interested in acquiring technical assistance." Voroshilov thereupon proposed to develop new types of tanks by including Soviet engineers in the German design offices and by building new production facilities in the USSR: "Under certain conditions, it is possible to construct here several special enterprises."[91] Voroshilov also wanted assistance from German industry to realize this scheme, which would enable Germany not only to circumvent the Versailles restrictions, but also to provide the Red Army with modern weaponry.

At the same time, the military cooperation with Germany was also linked to the internal political concerns of the Soviet leadership. That included cultivating caution toward the West and even fanning hatred toward it—essential components of Bolshevik strategy. In a conversation with Hammerstein, Voroshilov specifically emphasized that the social and political systems of Russia and Germany represent fundamental antipodes, and that hence it can only be a matter of business relations based on mutual self-interest. The Soviet leadership indeed sought to sustain a "siege mentality": only fear of military attack by the capitalist states could justify the regime's draconian measures to reconstruct Soviet society. That is why virtually every show trial involving "wrecking" included allusions to real foreigners or at least mythical connections with the White Guards abroad or the capitalist West. Thus the famous "Shakhty Show Trial" of 1928, for example, involved three German citizens (an engineer and two technicians), who were accused of sabotage. The German government, which had already learned something from its relations with Moscow, took a conciliatory position. The Soviet high court took into account the humble behavior of the Germans: two of the accused were acquitted, the third received (by Soviet standards) a mild sentence. However, right to the time that Hitler came to power, such "traffic accidents" failed to have a significant negative impact on Soviet-German military cooperation.

The essential fact is that Germany was still the most desirable partner for the Soviet political leadership. A draft of a 1929 Politburo resolution ("On the Current Mutual Relations with the Reichswehr") approved the cooperation of design facilities of the two countries in the fields of artillery, machine guns, and military chemicals. Simultaneously, it encouraged cooperation of their mutual intelligence services with respect to a common enemy, Poland.[92] Documents from January 1930 include the "theses" for talks by political instructors in infantry regiments. Based on Litvinov's speech at the second session of the All-Union Central Executive Committee, the theses defined the Soviet Union's relationship to the main capitalist states. In general, of course, the instructors were expected to express sharply negative attitudes. In the case of Germany, however, the political instructors were to communicate the following ideas:
USSR and Germany

> 1. Germany is one of the states with the most friendly attitude toward us.
> 2. Who oppresses Germany?
> 3. Attempts by German reactionary circles to disrupt the mutual relations with the USSR.
> 4. Growth of our ties (note: this means economic and *political* ties!) with Germany.
> *Conclusion*: Germany is the most friendly capitalist country, commercial relations with which are steadily growing stronger.[93]

Hammerstein proposed a tripartite formula that Germany and the Soviet Union should observe: friendship of armies, maximum possible friendship in foreign policy, and respect for the internal policy of each side.[94] But he noted that there were constantly the same stumbling blocks: the unofficial support of the German Communist Party by the Comintern and Soviet agents in Germany, as well as the overt sympathy for the German communists and its paramilitary organization (Union of Red Front-Line Soldiers) by Soviet officials on such revolutionary holidays as May Day. Indeed, the latter was even pro-

nounced the day "of inspection of the fighting forces of the international proletariat." As a result, there was recurrent conflict between
the two partners well before Hitler came to power in 1933. In his
conversation with Hammerstein, Voroshilov seemingly agreed that
the ties could only be "business-like," but added that there is no
point in "mixing up the Third International or the party with our
purely business relations."[95]

Reichswehr and Red Army: Ties

The question of direct ties between the German and Russian military
was a cause of continuing concern, but also utility for the Red Army.
The concern was predictable: fears of a breach of security, which
could apply even to the highest ranks of the military. That was apparent, for example, when the two sides signed an agreement on December 21, 1928 permitting oral and written relations between the Economic Section of the German embassy in Moscow and the various
Soviet commissariats. Once the agreement took effect (January 15,
1929), the embassy's Economic Section had the right to deal directly
with the Revolutionary-Military Council. To restrict free access,
Voroshilov immediately ordered that direct talks be conducted only
by the members of the Council and Berzin, the head of Red Army
intelligence (the Fourth Department of the general staff). The
Council's members theoretically could correspond through Berzin's
apparatus, but each time had to report about this to Voroshilov or his
deputy, Unshlikht.[96]

The high command of the Red Army showed some discomfort
and confusion when the officers and generals of the Reichswehr visited their military units. It was not altogether clear who these people were—allies or simply guests? Berzin reported on one such
episode directly to Voroshilov. During a banquet in honor of Hammerstein[97] (at the camp of the 1st Infantry Division, near Kazan in
late September, 1929), the corps and division commanders both
made speeches. Whereas the corps commander offered the standard
pablum about the struggle for peace and friendship of peoples, the
division commander expressed his hope that the Germans would be
liberated as soon as possible from the yoke of the Versailles Treaty.
That statement was patently political. It was certainly improper, in
Berzin's view, for a division commander to say such things without
the permission of his superiors. It turned out that, in "giving permis-

sion for Hammerstein to visit the camp," the corps commander had
also exceeded his authority.[98] On this memorandum from the head
of army intelligence, Voroshilov scribbled the following resolution:
"People who act on their own authority in so delicate a question as
the relations with the 'guests' are to be given a dressing-down and
personal reprimand. In the future it is necessary to instruct the command staffs and the political administration how they are to conduct themselves in similar situations."[99] Voroshilov himself scrupulously reported to the Politburo on his conversations with representatives of the Reichswehr. For example, in 1929 Voroshilov filed the
following report: "Secret. To Comrade Molotov, Secretary of the
Central Committee Secretary. I enclose a telegram addressed to me
from Hammerstein (Chief of Staff of the Reichswehr) for the information of members of the Politburo."[100] As the telegram was nothing more than an expression of thanks for the hospitality shown
during his visit to Moscow, it is obvious that Voroshilov sent the
telegram not to apprise the Politburo of an important matter, but
simply to keep himself above reproach and suspicion.

From 1925 the two sides arranged systematic exchanges of Red
Army and Reichswehr officers, including study at each other's military academies. In 1926 Uborevich spent several months in Germany, where he became acquainted with the Reichswehr training in
various areas, including officers in the General Staff.[101] The Soviet
military command attached particular importance to the stationing
of command personnel at the military academy in Berlin and
attempted to send its most capable people. Although in principle it
was deemed advisable to send people who already had some familiarity with the Reichswehr, the high command also had the goal of
acquainting "a certain circle of the command staff" with the military training and equipment of foreign armies.[102]

A constant stumbling block, however, was the fact that the officers had little or no knowledge of German. Thus an army commander named Belov requested that he not be sent to Berlin because he
did not know German. When Voroshilov confirmed the appointment of Bliukhner as military attaché in Berlin, he noted: "A weakness is the fact that he does not know the [German] language. However, the majority of our military attachés begin their work without
knowing the [local] language, so there is nothing extraordinary
here."[103] The officers deemed to be most promising included Uborevich, Iakir, Eideman, and Appoga. Moscow counted, in particular,

on Uborevich; in 1927 there was talk of posting him to Berlin for an entire year. Evidently, the Soviet military encountered resistance to such a long term, impelling Voroshilov to turn to Chicherin for assistance: "There is some kind of external force, which is exerting pressure on the Reichswehr in the question of the length of residence for comrade Uborevich."[104] In a letter to Uborevich (already in Berlin), Voroshilov admonishes him to avoid unduly close personal ties with officers in the Reichswehr:

> You are aware that we have friendly relations with the Germans. However, there are certain movements which orient themselves toward the West and attempt to exploit the connections with us for purposes of blackmail. . . . It is necessary to be exceedingly careful in one's relations with representatives of the Reichswehr. . . . To be sure, one must sometimes dine with the Germans, but such occasions must be kept to the minimum. On this point there is a firm resolution of superior authorities [Politburo].

The letter continues in the same paternalistic, pedantic tone:

> You must demonstrate to the Germans the model of our commander—a communist, hard-working, modest, frugal, not importunate, alien to bourgeois habits and all kinds of banquets, etc. This has to be emphasized to the Germans.[105]

As these documents show, the Soviet high command expected not only a detailed description and analysis of military training in the Reichswehr, but also awareness of the Reichswehr's role in German politics and its relationship to Soviet Russia. They were also expected to provide recommendations about the further development of relations with Germany in military affairs.

Two instructors at the Frunze Military Academy, Krasil'nikov and Svechnikov, described their impressions after returning from Germany in February 1927. They noted that the German general staff regarded the "Soviet republic" as a force capable of increasing its military might, especially in the presence of a common adversary: Poland. Their report, addressed to the head of the academy (R. Eideman), emphasizes the "genuine sympathy" and respect of middle-level officer corps for the Red Army, given their hostility toward France and Poland. But Krasil'nikov and Svechnikov also believed that "friendly feelings can be preserved for a prolonged time" in the higher ranks of the general staff of the Reichswehr, and hence it would be possible to use "these ruling circles to put pressure on the

German government in ways favorable to Soviet Russia."[106]

The most substantive comments appeared in a lengthy and infor-
mative report that Uborevich filed in January 1929 at the conclusion of his thirteen-month stay in Germany. The report concludes
that the Reichswehr is preparing for a transition "to a large army for
external war" and that German industry is being systematically prepared for this eventuality. On the political level, he warned of a possible repudiation of the Versailles terms by military means, although
most believe that the time for revanche was not yet ripe.[107] Com-
paring the Reichswehr with the Red Army, Uborevich came to the
conclusion that "German specialists, including those in the military,
are immeasurably superior to us." His recommendations are quite
direct and cynical. "It seems to me," he wrote, "that we should buy
off these specialists. . . . I do not think that German specialists are
politically worse or more dangerous than our Russian specialists. In
any event, one can learn a lot from them. . . . "[108] A half year later,
Uborevich retrospectively came to the conclusion that until the
autumn of 1927 the high command of the Reichswehr (Groener,
Haine, Blomberg) did not have a strong interest in strengthening
ties and further cooperation with the Red Army.[109]

As a rule, Red Army commanders posted to Germany were
astonished by the different preparation given to officers of the
Reichswehr. Army commander Belov (who, despite his own remon-
strations and lack of linguistic skills, was sent to Germany), wrote
an embittered letter to Voroshilov: "When you see how the German
officers kill themselves with hard work (from second lieutenants to
generals), when you see how they work to train their units and what
results they obtain, your entire being suffers from a consciousness of
our weakness. One wants to scream bloody murder and demand the
most intensive training, the decisive remaking of our commanders
in the shortest possible period of time. . . . The non-execution of
commands is simply unknown in the German Reichswehr."[110]

The value of the training that the Reichswehr afforded for the
professional knowledge of the upper echelons of the Soviet officer
corps is attested by the posts that they held in the Red Army. In
1927 they included the commander of military district, the chief of
staff in a military district, two division chiefs of the general staff, a
deputy head of division in the general staff, a corps commander, the
chief of staff in a cavalry corps, the commander of an artillery regiment, and the head of the military academy.[111] In 1929 the contin-

gent posted to Germany included the commanders of two military districts, two corps commanders, the chief of a section in the general staff, a division commander, two regimental commanders, the head of an artillery school, the artillery commander in a military district, and a deputy chief in the air force.[112] In 1931 the Soviets sent a specially selected group of top officers:

General Military Group: commanders from three military districts;

Military Technology Group: the deputy head of armaments, the chiefs of military-technical administration and artillery administration;

Military Transport Group (involving mobilization and railway transports): the heads of two sections of the general staff, the deputy head of a section, the head of a sector, and the military representative of the Moscow junction;

Staff Group: the heads of staffs from five military districts, the head of the staff for military training, a former military attaché, and a commander assigned to the NKVD;

Motorized Forces Group: two commanders, who were sent to Germany to study in German tank schools;

Specialists Group: seven commanders to study the preparation of troops under field conditions;

Military-technical Group: three commanders, including the head of artillery administration and a representative from the military chemical administration;

Cavalry Group: the head and his deputy from the military-horse administration.[113]

The Red Army, for its part, had special rules governing visits to its own installations by military representatives of foreign states. The rules, issued over the name of M. N. Tukhachevskii (chief of staff) and Ia. A. Berzin (chief of army intelligence) on January 30, 1928, regulated the behavior of Soviet commanders during formal receptions of foreign guests. The section entitled "Duties of the Local Military Command" included this instruction:

> Banquets are to be held in conformity with a strictly restrained political line at the given moment. The commanding officers are obliged to emphasize in their speeches the political uniqueness of the Red Army and its unbreakable bonds with the toiling population. Those present at the banquet should observe a sense of moderation, in particular with respect to the consumption of alcoholic drinks. One should treat the guests with politeness, but also show a sensitivity for

one's own dignity and the honor of the Red Army. . . . One should
channel [the guests'] attention in a direction most desirable for us.[114]

As to strictly military matters, the Soviet command was especially
interested in the organization of the German armed forces. That
involved several matters: (1) interrelationship of land and sea
forces, and of different types of military forces; (2) the organization,
armaments, technical means, and applicability of the cavalry (for
example, in Poland); (3) the Germans' attitude toward fortified
areas; (4) organization of rear areas and supplies in peacetime and
wartime; (5) daily life in the German army.[115] In a secret letter to
Uborevich (March 1928), Voroshilov asked for data on the normal
consumption of ammunition for firearms and artillery in wartime
and also the amount required for one year of war.

The German army also sought to learn from the Soviet side. The
Reichswehr's instructions for commanders directed them to pay particular attention to the use of motorized units, management of
defensive battles, systems of air defense, and the like. For their part,
the Germans also believed that they could learn something from
the Red Army. Von Blomberg, for example, cited such things as the
weapons and equipment of the army, sapper units (especially pontoon construction), air force, chemical weapons, propaganda, the
organization of anti-aircraft defense for the civilian population, and
the mobilization of the population in war time. Von Blomberg's
general conclusion was that both sides needed the cooperation and
both stood to profit from it. He emphasized as well that it was
important to disregard differences in state systems and not to allow
these to interfere with military cooperation.[116]

Notwithstanding the close surveillance of the OGPU, the
Reichswehr undoubtedly obtained high-quality information about
the condition of the Soviet armed forces and its military industries.
But the same is true of the Soviet side. It systematically intercepted
diplomatic mail, copied the correspondence from foreign military
attachés, and was particularly interested in their assessment of Red
Army units and field maneuvers. A letter from Voroshilov to the
OGPU chief (V. R. Menzhinskii) in October, 1927 indicates, however, an abiding concern to obtain the information, but to avoid
causing a diplomatic incident—especially with respect to the Germans. At issue was a complaint from two German officers (Colonel
Halm and Major Fischer), who had observed Soviet field maneu-

vers and subsequently complained about missing diplomatic correspondence (which had come from Berlin but failed to reach them).
Noting that "the Germans are deeply outraged," Voroshilov asked
the OGPU to make a full investigation and to apprise him of the
results. He concluded the letter with this revealing sentence: "Of
course, I hardly need to convince you that this kind of operation
must be carried out delicately and remain absolutely unknown to its
objects. One must take that into account, especially, when dealing
with Germans."[117]

During this period both sides' governments continued to prefer
Brokdorf-Rantzau as the German ambassador in Moscow. According
to Hencke, people in the German foreign ministry said the following
of Rantzau: "If the ambassador should someday die, he should be
mummified and left sitting in his post in Moscow."[118] Such witti-
cisms aside, after Rantzau died on September 8, 1928, the German
government designated Herbert von Dirksen as his successor. Dirksen believed that the military cooperation constituted a most important element in Soviet-German relations. It was beneficial to Germany insofar as it enabled his country to circumvent the terms of
the Versailles Treaty and thus to rearm clandestinely.

OGPU and Soviet Germans

The OGPU, as already suggested, played a not insignificant role in
shaping Soviet-German military cooperation in this first pre-Hitler
phase. It comes as no surprise that the secret police carefully moni-
tored everything that had to do with Germany—from the activities
of ambassador Rantzau to the conditions among "German colonists"
(Soviet citizens of German origin who migrated to Russia in the
eighteenth century). The OGPU found it especially disturbing that
Rantzau was so well informed about Soviet affairs. Suspicion inevitably fell on those officials in the foreign affairs commissariat
who worked in the section specializing on Germany. Brodovskii, the
OGPU official responsible for overseeing the commissariat of foreign affairs, complained specifically that Rantzau knew altogether
too much about internal Soviet affairs. Chicherin, commissar of foreign affairs, was obviously irritated by the insinuation and meddling
in his own domain. In a letter addressed to Brodovskii, he bluntly
questioned the veracity of the accusation: "Please send me the

material you have, for only when I have received these materials can I decide whether measures must be taken and what kind these should be."[119] In turn the head of the Fourth Section of the OGPU wrote on the top of Chicherin's letter the following resolution for his deputy: "Absolutely confidential for comrade Menzhinskii. The source of this information must be established, no matter what the cost. Is it not through Kopp's wife?"[120]

The OGPU head, Feliks Dzerzhinskii, was so interested in Brodovskii's report that he demanded not only all the pertinent information at his disposal, but also those reflections "which are perhaps inappropriate for you to convey to comrade Chicherin. This is a matter of the utmost importance." The OGPU head immediately listed the names of those who had conducted negotiations with the Germans and attended sessions of the Central Committee—i.e., those officials most likely to have leaked classified information to the Germans. These included Chicherin himself and several other top officials in his commissariat—Kopp, Krasin, Krestinskii. But Dzerzhinskii recommended looking for the culprit among their wives, sisters, and secretaries. He emphasized that "every petty detail is important. I have been told that Kopp's sister-in-law recently married a German who holds a high official post. Is that true?"[121]

In 1924–1925 Soviet-German relations fell victim to a series of untoward incidents—such as the cases involving Soviet agents in Leipzig (the "German Cheka") and German students in the USSR. In all these Rantzau showed a certain flexibility, trying to avoid any undue complications and to pursue the policy adumbrated at Rapallo in 1922. According to Chicherin, the German ambassador was convinced that the existing Soviet government (in February 1925) was ideal from the German perspective: any other would be favorably inclined toward the Entente. To be sure, Rantzau had no doubt that the OGPU played a major role in the conduct of Soviet foreign policy. A joke popular among foreign diplomats in Moscow (and jotted down by Chicherin in his own notes) observed that it would be better for the diplomatic corps if they received their accreditation from the OGPU.[122]

The OGPU did indeed harbor strong anti-German sentiments. It even reached the point where Dzerzhinskii himself could indulge in the most absurd fantasies: "the German government (together with monarchist and nationalist German circles) is conducting work to overthrow Bolshevism in Russia and orient themselves on a future

monarchist Russia." Still, the OGPU chief asked his closest associ-
ates (Trilisser and Iagoda) if that opinion had any validity. He also
requested material to resolve the following questions: do the Germans aid White Guard organizations? is it an accident that the firm
Junkers has provided virtually nothing? are the Germans really of
assistance in organizing the production of chemicals and other
goods? Dzerzhinskii demanded as well an analysis of the activity of
German concessions in the USSR.[123]

A half-year later Artuzov (chief of counter-intelligence in the
OGPU) filed five memoranda on the activities of Germans in the
USSR. His general conclusion: "Without doubt, German nationalists have performed an enormous work in all areas and significantly
overwhelmed our influence among German colonists in the USSR.
[Among] the latter [our influence] is extremely weak." He concluded that one should liquidate both Junkers and GEFU.[124] The
OGPU's counter-intelligence section discerned the greatest menace
in the organization "Auslanddeutsche," which focused on Germans
living in foreign countries. Since the Soviet secret police began
with the assumption that this organization was essentially an intelligence operation, it attempted to assemble proof that German
colonists wanted only to gather information for Auslanddeutsche or
to aid in the restoration of monarchy in Russia. The OGPU even
invented a name for the Russian section of Auslanddeutsche: "Central Committee of Germans residing in Russia." It allegedly had its
own representatives in the seven homeland territories of Germans
inside Russia.[125] This "Central Committee" was purported to have
three departments: one for propaganda and publications, a second
for finances, and a third for emigration. It published several periodi-
cals specially aimed at Germans residing in the USSR.[126] According
to the OGPU, these publications were "counter-revolutionary" and
propagandized "pan-German, nationalist ideas."[127] The OGPU also
accused the Financial Department of counter-revolutionary activity
through its economic assistance to needy colonists. For that matter
the OGPU suspected the German Red Cross of engaging in similar
"espionage and counter-revolutionary work" and shut it down in
early 1924. The OGPU asserted that the conglomerate "Kon-
kordiia" (a firm engaged in the production of spirits) was now the
center of espionage: its liquor shops were allegedly functioning to
gather intelligence. The firm also was said to have ties with the
White Guards and to be providing material assistance to German

national schools, which the OGPU also accused of counter-revolutionary activity.[128] The German consulates in the Soviet Union were also working actively in areas with the colonists.

Possibly aware that its report lacked sufficient proof, the OGPU sought to strengthen its argument with data on the "class composition" of the German colonists. The group, it declared, was composed mainly of "kulaks," who naturally inclined toward "fascist-nationalist" aspirations. The stratification of German colonists—so much desired by the Soviet state—"is advancing at an extremely slow rate," the OGPU concluded. Among German colonists in the Ukraine, for example, 40 to 50 percent were "big kulaks" and former estate-owners; this category also included the German rural intelligentsia. Except for a small stratum of poor colonists (5 to 6 percent), the rest belonged to the "independent middling peasantry"—i.e., those who were self-sufficient. A second piece of evidence for the "counter-revolutionary spirit" of German colonists was their refusal to join the Communist Party or its youth organization, the Komsomol. Thus in the 70 German colonies of Melitopol'skii District (with a population of more than 30,000), there was not a single member of the party or the Komsomol.[129] The OGPU claimed that anti-Soviet elements and kulaks were responsible for subversive agitation and counter-revolutionary agitation. To make matters worse, "activism in the colonies and the aspiration to form an independent national region are mounting and, horrible to say, enjoy support in the German Section of the Central Committee."[130] Approximately the same situation existed in other regions with German populations—in Ekaterinoslav and Odessa provinces.

The autonomous German republic on the Volga had more than a half-million ethnic Germans. Although the class composition appeared more innocuous (50 percent poor peasants, 30 percent middling peasants, and 20 percent kulaks), the OGPU still found cause for concern. One has the sense that, regardless of the class composition, the Germans appeared to be an unreliable ethnic group, although the OGPU nominally clung to a "class analysis": "This is not a real stratification of the population, for the majority of the population became impoverished through famine and repeated harvest failures. Consequently, its ideological relationship to Soviet power has remained that of the kulak."[131]

The conclusion of the Counter-Revolutionary Section of the OGPU was unambiguous: "All the German colonies and their leaders are used as an intelligence base that would be harmful in the event of war."[132] The OGPU drew particular attention to the fact that Germans occupied a borderland area and warned of systematic infiltration into the Soviet system: "Germans have penetrated deeply into our army, economy, state apparatus and in some areas control entire branches of industry."[133] To deal with the problem, the OGPU recommended measures to prevent the formation of separate national autonomous regions, to fragment colonists by exploiting national and religious tensions among them, to wage class war in the colonies, to create Soviet organizations among the colonists, and to permit the emigration of kulak elements.[134]

It is difficult to say whether agents in the Counter-Revolution Section really believed in this surrealistic picture or simply wished to accommodate the suspicious mind of their chief, Dzerzhinskii. Whatever the case may be, "incriminating" material against the Germans had been prepared a full sixteen years before the fateful decision in August 1941 to liquidate the Autonomous Republic of Germans on the Volga and to exile all ethnic Germans to remote areas in the East.

The official viewpoint of the OGPU toward the German policy was clearly expressed in a circular letter, endorsed by the deputy chairman (G. Iagoda) on July 9, 1924.[135] The letter asserts that after the conclusion of the Rapallo Treaty an enormous number of German businessmen, industrialists, and other operators had been "pouring into" the Soviet Union. The overwhelming majority of their enterprises (commercial-industrial and transportation concessions as well as travel bureaus) were accused of engaging in espionage. They chose their personnel from former officers of the German army (in part, from officers formerly in the General Staff) and from various fascist organizations. Some of them once lived in Russia and had been arrested on the grounds of suspected espionage.[136] Indeed, the OGPU accused all German nationals working in the Soviet Union of conducting military, diplomatic, and economic espionage in the interests of the German *haute bourgeoisie*. The OGPU repeated its accusations, moreover, against the German colonists as subversive and inherently disloyal. It also attacked the Red Cross, which was allegedly disseminating counter-revolutionary literature and gathering intelligence. The OGPU complained that "it is very difficult" to wage a battle against one intelligence-gathering circle—the German journalists accredited in Moscow. Nevertheless, it recommended the adoption of repressive measures against them, but "with great caution, since this can provoke an anti-Soviet campaign in the foreign press."[137] The main task of the OGPU, as formulated by its counter-intelligence section, was to penetrate the German institutions located on Soviet soil. The agency also demanded that no residence permits be given to German nationals without the permission of its office in that province. The OGPU also recommended a more zealous recruitment of agents from the ranks of German citizens residing in the USSR. Attention should also be given to Soviet citizens whose relatives had fled abroad as part of the White Guards. The OGPU also demanded a careful filtering and surveillance over German communists coming to the Soviet Union. The same suspicion applied to members of the Russian Communist Party who had ties to German representatives: "It is absolutely necessary to put an end to this, for the Germans can easily obtain information from party members about the most confidential matters in state and party policy."[138] Thirteen years later this idea acquired new meaning in the formula about "saboteurs with a party card in their pockets."[139]

No matter how the OGPU regarded Germany, German concessions, and German colonists, the fact remained that the Soviet government had a deep interest in cultivating good relations with that country. German firms were indeed "pouring in," to use the OGPU's phrase. According to documents of the Department of Foreign Orders in the Commissariat of Defense, some 250 German firms had business arrangements with the USSR. That was far more than all the other foreign firms combined: 77 French firms, 71 American, 58 English, 16 Italian, and 11 Austrian.

The End of Military Cooperation

Nonetheless, the days of military cooperation were numbered. The turning point came at a peace conference in July 1932 in Geneva, where the German government openly denounced its neighbors for arming against it and therefore declared itself no longer bound by the Versailles Treaty. As a result, the military cooperation in its original form had lost its former significance. At this point, however,

Germany still wanted to maintain some military ties, especially at the level of strategic planning in the event of a crisis-situation that threatened to unleash a new war in Europe. This fit well with the policy of Chancellor Heinrich Brünning, who supported a policy of balancing the West against the East. But his successor, Franz von Papen, who held the office of chancellor from July to September 1932, inclined toward France and Great Britain. He described his policy as an attempt to prevent a rapprochement between France and the USSR by creating a new diplomatic configuration: the West against the "menace of Bolshevism." As a result, he adopted a formal decision to terminate its secret military cooperation with the Soviet Union.

Hitler's accession to power in early 1933 therefore merely marked the culmination of a process already at work, and he acted quickly to close German military installations located on Soviet soil. Hitler, who had announced a major program to rearm Germany, no longer needed secret schools in foreign countries to train military personnel. Köstring argued that there was some reason to maintain a certain level of cooperation, given the two countries' mutual political interests. That view, however, did not evidently go much further than General Adam and resulted only in Köstring's removal as military attaché in Moscow.[140] Köstring recognized the many negative political factors that made military cooperation unlikely—Hitler's accession to power, Germany's resignation from the League of Nations, repudiation of the military limits in the Versailles Treaty, and the Soviet Union's decision to join the League of Nations. Nevertheless, he held that some German officers still favored military cooperation; that was especially true for those who themselves had previously participated in that cooperation. In 1939 Köstring was again appointed military attaché in Moscow and served as air force attaché as well. In dispatching him to the new post, Hitler said: "Our ideological differences with the Russians are irreconcilable. But I expect you to maintain good relations with the Red Army, as they are supposed to exist."[141] From this conversation Köstring had the distinct impression that Hitler had no inkling of the close cooperation that had existed for many years between the Reichswehr and the Red Army. It is possible, of course, that Köstring misinterpreted Hitler's remarks. After all, shortly after coming to power in 1933, Hitler issued an order to close all the German installations on Soviet territory; the order was carried out by the end of the year. It was for this purpose that the Germans dispatched General von Bockelberg to Moscow, where, to his surprise, he was given an extremely cordial reception. Hencke speculates, rightly, that Moscow still hoped that in the final analysis a pro-Russian sentiment would prevail.[142]

Hencke reports (although without factual corroboration) that a strong anti-German mood prevailed among local Soviet authorities in areas where the Reichswehr installations were located. According to Hencke, the confrontations, "which were inevitable in the dissolution of our military installations, often were difficult and sometimes unpleasant as well. One could hardly demand that the subordinate functionaries could suddenly liberate themselves from the influence of the anti-German propaganda that they had heard night and day in an extreme form."[143]

According to Hencke, once the military cooperation with the Soviet Union had ended, German military circles used their military attaché in Warsaw to maintain contacts with the Red Army.[144] In Hencke's opinion, this "Warsaw connection" was somehow linked to the Polish question. The Nazi takeover in Germany had induced a certain rapprochement on the part of England, France, the USSR, and also Poland. But it remained axiomatic for Soviet foreign policy that the Polish question could be resolved only through collaboration with Germany. Hencke recalls how, during his tenure as German consul in Kiev, the chairman of the Executive Committee for Kiev Oblast' (Vasilenko) offered the following toast at an official reception in April, 1935: "And together we shall be bombing Warsaw again!"[145]

Delivered in the presence of several staff people from the German embassy in Moscow, as well as Soviet officials, the statement was plainly intended to communicate to Berlin the thinking of the Soviet leadership. At any rate, that was Hencke's impression. Moreover, Hencke categorically rejected the notion that Soviet generals were conducting their own policy, behind the back of their government. Hencke contends that Berlin believes the Warsaw contacts were quasi-official and not some kind of "illegal Soviet-Russian feelers."[146] When the Soviet government attempted in 1935 to establish ties between its own military and the Reichswehr, it clearly overestimated the Reichswehr's political influence in the Nazi government and also the "German mentality." A capacity to understand the psychology of elites in Western governments was never a strong suit of Soviet leaders. For example, the Soviets exaggerated the possibility of influencing German policy by "soldier to soldier" appeals. At the same time, holding talks at the level of captain (the German military attaché in Warsaw) could easily be disavowed. Hencke writes that, at no point in the years 1935–1939, did he ever hear of any initiative coming from military quarters. As we shall see, however, that was in fact not true. It was not simply a matter of redrawing borders after the partition of Poland, but also the delivery of German weapons to the USSR.

The continuation of military cooperation in the early 1930s depended on a political decision by the two sides. The Germans found the vagueness of Soviet foreign policy highly disturbing: would the USSR join the Western powers (and hence act contrary to German interests), or would it continue the policy begun at Rapallo? Ebendorf holds that, among the most decisive supporters of the pro-German policy, was the chief of the Soviet general staff, Marshall A. I. Egorov, who was allegedly dissatisfied with the zigzags in Soviet foreign policy. Köstring quotes Egorov's response to rumors about a possible rapprochement between the USSR and France: "A bird in the hand is worth two in the bush! Shall we be friends? Yes, but it had better be soon!"[147] This came at a time when a growing number of German industrial engineers and Reichswehr officers were arriving in the USSR. It all reinforced the conviction that close German-Soviet cooperation was desirable. The last high-ranking visitor was General Adam, who supported the closest possible ties with the Red Army. In 1932 the Soviet government even provided him with a special train for his trip to southern Russia. Among other places he visited the Khar'kov tractor plant and attended maneuvers of the Moscow military district. During his discussion with Egorov he gave a detailed description of the Reichswehr's maneuvers on the Polish border. Twelve Soviet officers made their last visit to Germany in the autumn of 1933.[148]

German Military Installations in the USSR

For approximately a decade Germany and the Soviet Union constructed and operated several joint military installations on Soviet territory. Quite apart from the "high politics" of such collaboration, it is important to examine each concrete instance to see how the two sides cooperated and differed in their aims, expectations and assessments. An analysis of these cooperative ventures will suggest why, even before Hitler's accession to power on January 30, 1933, both sides had become increasingly dissatisfied with their cooperation in the military sphere.

The Junkers Plant in Fili

The first project of military cooperation was an aircraft plant that the German concern Junkers built in the environs of Moscow. The negotiations for the contract with the Junkers firm were difficult and protracted, lasting more than a year (from October 1921 to December 1922). But the two sides finally came to an agreement formally approved on December 12, 1922 by the Council of People's Commissars. The contract gave Junkers concessionary rights to construct an aircraft factory in Fili, near Moscow.[1] According to this agreement, the plant was to produce 300 metal airplanes per year.

Part of the output was to be sold to the Soviet defense commissariat; the balance was to remain at the disposition of the concern. Junkers was further obliged to set up the production of motors. In addition, a contract of November 1922 authorized Junkers to organize transit air connections over Soviet territory with Persia, Afghanistan, Finland, and Sweden. Yet another contract gave Junkers the right to organize aerial photography in the USSR as well as the option to engage in commercial activities.

Interestingly, the negotiations for the main contract of December 1922 elicited intense conflict within various Soviet institutions and vigorous opposition from two quarters—the commissariat of trade and the OGPU. The Commissariat of Foreign Trade, through its mission in Berlin, categorically opposed this agreement with the Junkers firm or indeed any direct arrangement between that concern and Soviet military authorities. As the archival record shows, Soviet officials at the Berlin trade mission claimed that the firm frequently failed to fulfill its obligations and hence should not receive concessionary privileges. The OGPU also opposed the agreement. The problem is to explain why the various organs should have taken such diverging positions.

The OGPU claimed that the founders of the "Aircraft Construction Company Junkers in the USSR" consisted of three components: members of the General Staff, the military-industrial sector, and the navy. One goal of the concession, declared the OGPU, was obviously to evade the restrictions of the Versailles Treaty: the German military understandably wished to find "a hiding place for German military property (concealed from the Entente, especially France) and to create a military base for Germany."[2] But the suspicious OGPU did not believe that this was the only objective, or even the main one: the real purpose of the concession, it claimed, was to establish "links with our General Staff, primarily in operational, intelligence, and organizational matters." If this indeed implies close cooperation between the general staffs of the two armies, then what was the purpose? Given the ostensible areas of contact (operations, intelligence, and organization), the cooperation theoretically amounted to a military alliance. But that plainly was not the case, encouraging the OGPU to imagine subversion or espionage as the real purpose. At any rate, the lingering suspicion probably contributed to the fabrication of the "case" against the Soviet general staff in 1937 that led to the purge of the Red Army elite.

The OGPU report then launches into the realm of sheer fantasy. Seeckt and his circle were actually leaning toward ties with England. Their main objective was purportedly "to prepare the soil in Russia, both in political and economic respects, for a monarchist coup in the USSR." It is difficult to believe that the GPU really believed that such a coup was possible, with or without the assistance of England and a new war in 1921–1922. It seems far more likely that the OGPU* was simply seeking to frighten and intimidate the Soviet leadership with the spectre of a monarchist conspiracy, as in operation Trust, which was blown out of proportion by the OGPU. The civil war was over, the white forces decimated; it was perfectly clear that there was not even the slightest chance that a monarchist conspiracy in the USSR could succeed. Rather, this was simply a device to create a siege mentality and to strengthen the security organs in a state still in the process of being built. It should be remembered that the OGPU memorandum was written no earlier than 1925, when problems with the Junkers concern had become apparent and the government was reconsidering the 1922 agreement.

The OGPU accused the concern of violating the terms of its concession: it had failed to meet its schedule for the delivery of planes and it had failed to meet quality standards.[3] It also levied a host of other accusations, which purported to demonstrate that the firm engaged in "wreaking" (*vreditel'stvo*, a Soviet term for criminal actions to harm the economy by deliberately destructive actions), promoted religion, and employed practices that were inimical to workers and trade unions.[4] The main accusation, however, was that the firm signed the agreement in order to "take over" the Soviet aircraft industry or, failing that, to "disorganize it."[5] After making several more sweeping allegations, the OGPU report offered the following indictment: "Junkers, as a whole, can be regarded as an espionage and counter-revolutionary organization that is working for the English (or at least oriented in their direction)."[6]

From the correspondence among representatives of the firm and Soviet institutions (but also from an exchange of opinions in the upper ranks of the Soviet administration), it is clear that this activity involved a quite different character. In any event, the

---

*Contemporary sources casually intersperse GPU and its new name, OGPU (1922–34),regardless of date; in most cases, regardless of source, OGPU is correct and will be used here.

Politburo commission on the Junkers concession (created in January 1925) concluded that it was desirable to retain the concession and to create more favorable conditions for it. Only then, it concluded, could the concession produce aircraft in Moscow at a cost not exceeding (at least not appreciably) the price of comparable planes manufactured abroad.[7] However, the OGPU did not give up. It obtained support from influential people in the Soviet aviation industry, who feared that the Junkers' contracts would limit prospects for developing the production of domestic military aircraft. There were also some unsubstantiated insinuations of bribery in the air-force administration.[8]

The head of the Soviet air force, Petr I. Baranov, proposed a scheme to terminate dependence on Junkers and to organize the domestic production of all-metal airplanes. His plan involved tapping the former personnel of Junkers for technical assistance and using the designs and blueprints that this firm had already prepared. In a highly classified report to K. Voroshilov (chairman of the Revolutionary-Military Council) on November 21, 1925, Baranov recommended that the Soviet Union take over the Junkers plant in Fili and organize aircraft production itself. Baranov proposed to use the plant's chief engineer (Schade) and his assistant (Cherzikh), both of whom were employees of Aviatrest (the Soviet trust for aircraft production); the new operation would also use the concession's technical staff, which had returned to the firm's home base in Dessau. Baranov also proposed that all the design work be assigned to A. N. Tupolev (an engineer at the Central Aerodynamic Institute). The air force chief did not shy away from simple larceny to ensure success of the new operation, recommending that "all the necessary blueprints, materials, etc. be secretly removed from the plant."[9] That Baranov unabashedly could tender such a proposal to the head of the defense commissariat suggests that such actions were not deemed reprehensible. He also reported that a group of Russian engineers, presently employed at the Junkers plant, had already been systematically stealing materials. According to Baranov, this group "on the basis of these materials and their experience in all details has worked out a production organization, molds, machine-tools, a record-keeping system for stocks and orders, etc."[10]

Interestingly, Baranov's description of the firm's operations inadvertently suggests that its operations were by no means so shoddy, as the OGPU charged. According to the air force chief, "we have all the blueprints and materials to begin immediately to set up the production of Iu-20 and Iu-21 (which Junkers had produced), but also Iu-22s. The start-up of production does not involve any special difficulties and requires a term of approximately two months."[11] A mere two months—notwithstanding all the pernicious activity as alleged by the OGPU! One can scarcely avoid the conclusion that it was not the Junkers firm that sought to "take over" the Soviet aviation industry. Rather, it was merely an attempt by the Soviet Union to confiscate foreign knowhow and to use the German firm's blueprints and technology for the "domestic" production of aircraft.

Apart from invidious attacks by OGPU and domestic competitors, the firm also suffered from financial difficulties. In the fall of 1925 it was on the verge of bankruptcy, saved at the last minute through the intervention of the German government. Two-thirds of the company's stock now belonged to the German government; correspondingly, the firm's governing board was altered to include people representing government interests. The firm's founder and head, Professor Hugo Junkers, retained his position as chairman of the board.[12] Schlieben, a former German minister of finance, was given the task of putting the firm back on its feet; he promptly removed virtually all those who had had disputes with the Soviet government (including the firm's director, Sachsenberg). In conversations with Georgii V. Chicherin, Schlieben emphasized that the Soviet government's attitude toward the fate of Junkers was very important, for "its demise would inflict a serious blow to the economic interests of Germany." Schlieben endeavored to avoid an open break and emphasized the need for an amicable resolution of the questions pertaining to economic relations between Germany and the USSR. For his part, Chicherin recommended that the appropriate Soviet agencies treat Schlieben's warning with the utmost caution, given the deteriorating relations between the USSR and England at the moment.[13]

However, the Soviet agencies with a vested interest remained militantly opposed to the Junkers firm. Thus the Soviet trade mission in Germany demanded that the government "openly declare full-scale war on Junkers over the agreement," and that the trade mission be given plenipotentiary authority for this.[14] The question was reviewed by a special commission of the Politburo, which adopted a resolution to liquidate the mutual obligations through an amicable settlement.[15] To carry out this order, the Main Committee on Concessions created a special commission.[16]

The negotiations were difficult and prolonged. The main stumbling blocks were the firm's financial claims with respect to liquidation and the Soviet refusal to accept twelve bombers from the plant.
To resolve the differences as quickly as possible (so that a Soviet
plant to produce metal airplanes could take over the plant), Deputy
Chairman Iosif S. Unshlikht recommended a certain increase in the
compensation to Junkers.[17] The total payment for liquidation of the
concession, confirmed in March 1927, amounted to 3 million rubles,
which constituted compensation for the plant, its equipment, and
fourteen airplanes with motors and spare parts.[18]

The entire history of the Junkers plant was a not very edifying
episode. Quite apart from the problem of employee theft, this concession—like most others during the New Economic Policy—was a
failure. Its military connection, rather than enhancing its prospects,
only elicited active opposition from the OGPU.

The German Pilot Training School in Lipetsk

Established under the terms of the military cooperation agreement,
the Germans formally founded this training facility in 1925 and
opened it the following year. Its Soviet acronym was VIVIPOL,
which stood for "Camp for Scientific Experimentation and Personal
Training." Its formation had been preceded by the appearance of German instructors in Moscow (in Autumn 1924) under a captain from
the German General Staff, Schröder. The group, which included four
officers and two NCOs, conducted tactical military games with
Soviet pilots. Naturally, the OGPU suspected the Germans of espionage and maintained close surveillance over them. But this group
had a very limited range of capability and ceased to operate in April
1926, although individual members did continue to serve in the Germans' military administration in Moscow.

On April 15, 1925 the Soviet air force signed an agreement with
a representative of the German group in Moscow to establish a pilot
school for Germans in Lipetsk and to construct the requisite buildings, hangars, warehouses, and other facilities. Baranov, as head of
the Soviet air force, signed for the Soviet side; Colonel Lieth-
Thomsen signed for the German side. The Germans assumed the
obligation to pay for all expenses connected with the school, which
was subordinated to the Weapons Directorate of the Reichswehr.[19]

By September 1926 the school was in operation. A representative of the Reichswehr (Wilberg) visited the school and expressed his satisfaction.[20] Nevertheless, there were some complications, especially in the shipping of equipment from Germany to the USSR. As the "Director" (Lieth-Thomsen) complained to Un-shlikht, Soviet customs officials had damaged much of the equipment and some materials had simply disappeared.[21]

During the entire time (1926–1932) that the Lipetsk school was in operation, some 220 military pilots participated in each of the half-year training courses. Altogether, approximately 1,200 German pilots received training in Lipetsk; some attended the training sessions repeatedly, either to improve their skills or obtain experience in other areas.[22] On May 31, 1928 the school reported that it employed sixty-five German staff members at the school.[23] Soviet pilots also received training there. A report sent to Stalin in December 1926 notes that sixteen pilots had been trained in fighters, and another forty-five mechanics had received technical instruction.[24] According to a note from Ian K. Berzin (head of the intelligence unit in the General Staff) in January 1929, thus far 8.6 million rubles had been spent on the school.[25]

Training focused on two main specialties: combat and reconnaissance. Each year, under the supervision of an officer from the Reichswehr, the school conducted training sessions, which included tests of new weapons and equipment, as well as maneuvers with Soviet pilots and service personnel. The Lipetsk school had ninety German fighters, as well as other types of aircraft. Each year the school cost the German military 3 million RM; another 2 million RM was spent on the improvement of equipment.[26] The Germans had an analogous school in Italy; they purchased airplanes for the future Luftwaffe in Sweden and the Netherlands.

To conduct the tests in Lipetsk, the Reichswehr sent a group under the supervision of a senior engineer, Hackmack. He came to the conclusion that the tests, as conducted in Lipetsk, simply could not be carried out in Germany. Above all that pertained to the weapons systems on the aircraft. Hackmack held that progress in this sphere was so significant that one must consider equipping a military installation for this purpose by the spring of 1927. That base could test the effectiveness of the firepower on the aircraft, its bombs, and also the system of control. "I have the distinct impression," wrote Hackmack, "that Russians firmly believe in cooperation in the area of technology."[27] He did not err: Unshlikht's letter to Stalin enumerated many advantages that the Soviet side was deriving from the Lipetsk school—in the sense of familiarity with the most recent technical improvements, knowledge of tactics, and creation of pilots and specialists for the air force.[28] In Hackmack's opinion, well-prepared testing could help create a German structure in this area in Russia. He therefore proposed to outfit the Lipetsk school fully and to assist with equipment and personnel. A site for the testing was found near Voronezh; it had been used previously by a squadron of Soviet bombers. If the testing proved successful, it was thought, the military ties between Germany and the Soviet Union would naturally be strengthened. Evidently fearing skepticism on the part of his superiors in Berlin, Hackmack declared bluntly that "these proposals are not utopian, and the problem was purely organizational."[29] The training included literally everything that concerns the construction of airplanes, their outfitting, weaponry and bombing (including tests of poison-gas bombs).[30] As the training program at Lipetsk shows, the school clearly played a significant role in preparing highly qualified cadres for the future Luftwaffe.

Lipetsk also tested a prototype of the German dive-bomber, known as the Stuka.[31] Köstring recalls that, when he visited Lipetsk in his capacity as military attaché, the senior officer reported for duty and, instead of the customary salute, exclaimed: "The German Luftwaffe is ready for take-off!"[32] Köstring notes that "for me this was an historic moment: it was the first time that I had heard a German officer report in like this."

In 1941, Soviet soldiers were to experience first-hand just how effective the training at Lipetsk had been. But in the 1920s all this was seen in a different light. In July 1933 the Reichswehr decided to close the school at Lipetsk. Buildings and equipment that could not be shipped to Germany were given without charge to the Soviet partners. While making this gesture, the Reichswehr command proposed to maintain reciprocal visits of officers and specialists (to inspect technical sites, factories, and flying schools) and to continue the exchange of experience in the areas of tactics and technology.[33]

Tomka

Eager to rebuild its military industry, the Soviet government gave particular attention to the production of airplanes, motors, tanks, military vessels, and toxic substances. By the mid-1930s the Soviet

Union concentrated production of the main military goods in sixty-eight plants.[34] Geographically, the plants for the production of war gases were located mainly in central Russia and in the Volga region.[35] A joint Soviet-German installation for the testing of poison gas was located on the Volga.

The beginnings of cooperation in the area of chemical warfare came in August and September 1923, when the German firm GEFU created a joint enterprise with the Soviet corporation Bersol. The concession involved a chemical plant located at a railway station, Ivshchenkovo, on the Samara-Zlatoust Railway Line. Its goal was to produce asphyxiating gases (phosgene and mustard gas) on Soviet territory. As a secret document from December 1924 reveals, however, the plant was also to produce "a broad range of chemical production" where "secrecy" had the highest priority. The two partners agreed that the Soviet side (called "Metakhim") would provide a chemical plant as its share of the investment, and the Germans were to supply new equipment (from the Stolzenberg firm in Hamburg), patents, and cash. The total capital of the enterprise amounted to 12 million gold rubles. The two sides agreed that for the first three years each side would make a guaranteed annual order for 2,000 poods (32,760 kg) of liquid chlorine and 5,500 poods (90,090 kg) of yperite, both of which were to be sold at cost. Metakhim assumed responsibility for ensuring that the equipment from GEFU was exempt from import tariffs and for shipping the finished product. The contract was for a twenty-year term.[36]

At a meeting on February 1, 1926, the Revolutionary-Military Council approved the report of the chief of the Military-Chemical Directorate (Iakov Fishman) about anti-gas defenses and chemical warfare. The Council drew particular attention to the study of the most recent developments in aerochemical substances for defense and attack, the use of poisonous mists, and the reduction of the cost and complexity of chemical warfare. One point in its resolution called for increasing the role of the Military-Chemical Directorate in the development of the peacetime chemical industry and planning for its possible mobilization in the event of war. That meant, in effect, establishing military control over the entire chemical industry. The Council further resolved to construct shelters to protect the civilian population from chemical attacks. As the resolution implies, the Soviet leadership regarded war as inevitable and was prepared, if need be, to use chemical weapons. The Council also decided to construct a test site, a chemical laboratory, and experimental plants.[37]

In May 1926 the venture conducted its first test firings of chemical shells—500 shells with yperite and 250 with diphosgene. Fishman reported that the first firing was a failure, but a second firing had better results: "A significant part of the animals showed a positive reaction. These animals are now in serious condition." The chief of the Military-Chemical Directorate spoke proudly of Soviet-made yperite, which was purportedly very potent. Indeed, by a mishap the toxin was tested not only on the experimental animals (cats), but also on human beings—two Red Army soldiers had been accidentally exposed to the toxin. According to Fishman, both were severely affected and required hospitalization. Fishman was obviously very satisfied with the gruesome effectiveness of the chemicals: "The moral effect on our units was very great. The Red Army units serving at the site, despite the gas masks were often overtaken by panic."[38] Enemy troops could be expected to display the same terror. Fishman also reported that Soviet respirators (model T-4) proved to be of first-rate quality. Encouraged by the results of this test firing, Fishman proposed to conduct large-scale tests (with all types of land forces) at the Luga site at the end of the summer.

Three months later Fishman informed Unshlikht that the plan to produce 500,000 shells with poisonous substances was possible, but only if the necessary means were provided in time. He complained that the quantity of chemical ordnance (bombs and gas mines) was insignificant and did not satisfy tactical requirements and strategic considerations. At present, he reported, his organization could manufacture only 40,000 gas shells. Half of these would contain mustard gas; the balance would consist of fragmentation chemical shells, mustard gas, type "S," and other new forms of toxic substances.[39] Eventually, Metakhim resolved some of these problems and concluded a further agreement with GEFU to supply the latter with 400,000 shells at a cost of eighteen million gold rubles. Six military plants were assigned to fulfill this order.[40]

In September Colonel Wilberg, the Reichswehr's representative, visited several sites of joint cooperation, including a test-firing range near the railway junction of Podosiniki (about 1.5 hours by automobile from Moscow). The range was later relocated to Vol'sk District in Samara province, where a German firm, Stolzenberg, had built a chemical plant. The construction of this plant had been begun in

1923, but did not go into operation until 1926—chiefly because of the firm's financial difficulties. These business problems, together with an explosion at its plant near Hamburg, attracted considerable attention in the German press. As a result, some details of the Soviet-German collaboration in the production and testing of poison gases came to light, leading to accusations in the press that Germany was violating the Versailles Treaty.

In his unpublished memoirs Hencke claims that the testing did not involve offensive chemical weapons, but only defenses against them. However, Soviet documents disprove that claim. In a letter to Stalin, Unshlikht reported that the Soviet air force had been conducting tests of chemical gases—jointly with the Germans, in accordance with the agreement of August 21, 1926. The tests had involved experiments in diffusing (from various altitudes) liquids with the physical properties of yperite; the tests had shown, according to Unshlikht, that "the aviation's use of mustard gas against live targets (to infect the area and populated settlements) proved technically feasible and has great value."[41] Unshlikht also took obvious satisfaction in noting that Soviet material expenditures, compared to the Germans', had been inconsequential.[42] He therefore recommended that the cooperative work with the Germans be continued at a joint tank school (to be established by the agreement of December 2, 1926), in Lipetsk and also in air-force testing. In contrast to these strictly military operations, Unshlikht was critical of joint military-industrial enterprises with the Germans, noting that these attempts to attract German capital (via the Reichswehr) had not been successful.[43]

That position was directly challenged by Gal'perin, an official in the Revolutionary Military Council and on the board of the Main Chemical Administration. His proposal, submitted in 1927, created quite a sensation: it recommended that the Soviet government seek foreign capital to invest in the Soviet chemical industry and, in particular, in the military-chemical branch. His main thesis was irresistible: the concessions would use domestic raw and semi-processed materials, thereby avoiding any dependence on the international market.[44] As in other sectors, this drive for autarky sprang both from a desire to be independent from the capitalist world and from the vested interests of a particular economic sector in promoting its own development. The Main Commission on Concessions discussed the Gal'perin report at a session in early January 1927 and endorsed its main principles. As chief of the Military-Chemical Directorate, Fishman supported the proposal and emphasized that one must coordinate the work of the concession with the defense needs of the country.[45] The OGPU also supported Gal'perin's proposal and drew it to the attention of the military administration.[46]

But the Soviet Union required not only capital, but also know-how. As the Military-Chemical Directorate declared in February 1931, "We need technical assistance." It was referring specifically to the production of toxic substances and the defense against chemical weapons. As earlier, the Soviet Union collaborated with a number of leading German firms: Dreger und Auer, Gustav and German Maining, and Hugo Stolzenberg were partners with the military-chemical service of the Red Army.[47] The Directorate urged immediate action to attract foreign firms for technical assistance. Moreover, in connection with the orders of the Soviet trade mission in Berlin, it proposed to send its own people to the foreign plants "in order to take everything possible from them and to pay as little as possible for it."[48] That statement neatly epitomized the Soviet attitude toward its German partners. Köstring also attributes the following remark to Fishman: "Germany has the most famous chemical industry in the world. We find it unthinkable that your leading men cannot develop something new."[49] As a result, the tests of poisonous materials were delayed until the next year: the Soviet side did not want to waste funds on testing until they were sure that the Germans had something new. A visceral distrust of the capitalist partner, reinforced by the OGPU's vigilant surveillance of both partners, were constant features of Soviet-German military cooperation.

All this was especially evident to the Germans working at Tomka. Of interest here is the correspondence between the deputy commissar for foreign affairs (N. N. Krestinskii), the commissar of military and naval affairs (K. E. Voroshilov), and the chairman of the OGPU (Viacheslav R. Menzhinskii). On December 15, 1928 Krestinskii informed Voroshilov that, according to Kork and Uborevich, the Germans at Tomka were extremely dissatisfied with "the regime of semi-imprisonment to which they are subjected by our side."[50] Krestinskii reminded him that Soviet military personnel in Germany were allowed unrestricted freedom of movement and that the authorities could not "meddle in their personal lives." But, noted Krestinskii, the situation was quite different for Germans in the USSR: "In our country, a trip not only to Moscow, but even to the nearest large city, is regarded as something absolutely extraordinary and is permitted only in exceptional circumstances." Voroshilov quoted at length from Krestinskii's letter, including his remark that Germans who might be turned into "a weapon to attract more sympathy toward us, instead lose those feelings of sympathy that they arrived with." Krestinskii proposed that an arrangement be made "with the comrades" in the OGPU and expressed the hope that Menzhinskii would issue the corresponding orders. These orders should, on the one hand, "ensure the necessary surveillance of the Germans," but on the other "not be so overt and demonstrative" as to create "all kinds of restrictions and degradation." Referring to comments by the chief of the Military-Chemical Directorate, Voroshilov nevertheless observed that "the Germans attempted to behave themselves brazenly in the joint ventures and it is entirely proper to call them to order."[51] Voroshilov thus attempted to strike a compromise and also to pose the question tactfully and thereby to avoid insulting Menzhinskii's OGPU.

In the autumn of 1928 General von Blomberg visited Tomka in addition to other German military sites. With an obvious sense of satisfaction, his report noted the good organization, smooth flow of work, and also the lively interest that the Russian side took in testing and in expanding the plant's capabilities.[52] Eventually, however, the two sides agreed to close Tomka. For its part, the Soviet side became openly dissatisfied with what it perceived to be the Germans' failure to offer "new ideas"—that is, new forms of toxic substances. Indeed, Fishman strongly suspected that the Germans were deliberately withholding the newest breakthroughs from their laboratories in Germany. In a Reichswehr document dating from 1931, Niedermayer recalls a business trip to Germany by Soviet chemists, who had been sent by the Revolutionary Military Council to learn about the research in German laboratories and to hold discussions with their leaders. It was also expected that the Soviets would participate in military tests and exchange opinions on technical problems and tactical questions.[53] The test schedule for 1931 included potent toxins, which bore code names like "yellow cross," "green cross," "blue cross," and shells loaded with poison gases. The tests also aimed to study the feasibility of diffusing toxins by means of artillery shells and bombs.[54] As earlier, the Soviet side continued to complain about the lack of new materials; on April 13, 1932 an irritated Fishman pointed out to his German colleagues that the tests offered absolutely nothing new: there were no new poison gases, no new toxic mists. Nor did the tests offer new methods for using the poisonous substances and gases. The only change, he complained, was the demand for larger expenditures that the Soviet Union was to bear alone. Fishman proposed that the two sides conduct joint laboratory work in order to improve the test program for 1933. Only if there were technological innovation, he warned, could Germany expect further financial support from the Soviet side. He therefore proposed to devote 1932 to theoretical research in the laboratories and to resume testing in 1933, when the two sides could evaluate the results and test the tactical use of the new substances. Only if 1932 concentrated on serious laboratory work could the next year lead to useful, qualitatively new testing. The Soviet side expressed a willingness to send its specialists to Germany—no doubt not only to conduct the laboratory research, but also to gather industrial intelligence. The Germans thanked Fishman for his candor and expressed the hope that the problems could be overcome.[55] During these discussions the Soviet side also made clear its desire that the work on toxins be conducted in direct collaboration with the German firm I. G. Farben (and specific plants, such as Leuna Werke and Bitterfeld).[56]

On May 16, 1933 a Reichswehr representative (Lieutenant General von Bockelberg) and the German military attaché in Moscow (Colonel Hartmann) met with Fishman. The latter adamantly insisted that Soviet chemists be admitted to the secret laboratories of German firms conducting research on toxic substances. He also showed himself to be surprisingly well-informed about the location of the laboratories and the kind of research that they were conducting. Given that the discussion took place after Hitler's access to power, it is hardly surprising that Bockelberg's replies were evasive. But Hartmann's comments reveal also that the Germans clearly understood the Soviet position: Soviet military circles would have liked to expand the collaboration, but the change in the political situation constituted a fundamental obstacle. The German side, however, had second thoughts about the implication of such cooperation: "One must give a full answer to the question—is friendship with Russia of value (from a military point of view), given the growth in its industrial might and independence?"[57]

Mikhail N. Tukhachevskii (deputy chairman of the Revolutionary Military Council) was also drawn into these discussions. He had

visited Germany in the fall of 1932, when the von Papen government had decided to disengage from military collaboration with the
USSR. Although he was told that the reason for this change was fis-
cal, the import was the same: the Reichswehr was to close all its military sites on Soviet territory. In response to this report, however,
Hartmann claimed that the plan for closings involved only Lipetsk
and that part of the enterprise was to be transferred to Tomka.

These discussions took place on May 15, 1933—three and one-
half months after the Nazis came to power in Berlin. Moscow was
still trying to understand the meaning of that event and its implications for Soviet-German cooperation in military affairs. That is why
Tukhachevskii sought to assume a balanced position on the issue.
Thus, on the one hand, he reassured the Germans that even the closing of Tomka would not signify a "fundamental change" in military
cooperation.[58] It is difficult to imagine, of course, that Tukhachevskii himself believed this. On the other hand, he supported Fishman's argument that so far the cooperation in military chemicals had
yielded minimal results. To be sure, explained Tukhachevskii, it
would be quite a different matter if the Germans want to revitalize
work in Tomka. But thus far he had found little evidence of a change;
during his own trip to Germany, for example, he had not been shown
the production process, but only plant site. Tukhachevskii also
deemed it essential that Soviet military chemists be admitted to the
laboratories and learn about the newest forms of military toxins.
Fishman was more categorical: without new toxic substances, the
work in Tomka must be suspended. Evidently, both the Germans and
their Soviet partners now had to adjust to the new policies of their
home governments—which were always prone to zigzags, but now
moving toward disengagement. In conversations with the Germans,
Voroshilov emphasized that cooperation between the two countries
was justified and even necessary, but noted an indispensable precondition: cooperation must be compatible with the general political course.[59]

In analyzing the experience of military cooperation at Tomka,
the Germans observed that the difficulties of the earlier years had
increased significantly during the tests of 1932–1933. The Russians
were not interested in merely having the Germans test their toxic
substances and equipment, but also in obtaining something new for
themselves. "Cooperation in such a form can hardly be a cause of
joy," as one document from the Soviet side impatiently observed.[60]

Berlin had clearly decided to find a suitable site in Germany itself, where it could conduct tests independently, even if on a small scale. As for large-scale operations that could not be conducted inside Germany, then a country other than Russia would be found. At any rate, by July 1933 it was quite clear that Germany had either to accept the Soviet conditions or shut down Tomka. Political calculations, no doubt, weighed heavily: A half-year after Hitler became chancellor, he was conducting not only an anti-communist but also an anti-Soviet campaign. On July 21, 1933 the minister of the Wehrmacht decided that all chemical tests must henceforth be conducted in Germany itself. For its part, the commissar of military and naval affairs issued a decree terminating the work at Tomka and ordering its immediate dismantlement.

The Soviet and German personnel at Tomka parted under rather cordial terms. The Soviet commandant noted that the old friendship should be preserved; politics had nothing to do with soldiers. Some Soviet commanders emphasized the common interests of the USSR and Germany, especially regarding their mutual enemy—Poland. "We shall never be friends with the Poles," said one of the Soviet commanders. In earlier times the Russians were in Warsaw on several occasions, the Poles also were in Moscow, but the Russians will again occupy Warsaw."[61] The also discussed the possibility of using chemical weapons in the event of war between the USSR and Poland or between Germany and France.[62]

Kama: The German Tank School

The fourth German military enterprise on Soviet soil was the Kama tank school and training camp in the environs of Kazan. The Reichswehr's commanding officer was a Major Marlbrandt. It commenced operation in 1926, its status determined by a protocol signed in October of that year.[63] The chief of the Reichswehr's General Staff, von Blomberg, inspected the school in the autumn of 1928 and spoke of its need for equipment. Voroshilov made also the same demand.[64] In March 1929 he informed Stalin that the Reichswehr had requested assistance in transporting ten tanks to the Kazan school. The German side proposed that, as a respectable cover for the operation, a German firm, Rheinmetall, sign a fictitious contract with the Red Army about the sale of tanks. Once the tanks arrived in the USSR, the contract would be destroyed. Voroshilov endorsed the proposal. As he explained in a letter to Stalin, the Versailles Treaty prohibited Germany from building tanks; if there were a breach of confidentiality, the blame for violating the ban could be shifted from the government to "industry."[65] The school in Kazan received the tanks in the summer of 1929.

In 1928 the Reichswehr dispatched to the school a young officer named Heinz Guderian, who would become famous later, during World War II, when his tank division reached the very outskirts of Moscow. According to German sources, Guderian significantly improved conditions at Kama. During maneuvers and testing of new models of tanks, Soviet tank crews also took part. In addition to the testing and training camp, the Germans also had two Krupp tank plants to manufacture the new models.

According to Köstring,[66] the cooperation between German and Soviet tank crews was exceedingly close. The deputy chief of the Mechanization and Motorization Directorate of the Red Army gave a rather high assessment of the work at Kama. He noted that activities at the tank school "up to now represent great interest for the Red Army from both the technical and tactical point of view."[67] Sixty-five Soviet tank commanders completed the school in a three-year period.[68] The cooperation was complete, even to the point where German tank crews sometimes wore Soviet uniforms (rather than the civilian clothes that they ordinarily donned).

After 1933 German tank building at home increased sharply, making the complex near Kazan redundant. The Germans closed Kama in August-September 1933, along with all other military sites in the USSR.

Military cooperation between the USSR and Germany lasted more than a decade and, at various junctures, was advantageous to both parties. The cooperation was possible because of the coincidence of political and strategic interests; each side had different needs, and different objectives, in establishing and operating these installations. And for different reasons, each side grew increasingly dissatisfied with the results of this cooperation, quite apart from the ideological confrontation between German fascism and Soviet communism that had emerged in the early 1930s. By 1933, as the balance of power began to shift, the USSR and Germany stood at a crossroads in their relationship.

3 Crossroads

E ven after Moscow began to pursue a policy of collective security, it continued to seek better relations with Berlin. Although Hitler showed no real
interest in arresting the deterioration in relations, Stalin continued
to seek ways to improve relations. Although the dualistic appeal to
both the West and Germany also aimed to play one side against the
other, the appeals to Germany revealed Stalin's affinity for the
undemocratic regime. Even though military cooperation had been
sundered, the two sides did actively seek to strengthen economic
ties. The task here is to elucidate why Moscow pursued these ties,
what impeded its efforts, and how the two reached a new nadir in
their relations in 1937.

Hitler in Power

To understand the history of Soviet-German ties, both in military
and political spheres, one must recognize an incontrovertible fact:
the most powerful proponent of close ties to Germany was none other
than Stalin himself. Stalin was not frightened when the Nazis suddenly surged in popularity and political power in the early 1930s;
indeed, he generally took a relatively tolerant attitude toward national socialists (at least those outside his own country!). He calculated

that, if they actually came to power, they would not only terminate the despicable Social Democrats but also—so obsessed were they with revising the Versailles Treaty— direct all their energy against the Western countries, to the clear advantage of the Soviet Union.

This line of thought was apparent in 1931 during Stalin's talks with Heinz Neumann, a member of the Politburo of the German Communist Party. Stalin implicitly revealed his views by the way he formulated a crucial question: "If the National Socialists come to power in Germany, will they be completely preoccupied with the West, so that we can construct socialism [in the USSR]?" In the final analysis, Stalin was concerned first and foremost with consolidating his own dictatorship; he was perfectly content to accept any friendly regime in Berlin, regardless of its internal policies. Indeed, Stalin probably preferred a dictatorial regime, for the thinking and behavior of a German dictator probably seemed more comprehensible than the mentality of politicians from democratic states.

Stalin's perspective naturally laid the foundations for the policies of the Comintern, which consequently explained fascism as "an overly terroristic dictatorship of finance capitalism" that found its social base in the petty bourgeoisie. It regarded Social Democracy as "social fascism," for which—to be sure—one can find no intelligible definition. Whatever the value of these abstruse definitions, the practical implication of this outlook was to deny the possibility of a united front between communists and social democrats. There was indeed no need to cooperate with the perfidious Social Democrats. The XII Plenum of the Comintern's Executive Committee declared that the rapidly maturing social and economic crisis would grow into a revolutionary situation, which in turn must lead to the establishment of a dictatorship of the proletariat in Germany, and the sooner the better. The myth that fascism could accelerate the revolutionary process was a fatal chimera of the Comintern.[1] History was to prove these prognoses to be catastrophically fallacious. Nowhere was the disaster greater than in Germany: at Moscow's order, the German Communist Party pronounced the Social Democrats "enemy no. 1," drove a significant proportion of the workers into the Nazis' arms, split the vote of democratic and socialist forces, and contributed to Hitler's triumph at the polls in 1932. Although the Social Democrats obtained 7.2 million votes and the German communists another 6.0 million, the Nazis emerged the dominant party, with 11.7 million ballots.[2]

Once Hitler came to power, however, Germany's relations with
the USSR rapidly deteriorated. Police raids, arrests, and beatings of
Soviet citizens accompanied a savage anti-Soviet campaign on the
pages of Nazi newspapers. At a world economic conference, Alfred
Hugenberg (the German minister of economics and agriculture)
pronounced Eastern Europe (including Ukraine) to be fields of German expansion. Moscow at first believed that these were merely the
"birthpangs" of a new regime, and that relations to Germany would
gradually return to normal. That expectation, based on an exaggerated assessment of the Reichswehr's influence, proved erroneous.

Military Contacts, Political Tensions

To assess the Soviet Union's relations with the Reichswehr during
the first year of Nazi rule, one must note the important qualitative
changes in Soviet military industry that had occurred by 1933. By the
second five-year-plan, Soviet industry had significantly expanded its
production of ordnance and equipment for the Red Army. It now
began the mass production of tanks, new artillery systems, and warplanes. The Red Army accordingly adopted such new tactics as air-
borne assault forces, which made a strong impression on foreign military observers during maneuvers in 1932.

Still more important in affecting Soviet-German military relations, however, was the change in political climate that is especially
apparent in the case of Soviet officers training in Germany, who
were naturally well aware of the Nazis' anti-communist (and, by
extension, anti-Soviet) campaign. They were not only more circumspect in making assessments of the Reichswehr, but also gave
more attention in their reports to political and ideological developments. One such Soviet officer (Mikhail K. Levandovskii, commander of the Siberian Military District) added a dose of sycophantic
flattery in a letter to Voroshilov explaining the focus of his report:
"The comparison [with the German army] is necessary chiefly in
order to show once again what colossal successes the Red Army has
made under your leadership."[3] Levandovskii then quoted an order
from Voroshilov on the very same subject. The Siberian commander also lodged a formal protest with Colonel-General Alfred Jodl
(chief of the Russian Section of the Reichswehr's General Staff)
against the hostile attacks in the Nazi press on the Soviet military
on the occasion of the fifteenth anniversary of the Red Army.[4] Nor

did Levandovskii forget to close the letter by hailing "the Leninist Bolshevik Party under its leader, comrade Stalin."[5]

Some German officers, however, tried to downplay the import of the political changes in Berlin, at least with respect to military relations. The Soviet military attaché in Berlin (V. N. Levichev) sent a report to Moscow, quoting the opinion of Colonel Schmidt (head of the Military Academy): "If there has hitherto been no contradiction between the Soviet Union and Germany, then of course there can be no talk of it now. . . . It is in the direct interests of Germany that there be a strong Soviet Union." Schmidt argued that the very essence of the new German regime excluded a contradiction between the Soviet Union and Germany, for in both countries "the aim is to build socialism." The only difference is that Germany is building socialism on a national basis. He concluded, not without a sense of irony: "True, the Soviet Union hoped that the German baby would be born now with red hair, but instead he was born with brown hair."[6]

The Soviet military attaché was himself struck by the similarity of "cultural" phenomena in Nazi Germany and Soviet socialism. Bewildered by the sight of Nazis marching to the beat of Soviet revolutionary march music, the attaché consoled himself with the thought that Nazism could hold onto power "only by draping socialist slogans and words around itself."[7] Hence the genetic bonds between the Soviet and Nazi regimes were not only apparent at the time, but also explicitly discussed.

Soviet officers continued to train in Germany throughout the first half of 1933. Despite their increasingly critical evaluations of the Reichswehr and praise for their own Red Army, they continued to note the Germans' high level of motorization, artillery, communications, and (most important, according to the Soviet officers) the capacity for independent work that is inculcated from youth.[8] The German military attaché in Moscow, Colonel Hartmann, made the reverse observation, identifying as a characteristic feature of Soviet commanders "a far-reaching fear of responsibility." At the same time, Hartmann gave a rather high general assessment of the Red Army, although he rejected its claim to be capable of fighting a defensive war against any adversary.[9]

In the first half of May 1933 a group of high-ranking German officers (under the leadership of General von Bockelberg) made a three-week visit to the Soviet Union. Formally, this was a return visit for the trip that Tukhachevskii had made to German military installations in the fall of 1932. When Voroshilov sent Stalin a list of enterprises that the Germans would visit, he explained apologetically that "in terms of reciprocity it is necessary to show both production facilities and some military units."[10] In a reception held in honor of the German delegation, Voroshilov specifically underscored the Red Army's desire to maintain friendly ties with the Reichswehr.[11] Tukhachevskii attended an elite breakfast (for "a small circle") and expressed the wish that the Germans build 2,000 bombers so that they could (in his words) escape from "a difficult political situation."[12] The Soviet side showed Bockelberg such features as TsAGI (the Central Aerodynamics Institute), aircraft and tank plants, arms plants in Tula and Kalinin, radio factories, and chemical plants. The conclusion drawn by Bockelberg and the accompanying officers was favorable: "Cooperative work with the Red Army and Soviet military industry, in view of the grandiose Soviet plans, is exceedingly desirable, not only from military-political considerations, but also from a military-technical point of view." Bockelberg's general political conclusion was that "there are no signs that the undeniable famine could lead to the overthrow of Soviet power."[13]

Soviet leaders could be entirely satisfied. At a reception held in honor of the German military delegation, Voroshilov emphasized that the Red Army wished to preserve friendly ties with the Reichswehr. But—and a large "but"—what were Hitler's real intentions? It was clear that the Reichswehr could not be expected to keep its virtually autonomous status. Still, Moscow as yet had no clear idea how relations with Germany were likely to develop. At a reception for Ambassador Herbert von Dirksen and Hartmann, N. N. Krestinskii emphasized that the decade-long cooperation between the Reichswehr and Red Army was now entering a new phase because of the deterioration in Soviet-German relations. He then demanded that the German government use an "iron hand" to terminate the anti-Soviet attacks.[14] Evidently influenced by Krestinskii's words, Dirksen wrote Hitler: "Historically, we should maintain good relations with Russia, with whom we shall sooner or later have a common border."[15] Dirksen was essentially repeating Seeckt's idea about the inevitable demise of Poland—only in this context did his remark about "a common border" make any sense.

In late October 1933 Dirksen sent Krestinskii an official communication from Berlin, declaring Germany's desire to resolve all issues through negotiations.[16] There were indeed many issues to resolve. According to a report from the Soviet diplomatic mission in Germany, forty-seven Soviet citizens had been arrested in 1933; nine of them worked for official Soviet organizations in Germany. But more painful for Germany itself was the sharp reduction in trade. If 1929 is the base year of 100 (for all goods except platinum), by 1933 exports to the USSR had declined to 82.6, while imports from the USSR dropped to 19.7.[17]

The future of relations with Germany thus was exceedingly unclear. On the one hand, official Soviet organs vehemently protested the abuse of its journalists and trade representatives in Germany. On the other hand, high-ranking officials told their German counterparts that they "understood" the difficulties that faced Hitler immediately after he became Chancellor. Thus Soviet leaders still hoped that, after an initial period when the Nazis had become firmly entrenched in power), it would be possible to restore the relatively harmonious relations that had prevailed earlier. Avel' Enukidze (a close confidante of Stalin and secretary of the Central Executive Committee of the government) candidly voiced such views in a conversation with the Ambassador Dirksen on August 16, 1933. According to Enukidze, Soviet leaders realized that, once the National Socialists came to power, the "propagandistic" and "governmental-political" elements in the Nazi Party had split into distinct groups. Enukidze expressed the hope that, once Germany had formulated a "political course" for its government and resolved its internal political questions, it would also acquire freedom of action in foreign policy. Particularly revealing of Stalin's view of National Socialism were Enukidze's words that "for many years already" the Soviet government has had such a free hand. Enukidze thus drew a direct historical parallel between what happened in Russia after the revolution and what transpired in Germany after Hitler came to power—what the Nazis themselves called the "national-social revolution." In elaborating this comparison, Enukidze emphasized that both Germany and the USSR have "many people who give priority to the political goals of the party. They have to be cowed into submission" and precedence given to the government and its political objectives. After all, Germany and the USSR have enormous interests in common, including a revision of the Versailles Treaty in eastern Europe—a transparent allusion to the extinction of Poland. "The national-

socialist rebuilding of Germany can have a positive consequence
for German-Soviet relations," concluded Enukidze.[18]

Enukidze held this conversation in the presence of two deputy
commissars of foreign affairs (Nikolai N. Krestinskii and Lev M.
Karakhan) as well as the counselor of the German embassy in
Moscow (Twardovski). Hence the discussion bore an unmistakably
official character. According to Dirksen, in 1934 Enukidze showed
himself to favor friendly relations with Germany.[19]

In late 1933 and early 1934, as the Soviet government deliberated
its foreign policy, it made repeated appeals to Germany to resume
cooperation. Thus on October 24, 1933 the counselor at the Germany embassy in Moscow informed Berlin of a proposal by a Soviet
"friend"—most likely, Karl Radek, Stalin's closest adviser on German affairs who headed the bureau for international information at
the Central Committee. The "friend" proposed to arrange a meeting
between Dirksen (who was leaving his post as German ambassador
in Moscow) and V. M. Molotov, chairman of the Council of People's
Commissars.[20] The goal of such a meeting was to clarify Soviet-German relations. Such a proposal could have come only from Stalin
himself. Shortly afterward, on November 6, 1933 (at a reception to
celebrate the October Revolution), Tukhachevskii carried out a similar mission: he informed the same Twardowski that "the Rapallo
policy remains the most popular in the Soviet Union." It shall never
be forgotten, he said, that the Reichswehr had been the Red Army's
teacher at a difficult point in its existence. He added that the Red
Army would welcome a resumption of cooperation. To do so, he
added, it is only necessary to overcome fears that the new German
government is pursuing a hostile policy against the USSR.[21]

However, the Soviet leadership itself was divided on how to treat
Nazi Germany. According to a curious archival document (for the
first time made public here), in July 1933 the Soviet ambassador to
Germany, Lev M. Khinchuk, informed Lazar Kaganovich (a Central
Committee secretary) of a change being planned in the relations
between the USSR and Germany. Khinchuk noted that "Soviet-
German relations, which had already experienced a certain crisis in
recent years, entered an extremely acute phase after Hitler came to
power."[22] He claimed that the Germans fear not only their own isolation, but also the strengthening of Soviet influence in the Baltics
and in the Balkans. Nevertheless, he contended, the Germans are
continuing to play "the Rapallo game" and will not sunder the eco-

nomic ties with the USSR. Khinchuk therefore advised caution
toward Germany:

> While seeking closer relations with France, Poland, and other gov-
> ernments, one should not prematurely cast off the mask and initiate
> an uninhibited anti-German campaign. One needs here to observe a
> certain proportion, which is determined entirely by foreign-policy
> expediency. If we openly admit that nothing remains of the Soviet-
> German ties, then this merely reduces our value in the eyes of Ger-
> many's adversaries.[23]

One may wonder whether Khinchuk's comments do not reflect
doubts in the Soviet leadership about the best foreign policy course,
all the more since it regarded relations with Germany (or any other
"capitalist" state) as simply a game of expediency.

As subsequent events were to show, Stalin decided to conduct
foreign policy simultaneously along two quite contradictory lines:
an "official" policy of rapprochement with France and her allies, as
well as an "unofficial" policy of seeking not only cooperation but
also a comprehensive agreement with Germany. Thus, at the fourth
session of the Central Executive Committee on December 29, 1933,
Maksim Litvinov reiterated that the USSR was undertaking nothing against Germany.[24] This statement came shortly after the Central Committee passed a resolution to adopt a policy of creating a
system of collective security in Europe.[25] The Soviet Union also
decided to join the League of Nations and become an active member of that organization.

In early 1934 the Red Army command launched another diplomatic campaign to court the Germans. The Soviet leadership evidently believed that the prospect of renewing military cooperation
would carry the greatest weight with the Germans. Moscow clung to
the illusion that the Reichswehr was still an autonomous force capable of influencing German foreign policy. Hence Kliment Voroshilov
and Aleksandr I. Egorov kept insisting to their counterparts in the
Reichswehr that the USSR wished to preserve the best possible relations with Germany.[26] Hitler, however, had no intention of sharing
power with anyone, especially the generals of the Reichswehr.

The Turning Point: 1934

The year 1934 was a decisive turning point for Stalinist Russia. Collectivization by now was virtually complete, with enormous conse-

quences for the whole social structure. The peasantry had been vanquished and ruined; its most productive elements were either physically liquidated, decimated by an artificially created famine, or dispatched to labor camps. The industrial sector obtained labor virtually free of charge. Having used the old party guard to engineer and execute this social revolution, Stalin now prepared to realize plans that he had long nurtured: to get rid of his old comrades, even those who had assisted in building his dictatorship.

The events transpiring in the USSR did not go unnoticed in Berlin. In January 1934 Karl Radek "confidentially" informed German journalists that the policy of collective security—which the Soviet Union had just announced—was provoked by tensions in the Far East. Nevertheless, he explained, this did not preclude a new rapprochement with Germany:

> We are not doing anything that would tie our hands for a long period of time. Nothing will happen that could permanently block our way to achieving a common policy with Germany. You know the policy that Litvinov represents. But behind him stands a firm, careful, and distrustful person with a strong will. Stalin does not know what the real relations with Germany are. He has doubts. Nor could it be otherwise. We can only be distrustful of the Nazis.

Stalin's expert on German relations proceeded to draw this conclusion:

> We know that the Versailles [Treaty] no longer exists. We know something of Germany's capability to arm itself. You should not imagine that we are so stupid that we shall fall under the wheels of world history. The [foreign] policy of the USSR is to extend the world's breathing-spell.[27]

Radek's use of the term "breathing-spell" implied that war was inevitable and, apparently, that the Entente powers and Germany were natural adversaries. The USSR should make a choice, but this would depend on its relations with Germany. For its part, the Soviet Union was prepared for the closest possible cooperation with Germany. But not only with Germany—such was the transparent message from Radek's remarks. Radek, who prepared foreign-policy materials for Stalin's report to the Seventeenth Party Congress (February 1934), knew what he was talking about.

That congress, proclaimed the "congress of victors" (to celebrate the successful social revolution in recent years), was really the "congress of *the* victor"—Stalin, who had decimated his own people. His official report (delivered nominally on behalf of the Central Committee) was deliberately circumspect in its characterization of "the German type of fascism." To be sure, he declared, "the most careful analysis cannot uncover a single atom of socialism."[28] But its other half—nationalism—had made a powerful impression on Stalin, also with respect to internal affairs. He had already begun to reconsider the Bolsheviks' traditional hostility toward nationalism, especially its Russian variant. That more positive attitude would soon shape comments of Stalin, Sergei M. Kirov, and Andrei A. Zhdanov about a new textbook on the history of the USSR; in essence, all these stressed the need to revise the party's negative attitude toward the country's past. Similarly, Stalin began to reconsider his attitude toward National Socialism in Germany, even if it was not yet possible to renounce the formula established for the entire communist movement— that fascism is "the weapon of monopolies." Nevertheless, he was unequivocal in declaring that, whatever the regime's ideology, businesslike relations with the USSR were possible: "We are far from feeling elated about the fascist regime in Germany. *But what counts here is not fascism*, if only because fascism in Italy, for example, has not prevented the USSR from establishing excellent relations with that country."[29] Declaring that the Soviet Union must put its own interests first, Stalin hinted that the country could align itself either with the Entente or with Germany: "We have no orientation toward Germany, just as we have no orientation toward Poland or France."[30] That was Stalin's way of saying that the USSR could join with either side, as circumstances—not predisposition—warranted.

The reconsideration of traditional views—on fascism, social democracy, and the Comintern's tactics and slogans—followed the arrival of Georgii M. Dimitrov in Moscow (after the Leipzig Trial).[31] The Comintern, of course, was simply an instrument of Soviet foreign policy. The Politburo itself approved the Comintern's budget each year, and the OGPU-NKVD ran security checks on its functionaries.[32] Stalin had only contempt for the Comintern (which he called a "shop") and regarded its foreign functionaries as incompetent hirelings.[33] The main tasks of the Comintern were to disseminate the communist doctrine abroad through any means possible, to support Soviet foreign policy with mass movements (in most cases directed against their own governments and in support of the USSR), and to expand the Soviet spy network abroad.

While living in Germany, Dimitrov came to the conclusion that the Comintern's dogma must be altered. In particular, he realized that the communists' struggle against social democrats was counterproductive and harmful. Moreover, the Bolsheviks (including Lenin) hated social democrats not so much for ideological as for political reasons. Seeking total, uncontested influence over the popular masses, the Bolsheviks could not achieve this through suasion and, after seizing power in 1917, resorted to repressive methods against all their political adversaries, including social democrats.[34]

In a conversation with Politburo members in April 1934, Dimitrov attempted to explain "why, in a decisive moment, millions of masses do not follow us, but the social democrats or, as in Germany, national socialism." He argued that the main reason was the Comintern's propaganda and its "incorrect approach to European workers."[35] For the moment, Stalin continued to uphold the traditional point of view that the real problem was the historic tie of European workers to the bourgeois democracies.[36] However, Stalin was evidently not entirely persuaded that this was really the case. Indeed, at the Seventh Congress of the Comintern, he agreed to have Dimitrov present a report on the main question—the emergence of fascism and the Comintern's goals in the struggle for unity in the working class. Still, Stalin's loathing for social democracy was unabated. Although he did agree to apply the epithet of "social fascists" only to their leaders, he would make no further concessions.[37] Hence it was that, for various reasons, both communists and national socialists had a common foe—social democrats.

As it turned out, Stalin and Hitler learned much from each other on how to resolve internal political conflicts. Stalin took a keen interest when Hitler liquidated his "old comrades in the party" on June 30, 1934. Iakov Surits (at about this time appointed as the Soviet ambassador in Berlin), states that Stalin asked for details about "the night of the long knives." Stalin was also interested to know whether Nazi propaganda was effective and spoke favorably of the propaganda chief, Josef Goebbels. Nor did Stalin say anything critical of Hitler personally.[38] Surits's account is fully consistent with the reports in the well-known memoirs of Walter Krivitskii and Gustav Hilger.[39] The latter recalled confidential conversations between Soviet officials (including Radek) and Professor Oberländer (a member of the circle around the Gauleiter for Eastern Prussia, Erich Koch), ambassador Rudolf Nadolny, and other officials at the

German embassy in Moscow. Radek's remarks plainly reflected the
views of Molotov and Stalin himself. Radek spoke warmly of Nazi
organizational tactics, the force of their movement, and the enthusiasm of the German youth. "On the faces of German students,
draped in brown shirts," declared Radek, "we note the very same
devotion and the same inspiration that once illuminated the faces
of young commanders in the Red Army and also the volunteers of
1812."[40] Radek, unstinting in his praise of the stormtroopers and
the SS, called them "splendid fellows," and exclaimed: "You shall
see—they shall yet fight for us, throwing grenades."[41]

The Soviet leadership was nevertheless concerned about the possible impact that the eradication of German communism might
have on Soviet-German relations.[42] Initially, however, Hitler clearly
separated Soviet-German relations from the task of eliminating
communism in Germany itself. Indeed, in a conversation with his
foreign minister, Konstantin von Neurath, Hitler declared that he
would not tolerate any changes in the political, economic, or military relations with Soviet Russia.[43] He repeated the same ideas in a
public speech before the Reichstag on March 23, 1933.[44] This was a
direct response to the wishes expressed by the deputy commissar of
foreign affairs, Nikolai N. Krestinskii, who had told the German
ambassador that a positive statement by the chancellor was essential
for Soviet-German relations to remain on a friendly basis.[45]

In fact, however, relations between the two countries were deteriorating rapidly. Thus, Germany continued making assaults on Soviet
citizens and officials and conducted a virulent anti-Soviet campaign
in the press.[46] German authorities, for example, arrested the correspondents of *Pravda* and *Izvestiia*, when they arrived in Leipzig to
attend the trial of those accused in the Reichstag fire. The German
ambassador in Moscow, Dirksen, vigorously urged his superiors in
Berlin to terminate the police actions against the staff of the Soviet
trade mission.[47] The Soviet side certainly had grounds for righteous
indignation: the Reichstag fire, which followed shortly after Hitler's
accession to power, was merely a pretext to arrest Georgii Dimitrov
and two other Bulgarian communists. Moscow interpreted the persecution of German communists as a signal that Berlin was deliberately
seeking to raise tensions between the two countries and that it no
longer had an interest in better relations.[48] Moscow, nevertheless,
did not abandon all hope; the Soviet leadership hastily accepted
Dirksen's proposal to extend the Berlin Treaty of 1926, although it

still found most signals negative, even menacing. When, for example, Alfred Hugenberg announced at the World Economic Conference in 1933 that Germany must expand to the East, Moscow could interpret this only as a summons to conquer and colonize Soviet territory. Statements by other leading Nazis (especially Josef Goebbels and Alfred Rosenberg) seemed to demonstrate that Germany no longer even desired good relations with the USSR.

Faced with provocative gestures and statements, Moscow reacted sharply. On May 10, 1933 *Pravda* published an article by Karl Radek about the dangers of revising the Versailles Treaty, an action that—in his view—would mean war.[49] His article caused an uproar in Germany: the Soviet Union, which had previously denounced the Versailles Treaty, appeared to be changing its policy. The Germans were especially incensed by the fact that Radek used "Pomerania" instead of the usual term "Polish Corridor," for that implied recognition of existing Polish borders and denial of German claims. The article, moreover, coincided with a warming in Soviet-French relations. Germany, naturally, interpreted all this to mean an attempt by the USSR to find a new partner; it viewed French and Polish policy, simultaneously, as seeking to drive a wedge between Germany and the Soviet Union.

As Litvinov explained to Dirksen, however, party circles feared that an improvement in Germany's relations with England and France would propel Berlin toward an anti-Soviet policy.[50] Litvinov emphasized that "the basic attitude of the Soviet Government toward Germany has remained entirely the same: that the Soviet Government is convinced that it could have friendly relations with a National Socialist Germany as with a fascist Italy." Litvinov added that both countries also had a common interest in Poland and in the struggle against the Versailles Treaty.[51] In effect, Litvinov had virtually disavowed Radek's article.

For his part, Dirksen sought to persuade his superiors in Berlin that if Germany and Russia acted together, they could overcome their present weakness and become a powerful political factor with which the other great powers would have to reckon. "Cooperation and friendship of the two states is undoubtedly a positive factor for world peace as a whole," argued Dirksen. The ambassador contended that "even today, therefore, the same reasons that led Germany to conclude the Rapallo Treaty in 1922 and the Berlin Treaty in 1926 are alive and operative."[52] It is possible, but unlikely, that Dirksen—

appointed to his post three months after Hitler came to power—failed to understand where German policy was headed. Nor was it likely that military cooperation between Germany and Soviet Russia would be "a positive factor for world peace." But things were going smoothly in the summer of 1933, as Moscow considered alternatives to the Rapallo course it had followed for more than a decade.

Stalin still intended to follow a dual course, officially seeking rapprochement with France and her East European allies, while unofficially trying to renew or even expand military cooperation with Germany. Hence, despite the deterioration in relations with Germany, Moscow continued efforts to preserve friendly relations in the military sphere. Assuming that the Reichswehr was an influential force, even after Hitler came to power, Soviet commanders were extraordinarily cordial toward German officers—behavior that would have been unthinkable without explicit sanction from on high. Thus, at a reception in honor of a German military delegation, Voroshilov specifically emphasized that the Red Army desired to maintain friendly ties with the Reichswehr.[53] It was at approximately this time that Stalin read a Russian translation of *Mein Kampf*; although a new edition had just appeared in Germany, it did not contain any revisions in the chapter about the struggle against Bolshevism and plans for conquest in the East. Not long afterward, Molotov (as chairman of the Council of People's Commissars) received the German ambassador. After exchanging rebukes, Molotov made it clear that Soviet policy toward Germany would remain unchanged if the latter did likewise.[54]

Throughout 1933 and early 1934, even as the Soviet leadership reconsidered its foreign policy, it continued making appeals one after the other to Germany for closer ties. Gel'fand, a counselor at the Soviet diplomatic mission in Rome (he defected to the United States in 1940), later declared that "Stalin had been nibbling for an agreement with Hitler since 1933."[55] In late October 1933 the two sides resolved the dispute over their journalists, who now resumed their work in both the USSR and Germany. The Soviet side promised that Moscow radio and the press would refrain from meddling in internal German affairs and from making aggressive attacks on the German government and its leaders.[56] On October 24 a counsellor of the German embassy in Moscow informed Berlin about the proposal by a Soviet "friend" (most likely Radek) for a meeting between Molotov and Dirksen, who was about to leave his post as Germany's top envoy in Moscow, to clarify Soviet-German relations.[57] This proposal must of course have come from Stalin or at least had his approval. When Dirksen left Moscow on November 1, he was honored with an extraordinary farewell ceremony. He received personal gifts not only from top officials in the Soviet executive committee (Mikhail I. Kalinin and Enukidze), but also from Voroshilov—as an expression of the Red Army's friendly regard and perhaps as a reminder of the "glorious days" of Soviet-German military cooperation.[58]

At this same reception Tukhachevskii—no doubt acting on orders from the Kremlin—held a long conversation with a German diplomat (Twardovski) about Soviet-German military cooperation and the future relations between the two countries. Tukhachevskii endeavored to implant two ideas. First, he emphasized that the Rapallo policy remained exceedingly popular in the Soviet Union; nor should it ever be forgotten that the Reichswehr had been the Red Army's mentor at a difficult time in its history. A resumption of military cooperation would be extremely well received by the Red Army. Second, the future of Soviet-German relations depended entirely upon Germany. It was merely necessary to disperse fears that the new German government was following an anti-Soviet course. Tukhachevskii declared that "it is politics that separates us, not our feelings, which are most friendly to the Reichswehr."[59] Tukhachevskii even claimed to have seen little chance of Soviet collaboration with the French army—a prospect that deeply worried the Germans. He also denied rumors that the Soviets had informed the French of their previous cooperation with the Reichswehr.

On December 4, 1933 Litvinov gave Benito Mussolini a candid assessment of Soviet policy. He explained that "We desire to have the best possible relations with Germany. However, the USSR fears a Franco-German alliance and is therefore attempting to achieve its own rapprochement with France."[60] Nine days later, Litvinov repeated all this to the new German ambassador in Moscow, Nadolny: "We are not undertaking anything against Germany. . . . We do not intend to participate in any intrigues against Germany."[61] Litvinov then reiterated the same theme at a session of the Central Executive Committee on December 29, 1933[62]—shortly after the Central Committee announced its new policy of seeking "collective security."[63]

Even at this late date, the military ties between the two countries seemed to favor better relations. Although the Reichswehr had already liquidated all its military installations and operations on Soviet territory, it seemed to want cordial relations with the Red Army. Colonel Joachim von Stülpnagel in the Reichswehr ministry noted that military sites had been closed in a friendly atmosphere once certain misunderstandings (involving local Soviet authorities) had been resolved. To the inestimable joy of their Red Army colleagues, the Germans left behind—free of charge—military property worth 2.9 million marks. In final conversations with the German officers, Voroshilov and other high-ranking commanders expressed the hope that it would soon be possible to restore close ties with the Reichswehr. They also sounded out the Germans about whether they were willing to accept Soviet officers for training courses in Germany.[64] In early 1934 the Red Army launched a new diplomatic offensive to woo the Germans. The Soviet leadership evidently believed that the Reichswehr was still interested in resuming military cooperation and, more important, that it still played a crucial role in policymaking. It should be noted, however, that London was guilty of the same miscalculation. In reality, of course, Hitler had no intention of sharing power with anyone, especially the Reichswehr. Nevertheless, because Moscow was oblivious of all this, Voroshilov and Egorov continued telling their German contacts that the Soviet Union wanted the best possible relations with Germany.[65]

Hitler was not totally blind to the dangers implicit in a shift in Soviet foreign policy. The instructions to the new ambassador, which Hitler himself signed on November 13, 1933, laid out the main lines of German policy toward the USSR. It specifically identified Hitler's speech in the Reichstag on March 23, 1933 as the guideline for Soviet-German relations. In essence, it declared that the basis of German policy was the Rapallo Treaty of April 16, 1922 and the Berlin Treaty of April 24, 1926 (prolonged through the agreement of May 5, 1933). Hitler affirmed the principal objective was to maintain friendly relations between the two countries and thus to dissuade the Soviet government from joining any alliance directed against Germany. Hitler also directed the ambassador to determine whether Soviet policy was still to oppose the Versailles Treaty. The instruction also emphasized that the question of Poland, as before, was of cardinal importance. It also drew attention to the need to establish stable economic relations, to expand the role of German industry, and to provide access for Soviet goods on the German market (so that the USSR would be able to meet its economic obligations to Germany). The instruction specifically emphasized that fundamental differences between the two political systems should not be a barrier to the further development of relations. There was to be no attempt, by either side, to interfere in the other's internal affairs. Nor did Hitler entirely discount the possibility of military cooperation: "Good relations between the Reichswehr and the Red Army should be fostered."[66] The Germans soon designated a new military attaché in Moscow as well.

As 1933 drew to a close, however, the Politburo made the decision to create a system of collective security and to join the League of Nations. Litvinov's speech at the Central Executive Committee was interpreted abroad, and especially in Germany, to mean a radical turn in Soviet foreign policy. Radek, however, gave his German contacts a very different interpretation, which indeed provided the core of Stalin's remarks at the Seventeenth Party Congress three weeks later. In all likelihood, Radek helped to draft this section of the General Secretary's report at the congress. In any event, Radek's explanations were quite clear: the Soviet Union was pursuing only its own interests and had no intention of pulling "the chestnuts out of the fire for other countries."[67] Radek's comments were probably attempts to reinforce private, oral reassurances communicated to Germany. In addition, Radek said that the situation in the Far East was crucial in determining Soviet foreign relations. According to Radek, it was quite likely that, if the USSR became embroiled in a military conflict with Japan, Germany would probably exploit the situation to strike at Poland, seize the Polish Corridor, and compensate the Poles with territory in the Ukraine. That is why, declared Radek, the Soviet Union was now taking steps to avert such a contingency.[68]

At any rate, that scenario was hardly credible. After all, Poland still had a powerful ally in France; Germany was hardly prepared to risk a war on two fronts. However, Radek defended his opinion by referring to the new edition of Mein Kampf, which left unaltered the portion (chapter 14) envisioning a campaign against the USSR. That text, he argued, was the true statement of German intentions, not public statements like Hitler's speech in the Reichstag, which were merely intended to camouflage Germany's real plans.[69]

At approximately the same time, Voroshilov presented the same argument to Nadolny, who was then leaving his post as German ambassador in Moscow. He warned that the USSR feared a German-Japanese alliance aimed at the Soviet Union. Here Voroshilov also alluded to *Mein Kampf*—a translation of which had just been distributed to Politburo members—to sustain the argument. The head of the Red Army declared that a few words from Hitler would suffice to dissipate Soviet fears on this matter. Voroshilov then returned to the old theme of military cooperation, reaffirming that collaborative work with the Reichswehr would evoke profound satisfaction in the Red Army.

Nadolny, heeding Hitler's directives, cast some bait in Voroshilov's direction: the suspension of ties with the Red Army, he claimed, had emanated from the Red Army, not the Reichswehr. It was therefore up to the Soviet side to raise the question of resuming these ties. As the ambassador reported, Voroshilov "fell into deep thought and made no reply." He evidently thought that if Germany itself took the initiative here, this would be powerful argument against Litvinov's new policy.[70] Of course it was not easy for the professional German diplomat to make sense of the Bolshevik politics in Moscow.

Two days later, the chief of the Soviet General Staff (Egorov) told Twardowski of the Red Army's desire to reestablish its old ties with the Reichswehr and added that there was but one obstacle: Germany's present policy: Germany itself had closed its military installations in the USSR; the USSR had ceased to send its officers to train in Germany because the latter had subjected Soviet citizens to persecution and abuse. The German ambassador naively interpreted these declarations of friendly feelings as a reflection of the Red Army's fondness for Germany,[71] without suspecting that Egorov merely carried out orders from the Politburo. A few days later Egorov had a long talk on the same subject with the military attaché, Hartmann. This time Egorov went still further: he invited the new commander of the Reichswehr (Colonel-General Werner Freiherr von Fritsch) to Moscow for talks. Egorov reminisced almost nostalgically about the German generals with whom he had worked earlier, expressing a special fondness for General Friedrich Paulus and Colonel Wilhelm Reinhard. Half-jokingly Egorov added that, if these two German officers were to resign from the Reichswehr, the Red Army would take them "with open arms," for they were the Red Army's irreplaceable mentors.[72] Hartmann had no doubts about the sincerity of

Egorov's sympathy for Germany. It should be noted that these conversations took place on the very eve of the Seventeenth Party Congress and that their potential results were taken into account in
Stalin's report to the congress. Stalin evidently still believed that the
Reichswehr could exert a decisive influence on Hitler; one might
wonder too whether Stalin also made a mental note of the Red Army
officers' apparent predisposition toward the Germans.

Hitler did not ignore Stalin's speech. In his own address to the
Reichstag on January 30, 1934 (to commemorate his first full year in
power), the German dictator expressed his satisfaction with Soviet-
German relations. The instructions to Nadolny remained in force:
treat with "cool reserve" any rapprochement between the USSR
and France. A new instruction to the ambassador, sent shortly after
Hitler's address to the Reichstag, formulated German policy toward
the Soviet Union as follows: "From the standpoint of our policy as a
whole, in any case, the time has not yet come for an active policy
toward Russia either in domestic or in foreign policy. There 'cool
reserve' is advisable."[73]

However, that implied only a freezing of relations at their current
level and had little chance: events themselves were taking their own
course. In the face of growing international instability, the Soviet
Union urgently wanted some way to secure its western borders and
therefore proposed an agreement with Germany that would guarantee the independence of the Baltic states and Poland. But Germany
rejected this proposal, since it would tie its hands in resolving the
problem of Poland and German territorial claims against Lithuania
(over Memel). Moreover, such an agreement implied a menace to
the Baltic states by one of the two signatories—either Germany or
the Soviet Union; it was absurd to think that any other country
(e.g., France) had hostile intentions in the region.[74]

Nadolny proposed to halt the deterioration in Soviet-German
relations through a joint démarche by Hitler and Molotov, in which
the heads of the two governments would agree (1) to renounce any
intent to threaten the other's territory or to intervene in its internal
affairs; (2) not to support the other side's emigrés operating on its
soil; and, (3) to ban any declarations, either written or verbal,
aimed at the existence of the state or regime of the other.[75] However, Berlin did not accept the proposal.

Given the unsatisfactory, even dangerous state of Soviet-German
relations, the USSR adopted a new policy of upholding the Ver-

sailles Treaty and moving closer to a traditional Russian ally—
France. This led to proposals for an eastern pact, which would guarantee the inviolability of borders in eastern Europe and thus constitute a counterpart to the Locarno Pact of 1925 (which guaranteed
borders in the west). However, the proposal proved stillborn. Germany refused to participate on the grounds of inequality in military
armaments; England also raised its own objections. But the new
Soviet policy eventually bore fruit. On September 18, 1934 the
USSR formally joined the League of Nations and the following year
concluded a series of new agreements, all with the intent of out-
flanking and neutralizing the German threat. Thus on May 2, 1935
the Soviet Union signed a mutual-assistance agreement with
France; two weeks later it made a similar arrangement with France's
ally, Czechoslovakia. Stalin could now wait to see whether Germany's new political isolation would impel Hitler to give serious
consideration to a Soviet-German agreement. In the interim, Germany did show an eagerness to strengthen economic ties and signed
an agreement on commercial and credit relations in 1934.[76] In the
summer of 1934, however, Twardowski told the Italian ambassador
in Moscow that, insofar as Soviet policy had become hostile to Germany, his country had no intention of showing any initiative to
improve relations.[77]

Repression of Ethnic Germans in the USSR

As is well known, on August 28, 1941 Stalin liquidated the autonomous republic of the Volga Germans—on the absurd accusation
that they included "thousands and tens of thousands of saboteurs
and spies, who, on a signal from Germany, will set off explosions in
areas settled by Germans on the Volga."[78] Less well known, however, is the fact that this repression had a long prehistory, for the
deterioration in Soviet-German relations ineluctably affected the
fate of ethnic Germans in the USSR, particularly those residing in
western Siberia.

Reacting to reports of famine in the USSR, German citizens
organized a campaign to assist their fellow nationals in Soviet Russia. The so-called "anti-Soviet protests" in Germany were, to a certain degree, connected not only with the arrests of German citizens
residing in Russia, but also with the mass repression of ethnic Germans holding Soviet citizenship. The regime closed, for example,

the German-language newspaper published in Moscow (*Deutsche Zentral-Zeitung*); its editor was accused of being a German spy and shot. The party also conducted intensive purges in areas with ethnic Germans, ostensibly as a campaign against "fascist agents." Thus on November 5, 1934 the Central Committee dispatched a coded telegram to top party organizations, asserting that, in areas populated by Germans, anti-Soviet elements "had become active and openly conduct counter-revolutionary work."[79] That date is revealing: it clearly controverts the traditional view that mass terror commenced only with the assassination of Sergei Kirov on December 1, 1934. In fact, mass terror had often been applied since the end of the civil war: against national minorities, against peasants during collectivization, and against religious groups. The intensity of the terror fluctuated—depending on Stalin's political calculations.

The most important factor was the party's vehement repudiation of the widespread rumor (even in local party organizations and the NKVD) that Soviet foreign policy required a certain "indulgence for Germans and other nationalities that reside in the USSR and violate the basic loyalty to Soviet power."[80] Since it was not easy to prove accusations of disloyalty, such cases were simply fabricated. One piece of "evidence" was the claim that inhabitants of German districts allegedly refused to learn the official language in the republics to which their districts belonged. In the case of Siberia and the Volga, this meant a failure to learn Russian, but that in fact was the case. Moscow not only ordered repressive measures against "counter-revolutionaries" (primarily, those who received food, packages, and money from the "Winter Help" fund in Germany), but also prescribed the punishments—arrest, exile, execution. In addition, it ordered local authorities to threaten the German population with expulsion from the USSR. They were also to demand that the Germans sever any connections with certain "bourgeois-fascist organizations," i.e., to refuse any packages and money.[81]

The West-Siberian Krai Committee, in collaboration with the NKVD, zealously went about its work. On November 13 the committee secretary, Robert Eikhe, dispatched the appropriate directive; its eighteen points prescribed ruthless measures against the unfortunate residents of the German district.[82] In accordance with party tradition, the arrests of "counter-revolutionaries" was preceded by a purge of party ranks, which was given top priority. By the time Eikhe issued his directive, the NKVD had already unmasked a

"fascist group" in the German raion. Its members included the former secretary and an instructor in the raion committee, the director
of a school for kolkhoz youths, and the instructor of the raion office
of public education. Next came the repression of "kulaks," changes
in school personnel, and an increased emphasis on the study of
Russian. At the lower level, the Golyshmanovo Raion Committee
was taking its own measures. On December 4, 1934 (three weeks
after Eikhe issued his directive) the raion committee boasted of its
success: meetings of activists in thirteen kolkhozes had exposed
"organizers" and "recipients" of aid from Germany, who were branded as supporters or agents of Hitler. The entire campaign focused on
the receipt of parcels. It was decided to transmit any future packages
to MOPR (the International Organization of Assistance for Fighters
of the Revolution), which was to forward them the workers and
peasants languishing in Hitler's prisons.[83] All the party, Soviet, and
judicial organs were mobilized for the campaign against "Hitlerite
agents" among the Soviet Germans in Siberia. The charges were
manifestly false; under the pretext of combatting "fascist agents" the
regime intensified the campaign of grain requisition (which was not
going well) by confiscating the reserves of independent Germans
and even kolkhozes.

The regional court then tried the accused, who were charged with
a host of counter-revolutionary acts: sabotaging grain requisition,
forming fascist organizations, and (through the German consulate in
Novosibirsk) appealing to Hitler for help. The show trials were
intended to intimidate; rallies of "shockworkers" (*udarniki truda*) were
to send representatives to the court proceedings (in Golyshmanovo,
for example, three to four people from each kolkhoz). The economic
effect was clear: at the start of the trials a kolkhoz called "Red Front"
had fulfilled only 41 percent of its grain quota, but within a week it
had delivered 100 percent. Some of the accused at the major trials
received death sentences.[84] Simultaneously, meetings of kolkhozniki
adopted resolutions prohibiting any from accepting aid from Germany. The secretary of the Karasuk Raion Committee reported that,
as a result of this "operational work," German kolkhozniki had
actively spoken out at the meetings, exposing the organizers of
Hitlerite assistance and demanding that the organizers and recipients
be arrested, tried, and punished.[85] Nor was the military command of
the Siberian Military District idle: at its initiative, the Red Army
excluded "alien elements"—conscripts from the German raion.[86]

The security organs of Western Siberia wasted no time. On December 25, 1934 (forty days after the campaign started), NKVD brigades reported that, in areas inhabited by Germans, they had unmasked and liquidated thirty-six "counter-revolutionary groups" with 199 participants, and two "counter-revolutionary organizations" with 58 participants.[87] Altogether, a total of 577 Germans in the West-Siberian Krai were arrested; many more, of course, were dismissed from their jobs or expelled from kolkhozes.[88] The security organs gave special attention to the activities of the German consul in Novosibirsk, who had allegedly recruited people to serve as armed bands to support Germany in the event of a conflict with Russia. The final paragraph of Eikhe's report boasted that local authorities "are continuing to take repressive measures against those who continue to conduct fascist agitation in German colonies."[89] This fantastic history prepared the country's population to accept similar accusations later at the trials of party leaders, who were accused of collaborating with Hitlerite Germany. Robert Eikhe, the zealous secretary in Western Siberia and a candidate member of the Politburo, would himself later be arrested, have his spine broken during the "interrogation," and eventually be shot.

New Soundings

Despite the deterioration in Soviet-German relations, Stalin continued to nourish hopes for an improvement. He continued to send some faint but positive signals. When a German dirigible crashed on Soviet territory, killing its crew, on May 14, 1934, Soviet organs (commissariat of foreign affairs, NKVD, and military authorities) displayed extraordinary zeal in searching for the wreckage and received an official acknowledgment of gratitude from the Germans.[90]

It was Radek's task to lead the campaign against fascist aggression, and on behalf of collective security personally, and he told the chief of Soviet intelligence in Europe (Walter Krivitskii) about the duality of his own position: "Only fools could imagine that we shall ever break with Germany. What I write is one thing; reality, however, is something entirely different. No one can give us what Germany can. It is simply impossible for us to break with Germany."[91] Radek had in mind not only military cooperation (with which he had been connected from the very beginning), but also the enormous technical and economic assistance that had been obtained from Germany during the first five-year-plan. No one would have dreamed of asserting that, without foreign economic assistance (including German), it would be possible to build and reconstruct so many branches of Soviet production.

Thus the Soviet Union continued to pursue both options, including the "German card." That included tantalizing offers to give Germany a mutual guarantee on the Baltic states and to participate in the "Eastern Pact" (which would guarantee the security of all its participants). When Hitler rejected both proposals, Moscow was driven to pursue its other option—i.e., a system of collective security and a rapprochement with France and Great Britain. Stalin seems to have also hoped that this policy would force Germany to seek an agreement with the Soviet Union. It bears noting, however, that Paris and London had a similar logic: fearful of encirclement, Germany would be driven to seek an agreement with the West.

When Mikhail Kalinin accepted the accreditation documents of the new German ambassador (Werner von Schulenburg), he dropped a transparent hint that the two countries had common interests. To quote Kalinin: "We shall not assign too much attention to the cries of the press. The peoples of Germany and the Soviet Union are too closely linked in many different spheres and, in many respects, depend on one another."[92] Although Schulenburg reported that officials at all levels in Moscow avoid talking about politics, even Litvinov—the official proponent of collective security—told the ambassador that "the Soviet Union too desires an improvement in relations with Germany." The ambassador also received information from an unidentified source, alleging that the Red Army "urgently" desires to establish better relations with Germany and "is even prepared actively to advocate this." Schulenburg believes that these rumors are not entirely unfounded.[93]

The sentiment in Berlin, however, remained unchanged. Under circumstances similar to Kalinin's speech, Hitler gave the new Soviet ambassador, Iakov Surits, an exceptionally cold reception. Hitler's behavior had perhaps other reasons (Surits, like many of his aides, was Jewish), but the net effect was to dash hopes for better relations. Stalin, in turn, renewed the Comintern's activities. In late October 1934 he approved Dimitrov's proposals to alter the Comintern's methods of work and to commence a gradual reorganization.[94] The result was a new policy: the popular front.

The Kandelaki Negotiations

Although military cooperation had ended and political relations had deteriorated,[95] the economic ties between Germany and the USSR actually improved somewhat in 1935. Berlin needed oil, manganese, and wheat; Moscow needed machine tools, equipment for its chemical industry, and military materials. The data on imported machine tools provide an index of these ties: Germany had supplied 54 percent of all imported machine tools in 1929–1933, and almost the same share (53 percent) in the years of tension (1933–1937). To be sure, the Soviet market had earlier dominated German exports; the USSR purchased 51 percent of all machine tools produced in Germany in 1931, and this proportion jumped to 74 percent the following year. And even after 1933 the Soviet Union remained a major purchaser: it acquired 40 percent of all metal-cutting machines in 1936, and two years later increased this proportion to 50 percent.[96]

In March 1935, Germany repudiated the military limitations imposed by the Versailles Treaty and introduced universal military training. Henceforth the Germans no longer needed to maintain clandestine military installations in foreign countries. Hence, if military cooperation between the USSR and Germany were to resume, it would have to assume a radically different character and correspond to the political goals of the two countries.

At the point when Germany openly repudiated the Versailles Treaty, the Soviet Union completed a formal review of its foreign policy and proclaimed its commitment to collective security in Europe. The shift in course was apparent in an article by Tukhachevskii, entitled "The Military Plans of Germany Today." The article appeared first in *Pravda*, but was then reprinted in two other major Soviet press organs—*Izvestiia* and the army newspaper, *Krasnaia zvezda*.[97] Its principal idea was that Germany, behind the facade of an anti-Soviet campaign, was actually preparing to launch an attack on the western countries. He also cited figures on German arms that were intended to have a strong impact on public opinion. Stalin himself reviewed the article prior to its publication and made some editorial corrections. In particular, he changed the title, which originally had been "The Military Plans of Hitler," substituting "Germany Today" for "Hitler."[98] Stalin also replaced the concluding paragraphs (including a toast to Stalin's health) with a new text, emphasizing the threat of German arms, above all for France. Thus the article bore a quasi-official character—although, of course, the Germans did not suspect that Stalin himself had had a hand in its preparation. The article was, in some sense, a response to Hitler's remarks in a conversation with Anthony Eden of Great Britain, where the German leader warned that the main danger to Germany and Europe emanated from the Soviet Union and the Red Army.[99]

The Germans complained that Tukhachevskii's figures were grossly inflated, even fantastic.[100] The German ambassador, Schulenburg, lodged an official protest with Litvinov, declaring that the article was "most venomous" and "based on tendentious information."[101] In a conversation with the chief of the foreign section of the defense commissariat, the German military attaché expressed the Reichswehr's "amazement" over Tukhachevskii's article. That was all the more the case since it came "from a person of such political and military significance as Mr. Tukhachevskii, who is regarded with particular respect in Germany." The attaché added that, in conversations with their German colleagues, the Red Army officers "had always advocated the view that Germany had only to disregard the military provisions of the Treaty of Versailles in order to rise once again."[102] It was obviously impossible to contest that claim.[103]

Tukhachevskii's article served two purposes. One was to impel the French and English to take the German threat more seriously and, in particular, to persuade the French of the necessity of a mutual-assistance pact with the USSR. But the article also had a second goal: to persuade Germany that its anti-Soviet course was doomed to failure.

That the Soviet Union was still trying to court Germany became apparent a mere three months later, when it once again sounded out Berlin on a possible improvement in relations. For the present, to be sure, it sought only to sign an expansive new credit and commercial agreement. In late October, at an official farewell dinner at the German embassy (on the occasion of Twardowski's transfer to Berlin), Marshal Tukhachevskii appeared for the first time since Hitler had come to power. According to Twardowski, the marshal was exceptionally candid and warm. In Tukhachevskii's opinion, Germany would be ready for war by next year—at the latest. She had everything necessary to achieve this. If, however, Germany should decide to make war on Russia, this would result in a terrible calamity for both countries, for Germany would have to fight a new Russia. The Red Army had learned much; it would be a terrible adversary. But the crucial point in these remarks came when the marshal expressed regrets that Germany and the USSR did not cooperate. That was a mistake, since the two countries could successfully complement each other and neither held territorial claims against the other. If Germany and the Soviet Union had maintained their former friendly relations, they would now be in the position "to dictate peace to the world." Ideological differences should not be allowed to interfere. Tukhachevskii expressed the hope that the two countries could again work together.[104] Tukhachevskii's choice of words and the entire tone of his remarks left the impression that he was serving merely as a transmission belt between the Soviet and German leaders.

The very appearance of Tukhachevskii, only a few months after his anti-German article, shows that Stalin was stubbornly returning to the idea of a rapprochement with Germany. Indeed, by declaring that Germany would soon be prepared for war, Tukhachevskii seemed to encourage such thinking in Berlin—with the proviso, of course, that it should not attack the USSR, but cooperate with Moscow to "dictate peace" to the rest of the world. The precise terms of such cooperation remained unclear; not until the fall of 1939 did the two work out the conditions for such cooperation. In the interim, however, the Soviet Union was officially still pursuing its other option of a rapprochement with France.

The Comintern, accordingly, was re-outfitted to serve this new assignment. The tactic of a popular front was designed to facilitate a mutual-assistance agreement with France and her East European allies. Moreover, if the worst predictions of war with Japan in the Far East were realized, simultaneous with a threat from the West, the organization of a mass movement to defend the USSR would be the Comintern's primary objective.

When Germany introduced universal military training in March 1935, Moscow showed understanding and even a veiled approval. After all, the USSR had always denounced the Versailles Treaty. But Moscow also showed considerable alarm. The previous month (at the Seventh Congress of Soviets), Molotov had called the Germans "a great people," but the hall had responded with shouts, "Long Live the World Revolution!"

When Eden arrived in Moscow to discuss the alarming course of events in Germany, he found precisely the same attitude on Stalin's part. During a conversation in the Kremlin on March 29, 1935, Stalin told the British Foreign Secretary that "sooner or later the

German nation would have to be freed from the chains of Versailles.
. . . I repeat, such a great people as the Germans would have to break
loose from the chains of Versailles."[105] Aware that his words might
well reach Berlin, Stalin praised the martial qualities of the Germans: "The Germans are a great and courageous people. We never
forget this."[106]

The Soviet dictator was alluding to the economic negotiations
then being conducted with Germany. Stalin's aim, no doubt, was
twofold: to intimidate Eden with the spectre of a Soviet-German
alliance, but also to reinforce distrust of the Germans so as to avert a
deal between the West and Germany. The latter possibility, so inte-
gral to Stalin's idea of capitalist encirclement, remained Stalin's
constant nightmare. Inspired by this set of dual—but contradictory—aims, Stalin blithely informed Eden that the negotiations
with Germany about credits include "products that are not easily
mentioned—weapons, chemicals etc." An alarmed Eden asked:
"What! Has the German government really agreed to provide
weapons for your Red Army?" Stalin replied that "Yes, they have
agreed, and in the next few days we shall probably sign an agreement about a loan."[107]

The Soviet-German economic discussions involved the president of the Reichsbank (Hjalmar Schacht) and Hitler's plenipotentiary for economic planning (Hermann Goering). The negotiations proved successful. On April 9, 1935 Schacht and David Kandelaki (serving as the Soviet trade representative in Germany since
December 1934) signed documents regulating the economic and
credit relations between the two countries. The USSR agreed to
place additional orders in Germany to the amount of 200 million
marks; the orders applied exclusively to investment purposes—factory equipment (including some for the chemical and petroleum
industries), machine tools, products of the electrical industry,
ships, transport, measuring instruments, and laboratory apparatus.
The special agreement foresaw on-site technical assistance. The
German bank consortium was to provide additional credits for
these orders.[108] In short, the agreement envisaged long-term economic cooperation. For its part, Moscow saw a favorable outcome
of the economic talks as a positive sign for the resumption of political negotiations. Moreover, the resonance in the German press was
entirely positive; its general tone was that the agreement was
advantageous for both partners and would help to stimulate Ger-

man exports.[109] However, although the Nazi papers (for example, *Völkischer Beobachter* and *Angriff*) initially refrained from any comments, on April 12 the former published a new anti-Soviet article on the USSR.[110]

In July 1935, Stalin directed Kandelaki to feel out the chances for improving relations with Germany. The choice of Kandelaki was no accident: apart from his closeness to Stalin (if only from common ethnic ties), the decision conformed to Stalin's assessment of German fascism as "monopoly capitalism." The trade representative was thus the natural conduit. To approach Schacht was to deal with the "real" bosses. Moreover, Moscow regarded Goering—the second-ranking official in the Third Reich—as the key link between the monopolies and the government. Together, Schacht and Goering were presumed to exert a decisive influence on German foreign policy.

Schacht, however, feared any involvement in inter-agency conflicts and did not regard foreign policy as his real domain. That explains his response to an approach by Kandelaki on July 15, 1935, when the Soviet diplomat raised the question of an improvement in relations between the two countries. Schacht replied that, although he personally regarded an agreement on commercial exchange a good beginning for improved relations, he himself was not responsible for such matters. He therefore recommended that the Soviet government approach the German foreign minister, Konstantin von Neurath.[111] This reply did not mean, however, that Schacht had himself been fully excused from the whole question. He obediently informed his superior that he had been approached—as indeed he had promised Kandelaki that he would do. Moscow honored Schacht's advice.

Indeed, it tried all avenues. Litvinov and Tukhachevskii in Moscow,[112] as well as the heads of the Soviet diplomatic and trade missions in Berlin (Surits and Bessonov)[113]—all made repeated attempts to convince their German counterparts of the need for a radical improvement in political relations between the two countries. Thus, at a reception on November 7, 1935, Litvinov raised the following toast to Schulenburg: "For the renewal of our friendship!"[114] The German military attaché also quoted the words of the commander of armored troops, Uritskii, who had spent two years in Germany: "I shall always be grateful for everything that I learned during our collaboration, and I shall never forget the many friends

that I had in your country."[115] A week earlier Kandelaki had had a
new meeting with Schacht, and the two agreed about the favorable
prospects for a credit and commercial agreement in 1936.[116] A significant share of the items that the Soviet Union sought to purchase
through the commercial agreement consisted of military goods.
These included submarine batteries, autopilot systems, automated
instruments for ships, and television and stereoscopical apparatus.
But the orders ran into barriers; not all German ministries wished to
sell military equipment to the USSR. Nor did Kandelaki's appeal for
Schacht's personal intervention produce results. The Soviets then
tried to use their old ties to the Reichswehr.[117] In late January 1936
Hitler categorically forbade any arms deals with Russia. However,
the Committee for Trade with Russia appealed Hitler's decision,
arguing that it could not apply to deals contracted prior to the law of
November 6, 1935. Nonetheless, the negotiations to purchase submarine batteries were suspended; only those deals made earlier
(such as the sale of stereoscopical equipment by the Zeiss firm) were
exempt from the new law.[118]

In early December 1935 Bessonov attempted to use his persuasive
powers on an official in the Foreign Ministry (Rediger) and, indirectly, the top leadership. His main argument focused on the desirability of supplementing the Soviet-German Berlin Treaty of 1926
(on neutrality) with a "bilateral pact of non-aggression between Germany and Russia."[119] In late December Bessonov, together with the
chief envoy in Berlin (Surits), made inquiries with Twardowski as to
what must be done to improve relations. The German diplomat
replied that the Soviet Union must show initiative, cease attacking
Nazis, improve consular relations, and stop oppressing German
nationals in Russia as well as Soviet citizens of German origin. The
Germans had the distinct impression that Surits had been given
strict instructions to clarify what the Soviet government must do in
order to improve its relations with Germany. Surits also attempted to
dispel the Germans' belief that Litvinov was their chief adversary.[120]

Tensions rose to a white-hot level after Molotov's vitriolic anti-
German speech of January 11, 1936. Yet even in this speech Molotov alluded favorably to the impending Soviet-German agreement
on trade and credits.[121] The Soviet leaders seemed to imagine that
there were two distinct Germanies: one driven by anti-Soviet
plans, the other a businesslike and invaluable trading partner. *Au
fond* Stalin's analysis hinged upon the assumption that the real

"rulers" of Germany were the captains of finance and industry, among whom a prominent place belonged to Hermann Goering. In early February 1936, at the request of Anatolii I. Gekker (chief of the foreign section in the defense commissariate), the German military attaché, Köstring, arranged to screen a film about his travel. Twenty high-ranking commanders of the Red Army came, including Gekker, Uritskii (corps commander), Efimov (chief of the Artillery Department), Fel'dman (chief of the Personnel Department), and Khmel'nitskii (Voroshilov's adjutant). For Köstring this was new evidence of the Red Army's friendly attitude toward the German army.[122] On the very day that the German troops reoccupied the demilitarized Rhineland (March 7, 1936), at a reception in the Italian embassy in Moscow, Tukhachevskii uncorked a bottle of champagne to congratulate Köstring and even added that in a few weeks the Germans would have sufficient forces in the Rhineland to attack France.[123] Köstring drew the conclusion that the Russians hoped that an armed conflict would erupt between Germany and the western powers.[124] It is safe to assume that Tukhachevskii personally was pleased that the predictions in his 1935 article had come true.

Stalin now lost no opportunity to explore ways to improve ties with Germany, notwithstanding the formal condemnation of Hitler's action in the Rhineland. On May 13, 1936 Kandelaki and his deputy (E. K. Fridrikhson)[125] saw Goering personally. The latter showed a lively interest in improving relations with the USSR. The Soviet trade representatives were elated when Goering expressed the hope that, given the positive development in economic ties, it would also be possible to improve political relations as well. Indeed, the hidden purpose of their whole visit was to determine the German reaction to these preliminary feelers. As to the sale of military materials and equipment, Goering was again encouraging: that too would be possible, he said, once Germany had satisfied its own military needs.[126] Goering also invited the Soviet representatives to come directly to him, if need be,[127] and expressed the conviction that the time would come when Soviet-German relations could be improved in all areas, political as well as economic.[128] His cousin, Herbert Goering, who was to conduct all the negotiations with the Soviet Union, believed that the "ice has been partially broken." But most important, in his view, was an opinion that Hermann Goering had expressed to several German industrialists: "Obtaining raw materials from Russia is so important that he shall raise this issue with Hitler himself—however much the latter might be ill-disposed to accept this."[129]

Goering himself categorically insisted that Soviet requests for military equipment (including its orders from the Zeiss firm) be accepted. His position was quite understandable: as the government's plenipotentiary for economic resources, he knew that the German military industry desperately needed certain raw materials, such as manganese ore and petroleum, and these could be purchased on a regular basis from only one source: the USSR. Schulenburg believed that Goering's opinion would significantly contribute to improving Soviet-German relations, for it was based strictly on economic considerations.[130] Less than a month after the two sides had signed the economic agreement of 1936, Bessonov and Evgenii Gnedin (secretary of the Soviet diplomatic mission) discussed political problems with A. Hencke. According to the latter's notes, the Soviets said that "it was absurd that the two states which were interested in mutual economic relations should be campaigning against each other in the political sphere in an almost unprecedented manner."[131] The task was to find a political solution.

Meetings in the German Ministry of Economics considered the issue of an agreement with the USSR for 1937, and came to the following conclusion. There were two main obstacles to an agreement: Russia had no obligations to provide Germany with the raw materials in the necessary quantities, and Russia preferred to avoid long-term commitments. For its part, Germany was unable to provide the USSR with military goods and materials. As for other goods, the prices and method of payment had still not been determined. The only reasonable solution was to extend the existing agreements and to sign them without any further delay.[132] In one document Herbert Goering noted that his cousin Hermann desired business ties with the Russians "at any cost."[133] In December 1936 the two sides agreed to extend the agreement to cover the following year.[134] Nevertheless, things did not proceed smoothly. In April 1937 the Soviet trade mission warned that, unless the Zeiss firm fulfilled its contractual obligations from 1935, the Soviet Union would suspend the delivery of petroleum and manganese ore.[135] The threat had its effect.[136] But the resolution of conflicts in the economic sphere still failed to produce any parallel improvements in the political relations.[137]

Nevertheless, Stalin still hoped for some arrangement with the Germans and continued to send out feelers through diplomatic channels. Thus in July 1936 Bessonov had talks with Hencke about possible variants of a nonaggression pact. Hencke deflected these proposals, with the explanation that such pacts made sense only if the two states had contiguous borders. That was obviously not the case here. Moreover, Germany definitely had no intention of attacking the Soviet Union.[138]

Such attempts, of course, clashed with "official" policy. Evgenii Gnedin,[139] the secretary of the Soviet diplomatic mission in Berlin and later a well-known Soviet political commentator, expressed dismay over Stalin's interest in "option no. 2." In his memoirs he candidly recorded his reaction: "I remember how we diplomatic personnel at the Soviet mission in Berlin were somewhat dismayed when Eliava (deputy commissar for foreign trade) passed through Berlin (in 1936, it seems) and, through connections with old friends having access to Stalin, gave us to understand that 'at the top' they assess Hitlerism 'differently' than does the press or the personnel at the embassy in Berlin."[140]

Indeed, Stalin continued to hope for a deal with Hitler right up to February 1937. The Foreign Section of the NKVD, according to Krivitskii, repeatedly warned Stalin that "all the Soviet attempts to appease and conciliate Hitler are doomed. The main obstacle to an understanding with Moscow is Hitler himself."[141] Stalin, however, did not agree; he regarded Berlin's decision to grant credits as a sign that it intended to come to a political agreement with the USSR. Hence his response to the warnings of the NKVD: "Well, now, how can Hitler make war on us when he has granted such loans? It's impossible. The business circles in Germany are too powerful, and they are in the saddle."[142]

Stalin therefore stubbornly pursued his objective. At the very end of December 1936, and again in late January 1937, Kandelaki and a colleague paid another visit to Schacht. In the latter's opinion, trade relations between the two countries could develop successfully if the Soviet government, through its ambassador, gave assurances that it would renounce communist agitation abroad. According to Schacht's notes, Kandelaki expressed his sympathy and understanding. He also reported that, during his trip to Moscow, he had met with Stalin, Molotov, and Litvinov, and that he had spoken with them in the same spirit as he had earlier spoken with Schacht. On January 29 the two Soviet representatives visited Schacht again and conveyed a verbal message from Stalin and

Molotov. Its essence was that the Soviet Union had never objected to the resolution of political issues, that its policy was not aimed against German interests, and that it was prepared to enter into diplomatic negotiations to improve their mutual relations. It was, moreover, willing to conduct these negotiations in secret. Schacht again suggested that this message be conveyed by the Soviet ambassador directly to the German foreign minister.[143] Even before this meeting, Stalin—firmly convinced that an agreement with Hitler was possible—ordered the chief of the Soviet espionage network in Germany to curtail intelligence operations.[144] As Stalin explained to the NKVD chief, Nikolai Ezhov: "In the very near future we shall conclude an agreement with Germany."[145]

In 1936, especially before the show trials in Moscow, European military and diplomatic circles regarded the prospects for a Soviet-German agreement as entirely realistic. Baron Geyer, the German military attaché in London, told the chief of the British General Staff (Dill) that the German army had strong pro-Russian feelings, and that an unexpected agreement between the two countries could become a *fait accompli*. Of course, Geyer had a specific goal in saying all this: he sought to impel influential circles in Great Britain to reach an understanding with Germany and thereby avert the danger of a Soviet-German rapprochement. English political spheres assumed that proponents of cooperation with the USSR were to be found in the Reichswehr, Schacht's entourage, and among some industrialists. There were even some in the Nazi Party. However, Hitler himself was firmly opposed to improving relations with Russia; the only exception was in commercial matters.[146]

The British erred in assuming that the initiative came from the German, not the Soviet, side.[147] The Foreign Office believed that the only chance to avert a Soviet-German pact was to maintain the system of collective security. Hitler's refusal to improve relations with the USSR drew new support from the show trials and onset of the "great terror" in Soviet Russia: the accused, who had been prominent figures in the party and state, confessed to performing espionage duties for Germany and Japan. At the end of January 1937, in the case of the "Parallel Trotskyite Center," a military tribunal tried seventeen top figures for state treason. The leading personage was Karl Radek, who had carried Stalin's directive and conducted real negotiations with the Germans.[148] The trial brought up the names of the German military attaché, Köstring,[149] and press-attaché Baum—not to mention Hitler's deputy, Rudolf Hess, who had allegedly met with Trotsky. Why did the producers of the Moscow show trials invoke Hess's name? Evidently because he held no government post, and served only as the deputy-chief of Hitler's party. That connection seemed to underscore the ideological degradation of Trotsky, who had even made a deal with the fascists, and indeed the main thrust of the trial was directed specifically at Trotsky. But Germans had been mentioned in earlier trials as collaborators, and many German citizens, as noted earlier, had also been arrested.[150] The Soviet government demanded the recall of Baum and Köstring—a demand that Berlin flatly rejected.[151]

Naturally, under these tense circumstances, an agreement between the two countries was out of the question. In February 1937 the German foreign minister, Konstantin von Neurath, informed Schacht that the proposals offered by Kandelaki were unacceptable. The reason, he explained, was the Soviet-French agreement of mutual assistance and the activities of the Comintern. However, explained Neurath, this decision was subject to reconsideration in the future: "It would be a rather different matter if things in Russia develop in the direction of an absolute despotism based on the military. In this case we certainly ought not to let slip the right moment for taking a hand in Russia again." The foreign minister proposed to formulate the reply to Kandelaki as follows: so long as the Soviet government supported close ties with the Comintern, it would be impossible to expect political negotiations to be successful.[152]

Hitler's decision to spurn ties with the Soviet Union derived, apparently, from two notions: the unstable situation in the USSR (at least in his view) and the Soviet foreign policy of collective security (which seemed to be targeted at Germany and its allies). Hitler also took note of the weak reaction of England and France to his action in the Rhineland and his denunciation of the Locarno Treaty. He was further encouraged by the strong pressure from influential political circles in England to come to terms with Germany. Hitler calculated on obtaining maximum concessions from the West by proclaiming the "anti-bolshevik" aims of National Socialism. Hence Stalin's hope for a conflict between Germany and the Western powers had little real prospect.

In April 1937, rumors of secret Soviet-German negotiations circulated widely in European political quarters and in the press.[153] The French and Italian ambassadors in Moscow persistently inquired of their German colleague about an impending resolution of political differences between the USSR and Germany. Litvinov speculated that the rumors emanated from Paris. At the same time, he noted in a conversation with ambassador Schulenburg that Surits was very much encouraged by Neurath's opinion that in the future it would be possible to return to a discussion of political problems. At the introduction of a new state secretary Hitler had declared that "Neurath's policy is my policy," and that too seemed to be a good omen.[154] But Moscow's hopes were once again dashed, when the German press categorically repudiated rumors of a change in Germany's relations with the USSR. On April 17 Litvinov flatly denied these rumors in a telegraphed circular to Soviet representatives in Paris and Prague, no doubt in an effort to reassure the Soviet Union's partners about the mutual-assistance agreement. To substantiate his claim, he recommended that Soviet diplomats note the recall of both its diplomatic and commercial representatives (Surits and Kandelaki) from Berlin.[155]

Schacht and Goering, who bore responsibility for promoting German economic development, were dismayed by this turn of events. According to Surits, Schacht feared that Germany would soon be deprived of Soviet petroleum and manganese, which would be "devilishly difficult" to replace.[156] When German authorities refused to grant export licenses to Zeiss, Surits reported that this also evoked Schacht's dissatisfaction.[157]

Despite these setbacks the Soviet side nevertheless sent out new feelers. For example, the new Soviet diplomatic chief in Berlin (Konstantin Iurenev) emphasized in meetings at the German Foreign Ministry that the Soviet Union advocated "the creation of normal relations with Germany and is not opposed to good relations. However, for this it is necessary that the German government be aware of the need for a concrete reconsideration of its present policy toward us."[158] Such efforts seem to have born little fruit. Indeed, German-Soviet relations reached a new low on November 15, 1936, when Germany and Japan signed the so-called "Anti-Comintern Pact."[159]

The Tukhachevskii Trial

Accusations that a so-called "anti-Soviet Trotskyite military organization" was preparing a military plot to seize power had resulted in three waves of repression against the officer corps of the Red Army. The first purge came in the mid-1920s (aimed at "Trotsky-ites") and the second in the late 1920s and early 1930s (focusing on former tsarist officers). The third wave began in the second half of 1936, as the "Great Terror" itself began to unfold. The "Tukha-chevskii case" was the culmination of this process. It included, with Stalin's approval, the most prominent military leaders in the USSR: Mikhail Tukhachevskii (marshal), Ieronim Uborevich and Iona Iakir ("commanders of the first rank," or General), Avgust Kork ("commander of the second rank," or Colonel), and Vitalii Primakov, Vitovt Putna, Boris Fel'dman and Robert Eideman ("corps commanders," or Lieutenant Generals). Although this important show trial is of interest in its own right (with the usual extraction of confessions by torture),[160] attention here is given only to materials pertaining to cooperation with the Reichswehr—namely, the allegation that the accused had "systematically given the German general staff completely secret information."

That accusation was completely false. After Stalin's death, inves-tigators found documents in his archive confirming that Stalin had been duped by German disinformation: the Germans had fabricated and transmitted incriminating materials against Tukhachevskii and the Soviet military elite. At the time, a careful review demonstrated the documents to be complete fabrications.[161] One came from the correspondent of *Pravda* in Berlin, A. Klimov, in mid-January 1937. It asserted that "the highest officer circles persistently talk of con-nections and work of German fascists within the elite command personnel of the Red Army in Moscow. In this connection the name of Tukhachevskii comes up."[162] It has also been suggested that the documents were fabricated by German intelligence, but on orders from Moscow. There is no evidence for such an interpretation, which, moreover, hardly accords with the tenor of Soviet-German relations at the time.

Stalin apparently used these documents for his speech at the Mil-itary Council on June 2, 1937, shortly after Tukhachevskii's arrest. Stalin warned of a "military-political conspiracy against Soviet authority, investigated and financed by German fascists." The lead-ers of the conspiracy, he claimed, came from the ranks of purported "Trotskyites"—Trotsky himself, the right-deviationists (Aleksandr I. Rykov and Nikolai I. Bukharin), his own loyal supporters (Avel S. Enukidze, Lev M. Karakhan, and even Ian E. Rudzutak), as well as

those officers already arrested and Ian B. Gamarnik (who had committed suicide). Stalin claimed that all these people (with the
exception of Rykov, Bukharin, and Gamarnik) were German spies,
and that some had even provided intelligence for the Japanese.
Stalin fulminated against the Reichswehr upon which he had once
pinned so much hope: "This is a military-political plot. This work
carries the signature of the German Reichswehr."[163] These materials did not figure in the investigation itself, evidently because there
was no need for them: according to Soviet jurisprudence of the
time, the confession of guilt sufficed for conviction.

Although in recent years much material has been published on
the role of Stalin and other Politburo members in staging the show
trial of military officers in 1937, one must still explain what role this
purge may have played in Stalin's strategy with respect to Germany.
Stalin excluded the military from future political relations with
Germany. He no longer needed or wanted the cooperation of his
own generals with the German Reichswehr, even if it operated
under his control and per his own instructions. It may be that he
finally came to the conclusion that the two countries' mutual relations could be changed only by direct negotiations with their leaders. It should be remembered that, until the outbreak of war with
Germany, Stalin avoided making negative references to Hitler; the
fact that he removed Hitler's name from the Tukhachevskii article
is revealing. Stalin himself held no state post; as a secretary of the
Central Committee, if the need or desire arose, he could permit
himself even the sharpest attack on an ideological opponent, even a
foreign head of state. However, the circumspect Stalin preferred not
to do that in public.

Almost all who participated in cooperation with the Reichswehr
before 1933, or in Soviet-German negotiations from 1933 to 1937,
were purged. The sole exception was Surits, who died of natural
causes in 1952.

In 1937 the Soviet Union expelled many German citizens being
held under arrest. The spy mania led to the closing of a number of
German consulates, with retaliatory measures being taken by Germany. It is possible that Stalin's purge of the military (leading to the
removal of 40,000 officers) suggested to Hitler the need to do the
same in his own Reichswehr. In 1938 he dismissed his minister of
defense (General von Blomberg) and the chief commander of land
forces (Colonel-General von Fritsch); many other officers suffered

as well. They were replaced by generals and bureaucrats, whose Nazi convictions and personal loyalty to the Führer were beyond doubt. Hitler's military purge had a further goal: reorganization of the military command and subordination of the armed forces directly to Hitler. The military minister was replaced by the "Supreme Command of Armed Forces," headed by Hitler himself. In contrast to the repression of Storm Troopers in June 1934, this purge of the officer corps was bloodless. Moreover, the Munich agreement of late 1938, whereby Germany won a great victory without war, significantly enhanced Hitler's authority among the officer corps.

4 | Partners

The events in 1938–1939 revolved around Hitler's methodical campaign to build a new empire: occupation of Austria through *Anschluss* (March 10, 1938), the Munich Agreement (September 30, 1938), and the seizure and dismemberment of Czechoslovakia (March 11–15, 1939). The western democracies had hoped Hitler's ambitions would finally be satisfied by the annexation of Austria and Sudetenland and the diplomatic victory at Munich. This policy of appeasement did not, of course, work. Hitler's unexpected seizure and dismemberment of Czechoslovakia in March 1939 shattered any illusions about his insatiable appetite and starkly exposed his designs on the rest of Europe.

Of all these events, the Munich Agreement was particularly alarming for Stalin: it demonstrated the danger of a political rapprochement between German and the Western powers. There was no assurance it would not be repeated, especially with respect to a regime so unbeloved in the West as the USSR. The nightmare that had tormented Stalin for so many years seemed more menacing than ever. As before, Stalin responded with a two-pronged tactic. On the one hand, he sought to reinvigorate the Soviet-French pact of mutual assistance (the Czechoslovak agreement being a dead letter after Munich); he also attempted to improve relations with

Great Britain. On the other hand, Stalin's diplomats explored the possibility of a political agreement with Germany.

By early 1939, London also became increasingly concerned about Germany's aims and even surmised what were likely to be his next steps.[1] With the occupation of Czechoslovakia, which in effect nullified the Munich Agreement, a powerful wave of Germanophobia swept Great Britain. As the Soviet ambassador in London, Ivan Maiskii, observed, this was initially "a semi-conscious, spontaneous feeling . . . of an impending danger."[2] On March 31 Prime Minister Neville Chamberlain issued a statement reaffirming Polish independence and, a few days later, extended this guarantee to include Greece, Romania, and Turkey. A month later, on April 29, Great Britain introduced universal military training. In the interim, Germany bullied Lithuania into ceding Memel, while Italy attacked and occupied Albania. Hitler's campaign against Poland was already in progress: on April 11 Hitler endorsed the plan of attack and on April 28 repudiated the German-Polish nonaggression pact of 1934 and abrogated the Anglo-German naval agreement of 1935. He also demanded the return of Danzig, the construction of an extraterritorial highway in the Polish corridor, and the immediate return of the former German colonies.

The escalating tensions led to an exchange of opinions among Great Britain, France, and the USSR about counter-measures in the event of further German aggression. The result was the first concrete proposal by the USSR (dated April 17, 1939) for mutual assistance in the event of aggression against any of the signatories.[3] That proposal initiated Anglo-French-Soviet negotiations on May 3 for a mutual-assistance pact. Initially, the commissar of foreign affairs was still Maksim Litvinov, but within a few weeks he was replaced by Viacheslav Molotov, who simultaneously served as chairman of the Council of People's Commissars. The discussions were later expanded to include negotiations of the military missions in Moscow in August 1939, but the latter were suddenly terminated when the USSR signed the nonaggression pact.

The Stalin Doctrine

When the Soviet mass media announced the radical turn in Soviet-German relations in August 1939, the rank-and-file party members adjusted remarkably well. To be sure, the Nazi-Soviet nonaggression pact did not elicit unanimous approval. Some had difficulty jettisoning what the party had drummed into their heads for years—namely, that fascism was the principal enemy of the USSR. Nevertheless, party members were well-versed in the theory of "exploiting contradictions in the imperialist world" and, especially, could appreciate the tactic of provoking the capitalists to fight among themselves— to the manifest advantage of Bolsheviks and socialism.

The personal archive of Andrei A. Zhdanov[4] contains a fairly extensive letter from one V. P. Zolotov of Moscow, who describes himself as a party member since 1928. Zolotov had sent the letter to both Molotov and Zhdanov. Reading the letter carefully, "with pen in hand," Zhdanov marked what he considered to be Zolotov's main thoughts:

> We must always keep in mind precisely and clearly that our main, fundamental enemy in Europe and in the whole world is not Germany, but England. . . . We must finally understand that the most acute differences in government ideologies by no means preordain a similarly acute antagonism of political and economic interests. . . . Entering into an agreement with England and France against Germany, even concluding a military alliance with them, we should not forget for one moment that in this alliance, England and France will conduct a policy of insincerity, provocation, and betrayal with respect to us.

Zolotov thought that the primary task of Soviet foreign policy must be to "lure Germany into a war against England." To achieve this, he proposed to strengthen the Soviet military (to dissuade the German army from attacking the USSR), to inflame anti-British sentiments in Germany by every possible means, and simultaneously to support anti-Nazi agitation and propaganda in the democratic countries. Zhdanov heavily underlined the author's final point: "In the event of war between Germany and France and England, promise Germany that we will maintain neutrality, facilitate the protection of her rear guard, while concentrating the Red Army on the western border in order to paralyze the possibility of Poland's entering the war on England's side."[5]

Zolotov's letter came astonishingly close to predicting the course Stalin eventually chose. His idea that the capitalist powers would exhaust themselves in war, enabling the USSR to "throw the sword of the Red Army into the scales of history," is a concise formulation of the "Stalin doctrine." Stalin had adumbrated this notion as early as 1925, but did not include it in any published works until after the close of World War II. Only when the seventh volume of his "Works" appeared in 1949 did the general public have access to a speech he delivered at a plenary session of the central committee on January 19, 1925: "Our banner remains, as before, the banner of peace. But if war begins, then we will not sit with our hands folded—we shall have to act, but act last. And we shall act in order to *throw the decisive weight on the scales, a weight which could tip the balance.*"[6]

The theory of exploiting contradictions in the imperialist camp was deeply embedded in Stalin's thinking. The key was the tactics: play the capitalists off against each other and induce them to fight among themselves—to the obvious advantage of the USSR. Stalin would use this tactic, with considerable success, in the first phase of World War II.

Relations with Germany, 1938–1939

The convulsions of terror had barely subsided when Stalin returned to the idea of a political agreement with Germany. The Munich agreement had revived Stalin's fear that England and France would seek a general accord with Germany; it was merely a question of terms.[7] Information from various sources confirmed, without question, that Germany's immediate objective was to reacquire former German territories. Stalin could sympathize with that idea and indeed had favored annulment of the Versailles Treaty in the 1920s. He also harbored deep distrust of the "Entente"—i.e., France and England; he suspected that they were constantly weaving intrigues against the USSR that sought to bring Germany over to their side and to divert its aggression eastward. That analysis was not entirely without foundation.[8] But Stalin realized that Germany had its aims and interests, and that these were contradictory to those of France and England. German aims included the annexation of Danzig and the Corridor, followed by the establishment of German hegemony throughout Europe. Stalin therefore concluded that conflict with England and France was inevitable.

Under these conditions Soviet interests were best served if the western powers became embroiled in war with Germany, while the USSR remained neutral and pursued its own plans. The main obstacle to this policy was Hitler, whose actions were unpredictable. Yet, Hitler's very unpredictability gave reason to hope that, at the next critical juncture, he might come to terms with Germany. Stalin could not imagine that, if Hitler truly believed in anything, it was the necessity of destroying Bolshevism. He used the tribune of the Eighteenth Party Congress in 1939 to warn the western democracies that the USSR would not permit any policy directed against its own interests. At the same time, he also made a positive gesture in Germany's direction.

In Stalin's view, a new war had already begun, even if it had not yet assumed the character of a world war. On March 10, 1939 he declared openly that "the new imperialist war has become a fact."[9] This comment, which scholars have ordinarily ignored, in fact is central to many of his subsequent actions. Stalin criticized British and French policy of appeasement as mere "nonintervention" and "neutrality,"[10] which tolerated aggression, while he himself proposed to fight back. The essence of the foreign-policy part of his speech sounded like an invitation to Germany to reassess its relations with the USSR, especially the part where he spoke of the "suspicious uproar" about the Ukraine, which "has the purpose of inciting the Soviet Union's enmity toward Germany, of poisoning the atmosphere, and of provoking a conflict with Germany without any apparent basis."[11] Stalin hoped for precisely the contrary: if Germany designated the western states as its primary enemy and became embroiled in a military conflict with them, the Soviet Union could calmly proceed with its own plans. Analyzing Stalin's speech at the Eighteenth Party Congress, the German military attaché Köstring perceptively summarized Stalin's strategy: "A conflict in Europe would be the best deal, so far as the Soviet Union is concerned."[12]

Berlin heard Stalin's appeal for better relations. Molotov later spoke about this at a reception held in the Kremlin on August 23, 1939 to celebrate the signing of the Soviet-German nonaggression pact. With a glass of champagne in his hand, Molotov declared that it was "precisely Stalin, with his speech of March 1939, which was correctly understood in Germany, who accomplished the shift in political relations."[13] That was not merely a customary display of byzantine sycophancy; Stalin's address at the Eighteenth Party Congress, along with other indirect approaches, had played a decisive role in enticing Germany to abandon (at least temporarily) its anti-Bolshevism in order to concentrate on more immediate objectives.

The logic of this shift was not lost on Hitler. His generals vehemently warned against a war on two fronts that could invoke the
experience of World War I, in which Hitler himself had participated. Nor indeed was Germany prepared for a two-front war, if
indeed it ever could be. Hitler was also aware that Germany was still
building its arms industry and had in no wise amassed such a preponderance of military-industrial might as to challenge west and
east simultaneously.

Moreover, Hitler's strategy had hitherto aimed at eliminating
adversaries seriatim and not allowing them to unite in a military-
political bloc. Until this point his strategy had worked brilliantly.
The next point of conflict was Poland; given that the latter had a
common border with the USSR, the crucial question was how
Moscow would react to German aggression. Danzig and the Corridor were now the immediate goals of German policy. The rising tensions in German-Polish relations in the spring of 1939, given the
relative weakness of the western powers, encouraged Hitler to continue with his anti-Polish policy. Still, Hitler realized that this
would not be easy; he could either untie or cut the Polish knot. To
untie it, he needed the support—or at least neutrality—of England
and France, as in the case of the stubborn Czechs; after the invasion
of Czechoslovakia in March 1939, that was highly improbable. The
alternative was to "cut the knot"—to solve the Polish problem with
force. For that, however, Berlin required the consent and perhaps
collaboration of Soviet Russia, thereby returning to the path advocated in the 1920s by Seeckt and Hindenburg.

For his part, from late spring 1939 Stalin gave increasing attention
to "option 2"—alliance with Germany. On April 7, 1939 (approximately two months after his speech at the party congress), Georgii
Astakhov—a Soviet diplomat in Berlin and a key figure in the ensuing negotiations—appeared at the German Foreign Ministry to make
new feelers. He told his German colleagues that there was no point
in continuing the ideological struggle between the USSR and Germany, and that they could conduct a concerted policy. Ten days later
(April 17), Soviet ambassador Aleksei Merkalov, in a conversation
with State-Secretary Ernst von Weizsäcker of the German Foreign
Ministry, emphasized that the Soviet Union saw no barrier to normalizing relations between the two countries. He added that "beginning with normal relations, the relations can become constantly better and better."[14]

Not that Stalin forgot "option 1"—alliance with the Western democracies. Literally on the same day, the USSR proposed to England and France that they sign a long-term agreement for mutual aid (for five to ten years) and for assistance to East-European states between the Baltic and Black Sea and bordering on the USSR in the event of military aggression against any of them. The Soviet proposal also foresaw military cooperation.[15]

In short, Stalin was still playing both options. Even as he approached Germany about the threat of the western states, he simultaneously used various channels to let them know that an agreement was possible, if the Polish problem were resolved in a way acceptable to the USSR. Thus he was also not averse to an anti-German coalition—if conditions could be met.

Hitler's situation became considerably more complicated once England and France announced their willingness to defend Poland in the event of an attack. Hitler was now overtaken by doubts: if England and France defended Poland, how would the Soviet Union react? Poland borders on the Soviet Union, which had its own view of Polish matters. The mounting tensions with Poland and the desire to avoid a two-front war impelled Hitler to seek a normalization of relations with the Soviet Union—despite his personal antipathy toward the latter.

Whether Stalin grasped the Führer's psychological state or not, he took a step no doubt calculated to influence his eventual partner: on May 3, 1939 he replaced Maksim Litvinov, a Jew, with Viacheslav Molotov, as commissar of foreign affairs. As a pretext for Litvinov's removal, Stalin used an unauthorized meeting between ambassador Ivan M. Maiskii with the Finnish foreign minister Erkko in Helsinki, which was reported in the press. On April 27 Stalin summoned Litvinov and Maiskii, where they were vehemently denounced by Molotov. Curiously, the real culprit—Maiskii—did not suffer in the least and calmly returned to his post in London. On the night of May 3 troops of the NKVD surrounded the offices of the commissariat of foreign affairs; the phone at Litvinov's dacha was disconnected. The following morning Molotov, Georgii Malenkov, and Lavrentii Beria arrived at the commissariat and informed Litvinov of his dismissal. Afterward many of his aides were arrested and beaten, evidently in an attempt to extract compromising information.[16] Litvinov's portfolio was given to Molotov, who retained his post as chairman of the Council of People's Commissars. A few months later Hitler told top

military commanders that "Litvinov's replacement was decisive."[17]
Stalin certainly recognized the political importance of removing
Litvinov because of his Jewish origins. Much later, Molotov recount-
ed the following: "In 1939, when Litvinov was dismissed and I took
over international affairs, Stalin told me: 'Remove all the Jews from
the commissariat.' "[18]

Stalin had made a deft psychological move just as Hitler began to
change policy toward the USSR. Two days after Litvinov's removal,
on May 5, 1939, Georgii Astakhov received an invitation to appear
at the German Foreign Ministry. There he heard some pleasant
news from Schnurre: the German government had decided to permit the Skoda plant to fulfill its contracts with the USSR, despite
the changes following the invasion of Czechoslovakia in March.
Astakhov did not conceal his satisfaction and declared that the
matter was of "cardinal importance" for the USSR. He also emphasized that Molotov would exert a major influence on Soviet foreign
policy.[19] The previous day, a counsellor at the German embassy in
Moscow (von Tippelskirch) informed his foreign ministry that
Molotov's appointment was a guarantee that the policy would be in
strict accordance with the ideas of Stalin.[20] It would be wrong to
infer, however, that Litvinov had conducted his own foreign policy;
whatever he did, whether from conviction or instruction, fully corresponded with the foreign policy adumbrated by Stalin himself.

Soviet policy underwent significant change in the spring and
summer of 1939. Moscow developed a broad program; its primary
objective was to expand borders along the western frontier, beginning with Finland. One of the two potential partners—either the
Entente or Germany—would have to satisfy this ambition.

On May 17 Astakhov invited Schnurre to the Soviet embassy in
Berlin. Nominally the meeting was to discuss the status of the Soviet
trade representation in Prague, which the Soviet Union wanted to
preserve in the protectorate of Bohemia and Moravia. Schnurre,
who obviously picked up Hitler's signal about a shift in policy,
expressed confidence that Berlin would not take exception to the
request. All this consisted of mere preliminaries. Astakhov noted
that the shrill anti-Soviet tone in the German press had abated and
then moved to his main point: Germany and the USSR have no
contradiction in interests and hence no reason for conflict. As an
example of good relations, Astakhov cited Mussolini's declaration

after the formation of the "axis" that there were no obstacles to normal political and economic relations between Italy and the USSR.[21]

On May 20, Molotov told the German ambassador, Schulenburg, that he was not satisfied with the German proposal to continue only economic negotiations. It was necessary, he declared, to establish a "political basis," but declined to explain precisely what he meant. According to the ambassador's report to Berlin, Molotov is "virtually summoning us to a political dialogue."[22] Schulenburg himself then developed this idea in a discussion with the deputy commissar of foreign affairs, Vladimir P. Potemkin.[23] In Schulenburg's opinion, laying a "political basis" should include a series of measures in foreign and domestic policy. In domestic policy, it meant a clear separation of National Socialism and communism on the basis of nonintervention; a cessation of attacks in speeches, in the press, and on the radio; unimpeded participation of scientists and researchers in scholarly conferences (including German scholars in the USSR); and the exchange of artists and teachers. In foreign policy the "political basis" meant: confirmation of the Berlin Treaty of April 24, 1926 ensuring neutrality; and recognition that the USSR and Germany had no disagreements in matters affecting their vital interests; a declaration of Germany's aims with respect to Poland; recognition that the nonaggression agreement between Germany and the Baltic states enhanced the security of the USSR.

Schulenburg believed that a Soviet-German agreement must guarantee the security of communications in the Baltic Sea and, especially, the delivery of iron ore from Sweden. Amazingly, the German ambassador discussed the problem of Poland merely in terms of complications in the Baltics. Schulenburg also deemed it necessary to reopen the German general consulate in Leningrad and, correspondingly, a Soviet general consulate in Hamburg. The normalization of relations should also include an amelioration of the plight of German citizens arrested in the Soviet Union.[24] Naturally, Schulenburg's thinking did not broach several potential areas of agreement: Poland, the Baltic states, or military and political cooperation. Only his superiors, especially Hitler, could determine issues to be addressed in constructing the basis of future relations. So far as Germany was concerned, the essential question was war or peace. For the Soviet Union, the main objective was to achieve its territorial and political ambitions by reaching an agreement with one of the two capitalist camps and in order to extract the maximum benefit for itself.

Both Stalin and Hitler waited to see who would speak first and most candidly. In the end it was Stalin, through Molotov. In his speech at the Supreme Soviet on May 31, 1939. Molotov complained that the Anglo-French proposals to the USSR were unsatisfactory, because they neither ensured assistance to the Soviet Union in the event a third party (Germany) attacked Romania and Poland, nor guaranteed the security of the Baltic states.[25] Molotov was plainly hinting that the Soviet Union might well reach an agreement with any state, Germany included, that could guarantee Soviet interests in the Baltics, Poland, and Romania.

Despite the clear import of Molotov's public speech, a pause ensued, as both Hitler and Stalin waited. Moscow was still trying to maneuver, first by signing an economic accord, but then starting talks on a political agreement. That was the essence of a conversation between Gustav Hilger (counsellor to the German embassy) and Anastas Mikoian (commissar of foreign trade). Berlin was, however, still uncompromising. Hitler decided to inform the Soviet representatives that economic negotiations on the terms proposed by the Soviet Union in January were out of the question, and that Germany therefore had no desire to resume the economic talks. For pragmatic reasons, however, Hitler deferred sending this communication for several days—at the insistence of his foreign minister, Joachim von Ribbentrop.

In the meantime, Stalin grew increasingly uneasy. He evidently sensed that time was slipping away: Germany was preparing to strike, and the three-sided negotiations were moving at a snail's pace. He therefore intensified his behind-the-scenes intrigues with Berlin through his representative, Georgii Astakhov. On June 15 the latter held a critical discussion with the Bulgarian ambassador in Berlin, P. Draganov, who served as a kind of unofficial intermediary for negotiations with the Germans. Astakhov explained that the USSR must chose from three alternatives: sign a pact with England and France, continue inconclusive negotiations, or reach an agreement with Germany. The third suited Soviet interests best. In part, the scheme developed by Astakhov became the basis of the nonaggression pact signed on August 23, 1939. In part, as Astakhov explained, the USSR did not recognize the Bessarabian part of Romania and feared a German attack on the USSR, either through the Baltics or through Romania.[26] If Germany would renounce any intention of attacking the USSR or would conclude a nonaggression pact, the Soviet Union would probably refrain from signing a treaty with England. Under the circumstances, it was in Russia's best interest to draw out the conversations with England and leave its own hands free. As Astakhov expected, Draganov promptly informed the German Foreign Ministry of his conversation.[27] Oddly enough, London also showed itself inclined to procrastinate in its negotiations with Moscow.[28] Perhaps because it was playing a "German card" of its own: English and German envoys conducted secret talks in 1939, sounding out each other about the possibility of reaching an agreement.[29]

In any event, by the early summer of 1939 both England and the Soviet Union—each for its own reasons—did not want to hurry the signing of a triadic pact (among Britain, France, and the USSR) on mutual assistance in the event of aggression. Of particular interest is an extensive memorandum from the British Foreign Office, dated May 22, 1939. Among the disadvantages of such a three-way pact was the danger that England might have to act not to ensure the independence of small European states, but to support the Soviet Union against Germany. The memorandum laid special stress on the need to involve the Soviet Union if war broke out in Europe. Otherwise, it warned, "by the end of the war the Soviet Union— with its army unscathed, with England and Germany lying in ruins—would dominate in Europe."[30]

The procrastination in Berlin and London become more understandable in the light of events in the Far East. On May 11 fighting broke out on the Mongolian-Manchurian border in the area of the Khalkhin-Gol River. The Japanese army launched a full-scale attack, expecting to occupy strategic areas in the event of war between Japan and the USSR. Given Japan's alliance with Germany, the Soviet Union suddenly faced the frightening prospect of fighting a two-front war, in the east as well as the west. This danger exerted a strong influence on thinking in the Kremlin, especially as tensions over Danzig mounted during the summer of 1939. England, for its part, had difficulties of its own in the Far East because of the blockade of its concession in Tientsien; the outcome of Khalkhin-Gol directly affected English interests in this region. The battle came to an end only in August, when the Japanese army suffered a defeat. Soon afterward Stalin reached his agreement with Hitler, and that in turn had significant implications for the Far East. On September 16 Japanese and Soviet representatives signed the protocol to terminate military hostilities.[31]

The normalization of political relations with Germany was supposed to have the same long-term effect on Soviet relations with Japan. That is why Soviet diplomats did not fail to remind their German partners that the attention to the Far East was essential to a future normalization. On June 28 Molotov told Schulenburg outright that an improvement of political relations with Germany was both possible and desirable, that the USSR regarded the 1926 Berlin Treaty for neutrality as still valid. The German ambassador, sincerely interested in reaching a broad political agreement with Moscow, reacted favorably to Molotov's remark.[32] Supporting Molotov's statement to Schulenburg, the next day *Pravda* published an article by Andrei Zhdanov—one of Stalin's closest confidants, a member of the Politburo and Central Committee secretary, and chairman of the commission on foreign affairs for the Supreme Soviet. Zhdanov asserted that the English and French would like to make a treaty that put the entire burden of obligations on the USSR, and warned that the Soviet Union would never sign such an agreement.[33] Berlin immediately understood the significance and meaning of this signal from Moscow. Nevertheless, according to a decision by Ribbentrop on June 30, enough had already been said about the political sphere, and he recommended the same restraint with respect to signing a new commercial and credit agreement with the USSR.[34]

By early summer Hitler, together with Heinrich Himmler and Ribbentrop, watched a film about the military parade on Red Square, which had been shot by the German military attaché. It was the first time that Hitler had seen the "live" Stalin. It evidently made a favorable impression on Hitler, who said to Köstring: "I did not know that Stalin was such a likeable, powerful personality."[35]

Final Negotiations

The Polish situation, as well as news of the British and French missions in Moscow, put pressure on Hitler to act. The Soviet-German economic discussions, which had been deliberately delayed, were resumed on July 22, 1939. Four days later Astakhov and Julius Schnurre had already concurred that it was necessary to reach an accord on political questions. "Time will not wait," declared Asta-khov. He emphasized that the USSR had its own vital interests in the Baltics and Bessarabia, that it endorsed the return of Danzig to Germany and resolution of the Polish Corridor question in a man-ner acceptable to Germany.

Interestingly, at this juncture, when the two sides were whetting their appetite for expansion, the subject of ideology suddenly came to the fore. It did so, curiously, at German initiative. For the first in the two countries' mutual relations, Schnurre drew the Soviet diplomat's attention to the affinity in Soviet and Nazi ideologies:

> Despite all the differences in their respective Weltanschauung, there is one common element in the ideologies of Germany, Italy and the Soviet Union: opposition to the capitalist democracies. Neither we nor Italy have anything common with the capitalist West. Therefore *it seems to us rather unnatural that a socialist state would stand on the side of the western democracies.*[36]

Astakhov made no protestations whatsoever. Both he and the trade representative E. Babarin wished to clarify one essential point in Soviet-German relations: "Why does National Socialism regard the foreign policy of the Soviet Union to be hostile? People in Moscow have never been able to understand this, although there they always understood the opposition of National Socialism to communism inside Germany."

Schnurre explained in detail how National Socialism regarded Bolshevism in its present reform, that is, after the merger with Russ-ian national history, the Politburo's changes in the Comintern, and Stalin's renunciation of world revolution for an indefinite period of time. National-Socialists, having excoriated communism in Ger-many, were now convinced that Moscow no longer was seeking to disseminate communist propaganda and therefore now envisioned new possibilities for cooperation with the USSR, which were previ-ously inconceivable. As to the role of the ideological factor in the future relations with Germany, it is possible to judge by Astakhov's reaction: he called the conversation "extremely important."[37] Berlin was also satisfied with the results of this discussion.

Schulenburg was instructed to inform Molotov that Germany was prepared to respect all Soviet interests in Poland and elsewhere. The sides began a preliminary discussion of the terms of the future agreement. On August 2 Ribbentrop formulated the two principal points: (1) nonintervention in the affairs of the other side; and (2) renunciation of any measures aimed at the vital interests of the other. The first point referred to Soviet neutrality in the event of a Polish-German war; the second point meant the cessation of Soviet negotiations with France and Britain. Ribbentrop emphasized that, if an agreement could be reached, then "from the Baltic to the Black Sea there will be no problems that we cannot jointly resolve among ourselves." He also hinted at the possibility of a Soviet-German agreement on the fate of Poland, i.e., a new partition. Although Ribbentrop pretended that Germany was in no hurry, he concluded his instruction to Schulenburg quite specifically: Germany is interested in "the quickest clear normalization."

That impatience for a quick agreement hardly characterized French and British diplomacy. On July 25 the British government finally made the decision to dispatch a military mission to Moscow. Accompanied by a French counterpart, the two missions departed London on August 5 traveling not by air, but on the passenger-freighter *City of Exeter*, which a had top speed of 13 knots per hour. The slow-moving vessel arrived in Leningrad on August 10.

By that time Astakhov and Schnurre were engaged in intensive negotiations in Berlin. The search for an acceptable basis for political discussions had begun in June, when the two sides considered inserting a few political phrases into the preamble of an agreement on credit and trade. They had ultimately decided against such a symbolic gesture, but now the discussion had taken on a concrete character. After Astakhov declared that he had been empowered once again to express the desire of the Soviet government to improve relations with Germany, Schnurre candidly explained that Germany must resolve the Polish question, if possible through peaceful means, although force would be used if necessary.[39] That scenario was hardly one to suit Moscow's taste and increased the pressure to resolve the choice—between option 1 and option 2—as soon as possible.

Amidst the talks in Berlin and Moscow, Hitler went to Salzburg to meet with the Italian foreign minister Count Galeazzo Ciano. At noon on August 12, he was informed by von Ribbentrop that the Russians were fully apprised of German intentions in Poland and prepared to accept a German plenipotentiary in Moscow to discuss political questions.[40] With the attack on Poland now made irreversible,[41] the talks next shifted to Moscow, where Schulenburg conducted intensive negotiations with Molotov. The Soviet For-

eign Minister first proposed to discuss the general terms of normalization[42] but agreed to receive a German envoy to accelerate the
talks. Germany first designated a minister without portfolio, Hans
Frank, but in the end decided to dispatch von Ribbentrop himself
to Moscow.[43]

The Soviet leadership wanted not only to sign a nonaggression
pact in Europe, but also to have Germany convince Japan to abandon its anti-Soviet policy.[44] In contrast to Molotov's earlier aim (a
gradual improvement in relations), he evidently now had strict
orders from Stalin to act energetically and quickly and not to allow
himself to be overtaken by events.[45] The official reply, which Stalin
personally approved and which Molotov transmitted to Schulenburg on August 18, was anything but simple. The first section raised
the question of the anti-Soviet policy that the German government
had followed earlier, including the anti-Comintern Pact. Stalin
now offered an interpretation quite different from what he had
given earlier, when he had tried to interpret the Pact as aimed at the
western powers. He now stressed that it was directed against the
USSR and, especially, that it sought to encourage Japanese aggression toward the Soviet Union. As a result, the USSR was forced to
take steps to guarantee its own security, including the creation of a
united front against aggression. Moreover, given Germany's pro-
fessed desire to improve relations, the USSR proposed first to sign
the agreement on trade and credits, and then, after a short time, to
conclude either a nonaggression treaty or to reaffirm the neutrality
treaty of 1926. In either event the two sides must sign a protocol,
which would affirm Germany's willingness to observe Soviet interests. Prior to Ribbentrop's arrival, Molotov proposed that the two
sides prepare drafts of the nonaggression agreement so that the visit
and talks have a businesslike, concrete character.[46]

Although aware that Moscow was simultaneously negotiating
with the Anglo-French military missions, Hitler expressed skepticism that negotiations with the western democracies would come
to anything. At a military meeting in Obersalzburg, Hitler offered
this assessment of the Soviet position: "Russia has no intention of
pulling England's chestnuts out of the fire and will keep out of
the war. A lost war is as dangerous for Stalin as a victorious army.
His interest at most extends to the Baltic states."[47] Hitler as yet
did not imagine that Stalin's intentions ranged much further than
the Baltics.

Early on the morning of August 19 Schulenburg received an instruction from Foreign Minister Ribbentrop. Posted immediately after the signing of the Soviet-German economic agreement, the instruction declared that the Polish question had now become extraordinarily critical. Every day, it declared, one should expect events that will make military conflict unavoidable. Under the circumstances, it was absolutely essential to conclude a Soviet-German political agreement immediately. Given this urgency, Berlin now announced its complete assent to the idea of a nonaggression pact, guarantees for the Baltic states, and the use of its influence on Japan. Ribbentrop also declared his willingness to come immediately to Moscow, where he had the full authority to sign an agreement on behalf of the Führer. In Moscow the two sides could discuss the details of the agreement, resolve any remaining differences, and sign the treaty while Ribbentrop was still in Moscow.[48] Foreshadowing the possibility of a treaty with Germany, *Pravda* published an article on August 21 declaring that the economic agreement of August 19 "may appear as a serious step in the cause of improving not only economic, but also political relations between the USSR and Germany."[49]

Berlin spent two more days in an intensive exchange of coded telegrams with its embassy in Moscow. It stressed that the attack on Poland, originally planned for August 26, could not be launched before an agreement had been reached with Moscow. The delays only irritated the Germans; from Hitler's perspective, the Kremlin seemed to be playing a game of procrastination, if not sheer extortion, to extract maximum benefit. It certainly seemed in no hurry to sign a nonaggression pact. Despite Ribbentrop's repeated statements (on Hitler's instruction) and despite the special request to inform Stalin of all this, Moscow still conveyed the impression that it saw no reason for haste and that it simply sought to extort the best possible terms from Berlin. In fact, however, the Soviet leadership was anything but idle: it was preparing drafts of a pact and a special supplementary protocol, where Germany agreed not only to satisfy the specific vested interests of the USSR, but also to join in a grand undertaking—the partition of Eastern Europe into spheres of influence for the two sides. Yet Moscow was still not satisfied: it demanded that Germany assist in normalizing relations with Japan in the Far East.

In the end Hitler was forced to communicate directly with Stalin.[50] The letter, transmitted on August 21, contained several key points. The nonaggression pact, he contended, really represented a return to a policy that had been mutually beneficial to both states over the centuries. That comment appeared to eliminate the chapter in *Mein Kampf* on German policy in the East. In any event, Hitler accepted the Soviet draft of the nonaggression pact. To be sure, it was necessary to work out certain details, as well as the supplementary protocol (which, in fact, was the basis for the whole pact), and Hitler proposed to send Ribbentrop to Moscow on August 22 or 23 for this specific purpose. By rejecting the dates proposed by the Kremlin (August 26–27, one week after the signing of the economic agreement), Hitler strongly hinted that he was on the verge of attacking Poland and could not wait so long for an agreement with Moscow.[51]

The situation had thus undergone a radical transformation: Hitler had gone to Stalin *first*. This concession no doubt flattered the vanity of the dictator in the Kremlin; he consented to Ribbentrop's visit. Stalin also sent a brief telegram, confirming his assent to the visit and calling the nonaggression pact a turning point in Soviet-German relations.[52] Stalin would later embellish this assessment of the nonaggression pact, pronouncing it a turning point in the history of Europe, indeed "not only Europe."

The following day, August 22, Hitler made two speeches to his general staff. The first, cited above, noted the gradual change in Soviet-German relations after Litvinov's removal from office. He made the same point in a letter to Mussolini on August 25; Litvinov's dismissal, he declared, demonstrated the Kremlin's readiness to alter its relations with Berlin, which in turn led to "the most extensive nonaggression pact in existence."[53] Hitler was also pleased that the pact provided for obligatory consultations on all questions affecting the interests of the USSR and Germany.

Hitler's first speech on August 22 also referred to Soviet military negotiations with England and France as well as the fate of Poland. He noted that he had established personal contact with Stalin and that "now Poland is in the position in which I wanted her."[54] A day before the pact was signed, Hitler felt certain that Germany did not need to fear any blockade, for it could obtain from the east all that it needed—wheat, livestock, coal, lead, and zinc. As a result, he declared, the basis had been laid for a final assault on British hegemony. He left no doubts, however, that the immediate objective lay closer to home: "The wholesale destruction of Poland is the military objective."[55] Although the pact had not yet been signed, on August 22 State-Secretary Weizsäcker signed a circular, which was sent to German diplomatic missions and general-consulates in a number of states. It began with this statement: "The normalization and improvement of relations between Germany and the Soviet Union has been under slow and constant development for months."[56] That comment directly controverts the assumption of many historians that the Soviet-German agreement of 1939 was a spontaneous, spur-of-the-moment deal and not the product of long preparation.

The Nonaggression Pact

On August 23, amidst great pomp and ceremony, Ribbentrop and Molotov signed the nonaggression pact as well as a secret supplementary protocol.[57] The latter document demonstrated that the real purpose of the ten-year nonaggression pact was to partition Poland and to define the two sides' sphere of influence in eastern Europe. The protocol specified that, in the event of any territorial changes in the Baltic states and Finland, the northern border of Lithuania was to be the dividing line between German and Soviet spheres of influence. In this case Vilnius—which the Poles had seized in 1920—was to revert to Lithuania. In the event of "changes" in the Polish state (as the pact so tactfully described the country's impending partition), the line separating the Soviet and German spheres of influence was to be the Narew, Vistula, and San rivers. A special clarification of the "territorial and political reordering of areas comprising the Polish state" was signed by Schulenburg and Molotov on August 28.[58] In short, the agreement consigned Finland, the Baltic states and eastern Poland to the Soviet sphere.[59] As for southeastern Europe (i.e., Bessarabia) the document explicitly proclaimed Germany's complete lack of *political* interest in these territories.[60] That formulation, however, was a tacit claim on Germany's part to an *economic* interest, particularly in Romania.

During Ribbentrop's three hours of talks with Stalin and Molotov, the two sides clarified Germany's obligation to assist in normalizing the relations between Japan and the USSR.[61] They also examined the specific obligations of the Soviet Union to provide strategic materials, oil, and foodstuffs for the Third Reich. After that late-night talk, Stalin could not have had the slightest doubt that Germany was on the verge of attacking Poland. To be sure, Stalin reiterated banal clichés that Germany had only peaceful intentions toward Poland, provoking Ribbentrop to exclaim that every German is ready to fight against Poland.[62]

Stalin and Ribbentrop expressed complete agreement about England's weakness. The Soviet leader also attributed British hegemony to the stupidity of other governments, which had permitted England to bluff its way to dominance. He found an eager listener in Ribbentrop. Nevertheless, Stalin cautioned the Germans not to underestimate the British, who, despite their weaknesses, could fight stubbornly and skillfully. As for France, Stalin held that its army deserved respect. The conversation had the tone of a discussion among partners. According to Ribbentrop's later account, he told Stalin and Molotov that—in contrast to the French and English—he had not come to Moscow to ask for assistance if the English should start a war with Germany. Germany, he said, was perfectly capable not only of dealing with Poland, but also of defeating its western adversaries. According to Ribbentrop, Stalin gave this response:

> The viewpoint of Germany, which rejects military assistance, deserves attention. However, the Soviet Union is interested in preserving a strong Germany and, in the event of military conflict between Germany and the western democracies, the interests of the Soviet Union and Germany coincide completely. The Soviet Union shall never tolerate letting Germany fall into difficult straits.[63]

The German foreign minister proposed to include this comment in his speech and asked for Stalin's opinion. The Soviet dictator did give a text, but in revised form:

> The viewpoint of Germany, which rejects military assistance, deserves respect. However, a strong Germany is a necessary condition for peace in Europe; consequently, the Soviet Union is interested in the existence of a strong Germany.[64]

Hence the Soviet Union could not permit the western powers to put Germany in a difficult position. All this, he declared, constitutes "the common interests of Germany and the Soviet Union." Stalin concluded the talks by saying that "the Soviet Government takes the new Pact very seriously," and gave his "word of honor that the Soviet Union would not betray its partner."[65] For his part, Ribbentrop assured Stalin that the anti-Comintern pact had really

been directed against the western powers, not the USSR.[66] Slightly
more than a year later, Hitler would offer Stalin the opportunity to
become the fourth partner—with Germany, Italy, and Japan—in
dividing up the world. On August 23 Stalin was unaware that Hitler
was so desperate for an immediate pact that he gave a written directive (no longer extant, however) to Ribbentrop to concede, if necessary, that Germany had no interest in Constantinople and the
Bosphorus.[67] Informed by telephone that the pact had been signed,
Hitler ordered that the champagne be opened and, despite his own
disinclination to drink, on this occasion he imbibed. After that he
started to pound on the wall with both fists, exclaiming that "now
Europe belongs to me. The others can have Asia."[68]

The day after the pact had been signed, *Pravda* published an article pronouncing the agreement an "instrument of peace" and a
"peaceful act" that would allegedly contribute to the "reduction of
international tensions."[69] Of course the pact connoted precisely the
opposite, for it did nothing less than open the door to a new round
of European warfare. Indeed, a week later Hitler launched his attack
on Poland, thereby casting Europe into another world war. The
Soviet government had no illusions about the import of the Molo-
tov-Ribbentrop pact. On the anniversary of its signing, Molotov
publicly reminded the Germans of the Soviet contribution to their
cause: The nonaggression pact, he said, "provided Germany with
calm reassurance in the East."[70]

Both Soviet diplomatic channels and propaganda intended for
foreign consumption zealously propagated Stalin's claim that the
Soviet-German pact would serve the cause of peace. As Moscow
prepared for war against Poland, it claimed that Anglo-French and
Soviet military conversations might still be resumed and declared
that the Soviet-German pact brought a new stabilizing element into
the international situation.[71] To these ideas Ribbentrop added a
more brazen distortion: the Soviet-German pact was the product of
attempts by England to surround and isolate the two countries.[72]

Soviet-German Cooperation

Ever since April 1939 Soviet relations in Berlin had actually been
handled by a special envoy, Astakhov, instead of the regular ambassador, Aleksei Merekalov, who remained in Moscow. Under conditions of close cooperation, this situation created certain complica-

tions for the immediate exchange of information and on-the-spot decision-making. The Germans, indeed, specifically raised the problem with Moscow.[73] In response, the Kremlin dispatched a new ambassador to Berlin—a rather colorless bureaucrat named Shkvartsev. Astakhov, after his recall, was later arrested and died while under detention; Stalin evidently did not wish to leave at liberty so important a witness to the Soviet-Nazi rapprochement. Moreover, Stalin preferred to handle German affairs personally; that meant, of course, that everything had to be done in Moscow, not Berlin. Hence the personality of the Soviet ambassador in Berlin, in Stalin's view, mattered little.

Ribbentrop, given the rapid escalation of the military-political crisis in Europe, was deeply concerned that the real subject of the talks in Moscow (as well as the documents signed there and any pertinent correspondence) be held in the strictest secrecy. On August 27 Ribbentrop forced all those who had participated in the talks to sign a sworn statement that they would not divulge the substance of what had transpired in Moscow.[74]

In the last week of August, as the crisis came to a head, Hitler attempted to use the Soviet-German pact to force the British to accept his demands. In a conversation with the British ambassador (Sir Nevile Henderson) on August 25, Hitler specifically underscored the change in the strategic situation in comparison with 1914. This time Germany did not face the threat of a two-front war. The agreement with Russia was not only unconditional but also signified a change in German foreign policy, which would last "a very long time." He declared that "Russia and Germany would never in any circumstances again take up their arms against each other."[75] Their alliance also would guarantee the economic security of Germany for a long period of time. The substance of this conversation was also communicated to Moscow.[76] Interestingly, however, Berlin did not apprise Moscow immediately of this conversation. It is likely that Hitler originally expected that the English would react quickly to his playing the "Russian card," but did not wait until the very end: the time approached for the Supreme Soviet to ratify the treaty, and Germany awaited Molotov's speech with great interest.

On August 25, contrary to Hitler's expectations, the British signed a mutual-assistance treaty with Poland. Hitler had originally planned the invasion for August 26, but was so taken aback by the British reaction that he decided to delay the military action from "day X" to September 1.[77] As it prepared to launch the attack on Poland, Berlin watched intently every step of its new partner. On August 25 the Swiss newspaper *Neue Züricher Zeitung* published the following report: the main subject of the Anglo-French-Soviet negotiations in Moscow was a guarantee from the USSR that it would not attack Poland from the rear. The paper speculated that the withdrawal of 250,000 Soviet troops from the Polish border demonstrated that Poland was not endangered, at least from that direction.[78] It thus appeared that, although the USSR had signed the pact with Germany, it was continuing to hold talks with France and England.

It is impossible to determine whether the report emanated from Moscow, Berlin or the two western powers. Interestingly, however, the European communist press expressed the view that the nonaggression pact did not prevent negotiations between the Soviet Union and the Anglo-French alliance. Rumors that the Soviet Union had pulled back its troops from the Polish border alarmed Ribbentrop, who requested an immediate denial from Moscow. The USSR finally complied, but in a peculiar admonitory fashion, evidently in case the Germans should think of advancing beyond the stipulated border of their spheres. Specifically, the Soviet Union announced that it was undertaking no particular measures on the Polish border because its forces there were already on military alert.[79] TASS issued an official denial of the rumor in the same spirit. So belated a reaction, and then issued only after strong pressure from Berlin, reinforced the suspicion that the rumor had emanated from Moscow, and indeed precisely at the point when England was signing its mutual-assistance treaty with Poland. Moscow repudiated the rumor only after it had no doubts about the imminent outbreak of war.

Germany also expressed concern about Moscow's schedule for ratification of the nonaggression pact. For Hitler it was important that ratification take place prior to September 1. Molotov tried to calm Schulenburg with the explanation that ratification was a mere formality (here at least he could be ingenuous). The Soviet people were satisfied with the pact, which would be reflected in its discussion at a session of the Supreme Soviet.[80]

On August 31, Molotov delivered a lengthy speech at the Supreme Soviet. On the eve of the German invasion of Poland, he emphasized the historic predestination of Germany and the Soviet Union to a common fate: both, he noted, had suffered more than any other combatant in World War I. ("Correct!" shouted a voice from the hall.) In fact, this had been Stalin's interpretation of the status of the two countries for a quarter of a century. Molotov then drew a straight line between that fact and the nonaggression pact. He noted that the Berlin Neutrality Treaty of 1926 had been extended by Hitler in 1933 and, indirectly, reminded the Germans that the Soviet Union had attempted to establish political cooperation in the 1930s: "The Soviet government *also earlier* considered it desirable to make a further step forward to improve political relations with Germany, but the circumstances were such that this has only become possible now."[81]

To Hitler's ears this must have sounded like a reminder of missed opportunities. Molotov also expressed regret that only a nonaggression pact had been signed: "True, in this case it concerns not a pact of mutual assistance, as in the Anglo-French-Soviet negotiations, but only a treaty of nonaggression. Nevertheless, under contemporary conditions it is difficult to exaggerate the international significance of the Soviet-German pact."[82] The very same evening the Supreme Soviet ratified the pact.

Ribbentrop was ecstatic over Molotov's speech; *Pravda* reported that the Führer's address to the Reichstag endorsed every word in Molotov's speech.[83] Once the Supreme Soviet ratified the nonaggression pact, its most important act was to promulgate a law on universal military training. In contrast to the earlier law on military conscription, the new decree ruled that the entire population of the USSR could be mobilized for military service, now including noncombat roles. Soviet strategic planning was also subjected to fundamental changes, essentially to accommodate its new expansionist ambitions. The policy of "collective security" had come to an end.

The Invasion of Poland

On September 1 the German army stormed into Polish territory. At the request of the German command, a radio station in Minsk broadcast a signal to help orient and direct the Luftwaffe toward targets in Poland. On the third day of the war Ribbentrop invited the Soviet Union to occupy that Polish territory assigned to its sphere of influence. Not that Germany was deeply concerned to protect Soviet interests; it simply wanted to ensure that the USSR became directly involved in the conflict and thereby ensure its commitment to the August agreement. And a second front would also, of course, facilitate German military operations against the Poles.[84] The USSR, however, had its own reasons for not making haste. Apart from awaiting the outcome of German military operations, Moscow wanted to see how England and France would react; it also needed time to make the necessary political and military preparations for the attack on Poland. Stalin also realized that he must prepare the population, politically, for this dizzying turn of events. Even if party members had the agility to reverse course instantaneously, it was still necessary to find some way to explain to the general population why the Soviet Union, which had inundated its people with anti-fascist propaganda, was now sending troops into Poland just after the Nazi attack. In the interim Berlin and Moscow were engaging in a rapid exchange of telegrams. When Ribbentrop asked Moscow to send its troops more quickly, Molotov urged his partner to be patient, because excessive haste could "harm us" and serve to unite "our adversaries."[85]

On September 3 the new Soviet ambassador in Berlin, Shkvartsev, presented his diplomatic credentials to Hitler. The beginning of Soviet-German military cooperation was marked by the appointment of a new military attaché in Berlin: General Maksim Purkaev, who had previously helped important commands in the Red Army (commander of a division; chief of staff in a military district). If the appointment of so colorless an ambassador signalled that the Kremlin itself would control relations with Germany, Purkaev's appointment showed that Moscow attached great importance to the two countries' military cooperation.

The day after the nonaggression pact was signed in Moscow, the Soviet embassy and trade mission in Berlin held short meetings to emphasize the significance of the new treaty. As a secret report from the Gestapo noted, the meeting transpired not only in an "official" but also in a "heartfelt" manner.[86] On August 30 the guard at the Soviet embassy in Berlin greeted passers-by with "Heil Hitler." The trade mission received numerous expressions of best wishes from firms interested in developing commercial relations with the Soviet Union.

As the two sides prepared to coordinate their activities, the Gestapo nonetheless maintained its routine surveillance of the embassy and trade mission. In the trade mission, for example, it discovered news clippings and photographs about Ribbentrop's visit in Moscow—from various German newspapers, including the Nazi party organ, *Völkischer Beobachter*.[87] The Gestapo also reported that the staff in the embassy and trade mission were sharply divided in their opinion on the nonaggression pact. One group (predominantly Russians) displayed sympathy toward German military successes and took seriously the apparent improvement in relations between the two countries. The other group ("consisting of Jews and those under Jewish influence") treated all this ironically, declared that England and France had not yet said their last word, and talked about the horrors that war would bring. The Gestapo came to the conclusion that, in general, uncertainty reigned among the staff at the embassy and trade mission.[88]

Thanks to the reports of the NKVD, Stalin knew perfectly well that many Soviet citizens saw no need for a pact with the German fascists, inveterate enemies of the Soviet Union. Hence Stalin worked intensively to find an acceptable explanation not only to justify the pact (Molotov had already done that), but also the ensuing mobilization, expansion of field hospitals, and the invasion of Poland. Stalin finally had his explanation ready. It begins by depicting Soviet policy as a rescue operation: given the breakup of the Polish state, the USSR must save its blood brothers—the Ukrainians and Belorussians living in the eastern part of Poland, who are "threatened" by Germany.[89] Soviet propaganda would return to this formulation after the German attack on June 22, 1941.

Moscow realized, of course, that it was not easy to kill two birds with one stone—to satisfy both the Germans and its own people. It therefore resorted to a different maneuver: the central papers published reports that the western Ukrainians and Belorussians needed protection.[90] Molotov then informed the German ambassador in Moscow that the Red Army was prepared to enter Poland. He also wanted to know when Warsaw would be taken so that once the Polish capital fell, Moscow could inform its people that since the government there had collapsed, it was necessary to intervene to protect the Ukrainians and Belorussians.[91]

The Germans were livid. Ribbentrop quite reasonably observed that, according to Moscow's scenario, the USSR and Germany would not appear as partners, but as adversaries. The Germans then offered Molotov the draft for a joint communiqué.[92] Moscow, however, had quite different plans. After further negotiations, the two sides reached agreement on a formulation that would justify Soviet intervention. Ultimately, Stalin used both the German and the Soviet drafts.[93] The official note, given to the Polish ambassador in Moscow and published in *Izvestiia*, noted that the Polish state had disintegrated, that the USSR therefore did not feel bound by prior agreements, and that it would send its troops into Poland to protect the "life and property" of the people of western Belorussia and western Ukraine. It also promised to render aid to the Polish people.[94] Molotov gave essentially the same explanation in a radio address informing the country that Soviet troops had been sent into Poland.[95] The new redaction of the Soviet-German communiqué, prepared by Stalin himself, made no mention of a German threat, but contained only vague references to "third powers," which might seek to take advantage of the chaos in Poland. Perhaps the most remarkable and accurate part of the communiqué was the statement that Soviet and German troops "pursue no goal contrary to the interests of Germany or the Soviet Union, or contradictory to the letter and spirit of the nonaggression pact signed by Germany and the USSR."[96]

On September 17, 1939 Soviet troops crossed over into Polish territory. That date, not the more traditional June 22, 1941, marks the point when the Soviet Union actually became a combatant in the second world war. And it entered the war as an aggressor, after concluding a secret pact with another aggressor, Nazi Germany. Thus commenced the second phase of Soviet-German military cooperation.

Prior to the invasion of Poland, the USSR conducted some mobilization measures—which, though camouflaged as the mustering of reservists, nonetheless provoked panic among the population. In the Krasnopresnia district of Moscow, for example, the call-up for "training" was regarded as tantamount to mobilization. By the evening of the next day long queues had already besieged food stores; people bought up large quantities of whatever they could (e.g., sugar, salt, soap, and kerosene). Party organizations were ordered to explain to the population that the army had not ordered a general mobilization, but was merely mustering reservists for training, and that Moscow had full stocks of provisions for an entire year. Nevertheless, the stores were soon bare. The regime was forced to requisition trucks from various enterprises to help deliver goods to stores and shops.[97] Party leaders, moreover, were especially discouraged by numerous requests for a draft deferment on various pretexts. A plenum of the Moscow party committee admitted that party organizations, including the city committee, were "taken by surprise and experienced many difficulties." The director at one hospital described the resulting panic:

> People decided that war had begun, ran off to lines at shops. . . . A mass of doctors left. . . . All departed in a panic; the sick are also in a panic. In fact, a person is sleeping, and at 4 A.M. receives a notice ordering him to report immediately. And no one knows anything. And this is happening not with a single individual, but with tens of thousands. . . . All the women keep coming and weeping. They are parting with their husbands, thinking that they are being taken off to war.[98]

And this transpired throughout the USSR, not just in Moscow. This test of the population's preparedness for war showed that it was neither psychologically nor organizationally ready. The same was true of the members of the Communist party. Several months later the first secretary of the Moscow committee, Aleksandr Shcherbakov, confessed that the partial mobilization of reserves for the Soviet-Finnish War had also revealed enormous deficiencies in the mobilization work.[99]

After Warsaw had fallen, Molotov agreed that the original text justifying Soviet intervention "contained a note jarring to German sensibilities."[100] Molotov—in talking to a partner—was completely candid and explained that the Soviet government had been unable to find another pretext for military action "since the Soviet Union had until now not bothered about the plight of its minorities in Poland."[101]

Stalin, however, grew nervous and began to fear that the Germans would deceive him and seize areas previously allotted to the USSR. He certainly did not trust the German military, which would not be eager to abandon territory it had already conquered.[102] His anxiety was so great that he could not conceal it from Schulenburg; Ribbentrop tried to reassure Stalin that their agreements would be strictly observed. Berlin, he stressed, regarded those agreements "as the foundation stone of the new friendly relations between Germany and the Soviet Union."[103] Meanwhile, a new Soviet military attaché and his aides arrived in Berlin; at the suggestion of the German side, Soviet communications officers came as well. The field staffs of the two armies also established contact in Poland. On September 21 a formal military agreement was signed in Moscow (by Voroshilov and chief of staff Boris M. Shaposhnikov for the Soviet side, and by Köstring, Aschenbrenner, and Krebs for the German side). The agreement coordinated the movement of Soviet and German troops in Poland. As for cities and towns that the Wehrmacht relinquished to the Red Army, article 4 explicitly refers to the "purging" of any "saboteurs"; it also required that the Red Army assist in the "destruction" of any "enemy" resistance.[104] This was the prototype of a new secret protocol that would be signed a week later in Moscow. Seeking to deceive the unfortunate Poles (and, above all, world opinion), Germany and the USSR promised to assist the population of Poland to redefine the conditions for their "existence as a state." Just one day later Stalin informed the Germans that he had reconsidered the matter, categorically opposed Polish statehood in any form whatsoever, and proposed that Poland immediately be partitioned along the Narew-Vistula-San rivers. He also insisted that the pertinent negotiations—which he himself intended to conduct—be held in Moscow.[105] This decision was fraught with momentous consequences: the immediate liquidation of Polish statehood and ultimately the mass execution of Polish officers in the Katyn forest in April 1940.

The L'vov Episode

Germany and the Soviet Union failed to coordinate the actions of their military forces in Poland. That led to accidental military skirmishes; for example, Soviet planes mistakenly bombed the 21st German Army Corps on September 17 near Bialystok and Jesow, causing some deaths and casualties.[106] It was not the only such incident.

Perhaps the nature of German-Soviet interaction is best illustrated in the L'vov episode. The fighting commenced when a Soviet tank unit, mistaking the Germans for Poles, launched an attack. The result was a firefight between German and Soviet tank units.[107] The incident, however, took on a broader significance because it involved a question of territory: which side should conquer and annex L'vov? According to previous agreements, L'vov had been allotted to the Soviet Union. The German high command proposed a joint assault on L'vov, which would later be handed over to the

Soviet side. The German ambassador, Schulenburg, became deeply concerned and asked that Stalin be immediately informed of the situation.[108] The two sides did come to an agreement. The German military attaché in Moscow, Köstring, reported that the commander of the German 18th Infantry Corps met with his counterpart from the Red Army and resolved the matter.[109] The entire affair ended in a joint parade in L'vov.

The Polish campaign had other consequences. One was the symbolic alliance of the two sides, with joint parades by the victors and exchange visits by commanders in Brest and elsewhere. Photographers have also recorded the presence of the commander of the 19th Army Corps (General Guderian) and the commissar of the Soviet tank brigade in Brest.[110] Moreover, the campaign brought casualties and prisoners. From the Soviet side an enormous army participated (more than 466,000 troops); casualties included more than 1,000 killed in action.[111] The Soviet Union also captured 452,536 prisoners, including 18,789 officers.[112]

It was only at the end of August that Stalin decided to liquidate the Polish state. Previously he had been dissuaded by the prospect that England would declare war on Germany; as Adam Ulam has observed, preservation of the "Lublin Voevodstvo" gave the impression that Stalin was not bent on liquidation.[113] With the outbreak of war, Stalin no longer had any reason to camouflage his aims. On September 19 Molotov informed Germany that the Soviet Union wished to hold negotiations immediately in Moscow to decide the structure of the "Polish region." He made clear that the Soviet Union preferred to partition Poland along the demarcation line.[114] But Stalin had not only decided to consign western Poland to Germany but also to begin the immediate integration of eastern Poland into the Soviet Union. He was also planning a similar amalgamation of the Baltic states. The Germans also wanted to settle all questions concerning Poland as quickly as possible. Ribbentrop agreed to come to Moscow once again. As a preliminary to these talks, Stalin increased the pressure on the Baltic states and forced them to sign mutual-assistance agreements. He also sent another proposal to Berlin: if Germany would concede Lithuania to the Soviet Union, it could take the Lublin voevodstvo and part of the Warsaw voevodstvo (up to the Bug, as well as Suwalki). As part of the concession of Suwalki, Germany would also acquire a small part of Lithuanian territory. The goal of such a proposal was to avoid future disputes between Germany and the USSR. Indeed, the Soviet Union—with Germany's consent—wished to proceed to the immediate resolution of the "Baltic question," in accordance with the secret protocol of August 23.[115] Stalin did not intend to waste time.

The Treaty on Friendship and the Border

The two days of talks (September 27–28, 1939) in Moscow resulted in a treaty on friendship and the border, along with secret protocols. The aim was to prevent future conflicts between German and Soviet interests. The treaty established their mutual border on the territory of the former Polish state. The order, which henceforth would be imposed in this area, was to be determined by Germany and the Soviet Union separately; each was responsible for its own territories.[116] A confidential protocol foresaw a mutual relocation of people from German, Ukrainian, and Belorussian origins to the respective German or Soviet areas.[117] A secret supplementary protocol transferred the Lithuanian territories to the Soviet sphere in exchange for Lublin and part of the Warsaw areas.[118] The two sides also signed a secret supplementary protocol for the exchange of information and for cooperation to suppress "Polish agitation" (i.e., Polish national resistance).[119] Finally, the Moscow talks dealt with the expansion of political and economic collaboration. Molotov and Ribbentrop jointly declared that collaboration on various matters would constitute a solid foundation for peace in eastern Europe.[120] In reality, however, the partition by Stalin and Hitler led to wars and conflicts that have persisted in the area ever since.

So that no one would doubt that the Red Army actively participated in the assault on Poland, Molotov specifically made mention of its involvement at a session of the Supreme Soviet on October 31, 1939. The deputies broke into "stormy applause," to invoke a favorite cliché of the Soviet press. Stalin emphasized the military cooperation of the two sides in a telegram to Ribbentrop (in reply to congratulations on his sixtieth birthday): "Thank you, Mr. Minister, for the congratulations. The friendship of the peoples of Germany and the Soviet Union, sealed with blood, has every basis for being long-lasting and firm."[121] A joke then made its rounds in Moscow: the friendship was indeed sealed with blood—Polish blood!

Stalin's insistence on taking all of Lithuania, contrary to the agreement of August, made a very negative impression on Hitler and Ribbentrop. The disagreement over Lithuania was not resolved until January 1941, when Moscow agreed to pay Germany 7.5 million dollars for a small strip of land (which the Soviet Union had pressured Germany to cede and had already occupied).[122] Nevertheless, in general, Ribbentrop's second trip to Moscow created a semblance of good will between the two partners. In explaining to Mussolini the changes that were occurring in Russia (viz., the repudiation of "world revolution" and rise of Russian nationalism), Ribbentrop cited the opinion of an old veteran of the Nazi party, who had attended a banquet with Stalin and members of the Politburo, and later declared that it had been like meeting "with old party comrades."[123]

After the destruction of Poland, it was essential for Hitler to have the Soviet Union support his political offensive against England and France. He called upon the latter to end the state of war since the cause—Poland—no longer existed. On September 19 in a speech in Danzig, Hitler declared that he had no territorial claims against England or France. To be sure, Hitler modified that position in an address to the Reichstag on October 6: while still disavowing territorial claims against France, he demanded that England return German colonies seized after World War I and that it resolve various economic problems between the two countries.

In France, where defeatism was strongly entrenched, Hitler's appeal fell on fertile soil. Clement Attlee, who participated in a meeting of Labourites and Socialists in Paris in February 1940, later wrote that the mood was one of despair and depression. Most French socialists, he wrote, were either pacifists or defeatists.[124] Various intermediaries also became involved. These included the Swedish industrialist B. Dalerus (who had repeatedly been used by the Nazis for disinformation in the preceding months), the American businessman William Rhodes Davis (who sold Mexican oil to Germany and, like Dalerus, had met with Goering), James Moony (president of the General Motors Overseas Corporation), Baron William de Ropp of England, and many others.[125] Hitler would have been delighted to achieve a peaceful resolution, since that was tantamount to capitulation by France and England without their ever having fired a shot. In the opinion of an English historian, Hitler thereby would have been free to engulf southeastern Europe, while the western powers and the USSR looked on with "heavy hearts" but indecisively.[126] In fact, while the politicians who had been at

Munich were still in power, the majority opposed negotiations with Hitler. The Soviet Union joined this "peace offensive." It warned the West that, unless Hitler's initiative received a proper response, the responsibility lay with the western democracies, and Germany and the USSR would consult about appropriate measures.[127]

Public Opinion

The Soviet press, with customary unanimity, enthusiastically endorsed the new agreements with Nazi Germany. Ambassador Schulenburg, obviously very pleased, included excerpts from the Moscow press in his reports to Berlin.[128] Of particular interest were the speeches delivered at a meeting in Moscow's Central Park for Culture and Recreation on September 21, 1939—that is, four days after Soviet troops had marched into Poland. That same day the Soviet press published excerpts from Hitler's speech in Danzig; its commentators explained that, whereas Hitler had previously been a fascist, he was now moving in the direction of socialism, and that his movement should be called national-socialism. They quoted Hitler's evaluation of Poland as an undemocratic state, which fully conformed to Molotov's view.[129] Party organizations were instructed to launch an intensive propaganda campaign to support the Red Army's invasion of Poland, to emphasize the theme of "brotherly assistance" to help Ukrainians and Belorussians left to the caprice of fate,[130] and to organize public meetings where Molotov's address of September 17 would be read aloud. Local communists, furthermore, were to organize the "response of the toilers," including an oath for greater productivity and, in agricultural areas, to "double or triple" grain deliveries.

Vigilance, unity behind the party and Stalin, a struggle against "speculators and marauders," and a strengthening of the country's defenses—such was the canned response nominally emanating from the general populace. The result was a wave of meetings, attended by thousands. A meeting in the city of Tomsk, for example, was attended by 30,000 people. It was followed by reports of the overfulfillment of production plans—some by 20 percent, elsewhere by 80 or 100 percent, even as much as 200 percent. The only amazing thing was that a planned economy was capable of such phenomenal leaps in output. The reports included the vow, given countless times already, to wage a merciless struggle against wreckers, spies, and

saboteurs.[131] Later, in November 1939, in conjunction with elec-
tions to local soviets, special attention was given to German-Soviet
relations. For example, a report from the Kuznetsk district committee for September claimed that it had organized 389 discussions
(with an audience of 8,750) on the ratification of the Soviet-German treaties, 287 discussions (with an audience of 12,878) on
Molotov's speech of September 17, and 467 meetings (attended by
7,320 people) on the international situation.[132]

This massive propaganda about Soviet-German relations indicated, above all, that it was obviously difficult for the population to
follow this sudden turn in Soviet policy, which had transformed fascists from mortal enemies into good friends. This bewilderment, to
be sure, was somewhat offset by the territorial gains in Poland:
Stalin was again triumphant, indeed, had saved the western
Ukrainians and Belorussians from Polish lords and German fascists.
Still, doubts lingered and cropped up in questions to the lecturers
and speakers at these meetings. In Novosibirsk oblast', for example,
listeners raised questions about the impact of the German-Soviet
nonaggression pact on the "anti-Comintern Pact," about America
and its attitude toward these events, and the position of the English
and French communist parties on war with Germany.[133]

Ideology and the Comintern

To dispel doubts about the prospects for friendship with Hitlerian
Germany (and perhaps to repress his own inner misgivings), Stalin
also endeavored to buttress the "theoretical basis" for a Soviet-German alliance. Molotov articulated all this in a speech by Molotov at
a session of the Supreme Soviet (convoked to ratify the treaty) on
October 31, 1939. He emphasized that the war meant the destruction of Poland ("this offspring of the Versailles Treaty"), which had
been totally obliterated by a swift blow from the German and then
Soviet armies. He declared, moreover, that one must dispense with
outmoded concepts of "aggression" and "aggressor." Molotov told
the astonished deputies that the real aggressors were England and
France, since they had spurned Germany's peace initiatives. Continuation of war at this point was senseless, for Poland no longer
existed. Indeed: "To continue war, as war for the 'destruction of Hitlerism' and masked by the false flag of a struggle for 'democracy,' is
not only senseless, but criminal."[134]

The Soviet press, of course, immediately picked up the new slogans. All across the Soviet Union, newspapers and the radio denounced England and France as warmongers. Together with the Nazi press in Germany, the Soviet media admonished the United States not to intervene on the side of England. After Germany invaded and occupied Norway and Denmark, Soviet authorities closed the latter's diplomatic missions in Moscow. Under the pretext of repatriation, the Soviet Union turned over to Germany approximately 800 German and Austrian citizens who, as anti-fascists, had taken refuge in the Soviet Union and at the moment were in Soviet labor camps and prisons.

Particular attention was also given to propaganda in the Red Army. Thus a telegram from the head of the Main Political Administration (Lev Z. Mekhlis) on September 29 (i.e., one day after the signing of the Soviet-German Treaty on Friendship and Borders) gave detailed directions to military councils and the heads of political administration units on how to familiarize the Red Army with the new policy. Specifically, it directed military newspapers to publish the text of the treaty with Germany, the mutual-assistance pact with Estonia, the declaration of the German and Soviet government on September 28, and the lead article from *Pravda* on September 30. In addition, the meaning of all these documents was to be explained in meetings with military personnel. Mekhlis directed that special propaganda be conducted among the population in western Ukraine and western Belorussia. He noted that the border changes, compared with the previous plans for a demarcation line, were an expression "of our concern not to split the Polish people into two parts."[135] Propagandists lay special emphasis on the dislocation of Soviet troops and the construction of naval bases and airfields on Estonian territory as measures taken to ensure peace in the Baltics. Ensuing events, of course, demonstrated how specious all this was.

Army agitators were also to wage a battle against "robbery and plundering." In a separate telegram to political administrative personnel in Volkovysk and Tarnopol' (October 2), Mekhlis cited numerous instances of plundering by Soviet officers and soldiers. "These facts," he wrote, "disgrace us in the eyes of the local population, while elements hostile to the Red Army can use them against our great cause."[136] He warned the heads of the political organs and commissars that they would be removed from their positions if they did not take decisive action. He also reminded them that the local population will compare the behavior of Soviet and German soldiers. At the same time, he warned against "provocative attacks on Germany by Soviet military personnel," as contradictory to the treaty.[137] As indeed this telegram implies, anti-German sentiments were probably rather widespread in the army. On November 14 the Political Administration of the Ukrainian Front ordered its subordinates to take prompt action to stop the mass purchases of goods, for it was "an intolerable phenomenon, bringing disgrace on the Red Army."[138] The struggle against plundering ran parallel with political indoctrination. On November 2 Mekhlis ordered that Molotov's speech of October 31 be given close study, that the military be taught that the aggressors are England and France, and that Germany was simply a victim of the Versailles Treaty.[139]

As Stalin endeavored to adapt Leninist-Stalinist ideology to the needs of the moment, he was changing his view of National Socialism. This process actually commenced as soon as the Nazis came to power in 1933, but reached its acme in the fall of 1939. The Comintern had treated the nonaggression pact as an "instrument of peace," but still branded the war between Hitler and the western allies as an "imperialist" war on both sides. It obviously followed that the peoples of the warring sides should, in accordance with Leninist precepts, actively oppose their own governments—in England, France, and Germany alike. Now, however, the Soviet Union had entered into friendly relations with Germany, and Stalin had no intention of risking these new ties because of the Comintern, which he had never liked anyway. Nevertheless, Stalin—at Dimitrov's insistence—was forced to give precise indication on how to treat communist parties and their head organization, the Comintern, under the new circumstances. The aim of his directive was to ensure that under no conditions should the Comintern jeopardize Soviet-German relations.[140]

Stalin declared that the war was a battle between two groups of capitalist states to partition and rule the world. "We are not opposed," declared Stalin, "if they have a good fight and weaken each other."[141] Stalin proposed to renounce a decision of the Seventh Congress of the Comintern (which had described fascism as "the main source of aggression") and to jettison the slogan of a popular front; since this was an imperialist war, the workers should oppose both the war and those responsible for it. In practical terms, this was a call for English and French workers to sabotage the military efforts of their own countries. But this goal did not apply to German workers, insofar as Germany was now depicted by Soviet leaders as the victim, not the perpetrator, of aggression. At the same time, Stalin designated Poland as a fascist government susceptible to annihilation.[142]

In mid-October Stalin advanced new slogans for the Comintern. They conformed entirely with the main thrust of his foreign policy: close cooperation and possibly an alliance with Nazi Germany. The slogans included an appeal to "throw out the governments that are for war!" To make absolutely sure that there was no ambiguity, Stalin told Dimitrov (in Zhdanov's presence) on October 25: "We will not speak out against governments that are for peace!" But at that point the magical word "peace" served only German interests, which of course is why Berlin was so magnanimously advancing its "peace proposals."[143]

In the fall of 1939 Stalin also toyed with another idea: the possibility that the Nazis would change their ideological position. He believed that, since the "petit-bourgeois" nationalists were independent of capitalist traditions, they were "capable of a radical turn" and "flexible." At a dinner following the November parade (with Kaganovich, Molotov, Andrei A. Andreev, Mikoian, Semon M. Budennyi, Kulik, and Dimitrov present) Stalin urged that one "cast off the routine, not cling to fixed rules, see what is new and dictated by changed circumstances."[144] For Stalin this was simply a logical extension of his ideas about German nationalists; it fit neatly with his view of Germany as a victim of the Versailles Treaty. He believed that when the Nazis seized power, their aggressiveness had been expanded from a narrow party mentality to a broader state perspective, with the elimination of more limited adherents. Such an approach by Hitler conformed entirely to Stalin's assessment of him as a realistic politician and, to judge from future events, Stalin never expected to find in his "partner" a monomaniacal ideologue. That proved a fatal miscalculation.

Henceforth, in all concrete instances connected with German aggression, the Comintern repeated Soviet assessments and aims. In April 1941, as the Soviet Union's foreign political position rapidly deteriorated, Stalin was already prepared to dissolve the Comintern: "The attempt to disband the Comintern in this situation must be evaluated as an attempt by Stalin, at the price of terminating the Comintern's existence, to preserve friendly relations with Germany."[145] But Stalin was always prepared to exchange the Comintern for the sake of agreements with the West. In the final analysis he did precisely that, issuing an order in May 1943 for the Comintern to dissolve itself and thereby help assure friendly relations with his current ally, the United States.

Hitler and Nazi Ideology

Hitler's programmatic aims were based on a recognition of the continuity in German policy, the cornerstone of which (according to Nazi ideology) was the acquisition of "living space" in the east. Destruction of the Versailles system and the return of territories lost after World War I were only interim objectives, which Hitler regarded as a preliminary to the establishment of German dominance on the continent. A further step could be war with England should it not voluntarily accept German hegemony in Europe and return colonies seized in the first world war. At first appearing only in the form of dreams, the notion of a grandiose Reich stretching from the Pyrenees to the Urals gradually took shape as strategic designs and operational orders. But to achieve this, Germany had first to drive England to its knees, smash the Soviet Union, and colonize its territory. These plans comfortably fit within the conception of the racial Great-German Nordic theories, which were tantamount to the purely Nazi scheme for the total annihilation of the Jewish population in Europe. For the interim, however, Hitler had to restrain himself, for Moscow was the only real partner in the struggle against England.

In a diary entry of November 8, the head of the propaganda department, Paul Joseph Goebbels, noted with satisfaction Molotov's recent speech: "Savage accusations against capitalist states. Also friendly words for us."[146] Assessing the Treaty on Friendship and Borders, Hitler concluded that it completely excluded the possibility of misunderstandings or conflicts in the future, for German and Russian interests had been separated into clear spheres of interest. Each was free, in its sphere, to pursue whatever policy served its interests.[147] On October 4 the two sides signed a supplementary agreement, which provided a more detailed demarcation of the border of their state interests.[148] According to Ribbentrop, members of the Nazi Party "had unreservedly welcomed the German-Russian agreement." He explained this by the "realistic political thinking" so characteristic of Nazis.[149] After Ribbentrop's trip to Moscow, Mussolini jocularly referred to him as "Comrade Ribbentrop."[150]

To judge from the secret reports of the German security service, the German population reacted rather cautiously to the change in Soviet-German relations, and indeed some circles were outright hostile. A flyer circulated in Stettin, for example, spoke of "a fatal union concluded between Nazism and communism," and denounced the pact as an act of high treason.[151] From the start of the Soviet-Finnish war many believed that the Finns had followed a foolish policy with regard to the USSR, but also feared that the war would make communism an even more powerful force. The propaganda of the previous years, which indicated the danger of an expansion of Soviet influence in the Baltics, was still fresh in the minds of the population. At the same time, many Germans also felt that Finnish policy had been unfriendly toward Germany.[152] The secret police also noted that reports on the USSR "do not always take the correct tone." On the one hand, the population demonstrated a growing interest in the problem of Russia, which was reflected in the organization of Russian-language courses and an interest in Russian literature; on the other, however, people found it difficult to relate this new policy toward the USSR to the irreconcilable differences between Nazi and communist worldviews. Illustrative was a report that called both governments "socialist," with the same goal: "give to the producers all that they earn."[153]

One of the constant themes of the secret reports was the fate of the Volksdeutsche. Nor was the plight of Soviet Germans forgotten. In late January 1940 it was pointed out that the status of Germans in the USSR had improved somewhat. Among Germans living in the Volga and Black Sea areas, hopes had increased that they would be able to emigrate to Germany. It was also noted that, of 300,000 Volga Germans, only an insignificant number had been "bolshevized."[154]

Within a few months, Europe had witnessed a profound diplomatic revolution: two ostensible arch-enemies, Nazi Germany and Soviet Russia, became partners in the dismemberment of eastern Europe.

As this analysis suggests, Stalin himself played a key role: his "doctrine" for exploiting European tensions, his strategy of letting the other great powers exhaust themselves, and his abiding interest and preference for the "German card" were crucial factors in leading to the nonaggression pact. By the fall of 1939 the two countries were no longer partners, but predators—seeking to expand their territories and power.

5

Conquests and Conflicts

Stalin had many reasons to be pleased with the Soviet-German agreements of August and September. They showed, first, the efficacy of exploiting contradictions among the great powers to the advantage of the USSR. Second, the Soviet Union now had an opportunity to expand its territory and push back the "capitalist world" with a minimum expenditure of military force. Third, Stalin and his aides could imagine that it lay entirely within their hands to decide when, and how, the Soviet Union would intervene in the larger theater of war. Fourth, the country obtained more time to prepare for that decisive point when the USSR in fact did become embroiled in the world war. Stalin had his own ideas on this; it is entirely conceivable that he did not share all his thoughts with comrades-in-arms, especially with respect to developing relations with Nazi Germany. Finally, the change in geopolitics transformed the USSR, in a short period of time, into the primary source of strategic materials and foodstuffs for Germany. The USSR also guaranteed the security of Germany's rear in the east and, indeed, assumed a more active form. The campaign in Poland was reaching an end when General Köstring, the German military attaché in Moscow, requested Berlin to increase his staff in view of the impending expansion of military ties with the Red

Army.[1] Theoretically, this status could serve to augment its influence in Berlin.

Stalin, however, committed some serious miscalculations in expanding Soviet territory, especially with respect to the country's geopolitical position. Although he had succeeded in obtaining new territories and separating Soviet and German spheres of influence, the effect was to reduce, not enhance, the security of the USSR. By annexing Poland and the Baltic states, the two partners eliminated the *cordon sanitaire* that had not only shielded the Soviet Union from its only real potential aggressor—Nazi Germany—but also served as a buffer, protecting Germany from a sudden attack by the USSR. Now the Soviet Union shared a common border with Germany and its allies, and at virtually every point along that 5,000-kilometer line the Soviet Union was vulnerable to attack.

The Baltics (Autumn, 1939)

Backed with German political support, Stalin did not tarry in realizing his plans for territorial expansion. Simultaneous with the negotiations with Ribbentrop, Moscow began twisting the arm of the Estonian foreign minister, Karl Selter, whom it browbeat into signing a mutual-assistance treaty with the USSR on September 29.[2] The other two Baltic states, Latvia and Lithuania, were forced to do likewise shortly afterwards (on October 5 and October 10 respectively). As the Latvian foreign minister at the time, Wilhelm Munters, wrote many years later, "after the collapse of the Anglo-French-Soviet negotiations in Moscow, our last hopes for assistance from the Western powers to support our neutrality disappeared. We remained alone."[3] At a joint session of the commission on foreign policy and defense (from the State Assembly and State Council), President Konstantin Piats made the following declaration on September 26, 1939: "We have no choice. We shall hope that in the future Germany will not want us to perish."[4]

The Baltic states, however, could no longer count on the support of Germany (with which they had signed a nonaggression pact on June 8, 1939) or, still less, Britain. They were now forced to sign agreements of mutual assistance with Moscow. According to these agreements, the Soviet Union obtained naval and air bases and the right to station its troops within the territory of the Baltic states. British Foreign Minister Lord Halifax told the Latvian ambassador

on October 10 that Latvia had acted sensibly in signing the agreement with the USSR.[5] Winston Churchill wrote in his memoirs
that these events in the Baltics forced the Germans to keep a significant contingent of naval vessels in the Baltic Sea, which in turn
alleviated the situation for Britain.[6]

The Soviet Union disregarded the Germans' request that the
Lithuanians not be informed, for the time being, of changes in its
status.[7] Molotov, in fact, did just the contrary; he informed the
Lithuanians of the agreement with Germany in order that they
abandon any hopes of German assistance.[8] Although, with Moscow's
agreement, Vilnius was returned to Lithuania,[9] that was only a sweet
coating for the bitter pill they would soon have to swallow.

The Soviet-Finnish War

Stalin sensed from the spirit of the times that this was the moment to
realize critical territorial ambitions and needs. Indeed, the Munich
agreement of September 30, 1938 and the capitulation to Hitler's
demands were a clear signal that he must not defer indefinitely his
geopolitical and strategic objectives. All this reached a critical point
in the fall of 1939. With Germany and the western powers locked in
combat, Stalin saw his window of opportunity. In the first instance
that meant the "resolution" of differences with Finland.

At the end of February 1939 (just a few days before the opening
of the Eighteenth Party Congress), the USSR proposed to Finland
that it lease part of its territory, specifically, several islands (including Gotland), which the Soviet Union would use to construct military bases. The proposal came from Litvinov, two months before
he was dismissed as commissar of foreign affairs. Although Moscow
offered to give in exchange the larger territory of Soviet Karelia (a
Finnish-speaking area much desired by Finland), the Finnish
firmly rejected the proposal. It bears noting that Litvinov, whose
name is so closely identified with collective security, saw nothing
shameful in seeking to persuade an independent state to surrender
part of its territory. The Finns, of course, had a different view; they
certainly did not regard the islands as useless and infertile, but part
of their homeland.

Recently declassified documents from the Russian archives have
demonstrated that in the summer of 1939—even as the USSR
was negotiating with Britain and France—the Red Army's Chief

Military Council was examining a plan (prepared by its General Staff) to invade Finland. General B. M. Shaposhnikov, chief of the General Staff, presented the plan personally. The plan foresaw direct support of Finland by Germany, Great Britain, France, and also the Scandinavian countries. Stalin, however, rejected the plan, not because of diplomatic complications, but because—in his view—the plan exaggerated the difficulties of the conflict. The new commander of the Leningrad Military District, K. A. Meretskov, who had only recently been released from prison, drew up a new plan. It envisioned a Soviet blitzkrieg: a powerful first strike, followed, within two or three weeks, by the destruction of the Finnish army. The plan presupposed not only surprise, but also a low assessment of the Finns' military potential—not unlike the arrogant underestimation that would later characterize the Nazi plans for operation Barbarossa.

It required approximately five months to plan the attack on Finland. All this time the Soviet Union exerted constant diplomatic pressure, making new demands not only to exchange territory and to lease areas for military bases, but also to demolish the "Mannerheim line" of fortifications on the Karelian isthmus. Had the Finns agreed, they would have been totally at the mercy of Moscow. However, the USSR used diplomatic maneuvers to conceal this preparation for war or, as General M. Moiseev (chief of staff under Mikhail Gorbachev) put it, "the final military-preparatory measures were hastily conducted."[10] Urho Kaleva Kekkonen, who was then serving as a minister in the Finnish cabinet and would be the country's president from 1956 to 1981, recalled the Finnish quandary: "We knew that surrender of the demanded territory would have left a fatal gap in the country's system of defense." It was obvious, he said, what such a gap would mean "in the presence of neighbor like Russia."[11]

The USSR began to prepare its population psychologically for war with Finland, indeed in a manner that was eerily similar to German preparations before the attacks on Czechoslovakia and Poland. Molotov set the tone in his speech to the Supreme Soviet on October 31, 1939, in which he acknowledged that Finland had been advised to dismantle its fortifications. To do so, declared Molotov, was in Finland's own best interest.[12] It bears noting that fortified lines are purely defensive, not offensive; only a power interested in aggression could possibly have been interested in removing the Mannerheim line—a fact that was not, of course, lost on the Finns.

What impelled Moscow to adopt so harsh a policy toward Finland? One might attribute its behavior in part to an arrogant confidence in its own military might and invincibility, as well as the Bolsheviks' hatred of social democrats, like those who were then the ruling party in Finland. Moreover, in the fall of 1939, it appeared to be completely safe to launch an attack on the Finns, since Germany had agreed that this area belonged to the Soviet sphere of interest and would not interfere. As far as the British and French were concerned, once the Polish state had fallen they were too concerned about their own military needs to worry about the Finns. In addition, by this point the USSR had already made the necessary military preparations: its troops were already stationed in the Baltic states and poised to attack. Once the Finns rejected the Soviet ultimatum, on November 28, Moscow declared its nonaggression treaty with Finland to be void. Two days later it attacked. As soon became apparent, the Red Army—despite five months of preparation—was not ready for the conflict.

The principle of ideological warfare, utilized during the Russian civil war, was applied to Finland as well. The Soviets fashioned a puppet government for Finland, which was to be headed by Otto Kuusinen, a former leader in the Finnish Communist Party and now a functionary in the Comintern. Moscow also envisaged the creation of a Karelian Soviet Republic that would unite the Karelian Autonomous SSR with parts of Finland.

Kuusinen played no independent role in such schemes. The architect was Andrei A. Zhdanov. A close confidant of Stalin, he was first secretary of the Leningrad party apparatus, a member of the War Council of the Leningrad Military District, and a member of the Central Committee. New archival documents provide some interesting details about the so-called "Finnish Democratic Republic," which Moscow immediately recognized and with which it signed a treaty of mutual assistance and friendship. One document, in Zhdanov's handwriting, is a communiqué about the formation of the new republic and a declaration of the "popular government." As an instruction on how the Soviet media should characterize the document, Zhdanov instructed that it be called a "radio interception" and that it had been "translated from Finnish."[13] A second, likewise in Zhdanov's hand, is a draft of instructions for political and organizational work in areas of Finland already "liberated from the whites."[14] The third document contained an appeal to Finnish workers; it too is in Zhdanov's hand. He also adapted the printed text of the military oath of Red Army soldiers, with only minor changes, for use by the "People's Army of Finland."[15]

Militarily, however, the Soviet campaign against Finland was a humiliating military and political fiasco. The Red Army proved unable to fight under winter conditions; the tactic of frontal assaults on the Mannerheim line failed miserably and merely resulted in massive casualties. It did no good to mobilize the Komsomol volunteers or the skiers, who were senselessly thrown into battle and sent to their death. As a later commentary by the Soviet defense ministry observed, "our troops did not succeed in a single area (but especially in the Karelian Isthmus) in carrying out the assigned task."[16]

It did not take Moscow long to find a scapegoat: Meretskov. He was replaced by Marshal Semon K. Timoshenko; General Grigorii M. Shtern was summoned from the Far East to assist. Only after significant forces of all kinds had been shifted to the Finnish front was the Red Army finally able to break through the Mannerheim line. Still, the Soviet forces had to fight for every yard they advanced. Altogether, Moscow had to send a significant part of its land and air forces as well as part of its navy; by March 1, 1940 it had dispatched more than 760,000 men to fight on the Finnish front.[17] Soviet losses were shockingly high—more than 127,000 killed or missing in action, not to mention a large number of wounded.[18] Nevertheless, it finally forced the Finns to sue for peace, and a treaty was signed in Moscow on March 12, 1940. In addition to the Karelian Isthmus (including Vyborg) and various other territories and islands, it also obtained a lease on the island of Hango, with the right to establish a military base.

Politically, too, the war was a great moral defeat, for the aggression led to the expulsion of the USSR from the League of Nations. The war also exposed the country's military weakness, which ultimately would encourage Hitler to press on with his designs on the USSR.

Economic Cooperation

On September 28, 1939 Ribbentrop and Molotov exchanged letters about mutual economic cooperation. This had indeed already been foreseen in the trade and credit agreement of August 19, 1939, and the following month the two sides began negotiations that would culminate in the Economic Agreement of February 11, 1940. The two sides had good reason to think that they could significantly expand the August agreement: their close political and military cooperation against Poland, division of Eastern Europe into spheres of influence, and concerted policy toward Britain and France—all had shown a capacity for collaboration and common interests. To be sure, the new talks proceeded slowly, not least because the Soviet Union was preoccupied by the difficult military and political consequences of the Finnish War. It was to take nearly four months before an agreement was ready for signatures.

The delay was certainly not in the interests of Germany, which had shifted its whole economy to a war-footing and desperately needed to procure strategic raw materials and to stockpile of food reserves. Indeed, representatives of Germany's Economic Ministry had participated in discussions with Soviet officials at the German Foreign Ministry on September 6 and raised the question of using Soviet transport and territory to ship goods to the Far and Near East.[19] On October 15 Hitler agreed with Chief of the German High Command Wilhelm Keitel that Germany should exempt Soviet timber exports to Britain from the general blockade, because the timber was traded for zinc and rubber, which were vitally needed for the German war economy.[20]

The USSR in turn had its own military shopping list. In late October 1939 Ivan F. Tevosian (commissar of the ship-building industry) visited Germany and brought along a list of the items most desired by Moscow: blueprints and materials to construct light cruisers of the *Admiral Hipper* class, a battleship of the *Scharnhost* class, an aircraft carrier of the *Count Zeppelin* class, and hulls for two other categories of ships. The list included sea and ship artillery, hydroacoustic equipment, mines, torpedoes, minesweepers, and various other items. The Soviets also sought to purchase field artillery, antiaircraft guns, fighters, poison gases, pontoon equipment, explosives, and industrial machinery for peaceful purposes.[21] In March 1940 Tevosian and a division commander (Savchenko) spent three weeks in Germany, where they met with Goering and discussed the possibility of cooperation in arms production. The two sides agreed that Germany would supply models of its military aircraft, various artillery systems, and some other items.[22] Indicative of the tenor of relations was the Germans' decision to show Soviet specialists the Messerschmidt, Junkers, and Heinkel aircraft factories. The Soviet guests included an aircraft designer (A. S. Iakovlev), the director of a Soviet aircraft plant (P. V. Dement'ev), and the first deputy commissar of aircraft construction (B. P. Balandin, a specialist on motors). As a former commissar of aviation (A. I. Shakhurin) reported, the Germans showed Soviet specialists everything—the manufacturing plants, design bureaus, and newest technology for airfields and planes. Indeed, Soviet pilots were even allowed to make test flights in German miliary aircraft. Germany also agreed to allow the Soviet Union to purchase several models of its newest warplanes, including fighters (Messerschmidt-109 and 110; Heinkel-100) and bombers (Junkers-88 and Dorne-215). It goes without saying that the Soviet pilots and engineers made a careful study of the Germans' airplane technology.

The Germans, in turn, visited the Soviet Union to see what the Russian aircraft industry had to offer. While Shakhurin claims they were impressed by the unexpectedly high level of Soviet aviation production, the Germans actually drew a totally different conclusion: their own aviation industry, they made clear, was definitely superior to the Soviets.'[23] No doubt in response to this humiliating assessment, the Soviet Union hastily took steps to upgrade and expand their air force; the commissariat for aviation issued, for example, 300 directives in 1940 and another 488 the following year.[24] The passion for directives, resolutions, and ukases was of course characteristic of the Stalinist system, which invariably suspected subordinate bodies of whitewashing and coverups. The suspicion frequently had good cause. It even reached the point where Stalin himself demanded that Shakhurin and his deputies send him a sworn statement that the aircraft production would be increased to fifty planes a day.

The Soviet-German economic agreement of February 1940 without doubt laid a solid basis for close relations and cooperation. Although the general agreement was valid for a term of 27 months (i.e., until August 1942), the provisions on Soviet obligations to deliver various goods ran for only a term of 18 months. The negotiations were so difficult that Ribbentrop finally made a personal appeal to Stalin in order to bring them to a successful close. The German foreign minister reminded Stalin that this agreement was intended to go beyond mere economic matters. Its basis, he declared, was "the promise that the Soviet government was willing to support Germany economically during the war that had been forced upon her."[25] In other words, the economic agreement had to take into account political and military-strategic considerations, namely, that Germany was at war and could only gradually fulfill its obligations to the USSR.

At a meeting in the Kremlin on February 7, 1940, Stalin suggested a compromise: to conclude one treaty, not two (as the Germans had proposed). According to the agreement, the USSR would ship to Germany goods with a value of 220–230 million marks during the first six months of the agreement, then goods worth another 430 million marks in the ensuing twelve months (for a total of 650–660 million marks during the entire 18-month period). Germany, in return, was to ship goods of an equivalent value, but over a 27-month term. Stalin, for his part, asked that the Germans not raise the price on the goods that they were to deliver.[26]

Schnurre calculated that Soviet deliveries and services in the first twelve months of the agreement to have a value of approximately 800 million marks.[27] Specifically, the Soviet Union agreed to supply Germany with grain, petroleum, cotton, various ores, phosphates, timber, and platinum. As for German deliveries to the USSR, a significant share consisted of military equipment and equipment for manufacturing plants. Moscow also gave Germany permission to ship goods across Soviet territory to Romania, Iran, Afghanistan, and countries in the Near East. German plants that manufactured goods for the USSR were also to be compensated with copper, nickel, tin, molybdenum, tungsten, and cobalt. The Soviet Union also agreed to procure metals and raw materials for Germany in third countries. A special stipulation provided that, if either side should fail to deliver goods on schedule, the other could cease making deliveries.

Both sides were highly satisfied with the agreement. It was, after all, signed in the midst of the Soviet-Finnish war—and after the USSR had been expelled from the League of Nations and had heard threats that an Anglo-French expeditionary force might be sent to assist the Finns. As the German negotiators reported to Berlin: "Despite all these difficulties, during the long negotiations the desire of the Soviet government to help Germany and also to consolidate firmly the political understanding in economic matters became more and more evident."[28]

In the early spring of 1940 Stalin was still persuaded that partnership with German would be close and long-lasting. That assessment informed, for example, a document prepared in the Commissariat of Foreign Trade in March 1940: "The realization of this Economic Agreement (which, in its scale and significance, has no precedent in the history of world trade) has already commenced. Every day the USSR is dispatching trains laden with raw materials for Germany. Once navigation in the Baltic Sea reopens, the raw materials will go to Germany by ship as well. German industry, in return, is becoming increasingly occupied with Soviet orders."[29] In an interview with the foreign section of the American journal *Business Week* in April 1940, Anastas Mikoian (commissar of foreign trade) declared that the trade in the first year of the agreement had already exceeded the largest volume reached at any point since World War I (the 1.1 billion marks of 1931). Mikoian emphasized that the USSR had improved its shipping capabilities through the acquisition of the Baltic ports.[30] The German shipping line of A. Kirsten and Ernst Russo also opened a freight and passenger service between Leningrad and Hamburg.[31]

Once Germany had completed military operations in Poland, its military command immediately took steps to restore railway connections with the USSR in order to expedite the exchange of goods. The Soviet Union did likewise on its side of the demarcation line.[32] By mid-October the railway line was ready for regular operation, enabling a massive stream of nonferrous metals, oil, and foodstuffs to flow into Germany. Ribbentrop held that "the relationship [between the two countries] was fortunately growing closer and closer."[33]

The German press wrote at the time that, thanks to the Economic Agreement with the USSR (reinforced by the nonaggression pact), the British blockade around Germany had become a total fiasco. It also emphasized the prospects for long-term economic cooperation between the two countries.[34] In late November 1940 the Moscow correspondent for the central Nazi party organ, *Völkischer Beobachter*, emphasized the radical change in the European economy that had occurred since the German economic delegation arrived in Moscow: "The territorial-political revolution—which began after Germany acquired Austria and Czechoslovakia and after establishing the boundaries for German-Soviet interests—has gradually penetrated all of Europe. It is accelerated by the development of a new conception: the economy of a great space."[35] All this was linked, on a theoretical level, with the construction of a "new Europe," which would replace the traditional liberalism of Britain and France with socialism.

Just what did this "socialism" mean? As the September–October issue of a Nazi journal for social policy (*Deutsche Arbeitsfront*) explained, "the teaching comes this time not from the West, but from the center of Europe. . . . We Germans are socialists by our very nature. . . . Now, with the assistance of fire and the sword, a new social epoch should be born. . . . But national socialism is not, of course, an export good. *We do not want to prescribe to a single people, how this socialism will be realized.*"[36] Indeed, the ideological cliches of Soviet and Nazi propaganda were amazingly similar—for example, the notion that "the peoples of Europe await a new era, the era of socialism." As the Nazi journal explained, "how this will be done in particulars is left to the free decision of the peoples themselves, but they cannot be freed from the obligation to reorganize their internal life."[37]

The Nazis also decided to make their contribution to the development of economic relations with the USSR. As the deputy chief of the Import Administration in the Commissariat of Foreign Trade (Gendin) told his superiors, the "Foreign Organization" of the Nazi Party intended to take an active part in the development of German-Soviet economic ties and could recommend Russian-speaking experts to assist in expanding business ties with the USSR. Gendin welcomed this initiative and emphasized the "necessity" of exploiting this opportunity through an agreement with the Foreign Organization. After reading the memorandum, his chief (Mikoian) wrote: "Agreed. A.M."[38] It was as if there were no ideological prejudices. The idea of close economic cooperation with communist Russia and fascist Germany was not alien to the party apparatchiki in either country. Significant attention in this cooperation was given to the use of the Soviet Union's potential for making purchases in third countries and for the transit of strategic raw materials through Soviet territory, particularly rubber, tungsten, and tin—all of which were desperately needed by the German war economy. The proposals for trade included the export of German vehicles to Tsintsan via the USSR, with the shipment of tungsten and tin in return.[39]

The firm of Otto Wolff, which implemented this proposal, requested a visa for its representative to meet with agents of the firm in Alma Ata and Urumcha. But the deputy commissar of foreign affairs (Dekanozov) raised objections.[40] One can only speculate about the reasons for this opposition, but Dekanozov's status—he was simultaneously a deputy commissar in the NKVD—hints that police considerations may have played a role. Mikoian categorically demanded that the trans-shipment remain completely secret and that only a few people be aware of the operation.[41]

Each side, at least indirectly, made a contribution to the military campaigns of the other. The Soviet authorities were hardly neutral in the military conflict between Germany and the Allies. Thus, when war first broke out, Soviet authorities detained all the ships of Britain and her allies for three days in Murmansk in order assist the German raider *Bremen* in breaking through the British blockade to reach German waters. A Soviet icebreaker took a difficult route through the Arctic Ocean to bring the German raider *Schiff-45* through the Bering Straits to the Pacific Ocean. The German ship then successfully sank several vessels belonging to Britain and its allies.[42] Some German ships also took refuge in Murmansk in the course of naval operations. That same Soviet port also provided fuel and foodstuffs for German cruisers engaged in naval operations against Britain. The USSR also supplied meteorological information, which the German Luftwaffe used for its blitzkrieg against the British Isles. For its part, Germany restricted the movement of its own vessels in the Baltic and Black seas during the Soviet-Finnish War. One could cite still other cases of direct military cooperation.

After the Germans annexed Czechoslovakia, they reorganized the Skoda firm. Its new director, Gromadko, visited Moscow in early 1939 to meet with the people's commissars Boris L. Vannikov and Ivan F. Tevosian (the latter made a return visit to Germany in 1940). In Moscow Gromadko offered to sell products like howitzers, antiaircraft guns, naval weapons, and equipment and machinery to produce rifles and artillery pieces, armor plates, diesels, compressors for submarines, and much else. He proposed that the USSR render compensation in kind—with deliveries of iron and manganese ores, nickel, tungsten, copper, tin, ball-bearings and foodstuffs. Skoda also requested permission for the transshipment of its products across Soviet territory to the Manchurian government and other eastern countries.[43] During the next visit by Schnurre and other German plenipotentiaries on economic cooperation, Stalin showed irritation over the delays in German deliveries and declared, with obvious vexation, that he regarded the Soviet-German Economic Agreement as one of *mutual* assistance.[44]

According to German intelligence, from early June 1940 the German public was carefully monitoring press reports about the Soviet Union. Less than a year had passed since the signing of the Soviet-German pact, but skepticism toward the USSR persisted. The security service in Innsbruck, for example, reported a widespread belief that the British attempts to woo Moscow underscored the importance of maintaining friendly relations, since these were necessary for obtaining raw materials and goods from Russia.[45] In Lublin and Warsaw it was rumored that the USSR would soon occupy Lublin and then push the demarcation line to the Vistula. It is reasonable to assume that the Polish resistance spread these rumors in order to encourage Poles living in the German zone of occupation. To this category belong as well fantasies of an impending "Bolshevik revolution" in France, which would be followed by Soviet efforts to mediate a peaceful settlement.[46] At this time too, in Germany itself, the population discussed the prospects for peace in the near future. The German secret police also picked up rumors from Bohemia and Moravia about the purportedly hostile attitude of the USSR toward Germany.[47] In brief, people in each area speculated about the situation, depending upon their plans, expectations, and hopes.

But the economic nexus was also a source of mounting tension, for the German war economy was far more inclined to receive than to give. First in the spring of 1940 but especially toward the end of the year, German firms encountered growing difficulties in filling Soviet military and industrial orders. In mid-March 1940 Evgenii Babarin drew Karl Ritter's attention to the serious problems in arms deliveries to the USSR, to the long delays in building ships for the Soviets, and to the increased price of constructing a chemical plant.[48] In May 1940 the chief of the Import Division at the Commissariat of Foreign Trade (Sergeev) informed Mikoian of numerous difficulties that had arisen in dealing with German firms over the last few weeks: in eleven cases German firms had not made any production offers, in fifteen cases they had been late in making the offer, in eleven cases they offered an unacceptable schedule for delivery, in seven cases they had unilaterally repudiated the agreed-upon terms, in six cases their goods had failed to meet the contractual technical specifications, and in twenty-eight cases they had been late in final delivery.[49] The archival files of the Commissariat of Foreign Trade contain long lists of German firms that were late in meeting their contractual obligations or failed to deliver at all.[50] In a word, the punctilious fulfillment of contractual obligations by the Soviet Union contrasted sharply with the endless delays on the part of the Germans. This was a significant hint of problems in the relations between the two "partners."

During the seventeen months between the signing of the Economic Agreement and the outbreak of the Soviet-German War, the USSR shipped Germany the following raw materials and goods:

Item	Amount (in tons)
grain	1,463,000
timber materials	1,000,000
phospates	184,000
manganese ore	140,000
raw cotton	101,000
chromium ore	26,000
asbestos	15,000
copper	14,000
flax	11,000
nickel	3,000
platinum	2,736kg

In addition, transshipment across Soviet territory had provided Germany with strategic raw materials and food products from countries in the Pacific basin and the Near East.[51] In exchange the USSR had obtained primarily plant equipment to manufacture military goods, as well as various types of arms for the army and navy.[52]

The heyday of military and economic cooperation between the two countries was the period from the autumn of 1939 to the spring of 1940—that is, prior to Germany's victory on the western front. Germany supplied the USSR with machines and equipment; the latter assisted the German war effort with deliveries of strategic raw materials. Karl Schnurre, who played a major role in preparing and implementing the Soviet-German Economic Agreement, wrote an article for an issue of *Der deutsche Volkswirt* that appeared on May 10, 1940—the very day the Germans began their offensive in the West. He lauded the success of the agreement: "All in all, German trade with Eastern Europe, as a result of the Economic Agreement with the Soviet Union, has attained a volume that it never reached in previous years."[53]

In August 1940 (for the first time since 1932), the Soviet Union participated in the twenty-eighth "German Eastern Fair" in Königsberg. At the ceremonial opening, the gauleiter for East Prussia, Erich Koch, emphasized "the almost unlimited possibilities" inherent in the Soviet-German Economic Agreement. He also alluded to a proposal to build a waterway linking the Mazura Canal (itself under construction) and the upper Vistula with the Russian river system that reached all the way to the Black Sea.[54] In reply the Soviet ambassador Shkvartsev noted "the close economic and political mutual work," which was based on more than a temporary conjuncture of interests.[55] One may well assume that the text of Shkvartsev's remarks were approved, if not simply prescribed, by his superiors in Moscow.

Three days after the signing of the Soviet-German Economic Agreement, Ribbentrop made a deliberate effort to impress Sumner Welles—a special emissary from U.S. President Franklin Roosevelt. The German foreign minister stressed that Germany was now invincible, economically as well as militarily. In addition to its own *Lebensraum*, Germany had "access to a large portion of Europe, the whole of Russia, and, by way of Russia, to wide areas of the world."[56]

In a letter to Mussolini dated March 8, 1940, Hitler gave a rather extensive explanation of his policy toward the Soviet Union. He contended that the USSR was undergoing a profound transformation, which consisted in the replacement of bolshevism by Russian nationalism. It is necessary, he wrote, to take this into account and use it to one's own advantage. Moreover, and most important from Hitler's viewpoint, there was no reason to presume that anyone in the present Soviet regime would try to intervene in Germany's internal affairs. The two countries had lived in peace and friendship for many years, their economies supplementing one another. The Economic Agreement was a major accomplishment in the present situation.[57] As Ribbentrop explained to Mussolini and Italian Foreign Minister Ciano, the present situation allowed Germany to free divisions that would ordinarily have been tied down in the east and use them for the battle in the west.[58]

At this point, while Hitler was preoccupied with the single task of establishing German hegemony over the entire European continent, he could hardly have imagined a better partner for this goal than the Soviet Union. But, within three months, Germany's victory in the West gave grounds to reexamine military and economic priorities, including the policy toward the Soviet Union. Continental Europe was in German hands; the Reich now could envision new perspectives, including the creation of an economic space that would change signficantly the Soviet Union's role as the main supplier of raw materials and foodstuffs. The reason was simple: Germany already had access to raw materials in many other European countries. After July 31, 1940, when Hitler ordered his General Staff to plan a military operation against the USSR, the latter no longer loomed as its main European partner, but as a territory intended for German colonization—with all the political and economic consequences that this would entail.

Base "Nord"

Among the firm projects for close cooperation that Ribbentrop and Molotov had discussed, one was to grant German naval vessels a base in Murmansk for the concealment, repair, and refueling of both surface ships and submarines. Molotov proposed to use Terberk Bay (northeast of Murmansk), as the site that offered maximum shelter and concealment from outsiders. As a result, the Germans constructed a naval base at this site, known as the base "Nord" in all the official documents.[59] In a long memorandum to Ribbentrop on October 12, 1939 Fleet Admiral Erich Raeder declared that it was highly desirable to obtain from the USSR not only a base near Murmansk, but also bases in the Far East, in the vicinity of Vladivostok, in order to refuel, supply, and repair German submarines and cruisers operating in that theater. It would also be desirable, he added, if Russian ships were outfitted as supply vessels (with food and fuel), enabling the Germans to conduct more protracted operations at sea.

Raeder listed all kinds of possible assistance that the Soviet navy might render German warships, even to the point of having the Soviet navy escort cargo vessels laden with food and fuel for Germans in areas where German raiders would operate. He also proposed that German ships supply fuel and food to its raiders within Soviet territorial waters. In this case the Soviet side should ensure safe passage through its minefields and barriers, permit the repair of German ships in Soviet wharves in the north and Far East (the repairs would be performed by German specialists), ensure the security of these bays from enemy attack, and supply intelligence about military and commercial vessels of the enemy. Raeder emphasized the need to exploit the advantages that could be obtained from the Soviet government and thereby facilitate the tasks of the German navy, above all by providing refuge, fuel, and foodstuffs in Soviet ports.[60]

In a coded telegram to the German ambassador in Moscow, Weizsäcker reported that the Soviet government had given a positive response to the German requests for certain support of its naval forces as long as the war continued. A similar report was dispatched to the chief command of the German navy.[61] On October 22 the German naval attaché in Moscow (a Captain Baumbach) reported that the People's Commissariat of the Navy had issued an order to the naval command to transfer base "Nord" to the German navy.[62] The command of the German navy was also interested in servicing its submarines.[63] Commissar of the Navy Nikolai G. Kuznetsov completely satisfied these requests. In reply to a letter from Fleet Admiral Raeder expressing gratitude, Kuznetsov gave an assurance that he put deeds before words and that only afterward would he send a written response.[64]

The Soviet government had requests of its own. At the start of the Soviet-Finnish War, the USSR attempted to use submarines to establish a blockade of the Gulf of Bothnia, and it inquired whether Berlin would be willing to provide fuel and provisions from its ships heading toward northern Sweden. The Soviets, indeed, asked for a prompt decision and for deliveries within three to four days. The German ambassador in Moscow, Schulenburg, recommended that Berlin give a favorable answer to the request. In his opinion, such assistance would not really weaken the Finns and would not have a serious impact on the outcome of the Soviet-Finnish conflict. And it would open the door for Berlin to make new demands of its own—especially, for the provisioning of German raiders in the Far East.[65]

At approximately the same time, three Soviet naval officers journeyed incognito to hold talks with the German naval command.[66] Their official goal was to map the safe route through Soviet minefields west of the Aland Islands.[67] It was expected that they would board a German ship for the meeting. When Moscow suddenly withdrew its request for assistance for its submarine, the surprised Germans were left wondering just what goal the Soviets actually had in mind.[68]

German submarines and raiders, with support vessels, appeared in November at a Soviet inlet in the north, at the bay of Jokanski-

Reede, where they established Base Nord to supply, refuel, and conceal their ships. The base command was located on the German
ship *Phönizia*. As classified German documents make clear, this base
on Soviet territory was the mainstay of the German navy—its *only*
base—until the seizure of the Norwegian shoreline.[69] Almost a year
later, the German high command decided that it no longer needed
Base Nord and issued an order on September 16, 1940 for its liquidation.[70] Simultaneously, the Germans destroyed all the communication codes that they had been using at the base.[71]

In Moscow Baumbach visited Kuznetsov and gave him a personal
letter from Raeder, which expressed Germany's gratitude for use of
the base.[72] In fact, the parting was hardly so amicable: the NKVD
searched one of the two German ships that participated in the base
closing and, hoping to find classified documents, attempted to open
its safes. In the case of the other vessel, the *Phönizia*, the NKVD
demanded that the captain open the safes. When he categorically
refused and appealed to the German naval attaché in Moscow, the
NKVD responded by blocking the ship's departure for several hours.[73]
The former head of Base Nord, Auerbach, subsequently wrote several
memoranda, recording his impressions of the base, Murmansk and its
port, the railway line between Murmansk and Leningrad, and the
Soviet navy. He noted that the NKVD regarded the German base as a
nest of German spies, but that was of course hardly surprising, given
the mentality of people in the NKVD. It must be said, however, that
the suspicion was not entirely without foundation: the Germans naturally reported to their own intelligence service whatever they found
of interest inside Soviet territorial waters. This included a description
of the ships in port, the loading equipment at the port, and even special maps of the Murmansk shoreline that the German military command had hitherto not possessed.

Katyn

Although the Soviet Union (to its own surprise and that of the
world) was preoccupied in the winter of 1939 with the Finnish war,
it did have other concerns: the "Sovietization" of territories in eastern Poland that had been annexed to the Belorussian and Ukrainian republics. This process included purging operations by the
NKVD, which seized those who belonged to the catch-all category

of the "socially dangerous"—a great many of whom were ethnic Poles. The main objective of these operations was to make the restoration of of the Polish state impossible, and that meant the physical destruction of those who belonged to the former Polish army and the Polish intelligentsia. Once the Soviet Union had finally defeated the Finns in March 1940 and eliminated any threat of Anglo-French intervention, it was able to focus all its attention on this purge process in the newly conquered areas. On March 5, with the Finnish conflict virtually resolved, the Politburo adopted a resolution ordering the execution of interned members of the Polish army as well as "socially alien elements" from the civilian population. There was to be no prior investigation or trial; responsibility for implementing the order was given to the NKVD. Here is the text of the resolution:

> Transfer to the NKVD the papers concerning 14,700 former Polish officers, officials, landowners, policemen, and gendarmes held in camps for prisoners of war, as well as the papers concerning members of different subversion and espionage organizations, former land and factory owners, former Polish officers, former officials, and former clergymen arrested and held in jails in the western regions of Ukraine and Belorussia—a total of 11,000 people, whose cases must be considered in keeping with a special procedure and who must be subject to the supreme punishment—execution by a firing squad. The consideration of the cases must be carried out without summoning the arrested people to court and without presenting them with indictments.[74]

The resolution bore the signatures of Stalin, Voroshilov, Kalinin, Kaganovich, Mikoian, and Molotov. During the first few days of April the NKVD carried out this order in the Katyn forest near Smolensk and in three other camps that held Poles under arrest. The executions at Katyn forest first became known when the Germans discovered the graves in 1943. The executions at the other sites, however, did not obtain official confirmation until October 1992, when Boris Yeltsin, as president of the Russian Federation, for political reasons decided to make the matter public and to give the pertinent documents from the Politburo's archive to the Polish president, Lech Walesa.

The mass executions of Poles on Soviet territory came immediately after the Germans had destroyed Polish intelligentsia within their sphere of dominance. A tragic fate thus awaited the Poles, no matter whether they were in the Nazi or Soviet zone.

The Balkans

The interests of all the European great powers intersected in the Balkans, but here Germany tended to pursue a different tack: it aimed to preserve the stability of the existing states in the region. The reason was that it obtained raw materials and foodstuffs essential to its war effort, and it therefore put the highest priority on stability and status quo. In particular, Germany was prepared to protect its Romanian petroleum sources in Ploesti at any cost. In the wake of Poland's destruction, revanchist sentiments intensified in Hungary and Bulgaria; Romania reacted by becoming even more pro-German. The economic agreement between Romania and Germany, signed on March 23, 1939, conferred significant advantages to the latter. The influence of pro-French and pro-British circles weakened, although British ties to the economy remained quite strong. In April 1940 the British government established the United Kingdom Commercial Corporation, Ltd, which was specifically aimed at trade with the Balkan states.

The weak link in Germany's Balkan politics proved to be its own ally, Italy, which had its own aggressive designs on Yugoslavia, Greece, and parts of Turkey. What Rome lacked, however, was the means to realize these ambitions. On the opposing side, Britain endeavored to support those forces in Romania, Yugoslavia, Greece, and Turkey that were interested in preserving the territorial and political status quo. The immediate aim of British policy was to form a neutral bloc from those four states (and, if possible, Bulgaria). These states already constituted the so-called "Balkan Entente," which was under strong French influence. If this rather improbable scenario had succeeded, it was supposed to provide from 70 to 110 divisions. On April 24, 1939 the British foreign minister, Lord Halifax, explained to his Romanian counterpart that the main objective of his government's plan of "guarantees" was to foster unity and strength of the Balkan states.[75] This plan of course had little chance of succeeding, given the hostilities among the Balkan states, especially in the conflicting claims of Romania and Bulgaria to southern Dobruja.

December 1, 1939 marked the anniversary of the Trianon Peace Treaty of 1920, which transferred Transylvania and eastern Banat from Hungary to Romania. On that very day Hungary summarily demanded that the treaty be abrogated and the territories returned. Two months later a conference of the Balkan Entente (convening in Belgrade in early February, 1940) considered the question of creating a Balkan block (including Bulgaria). The conference proved a complete failure. Britain's plan for a neutral bloc entirely disappeared later that month when a pro-German government came to power in Sofia. But Bulgaria had another claimant to its attentions—the Soviet Union, which had its own traditional and strategic interests in the Balkans. In the final analysis, in 1940 the fate of the Balkans depended upon two main factors—the outcome of fighting in the West and the relations between Germany and the USSR.

The situation was considerably more complex in Turkey, where great political skill on the part of the Turkish leadership was required to resist the temptation to become embroiled in war in order to "round out" its borders at the expense of neighboring states. Turkey's geopolitical position, together with the conflicting interests of the great powers and neutral states, opened the door to considerable maneuvering on the part of Ankara. The Turkish government exploited these to the hilt when it signed a mutual-assistance pact with Britain and France on October 19, 1939. By the following January the agreement had brought the Turks £42 million in credits and loans. That same January Turkey agreed with Bulgaria to make a mutual pullback of their troops from border areas. In April London believed that Turkey would soon enter the war on the Allied side.[76]

The Allies also counted on Turkish assistance in carrying out a decision by the high command to bomb Soviet oilfields in Baku and the shipping and storage facilities at Batumi, the aim being to deprive Germany and the USSR of a vital oil source. The operation, it should be noted, was planned in the winter of 1939–1940, at the height of international indignation over the Soviet attack on Finland. In late January 1940 the American ambassador in Paris, William Bullitt, informed Washington of French proposals to shift the war to the south, but added that the scheme had failed to elicit support in either London or Ankara.[77] By March, however, Britain had changed its views. The commander of French armed forces in the Near East, General M. Weygand, later gave the following testimony before the French parliamentary commission investigating France's capitulation in 1940:

On March 1, 1940 British air force authorities informed me of the
desire of the British government that, on the territory under my command, reconnaissance be conducted with the goal of determining the
feasibility of organizing an attack on the Baku oil region. On March
13 I received a communication from General [Maurice] Gamelin
[head of the French General Staff] about a project, which had been
long since prepared, on British-French policy in the Balkans. This
project took into account the operation against Baku.[78]

As Weygand's aide for military air power told the French minister of
aviation: "I do not have enough aviation. Give it to me, for the war
will be decided in the Caucasus, not on the western front. We shall
not fight in the West; we shall fight in the Caucasus."[79]

Prior to the Soviet-Finnish War, Germany assumed that Soviet
territorial ambitions would be limited to the return of Bessarabia.
Berlin thus failed to appreciate not only Stalin's personal appetite,
but also Russia's ancient dreams of taking the Straits, as well as its
Pan-Slavist schemes regarding Bulgaria. Moreover, Ribbentrop certainly erred in thinking that Stalin had renounced the idea of world
revolution.[80] The tactics, not the telos, had changed. When Stalin
met with Dimitrov on January 21, 1940, at the very height of the
Soviet-Finnish War, he expressed the following opinion: "World
revolution as a single act is nonsense. It occurs at different times in
different countries. The actions of the Red Army are also the cause
of world revolution."[81] In Stalin's mind, at least, the notion of world
revolution was replaced by "world socialist system," which to a significant degree would be created through the efforts of the Soviet
armed forces.

From the perspective of the German Wehrmacht, it was highly
desirable to divert Moscow's attention from the Balkans to the Near
East and India and thereby embroil Russia in the war against Great
Britain.[82] The Germans deemed it useful, to be sure, to invoke the
Soviet specter to frighten the Balkan countries and thereby impede
the formation of a Balkan bloc. Berlin was also fully aware that Italy
feared Soviet competition in the Balkans.[83] In a letter to Mussolini
on March 8, 1940, Hitler dropped a thinly veiled hint of the Italian
fears, claiming not to believe that the Soviets posed a threat to the
Balkans. Hitler added that one should be more fearful of those with
revanchist ambitions—a clear reference to Italy's client, Hungary.
At the same time, the attempt by Britain and France to involve
Turkey on its side posed a threat to Russia, Italy, and even Romania,

if it was a matter of depriving authoritarian regimes of sources of vital raw materials.[84] In response Mussolini wrote that he counted on Germany to use its good offices to ensure that Moscow "leaves the Balkans alone," indeed that it even issue a public announcement to that effect. He added that such an action would lead to an improvement in bilateral relations between Rome and Moscow.[85]

But Stalin had his own ideas. The war with Finland had barely ended; Stalin had not yet had time to take his next step. The first priority was to conclude the Soviet-Finnish War: on March 6 the Soviet government invited Finland to send a delegation to Moscow for peace talks.

Cultural Links

Cultural ties between Germany and Russia, which had been so intense in the 1920s, virtually disappeared after the Nazis came to power, but resumed in 1939, after the successful joint operation to partition Poland. In late January 1940, Peter Kleist (the counselor in the German Foreign Ministry responsible for cultural relations with the USSR) journeyed to Moscow. He held preliminary talks at the All-Union Society for Cultural Relations with Foreign Countries, known under its Soviet acronym as VOKS (*Vsesoiuznoe obshchestvo po kul'turnoi sviazi s zagranitsei*), a front organization for ties with foreign countries, which had close links to the commissariats of foreign affairs and interior. Its chairman was the art critic Vladimir Kemenov.[86]

The Institute of Eastern Europe in Berlin established a section called Die Dienststelle Osteuropa, which established a cultural liaison with the USSR. Subsequently, in October 1940, "competent" German institutions and ministries (according to the German embassy in Moscow) established a Zentralstelle Osteuropa. The Germans reported that the decision to establish their own organization was the result of competition with that body. The goal of the German partner was "the unification of all diverse questions, proposals and wishes that arise in the sphere of cultural relations between Germany and the USR and to ensure their prompt and full resolution."[87]

The date is noteworthy: October 21, 1940—just two weeks before Molotov came to Berlin for talks. Kleist, in order to lay the groundwork for close cultural collaboration, had arrived with pro-

posals for immediate discussion and implementation. His plan carefully circumvented the dangerous reefs of ideology and sounded out
areas of cultural ties that were mutually acceptable. He proposed to
organize, as early as February 1941, a Soviet exhibition of folk culture in Berlin. A German economic delegation headed by Schnurre
would first go to Moscow to go over the plans. Kleist also proposed
an exchange of films.

The center of attention in 1940 was to be a German exhibition
about road and vehicular construction. The Germans also offered
their help in staging Richard Wagner's *Die Walküre* at the Bolshoi
Theater. As an attaché at the German embassy in Moscow noted,
the staging of an opera by a composer Hitler adored but who until a
short time before had been routinely denounced as a fascist in the
Soviet press—aroused "considerable attention among those of us
working in the embassy."[88] To the premiere were invited the ambassador and top-ranking staff of the embassy. One observer called the
performance, which included a film directed by Sergei Eisenstein,
"sensational and completely original." Although the number of
performances was limited, the German side duly noted and appreci-
ated the significance of the staging.[89]

For their part, the Germans were prepared to accept Soviet consultations for the performance of the opera *Ivan Susanin* in Berlin,
and even proposed to offer the piece in its Moscow version. The
thinking here was strictly political: the opera concerned the struggle
of the Russian people with the Poles. But then something inexplica-
ble occurred: despite promises, the musical scores were not sent to
Berlin—ostensibly for lack of suitable paper. The German embassy
carefully recorded a steady increase in the display of nationalist-
patriotic sentiments in art—for example, the staging of *Bogdan
Khmel'nitskii* (as a blatantly anti-Polish opera) and Tikhon Khren-
nikov's patriotic *Into the Storm*. Even the publication of the memoirs
of General Ignat'ev, an emigré who had returned to the Soviet
Union and joined the Red Army, appeared to be evidence of a shift
away from Bolshevik ideology.

All these efforts involved cooperation in the cultural sphere,
based on a recognition of national patriotism—German and Russian respectively. In Germany there were ceaseless attempts to deci-
pher the inscrutable "Russian soul," as in the widespread staging of
Anton Chekhov's *Three Sisters*.

With respect to science and scholarship, Kleist was especially interested in cooperation in meteorology. In 1940 the Soviet side provide the Germans with weather reports on the northern latitudes, which the German aviation then used in planning the air attacks on Great Britain.[90]

Many letters and proposals began to arrive from Germany shortly after the second Soviet-German treaty was signed. A consultant for the first western section of VOKS, Kamenkovich, sent the following confidential report to the deputy chairman of VOKS, G. M. Kheifets:

> After the signing of the treaty on friendship between the Soviet Union and Germany, a great change occurred in work at VOKS concerning Germany. If prior to the treaty not a single inquiry from private individuals or private firms came from Germany, in the period following the treaty German scholars who had previously corresponded with Soviet scholars, began to renew this, appending to the letter [copies of] Hitler's speech in the Reichstag. This was the first stage.
>
> Then came a rash of inquiries of the most diverse types: offers for the exchange of photographs, for the sale of machines, for the publication of German books in the USSR; invitations to Soviet ballerinas; requests for the sending of various materials, e.g., information on synthetic rubber, etc. These correspondents, who are not known to VOKS, refer in their letters to the signing of the agreement and indicate that the German Ministry of Propaganda and Enlightenment welcomes the establishment of contacts. One gets the impression that all the requests sent to the USSR are in fact organized on someone's order.[91]

This letter from the VOKS adviser is quite typical for the psychology of a Soviet official at the time: one had to be vigilant with respect to everything emanating from abroad and to measure it in terms of Soviet practice, where foreign contact was inconceivable except when authorized and supervised by "competent organs."

Interestingly, Germans now coming to the Soviet Union expected to find an order analogous to what existed in Nazi Germany. A female correspondent (a "Frau Dill") from the newspaper *Berliner Tageblatt* arrived on the first flight of the new Berlin-Moscow air connection, but was amazed to find a Jewish lawyer in a court that she visited. She then had the following conversation with the VOKS consultant, Kamenkovich, who gave this report of the encounter:

"Is the defense lawyer a Jew?"

"Yes, it seems so," I replied.

"No, what do you think, is he really a Jew?"

I then replied: "Why don't you ask this in his presence—I could then tell you for certain, since I would ask him about it. In our country one is not embarrassed to be a Jew and he would tell you. I think he's Jewish, indeed, he has a Jewish surname."

"What—have you really not driven the Jews from all leading positions, from the government?"

"No."

"But Litvinov was a Jew after all, and he was removed from his post as commissar of foreign affairs. Moreover, I was told at the embassy that the Russian people, in spirit, are anti-Semitic.

I explained to her that the Russian people were never anti-semitic, that they only tried to rear it this way, to inflame anti-Semitism, and that now anti-Semitism—like every other kind of nationalist discord among nationalities—is prosecuted by Soviet law, and that the information given to her at the embassy completely fails to accord with reality. After that citizenness Dill declared:

"This means that I cannot abuse someone on the street by using the curseword of 'Jew'?"

"No, it is possible," I said, "but you risk having to answer for this before a court."

"But for you, as a Russian," said citizenness Dill, "it must be entirely incomprehensible what is happening in Germany with respect to the Jews."[92]

In general, this journalist proved a "hard nut" for VOKS to crack: after seeing a film about Peter the Great, she compared him to Mussolini—which shocked and outraged the VOKS personnel handling her visit.[93]

Moscow did not make haste in responding to Kleist's proposals. In all likelihood, people at the top were too preoccupied with the Finnish war to deal with the question right then. However, on March 14, 1940 (just two days after signing the peace treaty with Finland), the commissariat of foreign affairs held a meeting to discuss the matter with the heads of VOKS.[94] The group approved Kleist's proposals, with some modifications. Specifically, the list of Soviet films for screening in Germany was expanded to include movies based on the works of Gor'kii and Chekhov. The list also includes *Chapaev*, a famous film about a Red Army hero in the Civil War, presumably to impress upon the Germans that Russian military prowess was to be found not only in the Petrine era, but also under the soviets.[95] However, the film *Peter the Great* was shown to the German economic delegation in Moscow and recommended for screening in Germany. The Germans attentively noted the intensification of national, patriotic ideas in the USSR—at the apparent expense of ideas about world revolution. The appearance of films about the military like *Aleksandr Nevskii*, *Kutuzov* and *Suvorov* all seemed to confirm the possibility of a Soviet-German rapprochement on the basis of recognizing national values and renouncing internationalist revolutionary ideas. The program for cultural exchange also included radio concerts of the works by Russian and German composers; during these years the music of Tchaikovsky was especially popular in Germany.

At the Soviet embassy in Berlin, responsibility for cultural cooperation devolved on Bogdan Kobulov, a plenipotentiary of the NKVD.[96] The Germans had no illusion about Kobulov. Although he attempted to delay a decision on the opening of a German road exhibition in Moscow, he finally approved the exchange of exhibitions. The Germans were firm in pressing their demands; one letter bluntly said that approval of the German exhibition in Moscow was a precondition for the Soviet economic exhibition in Berlin.[97] In late August 1940, a new meeting was convened at the foreign affairs' commissariat in Moscow, but this time at a higher level: it included the two deputy commissars (V. G. Dekanozov[98] and S. A. Lozovskii[99]), the general secretary of the commissariat (A. A. Sobolev[100]), a representative of VOKS (V.S. Kemenov), and several others. For the Soviet exhibition in Berlin, the group approved as its theme "the Mechanization of Agriculture in the USSR," rather than its alternative, "Soviet Architecture and Urban Construction." The choice was scarcely accidental, presumably intended to remind visitors that Germany was obtaining agricultural products from the USSR and to convince them that the food deliveries were reliable.[101] In a draft letter to Molotov justifying the proposal for an agricultural exhibition (which they originally intended to call "Sovkhoz Giant"), Kemenov wrote that this exhibition will display the achievements in Soviet agriculture machinery and correct the one-sided impression that the Soviet Union was a country rich in natural resources but backward in machine-building.[102]

At the September fair in Leipzig, the Soviet pavilion attracted much attention, "especially in workers' circles," as the German security service pointed out. In their responses visitors approvingly noted that, after several years of "false information" about "world enemy number 1," they had finally received the truth. The notebook of the security officers included examples like the following:

"Why not fifteen years earlier?"

"Yes, if it would only stay this way forever."

"My second fatherland" (words of a Yugoslav visitor)

"Hopefully, it is all true."

"This exhibition strengthens the unshakable trust in our Führer, Adolf Hitler."

"This is as it should be: Germany and Russia, arm in arm; nothing can happen to us!"

"The cooperation of both countries can only be a blessing for mankind."[103]

The display devoted to the natural resources of Russia produced a particularly strong impression. The observer from the security service noted, with approval, that the assessment of Russian resources provides good propaganda in favor of the German-Soviet economic agreement.[104] Soviet assessments on popular response conformed entirely to those of the German security apparatus.

The entire work of VOKS naturally bore a clear political tone, and any cultural undertaking had to have a political purpose and justification. The archive of VOKS confirms this quite clearly, as in the following cases.

One example is a document dated December 1940 and addressed to Aleksandrov, the chief of the section in the commissariat responsible for central European affairs. A deputy chairman of VOKS, A. Detistov, proposed to reject an offer from a German firm to arrange a tour for Soviet musicians in Germany, and give the following reason for the negative response: "Insofar as the fact of sending musicians to Germany would have a political character [sic], VOKS believes that a proposal to organize a tour on the basis of private initiative (and dictated by overtly commercial considerations) does not merit attention."[105]

In 1940 the Central State Library of Foreign Literature organized an exhibition of old German books—from the thirteenth to the seventeenth centuries. The display included some 300 to 400 books, as well as illustrations, photographs, and reproductions. The

exhibition offered a set of lectures in German as well as literary
soirées devoted to Schiller and Goethe. Plans were also being made
for exhibitions devoted to the works of E. T. A. Hoffmann, A.
Chamisso, G. E. Lessing, Heinrich Heine, F. Spielgagen, S. Brandt,
G. Freytag, and others.[106]

Among the Germans who visited the Soviet Union in 1939–
1941, one of the most interesting was Colin Ross, described in an
"objective report" from VOKS as a professional journalist.[107] Ross
was in fact a fairly well-known German writer-traveler. In recommending that VOKS give him proper attention, he was described as
"one of the most productive writers and political commentators in
Germany."[108] His tour of the Soviet Union in October 1938, with
his wife and teenaged son, was the last part of a worldwide trip. His
itinerary included among other places Moscow and Kiev. The
Moscow schedule was fairly routine: Tret'iakov Gallery, crèche,
schools, the textile factory "Trekhgornaia," and one unusual point:
a conversation with Soviet writers. Naturally, such a traveler, especially one who served as a correspondent for several German newspapers (including the widely-read *Deutsche Allgemeine Zeitung*)
could not fail to arouse attention in the USSR.[109] The following
confidential document reveals clearly how Moscow responded to
Ross's arrival:

> Confidential Report No. 1
> Concerning the arrival of the German writer, K. Ross (with wife
> and son) in Kiev. . . .
> When the factory director asked Ross to share his impressions of
> the USSR, Ross replied that, in his judgment, the USSR and Ger-
> many, although by different paths, are moving toward the same goal
> and that there is much more in common between Germany and the
> USSR, than between the USSR and USA. He sees much in com-
> mon in the upbringing of children in Germany and the Soviet
> Union. On the question of his political views, Ross declared that he
> is non-party, but also that the USSR has "non-party Bolsheviks," just
> as in Germany there are "non-party National Socialists," among
> whom he includes himself.[110]

In Kiev, Ross attended a formal meeting to commemorate the six-
teenth anniversary of Lenin's death, carefully jotted down the translation of the speeches, and asked that Nikita S. Khrushchev (the
Ukrainian party boss) be pointed out to him. Ross paid particular
attention to the section of the report on the signing of a pact

between the USSR and Germany.[111] Ross himself used every opportunity to underline the common interests between Germany and
the USSR, which were aimed against Britain. In Kiev, for example,
at a meeting of the Ukrainian Society for Cultural Ties with Foreign
Countries (where the writer Arkadii Liubchenko participated), he
raised a toast to the eternal friendship between the USSR and Germany, declaring: "The friendship between Germany and Russia
(which has formed over the centuries) sickens Britain, which has
made every effort to undermine this amity, by instigating trouble
between these countries, one after the other." He also ascribed to
British intrigues the dissemination of rumors about German plans to
seize Ukraine. Ross made ample use of the lexicon of Soviet and
Nazi propagandists, declaring, for example, that "the sagacity of
Stalin's and Hitler's policy has undercut the British policy" of spoiling their mutual good relations. He noticed, moreover, that film
clips of the May Day parades in Moscow reminded him of parades in
Germany: "Such enthusiasm and inspiration is only to be seen in
these countries—the USSR and Germany." He declared that "I do
not have words to express the feeling that overcame me when I
learned about the pact between the USSR and Germany."[112]

Ross was not alone in his impressions regarding the similarity of
the Soviet and Nazi regimes. The architect Kopp, who visited
Moscow in May 1940, expressed the hope that both of these great
peoples, Russian and German, will find the path to complete
mutual understanding, since "in essence they have one and the
same form of governance and are moving toward socialism by different paths. Somewhere in space there is a point where both peoples will meet at the final goal."[113] Impatiently and (no doubt) anxiously, Moscow awaited the publication of impressions that the
German journalists had obtained through the mediation of VOKS.
Their articles were read with considerable suspicion that they
might contain some dirty trick. In November 1940, VOKS, at the
recommendation of the press section of the NKVD (the journalist
Krauss), the representative of the Berlin economic newspaper,
Südosteko was given VIP treatment, including a visit to Red Square
during the military parade on November 7. However, the article he
published on November 29 bitterly disappointed his hospitable
hosts in Moscow. In a letter addressed to Aleksandrov and Pal'-
gunov,[114] Kheifets called the article "tendentious" and in places
even "hostile," and also accused the author of being two-faced. In

fact, however, Krauss's text was written in a quite well-meaning tone. Kheifets was probably upset by the comparison of new laws that increased the workday, made tardiness and absenteeism a criminal offense, and prohibited job changes. Nor could Moscow have liked his reference to the huge difference in wages among various categories of workers.[115]

The Germans took a particular interest in Soviet ballet. Lauks, Ribbentrop's personal photographer, was extremely irritated when the ballerina Marina Semenova refused to pose for him at her home—purportedly after learning that Lauks also planned to photograph another dancer, Olga Lepeshinskaia. The real reason for her refusal, however, probably lay elsewhere: Lauks had asked the ballet master of the Bolshoi Theater, Rostislav V. Zakharov, not to summon Semenova's partner to the rehearsal—the Jewish dancer, Asaf Messerer. Zakharov fulfilled the humiliating request rather than show Lauks the door.[116] Lauks proved himself an agile courtier in dealing with his Soviet hosts, as a curious memorandum in VOKS attests. No doubt attempting to obtain permission to photograph the Soviet-Finnish front, he told the head of the protocol section of VOKS that the entire international press had given a one-sided report on the Finnish front. He said that he himself had seen splendidly equipped Red-Army soldiers in Leningrad heading for the front, adding that all this "completely contradicts the slander spread by the bourgeois press of the entire world."[117]

In January, 1941 a cycle of lectures on the "peoples of the USSR" was organized at Königsberg University by the Institute for Research on the East. The general consulate in Königsberg immediately signaled Moscow about the need to provide the institute with Soviet materials, which would cause the authors of the lectures to use them in their talks.[118] In this case VOKS also merged as an intermediary for collecting information about individual German institutions that had some interest in the study of the USSR. In a letter to the Soviet general consulate in Königsberg on April 4, 1941, VOKS asked for a transcription of the lectures and for information on the institute's activities, publications, and the like.[119]

According to Schmidt, in the summer of 1940 he presented a memorandum on the need for the systematic development of Soviet-German cultural relations in all spheres, given the long-term cooperation between the two countries. His memorandum was sent on to Berlin, which, however responded with skepticism.[120]

In the winter of 1940–1941, amidst signs of a cooling in Soviet-German relations, the Historical Museum in Moscow held an exhibition called "The Fatherland War of 1812–1813." It reminded visitors of Russia's endless expanse and harsh winter, partisan warfare, and the heroic resistance of the Russian people that had smashed Napoleon's army. The German embassy hastened to inform Berlin of the exhibition.

Complications

Ribbentrop, having made two trips himself to Moscow, very much wanted—for reasons of prestige—to arrange a return visit by Molotov or even, at the invitation of Hitler, of Stalin himself. Evidently, Hitler initiated inquiries on that very subject. Although Molotov in principle had agreed to such a visit, in fact he did everything in his power to delay a trip to Berlin. That attitude was clearly evident during the Soviet-Finnish War, when TASS issued a formal disavowal of rumors that Molotov was to come to Berlin. When Ribbentrop suggested that Molotov be reminded of his promise,[121] Schulenburg persuaded him to abandon the idea: Molotov, he warned, would simply avoid any trip in the immediate future, since the USSR was determined to demonstrate its ostensible commitment to a policy of strict neutrality.[122] Ribbentrop wrote "for the F[ührer]" on the report, suggesting indeed that Hitler may have instigated—or at least endorsed—the idea.

As the experience of the Soviet-Finnish War demonstrated, the USSR had to exercise extreme caution in order to avoid becoming embroiled in war with the Western democracies. The Kremlin became especially sensitive to this danger in December 1939, when it was expelled from the League of Nations for aggression against the Finns. This circumstance impelled the Soviet Union to hasten the signing of a peace treaty with Finland on terms that were more or less acceptable to Helsinki. In addition, the USSR endeavored to demonstrate to the West that it strictly adhered to a policy of neutrality and did not lean toward Germany. Stalin formed his opinion on this question at the peak of the German-Polish War, just ten days before the Red Army attacked the Poles from the rear: "We can maneuver, incite one side against the other, so that they fight all the harder. The nonaggression pact, to some degree, helps Germany. The next step is to spur on the other side."[123]

In this case, however, Stalin made a serious political miscalculation. He did not succeed in "inciting" Britain against Germany; events took a different turn. Stalin succeeded only in achieving a steady increase in Germany's vexation with the needless machinations. Schulenburg later observed that the USSR repeatedly created difficulties in its relations with Germany; these included such matters as the issue of visas, delays in releasing the ethnic Germans imprisoned in Poland, a sudden stop in the deportation of German citizens held in Soviet prisons, and limits (without prior warning) on the use of Base Nord.[124]

The same considerations evidently prompted Moscow, in these same months, to stop supplying Germany with certain categories of raw materials and to refrain from purchasing strategic materials in third countries and transshipping these goods across Soviet soil. To justify this decision, Mikoian claimed that Japan was informing the British of each ship heading toward Vladivostok or Dalien (Dairen), with the provocative claim that the Soviet Union was purchasing these goods for Germany.[125] Tevosian and Savchenko, who spent three weeks in Germany, failed to obtain a satisfactory response to Soviet complaints about delays in the shipment of military materials to the USSR. Resolution of these matters required the direct intervention of Göring, who knew that the German economy critically needed Soviet deliveries foreseen in the agreement of February 11.[126] Göring, in his role as plenipotentiary for the Four-Year Plan, became the highest official for resolving conflicts; in extreme cases, Hitler himself settled any disputes. The key problem in the delivery of arms to the USSR was the priority accorded to supplying arms for the Wehrmacht. Göring's decision meant that Germany would resume supplying the USSR with coal and military materials. For his part, Mikoian agreed to resume the delivery of grain and oil by the end of April, but on condition that Germany by then deliver coal to the USSR.[127]

The question of the deliveries was not an isolated event, but rather formed the backdrop for a rapid change in the military and political situation in Europe. On March 20, 1940, the French government of Eduard Daladier resigned. Five days later the new administration under Paul Reynaud sent the British government a memorandum proposing to establish control over the Norwegian territorial waters, to seize the key defensive points on the Norwegian coast, to take measures to cut off German access to the Caucasus oil fields (even at the price of a "break with the USSR"), and to study the feasibility of sending submarines into the Black Sea.[128] The risk that war would be extended to the Caucasus and Black Sea area impelled the Soviet Union to continue its policy of maneuvering and equivocation. However, by the time of Mikoian's reply on April 6, rumors had already spread that German troops were being amassed at the Baltic ports and that they were being loaded onto military transports. German military operations in Scandinavia put an end to Allied plans to involve the Soviet Union in a war in the south. In all probability, this factor provided the primary motive for Stalin's decision to continue his pro-German policy. On April 8 the Allies partly mined the Norwegian territorial waters, but it was already too late: in a prelude to the impending catastrophe on the western front, German forces landed in Norway and Denmark the following day.

Moscow was extremely frightened: Germany was acting far too decisively. The Kremlin sought to mollify the Germans by making the deliveries, but in exchange wanted a promise that Berlin would observe the neutrality of Sweden.[129] Should the Germans be successful in enticing Sweden to join their cause, the Soviet position in the northwest would be catastrophic. However, the Germans themselves preferred a neutral Sweden, at least for the time being.[130]

The very day the Germans landed in Norway, Molotov informed Schulenburg that the suspension of the delivery of oil and grain to Germany was not due to a lack of zeal on the part of Soviet export agencies. Göring's reassurances proved sufficient for an immediate resumption of deliveries.[131] At the same time, Molotov offered the Soviet government's best wishes for Germany's "complete success in its defensive measures" in Denmark and Norway, and added that the British had gone too far in their total disregard for the plights of neutral states.[132] On April 12 Tevosian told Göring that Stalin had asked him to convey his gratitude for the promise to resume the delivery of German war materials and weapons. "Germany and the Soviet Union," wrote Stalin, "depend on each other." Stalin therefore expressed the hope for "really long-term" relations.[133] But these reassurances did not entirely satisfy Berlin. Countless rumors continued to circulate that Britain and the USSR were holding economic talks, and Berlin linked these purported negotiations directly to the USSR's failure to fulfill its promise to purchase strategic raw materials in third countries and to reship them to Germany.[134]

In fact, in the period between October 1939 and May 1940, Britain and the Soviet Union did open, suspend, and renew trade talks within the conditions of the war. These conversations were first linked to the military situation and later to Soviet ties with Nazi Germany. In the fall of 1939, immediately after the partition of Poland, Britain endeavored to extract an agreement from the USSR to respect the economic blockade that it had declared. Although Soviet sources claim that nothing came of all this,[135] in fact Molotov reassured the British that Soviet purchases in Britain were aimed exclusively at satisfying Soviet needs.[136] The negotiations for a wartime commercial agreement were suspended because of the Soviet-Finnish war; a further factor was the British decision not to return two Soviet ships, but to intern them in France. But the two sides reached partial agreements on the delivery of timber that the British had purchased in Arkhangel'sk. A week after the end of the Soviet-Finnish War the trade talks were reopened.[137]

On April 18, 1940, Germany occupied Norway. Afterward, Britain demanded guarantees that goods it exported to the USSR would be used only for internal consumption and not be transhipped to Germany. For its part Germany continued to make energetic demands that the USSR fulfill its obligation to purchase strategic raw materials on its behalf. In order to ensure Soviet compliance with its obligations, but chiefly to obtain a new agreement for the delivery of Soviet oil, the Germans offered to raise the price on Soviet oil, lower the price on German coal, and throw a cruiser into the deal.[138] The fact that the Soviet Union was providing Germany with strategic raw materials and foodstuffs finally brought the Anglo-Soviet negotiations to a standstill in the second half of May 1940, when war on the western front was full-blown.[139] By then Soviet and German emissaries had already reached a written agreement on oil and the cruiser had been transferred to Soviet representatives.[140] The situation, however, changed radically in June and July after the German victory in the west.

War in the West: Its Impact on Soviet-German Relations

On May 10 the German army stormed into Belgium, Holland, and Luxembourg. The same day the cabinet of Neville Chamberlain resigned, to be replaced within a few days by a coalition government led by Winston Churchill. Schulenburg informed Molotov of the

German attack in the West on May 10, following instructions issued by Ribbentrop three days earlier.[141] Molotov had probably already received the same information from Soviet sources. As was customary in such cases, Molotov took the line that Germany had been "forced" to act and averred his confidence in Germany's success.[142] On May 14 German tanks crossed the Meuse River and sped on toward Sedan. The defense lines in Belgium had been breached, driving the Allies back; on May 16 the Germans had crossed over into French soil. By evening French premier Paul Reynaud sent the following message to Churchill: "Yesterday evening we lost the battle. The road to Paris is open. Send us all the aviation and all the troops that you can."[143]

As the German war machine shifted into high gear, its demands that the Soviet Union deliver raw materials and foods became increasingly insistent. Two days after the start of the attack, Berlin directed Schulenburg to warn Molotov that, because of nonfulfillment, the German side was on the verge of cancelling the February agreement.[144] The Germans considered sending a special mission to hand deliver a letter from Ribbentrop to Stalin about the unsatisfactory state of their bilateral economic relations and the failure to deliver oil and metals to Germany. This nondelivery had come at a critical juncture because of the military operations against the west.[145] However, the mission was called off because a new British ambassador (Stafford Cripps) had arrived in Moscow to lead Soviet-British trade talks; the Germans wanted to avoid giving the impression that they were competing with the British in seeking Moscow's favor.[146] Simultaneously, Schulenburg emphatically denied any basis for doubting the Soviet Union's loyalty to Germany. The ambassador dismissed rumors of the Soviet government's alarm at Germany's success as enemy propaganda designed to cause friction between the two partners.[147] As far as the reaction of the Moscow elite was concerned, Schulenburg was certainly wrong. The Soviet leadership *was* stunned by the devastating defeats inflicted on the French army and the German breakthrough at the Maginot Line, completely shattering expectations of a protracted, stationary war in the west.

By late May Hitler himself expected that Britain would be forced to sue for peace. On May 17 he went to army group A (under the command of Gerd von Rundstedt) and delivered a long speech. He declared that, after the conquest of northern France, Britain would be ready to come to an agreement that would grant it supremacy at sea, while Germany ruled throughout Europe. According to one of the officers present (the head of the operational section, General Gün-ther von Blumentritt), Hitler declared that "in six weeks there will be peace" and that he would conclude a "gentleman's agreement" with Britain.[148] On June 2 he told the same group that once Britain was ready for peace, he could settle scores with the Bolsheviks.[149]

Besides temporary complications over deliveries, what had Stalin done to push Hitler toward the fateful decision to launch a war on the USSR? Above all, one must note Stalin's decision—in the wake of France's defeat—to sovietize the Baltic states. The German victory in the West had inspired the Baltic states to believe that Soviet pressure would now abate. Just the opposite occurred. The entire operation was conducted with lightning speed. Within the space of one week (June 14–21, 1940), the Soviet Union accused Lithuania, Latvia, and Estonia of violating the treaties of mutual assistance. This was followed by the "popular overthrow of fascist dictatorships" and the establishment of so-called "popular governments." The operation was completed on the eve of the signing of the armistice at Compiegne between Germany and France (June 22, 1940). The Soviet Union seemed to be attempting to equalize its own military and political situation with that of Germany, evidently to avoid appearing to fall behind.

The Soviet annexation of the Baltics occurred during the great drama on the western front and seemed to have gone unnoticed in Berlin. The latter, initially, did see the Soviet step as merely the fulfillment of old agreements. But a little later, when the Soviets raised the issue of repatriating Baltic Germans, the mood in Berlin underwent a fundamental change. Distrust toward Soviet intentions mingled with fear of a military conflict. At this time rumors spread through Germany about the construction of "eastern ramparts"—a defense line in eastern Prussia to thwart an attack from the USSR.[150] In July, according to a message from the security service (*Sicherheitsdienst*), "mistrust of Russia has seized wider and wider circles." There were also remors of disputes, especially over complications in their economic relations because Russia had failed to fulfill its obligations. People also suspected that Russia intended to exploit the shortage of oil in Germany for its own purposes.[151] If one takes into account that these rumors coincided with Hitler's decision to launch a war against the Soviet Union, they may well have been planted by the regime to prepare the population psychologically for the coming conflict.

Germany had given its assent to Soviet annexation of the Baltics back on August 23, 1939. It was therefore natural for state-secretary Weizsäcker, in a circular to German diplomatic missions on June 17, 1940, to declare that the Baltic events were the concern only of the Soviet Union and three Baltic states, and that Germany had no reason for concern "in view of the constantly friendly relations" with the USSR.[152] The following day Molotov formally apprised ambassador Schulenburg of the Soviet actions in the Baltics, sweetening the bitter pill with the explanation that it was necessary, once and for all, to put an end to the British and French intrigues. The latter had attempted, he intimated, to sow discord between Germany and the Soviet Union in the Baltics. At the same time Molotov expressed the "warmest congratulations of the Soviet government on the splendid successes of the German Wehrmacht."[153] This ritual attempted to reaffirm the harmonious partnership: the Wehrmacht defeated the enemy in the West, the Soviet Union struck the same foe in the east.

Nevertheless, both Hitler and Stalin must have understood perfectly that relations between their two countries were anything but idyllic. Soviet troops in Lithuania had advanced to the German border.[154] TASS published a categorical official denial of rumors that 100 to 150 Soviet divisions had been stationed in the Baltics—a figure that was plainly fantastic. It emphasized that Soviet-German relations were based "not on transitory motives of a short-term character, but on the fundamental state interests of Germany and the USSR." Molotov, in Schulenburg's words, was obviously very satisfied with this communiqué.[155] The ambassador himself suggested that the TASS message had been drafted by Stalin himself and would be followed immediately by a scrupulous fulfillment of the agreement concerning Bessarabia.[156]

That proved to be the case. On June 23 Molotov informed Schulenburg that his government intended to resolve the Bessarabian problem forthwith and, if need be, through the use of military force. To the amazement and distress of the ambassador, Molotov informed him of plans to annex Bukovina; he alleged that its population was Ukrainian.[157] Molotov bluntly told him that the Soviet government was counting on an official statement by Germany before midnight on June 25. The Germans, for their part, were unpleasantly

surprised by the Soviet claims to Bukovina. This was the second surprise, after the stationing of troops in Lithuania, that their Soviet
partners had sprung on them. In the end Stalin agreed to limit
Soviet claims to "only" northern Bukovina.[158] Given the fact that
Bukovina had once belonged to the Austro-Hungarian monarchy,
the seizure of any part of that territory was nothing other than an act
of raw annexation.

Germany made perfectly clear that it did not wish for Romania—
where it had important economic interests, especially in oil and
foodstuffs—to be turned into a battlefield.[159] Ultimately a proposal
by Molotov prevailed; the USSR and Germany would decide the
question jointly and through peaceful means. The USSR issued an
ultimatum, while Germany advised Romania to resolve the dispute
peacefully—that is, to accept the terms of the ultimatum. Germany
ostensibly laid responsibility for the crisis on Romania itself: Hitler
reminded the Romanian king that his country had agreed to accept
a guarantee from Britain in 1939.[160] At the same time, the Germans
reminded Moscow that their agreement pertained solely to Bessarabia. Ribbentrop also warned that 100,000 "Volksdeutsche" lived in
Bessarabia, and that Germany was vitally interested in their welfare
and safety.

On June 28–30 the Red Army occupied Bessarabia and northern
Bukovina. Soon a rather significant number of Volksdeutsche were
evacuated to Germany, in a process similar to what transpired in
Lithuania. From Bukovina and Bessarabia came a steady stream of
rumors about outrages committed by local bands of "Jews and communists," who plundered the shops and hotels belonging to Germans, but the Red Army—when units arrived—conducted itself correctly.[161] On August 2, 1940 the "Moldavian SSR" was formed from
territories formerly comprising the Moldavian ASSR, Ukrainian
SSR, and Bessarabia; it survived until the collapse of the USSR in
1990, when the independent republic of Moldova was established.

German citizens expressed dissatisfaction that the Soviet Union
had resolved the Romanian question at a time when Germany was
preoccupied in the West. The German population, like the Soviet,
of course knew nothing of the secret agreements between their two
countries. The German government, it should be noted, was actually happy to have its citizens stunned by the news of the Soviet
ultimatum to Romania. The German radio and press reported about
these events only when they were already at their peak.[162] Nor did

the Germans fail to notice that the Soviet regime had increased the work week from six to seven days, and had new symbols of rank and greeting in the Red Army.

Uncertainty about the durability of Soviet-German relations, at least over the long term because of the existing regime in the USSR, became a leitmotif in popular thinking.[163] The German populace even heard rumors that Molotov—who represented a pro-German policy—would shortly be replaced, and that an anti-German government would come to power in Moscow.[164] This rumor was somewhat dampened by countervailing reports that Moscow had abolished the institute of political commissars—this was interpreted to mean that the USSR was abandoning Bolshevism in favor of a national Russian state.[165]

It is worth noting that the Czech population in Bohemia and Moravia regarded Soviet actions in Bessarabia and northern Bukovina as increasing the influence of the USSR and the idea of panslavism in central Europe and the Balkans. In the final analysis, hoped the Czechs, this would put pressure on Germany and lead to a reestablishment of their independent state.[16] Among Czech peasants, however, the dominant sentiment was cold fear of Bolshevization should the Russians come: however onerous the German rule might be, it was preferable to that of the Soviets.[167]

The population in occupied Poland, by contrast, hoped that the Slavs would be unified under the aegis of the Soviet Union and that room would be found for a Polish people's republic. Rumors circulated too that a Polish Red Army had been created in the USSR.[168] The German intelligence service, in analyzing the hopes of various and even overtly hostile forces (such as the Ukrainian and Belorussian nationalists, Russian emigrés and Polish nationalists), noted that any formulation of Panslavism was rooted in antipathy for everything German: "Panslavism surely means Germanophobia."[169]

Rumors about probable conflict with Russia were based on fears that Britain's rejection of peace talks would lead to a protracted war, the outcome of which was anything but clear. Specifically, German public opinion was divided into two camps: one believed in a speedy end to the war, the other foresaw a prolonged conflict. The signing of the Berlin Pact in September 1940 seemed to confirm the second view: why conclude a military union if the main adversary—Britain—is on the verge of defeat, if no hostile plans are being laid against Russia? Part of Hitler's speech to the Reichstag in

July dealt with the reactions to the USSR, and it contained some statements intended to allay fears and anxieties. Nevertheless, the same speech exhorted Britain to open peace talks.[170] The Soviet press gave a rather positive assessment of the speech.

When Britain categorically refused to negotiate, this automatically raised the "Russian question:" could one presume a peaceful development of German-Soviet relations after the Soviet Union had so hastily annexed the Baltic states? The USSR had acted decisively; between August 3 and August 6, the new "socialist republics" were incorporated into the USSR. East Prussia now had common borders with the Soviet Union—a new, unpleasant experience for the ordinary German, who was not psychologically prepared for this rapid development of events. The German provincial press (for example, in Karlsruhe, Dortmund, Neustadt, Salzburg, Innsbruck, and Allenstein) wrote openly about this popular concern.[171] To all this must be added anxiety concerning the fate of the Baltic Germans. Reports by the security service cited numerous instances of searches and arrests in Lithuania and the persecution of the so-called "people's militia" of the Volksdeutsche, together with the inevitable accusations of espionage. The problem of the Baltic Germans was resolved by a Soviet-German agreement to give them a choice of citizenship.[172]

The German people, nonetheless, still hoped for a quick end to the war, all the more since the capitulation of Britain seemed inevitable. In the wake of Germany's impressive military victories and the ceaseless pounding of British cities by the Luftwaffe, a mood of smug self-assurance spread throughout the German populace. Especially popular were the illustrated publications showing photographs of British ports under attack from the air.[173] In mid-September the German population believed that the landing of German forces on the British Isles was imminent. However, a note of anxiety was also becoming apparent: if the German air offensive failed to break the British and if they managed to survive the winter, the United States appeared likely to enter the war. And the German populace still felt a nagging fear of the Soviet Union: what would it do in this situation? The sudden shifting of German troops to the east fed these doubts and rumors that fifty Soviet divisions had been concentrated on its western borders.[174]

As if seeking to counteract rumors of tensions in Soviet-German relations, the USSR attempted to reassure the Germans through

punctilious fulfillment of its delivery obligations. A memorandum
by Schnurre, for example, emphasized not only that the development of German-Soviet trade was entirely satisfactory but also that
the Soviet Union was making a significant effort to produce and
deliver the materials needed in Germany. Of the total number of
deliveries in May–June 1940 (valued at 160 million Reichsmarks),
thirty-two arrived in May, fifty-three in June, and the rate rose still
higher in July. By June 30, 1940, the USSR had sent Germany
376,000 tons of grain (worth a value of 52 million RM), and
279,000 tons of oil (with a value of 39 million RM). Most important, the increased delivery appeared to be directly linked with the
military success of Germany and reflected the growing fear in the
USSR. Germany received 61,000 tons of oil in May but 102,000 in
June. Still more striking were the data on grain deliveries, which
jumped from 76,000 tons in May to 197,000 tons in June. The
Soviet side even overfulfilled its obligations in the sphere of strategic materials: the target for an entire year (5,000 tons of copper and
450,000 tons of tin) was met in the space of four months. In addition, the Soviet Union transshipped raw materials that it had purchased in third countries: 5,800 tons of copper, 535 tons of tin, 75
tons of cobalt concentrate, 75 tons of scrap nickel, and 1,300 tons
of rubber.

On July 4 Mikoian confirmed that the Soviet Union would sell
Germany one-half of the nonferrous metals purchased in third
countries since February 1940. But, as the February agreement had
foreseen, Germany had a longer time-frame for the delivery of goods
on its part. By the end of June, of the Soviet orders for 600 million
RM, only 82 million RM in goods had been delivered (including 25
million RM were for the cruiser *Liutsov*).[175] Because of delays in the
delivery of German equipment and arms (in the midst of mounting
complications in the Baltics, Finland, and the Balkans), Stalin
resorted to the only form of pressure at his disposal—a delay in
Soviet deliveries to Germany. Negotiations of trade delegations
(held in Moscow, from August 24 to September 12, 1940) to verify
implementation of the Economic Agreement of February 11,
showed that the Germans were systematically failing to fulfill their
obligations. A check by the German economic ministry and the
Supreme Military Command showed that, in order to realize plans
to increase the German armed forces to 180 divisions, it was impossible not only to reduce Germany's backlog of late deliveries (worth

73 million RM), but also to meet its obligations with respect to other goods. Moreover, realization of the program for military deliveries ran contrary to an order from Hermann Göring forbidding the export of any machinery and equipment to the USSR that might be used to increase its military potential.

The German economic ministry understood fully that a cutback in Soviet deliveries of strategic raw materials and grain would deal a blow to the military and economic condition of the Reich. Meanwhile, the Soviet Union had decided to cancel all long-term orders and to limit imports primarily to military goods that could be delivered within eight to ten months (i.e., before the end of June 1941— a date worth noting indeed). In a memorandum to Ribbentrop, Schnurre laid particular emphasis on the fact that deliveries from the USSR comprised a substantial part of the German war economy. Since the signing of the agreement in February 1940, the Soviet Union had delivered Germany raw materials worth more than 300 million RM (including 100 million RM in grain), but in return had received goods worth only 150 million RM. Schnurre especially stressed that Germany's economic ties to Iran, Afghanistan, Manchuria, China, Japan, and South America ran across the USSR.[176]

The Balkan Question

Perhaps more intensively than anywhere else, the Balkans gave rapt attention to rumors (probably disseminated by German intelligence) that on September 15 Hitler would accept the capitulation of Great Britain in Buckingham Palace. This region had been profoundly frightened by the quick defeat of France, by the German-Soviet partnership and cooperation, and also by its own internecine disputes.

The balance of power in the Balkans now underwent a radical change. Britain sought to sustain its position, bearing in mind that the Balkans were the gateway to the British Empire. Germany sought to avert bloodletting in the Balkans, at least until it had secured the defeat of Britain. Italy endeavored to claim equal rights with its German ally and to satisfy its own claims and pretensions. The Soviet Union feared that Germany and Italy would grow stronger, still more that German troops would march into Bulgaria, and also that Turkey would side with one of the combatants.

At a more practical level, in the summer of 1940, while Germany had not entirely abandoned the idea of a frontal assault on Britain, it continued seeking to isolate and encircle its foe. Berlin considered various plans to join Spain in seizing Gibraltar, while Italy was to take the Suez Canal. At the same time, Germany endeavored to dissuade Italy from attacking Yugoslavia and Greece, even while recognizing that both states belonged to the Italian sphere of interest. The Supreme Command of the Wehrmacht explained to Italy that, "the 'Axis' is at present engaged in a life-and-death-struggle with Britain and that it would therefore doubtless be inadvisable to tackle any new problem at all that did not absolutely have to be tackled in connection with this effort to crush Britain."[177]

Germany had earlier forced Romania to capitulate before Soviet demands. Hitler now decided to purge the Romanian political horizon of any pro-British and pro-French supporters and to establish total control over that country's resources and politics. It was now a matter of forming a Greater German economic sphere, which meant the reorganization and total subjection of foreign companies to German control.[178]

At the same time, the Germans carried out a "territorial" reorganization. Their first step was to support the territorial demands of Bulgaria. On March 21 Bulgaria and Romania signed an agreement at Craiova to reestablish their 1912 borders and to transfer Dobruja to Romania. On August 29, as a result of this new German "arbitration," Romania was forced to cede to Hungary a significant part of Transylvania—an area embracing 2.5 million inhabitants, of whom 1 million were Romanians. Simultaneously, Germany and Italy imposed on Romania their guarantee of its integrity—which, in essence, was a euphemism for total subjugation to German policy.[179] Within a short span of time, King Carol II abdicated in favor of his son, but the real dictator became General Ion Antonescu.

However much the Soviet Union may have disliked these developments, it had no alternative but to accept the new Romanian border as a *fait accompli*.[180] This meant that the USSR recognized German interests in Romania, although Molotov was sufficiently careful to refer only to petroleum.[181] The USSR also assumed a favorable stance toward Hungary's revisionist demands and its request for the relocation of several Hungarian villages in northern Bukovina.[182] The Soviet government was basically testing the ground for its

Balkan policy; it focused primarily on Bulgaria and Turkey, where it expected German support—as in the case with Romania.

But here Stalin went too far: the agreements of 1939 had not recognized Soviet interests in this region. Hitler told the Bulgarian minister-president and his foreign minister in no uncertain terms that the definition of German and Soviet spheres of interest pertained only to the Baltic states and Bessarabia, not to the Balkans. Nevertheless Hitler felt obliged to make certain reservations: "Of course he had had to concede Russia the right to rectify wrongs of the past, since he claimed this privilege also for Germany."[183] Hence Hitler left himself free to deal with any future political combinations involving the Soviet Union. At the same time, he implicitly warned Bulgaria not to indulge in adventurous policies contrary to German interests. It should be noted that Hitler's action here preceded his decision to attack the USSR, but that decision was already—as this case suggests—in the making. In short, by mid-August 1940 Germany definitely opposed Soviet involvement in Balkan affairs, insofar as this would lead to the discussion of purely territorial questions and involve ideological issues as well.[184]

Following the victory in the West, Berlin was equally restrained in its response to the suggestion that it help improve Soviet-Turkish relations. In any case, when the German ambassador in Turkey, von Papen, made such a proposal,[185] that was Berlin's response.[186] Nevertheless, von Papen insistently advised Berlin that, if not through a Soviet-Turkish agreement, then through negotiations between the Axis Powers and the USSR, some settlement of the status of the Straits could be achieved.[187] For its part, the USSR regarded the Montreux Convention of 1936 as unsatisfactory and contradictory to its vital interests. In von Papen's view, a non-combatant Turkey was crucial to the preservation of the British empire. But the situation would change radically if the Soviet Union wanted to exploit the new situation and move toward the Indian Ocean and Persian Gulf.[188]

In any event, the question had to be resolved, one way or the other. Papen's idea of exploiting Soviet interest in the Straits question—to draw it into the war on the side of Italy and Germany and against Britain—fell on fertile soil. In early July, Germany published "White Book No. 6," which revealed the French plan (March 1940) to bomb the Baku oilfields by using Iranian or Turkish airspace. In one document the French ambassador in Ankara reported that the Turkish foreign minister, Saracoglu, saw no obstacles so far as Turkey was concerned.[189] The Soviet Union used the incident to question whether the Soviet-Turkish and Soviet-Iranian nonaggression pacts were still in force. However, in the end Germany did not succeed in exacerbating Soviet-British tensions. According to information that the Germans obtained from a Turkish diplomat in Berlin, Turkey had no intention of surrendering to Soviet pressure over the Straits or other territorial demands, even at the risk of war.[190] In the summer of 1940 relations between the Soviet Union and Italy improved markedly, especially because of their common interest in the Balkans and in the Straits. For its part, the USSR was prepared to recognize Italy's interests in the Mediterranean Sea, if Italy would acknowledge its own rights in the Black Sea.[191]

The USSR and Britain

Winston Churchill decided to appoint a new ambassador to Moscow: a prominent Labour politician, Stafford Cripps. He arrived in Moscow on June 12, 1940—at a time when the German army was driving toward Paris. On July 1 Cripps handed Stalin a communication from Churchill, who explained that Britain had two goals: to save itself from the threat of German domination and to liberate Europe. Emphasizing that the Soviet Union must judge for itself whether German pretensions to hegemony threatened its own interests, Churchill expressed a willingness to discuss any of the vast problems created by Germany's recent campaign of conquest and absorption.[192] But the commercial and other negotiations conducted by Cripps in the summer and fall of 1940 did not lead to any practical results. Nor could they: the Soviet Union was too terrified by Germany's stunning military victories to countenance an agreement with Britain. The latter, however, still hoped that circumstances would nonetheless force the Soviet Union to move in its direction. As the *Economist* wrote at the end of July 1940: "We cannot defeat Germany fully without allies, and what more obvious ally could there be than the State whose alliance with the West Hitler has already shown his anxiety to prevent at any cost? . . . Patiently, if need be, but with the great persistence, we must work for a Russian alliance."[193]

Hitler understood clearly that Britain based its hopes on enduring until an inevitable and radical shift in Soviet foreign policy. There were several possible ways to involve Stalin in the war—tempting him through new territorial acquisitions and the prospect of participating in a new partition of the world. The counter-strategy was to entice Stalin with a partnership in the Greater German economic sphere—a role that in fact elicited support from some German industrialists. The only danger was that Germany might become too dependent on this partner. More important in the long run, however, was Nazi ideology, which began to cast a dark shadow over Realpolitik.

On May 27, 1940, when part of the British expeditionary corps in France was desperately resisting the German assaults around Dunkirk, the British war cabinet discussed a report from the general staff, "British Strategy in a Certain Eventuality." The report assumed that as soon as Italy formally entered the war on Germany's side, France's north African colonies would fall to Germany; that Spain, Portugal, and the Balkan states (with the exception of Turkey) would remain under the Allies' control; that Britain could expect complete financial and economic support from the United States; and that the USSR would be highly alarmed by Germany's waxing military might. From these four premises, the general staff came to a rather optimistic prognosis for the outcome of the war, and concluded that Britain was capable of continuing the war alone and ultimately prevail in the conflict.[194]

Oddly enough, Hitler also believed that Britain was capable of continuing the war as long as it had hope of support from the USSR and the United States. As yet he was reluctant to seek peace with Britain, for he correctly perceived little readiness on his adversary's part to conclude "peace" as he understood it, that is, capitulation. A diary entry of June 30, 1940 by Colonel-General Franz Halder gave this summary of his conversations with state-secretary Weizsäcker, who no doubt reflected the Führer's thinking:

(a) We can preserve the victories of this campaign only with the means with which they were achieved, that is, with military power.
(b) No concrete basis for any peace treaty exists yet.
(c) We shall keep a steady eye on the East.
(d) Britain probably still needs one more demonstration of our military might before she gives in and leaves us a free hand in the East.[195]

Both for himself and his subordinates, Hitler attributed Britain's stubborn resistance to the continuing hope that it could reach an agreement with the Soviet Union. In fact, that was only a half-truth: Britain would not have capitulated even if it had to fight alone, for it could count on the increasing support of the United States. Nevertheless, in Hitler's thinking the Soviet Union assumed exaggerated importance as an obstacle to victory in the West and gradually came to the forefront of his military and political strategy.

Halder's diary provides abundant and eloquent testimony on this point. Thus in a notation on July 11, 1940, Halder quotes a high-ranking official in the foreign ministry (who no doubt reflected the thinking of his superiors) to the effect that both the USSR and Britain "are seeking a rapprochement."[196] Two days later Halder wrote: "The Führer is greatly puzzled by Britain's persisting unwill-ingness to make peace. He sees the answer (as we do) in Britain's hope on Russia."[197] On July 16, 1940 Hitler signed Directive No. 16 on the campaign against Britain (with the code name "Sea Lion"). Its objective was to eliminate Great Britain as a base of military action against Germany and, if need be, to occupy that country. Three days later Hitler delivered a speech at a Sports Palace, pro-claiming his willingness to make peace with Britain.

Simultaneously, Germany actively pursued contacts through var-ious intermediaries and attempted to sound out British willingness to reach agreement. It bears noting that Hitler's information about the mood and political situation in Britain bore scant resemblance to reality. The official position of the British war cabinet was quite clear: in its name Halifax categorically rejected Hitler's proposals for peace.[198] As Churchill later observed, Hitler naturally would have liked to make peace with Britain while holding onto his conquests, but that of course would have been no peace treaty, but simply capitulation on Britain's part.[199]

Hitler gradually came to the conclusion that if he eliminated Churchill's hope for Soviet intervention, Britain would no longer refuse to capitulate. On June 22, 1940 Hitler made a speech at a meeting organized by Field Marshal Walther von Brauchitsch and spoke at length about the problem of Anglo-Soviet relations. For the meantime Hitler found no evidence that the USSR was ready to launch an attack on Germany: "The Russians are afraid of compro-mising themselves in our eyes; they don't want any war."[200] This statement probably reflected the information that he had received about the meeting between Stalin and the British emissary, Stafford Cripps. Cripps had endeavored to convince Stalin that German domination was a threat not only to Britain but also to the USSR, and therefore that the two countries should unite in the name of self-preservation and the restoration of a balance of power in Europe. Britain also proposed to acknowledge Soviet leadership in the Balkans in order to maintain there the status quo. It was also willing to recognize Soviet interests in the Black Sea and Straits.

All this, it would seem, should have satisfied Stalin's wildest dreams, but in fact the British made a miscalculation: they sought only to reestablish the prewar status quo, but Stalin wanted a new balance of power. Moreover, he simply did not trust the British. That is why the Germans were so well informed about Cripps's proposals and Stalin's response. Indeed, Stalin's reaction was intended to soothe German fears: the Soviet Union saw no threat of domination by a single power, especially on Germany's part. Moreover, Germany's military success posed no threat to the USSR, for their relations were based on respect of the national interests of both parties. The former balance of power in Europe was oppressive not only for Germany, but also for the Soviet Union. Hence the USSR had no interest in reestablishing the former balance of power in Europe. Stalin also emphasized his belief that no state could pretend to exercise a dominant role in the Balkans. The USSR did not claim such a role, although it was of course interested in Balkan affairs. As far as the exceptional jurisdiction exercised by Turkey over the Straits, the USSR's opposition to that status was well known to the Turkish government.

The only point where Stalin showed interest in the British approach was the matter of trade, but here too he categorically rejected any hint of British meddling in Soviet-German commercial relations. Moreover, Stalin announced that the USSR would continue to resell to Germany some of the nonferrous materials acquired from third countries, for Germany requires them to produce the goods that it in turn sold to the Soviet Union.[201]

In short, Stalin's response to Cripps was intended to clarify Soviet-German relations and, in some measure, reassure Hitler. It presupposed, of course, that Hitler himself wished to preserve peaceful relations with Moscow. Stalin firmly emphasized that he wished to cooperate fully with Germany, since both countries shared a common interest in changing the prewar status quo, in

cooperating in the Balkans, and maintaining the economic agreement. So far as the USSR was concerned, the only outstanding issue
was the need to revise control of the Straits. At no point did Stalin
claim any exceptional rights. In sum, Stalin's response conveyed the
impression of a highly rational politician. If Hitler did have hostile
intentions against the USSR, Stalin's reply seemed to invite him to
reconsider one more time.

Hitler, however, wavered for only one more week. After that
period of vacillation, he came to a irreversible conclusion that
would ultimately doom the Third Reich: on July 31, at a conference
of commanders at Berghof, Hitler announced his intention to
attack the USSR:

> Britain's hope is Russia and America. If the hope of Russia vanishes,
> America too will abandon Britain. If Russia is vanquished, Britain
> shall lose its last hope. . . . The conclusion: on the basis of this con-
> sideration, Russia must be liquidated. The term [set for an attack] is
> the spring of 1941.[202]

Although the date had already been set for an invasion of Britain
(September 15, 1940), Hitler did not abandon his hopes to vanquish
Britain through nonmilitary means. This view had the support of
the navy. Admiral Erich Raeder feared that an unsuccessful landing
could decimate the small German navy. That led to repeated proposals to defer implementation of "Sea Lion" until more propitious
times. Preparations, nonetheless, went ahead. Still, the most significant change in war plans concerned priorities: instead of "first
Britain, then the Soviet Union," planning now presumed "first the
Soviet Union, then Britain."

From August to October the Luftwaffe conducted an intensive
air campaign against Britain. It failed, however, to break British
resistance; German losses were twice those of the British. The
British aviation industry was able, even amidst conditions of inces-
sant bombing, to replace the lost aircraft.[203] On November 12 the
invasion plan was deferred until the following year.[204] In fact, the
Germans were never again to give serious consideration to the plan.
Nevertheless, simultaneous with the planning of operations against
the USSR, Germany made repeated attempts to draw Britain into
peace negotiations—efforts that included unsuccessful ploys to
operate through the Duke of Windsor (the former King Edward
VIII).[205] After the British government appointed him governor of

the Bahamas in August 1940, the Duke and his wife left Lisbon to assume his new post, ending the German attempts to use him as an intermediary.

In the interim rumors of tensions and a possible conflict between the USSR and Germany continued to circulate widely in the summer of 1940. Such ideas were especially appealing in Balkan governments (with the possible exception of Yugoslavia), which—like the Baltic states earlier—may have feared both Germany and the USSR, but if they had to choose between these two would prefer Germany. This situation naturally evoked concern in Moscow, which responded by issuing official statements on its strict observance of Soviet-German agreements and by taking special defense measures (e.g., by increasing the workday from seven to eight hours, by prohibiting unauthorized job changes, by making absenteeism and tardiness at the workplace a criminal offense, and by expanding its military program). At the session of the Supreme Soviet that approved these measures, Molotov reminded Berlin of the mutual advantage of German-Soviet relations (which were founded on "basic state interests"), but declared that the Soviet Union must prepare itself militarily.[206]

None of this came as a surprise to Germany, which was supposed to assist in modernizing Soviet military enterprises and its arms program. Simultaneously, Ribbentrop's diplomats began to collect facts to prove that the Soviet partner, in letter or spirit, was violating the terms of the 1939 agreements.[207] Disputes also erupted over the Soviet concession for the German firm of I. G. Farben to mine nickel at Petsamo and the respective shares of the output.[208]

Molotov voiced the Soviet grievances: in the event of arbitration in Vienna, Germany would violate Article 3 of the Nonaggression Pact stipulating mutual information and consultation in questions of mutual interest. Germany rejected that claim and, for its part, had grievances of its own: the USSR had seized Lithuanian territory which, by prior agreements, properly belonged to Germany. In addition, the Soviet side had seized Bessarabia and northern Bukovina with undue haste, which in turn had intensified revisionist demands of the Balkan states vis-à-vis Romania.[209] Other problems that contributed to tensions in Soviet-German reactions concerned the resettlement of Germans from the Baltics and Bessarabia (and satisfaction of their property claims)[210] and the appearance of German armed forces on Finnish territory and later in Romania. In some

cases the two sides could reach agreement (e.g., when Molotov proposed that the USSR participate in the commission to supervise the
Danube, the Germans agreed).[211]

The Berlin Pact

Background

In mid-September, shortly before the signing of the Berlin Pact
(September 27, 1940), Germany presumed that the USSR had no
alternative but to acquiesce. Militarily, the Soviet Union was rather
weak; it was highly unlikely that Stalin would take an antagonistic
position, given the danger of war on two fronts. Hitler declared that
the war against Britain had been in effect won, although it was still
too early to say precisely when the British would finally capitulate.
Britain's hopes, no doubt, rested on the eventuality that the United
States and the Soviet Union would enter the war on its side. Hitler
believed not only that the USSR was too cut off from the United
States and Britain to expect any help from those quarters but also
that Stalin was too rational to allow himself to be drawn into a confrontation: he could hardly fail to understand that the German army
could vanquish the Soviet side at any moment, threaten the very
existence of the current regime in Moscow, and inflict terrible
destruction on the industrial centers of European Russia. In the
judgment of top Nazis, Stalin would prefer to take advantage of his
current policy. Hence Germany should be able to distract the Soviet
Union with offers for expansion in the area of the Persian Gulf and
India—as Hitler in fact did propose in talks with Molotov two
months later.

    By contrast, Soviet meddling in Balkan affairs was highly un-
desirable; in particular, an agreement between Russia and Turkey
would clearly contradict the interests of the Axis Powers. Germany
and Italy, as Ribbentrop and Mussolini had concurred, should take a
friendly posture toward the Soviet Union, which might draw the
latter into closer relations with the Axis.[212] At the same time the
Germans very meticulously noted the smallest hints that the Soviet
Union was expanding its cooperation with the United States and
Britain. The German embassy in Washington reported in September 1940 that Russia had made repeated requests for assistance.

Specifically, Moscow asked the Americans, notwithstanding the embargo, to sell machine-tools for military plants and to send American specialists to the USSR to help construct plants for the construction of high-octane gasoline, which Washington had on numerous occasions declined.[213]

Hitler had a rather good grasp of Stalin's thinking: from the outbreak of war the Soviet dictator had counted on a prolonged conflict, which in fact served Soviet interests perfectly. But Stalin had miscalculated; he had not expected Germany's overwhelming military success. By March 1941 Hitler expected to have 100 first-class divisions under arms, including 24 that were fully motorized. As Hitler told Mussolini in October 1940, he "considered [it] out of the question that Russia would undertake anything" given the total preponderance of German might.[214]

The Signing of the Pact

Two events of this period exerted a significant impact on Soviet-German relations. The first came on September 27, 1940, when Germany, Italy, and Japan signed the Berlin Pact (Tripartite Agreement), which divided the world into spheres of influence and which was primarily directed against the United States. The second event came in November 1940: negotiations with the USSR about its participation as the fourth partner in this division of the world.

Molotov learned of the Axis treaty just one day prior to its signing. Ribbentrop's note on the political pact excised every hint that it was aimed at the United States and emphasized that the participants of the pact were completely agreed that it did not concern their individual relations with the USSR (article 5).[215] Molotov claimed that Moscow had actually known about the pact well beforehand—from its own intelligence sources in Japan. Molotov, in particular, was interested in anything that had to do with the Japanese pact.[216]

The letter of the German ambassador in Tokyo (Eugen Ott) to the Japanese foreign minister Yosuke Matsuoka specifically emphasized Germany's willingness to do everything in its power to promote friendly relations between Japan and the USSR. "With regard to the relations between Japan and Soviet Russia," he wrote, "Germany will do everything within her power to promote a friendly understanding and will at any time offer her good offices to this end."[217] Molotov, however, worried that the pact nevertheless had secret codicils pertaining specifically to the Soviet Union. He attempted to extract information on this from the Japanese ambassador in Moscow, Togo.[218] In sum, news of the pact was greeted in Moscow without the slightest sign of enthusiasm. A lead editorial in *Pravda* emphasized that the signing represents "a further intensification of the war and an expansion of the sphere of its operation." The editorial drew particular attention to article five on the Axis powers' relations to the USSR and asserted that the article should be interpreted "as confirmation that the nonaggression pact between Germany and the USSR and nonaggression pact between Italy and the USSR were still in force."[219] A few days later the same newspaper published a detailed report from a TASS correspondent who had visited one of the London antiaircraft batteries and who obviously had considerable sympathy for the British.[220] At the same time, the Soviet press continued to brand Britain as the "aggressor," but now suppressed the inane campaign against American intervention in the war—even if this meant support for the "aggressor."

According to reports from the German secret police, the population in Germany itself did not have a clear understanding of the Tripartite Pact and its implications. Despite the unambiguous text of article 5, affirming that the pact bore no relation to the USSR, the secret police reported numerous rumors of major disagreements between Germany and the Soviet Union, especially with regard to the Balkans.[221] "Although the general confidence in victory in the population is in no way eroded, a certain impatience with the further development of the military events is noticeable."[222]

Both before and after the singing of the Tripartite Pact, Berlin discussed the feasibility of drawing the USSR into the pact as a fourth partner. The aim was to divert Moscow toward the Persian Gulf and Indian Ocean—in other words, toward another sphere of the British Empire. During a home visit by the German military attaché in Moscow, Köstring, General Karl Bodenschatz (Göring's adjutant), and General Ernst Udet asked whether the Soviet Union appeared willing to join the Tripartite Pact. The generals also indicated the price that Berlin was willing to pay for such participation: a free hand in the south, in the Dardanelles, and the region eastward of that. At the same time, Udet also asked whether Ukrainian peasants would support Germany if the latter abolished the kolkhozes and gave them back their land. The conversations also raised the question of a possible meeting between Hitler and Stalin in a third country. In short, these discussions revolved around alternatives to the future relations with the USSR—either as a partner in dividing up the world, or as Germany's next adversary.[223] One should keep in mind the failure of the bombing campaign to break the British will to resist; the country clearly had no intention of capitulating. On October 12 Hitler ordered that the plan to invade Britain be deferred until the spring of 1941 and became increasingly convinced that he must win the war in the west by war in the east. Indeed, Hitler explicitly made this point in talks with Mussolini in October[224] and with the Hungarian premier, Count Paul Teleki, in November, 1940.[225]

Köstring by now had a good sense of how the winds were blowing in Berlin. His reports, like that of October 31, 1940 (which followed a three-day visit to engineering, artillery, and infantry units in Leningrad), stressed that "the impression is steadily growing in me that the Russians want to avoid any conflict with us."[226] On November 6 the attaché wrote that, "since Göring has now put our military deliveries in balance with the Russian deliveries, one may hope that the negotiations will end in peace and friendship."[227] On November 14 Köstring reiterated his conviction that the Soviet Union has no aggressive designs—indeed, just the contrary: "Molotov's trip [to Berlin] is for me just further proof of an idea that I have long held—namely, that the Soviet Union wants to have peace with us, since it cannot expect any advantage from a conflict with us. . . . The decisive factor in [evoking] the Soviet desire for peace is and remains the demonstrated strength of our army."[228] Köstring supported that opinion by referring to the population's mood, which unquestionably lacked any enthusiasm for expansionism and dreamt only of tranquility and sustenance.[229]

A final decision was supposed to come after the goals of the Soviet leadership had been clarified. Germany once again extended its invitation for Stalin and Molotov to visit Berlin. Ribbentrop's letter to Stalin is indubitably one of the most important documents from this period.[230] At the very time that Berlin was working out plans for war against the USSR, it had still not taken a final political decision to attack. Ribbentrop laid special emphasis on the fact that the European war had proven Britain and France to be an enemy not only of Germany but also of the Soviet Union—given their posture during the Soviet-Finnish War and their plans to bomb the Baku petroleum fields. By contrast, wrote Ribbentrop, the Soviet-German collaboration had unquestionably yielded positive results and had been built on the firm basis of their common geo-political interests.

In Ribbentrop's view, three factors now determined the real alignment of power in the world: the friendly relations between Germany and the USSR, the good relations between the USSR and Japan, and the friendship between the Axis powers and Japan. Ribbentrop explained that, in many instances, Germany had been forced to make decisions on the spur of the moment, such as the dis-patching of troops to Kirkenes, the Vienna arbitration, and the like. Foes had portrayed these actions as aimed against the Soviet Union, but Ribbentrop strenuously denied such accusations. The German foreign minister endeavored to persuade Stalin—unsuccessfully, as it turned out—that Britain was doomed to defeat and that its capit-ulation was only a matter of time. The core of Ribbentrop's letter (addressed to "Dear Mr. Stalin") was its restatement of Hitler's view that the four great powers—the Axis powers together with the Soviet Union—could cooperate in dividing up the world. Ribben-trop described the main task as follows: "In summing up, I should like to state that in the opinion of the Führer, also, it appears to be the historic missions of the four powers—the Soviet Union, Italy, Japan, and Germany—to adopt a long-range policy and to direct the future development of their peoples into the right channels by the delimitation of their interests for the ages."[231] Ribbentrop argued that all four powers were fully autonomous and hence could easily coordinate their interests.[232] To discuss all these questions, Ribbentrop invited Molotov to meet with Hitler in Berlin.

Moscow could hardly refuse the invitation. In his reply Stalin wrote that he deemed it "entirely possible" that there could be a fur-ther improvement in Soviet-German relations if the long-term interests of each nation were negotiated.

On November 12, 1940 Molotov, together with a large entou-rage of aides and security protection, arrived in Berlin. Although customarily described as the Molotov-Hitler talks, that label is not entirely accurate. Stalin himself took a most active behind-the-scenes role, constantly supervising Molotov's actions and cor-recting his blunders. This close control from Moscow became known only recently, when a Moscow journal published the corre-spondence between Molotov and Stalin during the Berlin talks.[233]

Unfortunately, Stalin's instructions to Molotov—issued shortly before his departure and cited in the correspondence—have not yet been published.[234]

Molotov held preliminary talks with Ribbentrop before beginning the direct negotiations with Hitler. In response to Ribbentrop's proposals to divide the world into four zones of interests, with one belonging to the USSR, Molotov pronounced the idea "very interesting" and worthy of discussion first in Berlin, then in Moscow (with the participation of Ribbentrop himself).[235] Stalin found Ribbentrop an entirely acceptable partner. The new agreements were to be completed in Moscow—a procedure that had worked well in 1939. The final word on this proposal was left to Stalin.

Stalin's reply to this first telegram came four and a half hours later. He was especially critical of Molotov's comment that the 1939 agreement was "exhausted," with the exception of the Finnish question. Stalin found Molotov's phrasing inaccurate, for it might lead the Germans to conclude that the nonaggression pact had lost meaning, when in fact it was a matter of attaching addenda to that agreement—which Stalin still regarded as the fundamental basis of Soviet-German relations.[236]

As yet, we have only the official German minutes of the negotiations with Hitler, for Russian authorities have not yet declassified its version of the talks. According the German records, Molotov expressed his agreement with Hitler about the role of America and Britain. He regarded the participation of the Soviet Union in the Berlin Pact as, in principle, completely acceptable but only if Russia were to cooperate as an active partner, not simply an object. In this case Molotov foresaw no reason why the USSR could not participate in the general effort.[237]

Molotov concurred completely with Hitler that, with the exception of the Finnish question, there were no unresolved problems in Soviet-German relations. For his part Hitler agreed that, politically, Finland belonged to the Soviet sphere of interest, but stressed that during the current wartime conditions Germany had a legitimate interest in obtaining nickel and timber from Finland. He added that, from Germany's perspective, any new conflict in the Baltic region was highly undesirable—a clear indication that Germany opposed a resumption of Soviet-Finnish hostilities. Should the latter happen, this would lead to a severe strain in Soviet-German relations, with unforeseeable consequences. After hearing Hitler's categorical statements, Molotov concluded that nothing good could come from further talk about the Finnish question and merely declared that he could see no signs of a resumption of such a conflict. Hitler thereupon declared that the discussion bore a purely theoretical nature. In fact, however, both sides understood perfectly well that the situation was quite different.

The most important thing, argued Hitler, was the impending dismemberment of the British Empire, encompassing 40 million square kilometers and a population of 600 million. This would open the brilliant prospect of creating a coalition of states interested in sharing the British legacy, ranging from northern Africa to east Asia. The coalition would include, besides the four Axis powers, France and Spain. At issue too was a greater East Asia: Germany was now ready to recognize the area south of Russia's border as its own proper sphere of interests. Molotov, however, was not deluded by Hitler's scenario for the next fifty or hundred years. Stalin, in particular, was interested in less grandiose, more pragmatic objects—such as the Turkish question, participation in the commission to regulate navigation on the Danube, and the Soviet-German disagreement over Romania (which had received guarantees from Italy and Germany without prior consultations with Moscow). In Stalin's view, it was essential to review this situation.

Molotov also conveyed Stalin's interest in reviewing the status of the Straits, arguing that Russia allegedly found itself in a threatened position and that it had therefore extended guarantees to Bulgaria (like those given to Romania by Germany and Italy). Despite Molotov's effort to extract a German guarantee for Bulgaria, at least in principle, Hitler declared that any decision must await his talks with Mussolini and that any guarantee had to follow its own request.[238] According to Molotov's report to Stalin, the foreign minister had told Hitler that "the time has now come to discuss a broader agreement between the USSR and Germany," but first he would like to know the precise meaning of "the new order in Europe"—which countries and under which conditions will participate in this, and what tempo is foreseen for realizing the basic ideas of the pact.[239]

Molotov's telegram to Stalin underscored "Hitler's great interest in reaching an agreement and strengthening friendly relations with the USSR with respect to spheres of influence."[240] Molotov telegraphed Stalin that neither his second meeting with Hitler nor a concluding talk with Ribbentrop (the latter, because of British air attacks, were held in the bomb shelter of the Foreign Ministry) had produced "the desired results."[241] Molotov's disappointment is understandable: he had failed to resolve the problems of either Turkey or the Balkans. But, in his telegram to Molotov before the second meeting with Hitler, Stalin categorically insisted that the question was not only egress from the Black Sea but also entrance: historically this had been a source of continuing threat to Russian security. Therefore, wrote Stalin, the security of the USSR cannot be ensured "without securing tranquility in the area of the Straits." That in turn was directly linked with the Soviet-Bulgarian agreement on the passage of Soviet troops for "the defense of entry into the Black Sea." Stalin added that "this question still bears current importance and does not allow any procrastination."[242]

Ribbentrop reiterated that the chief goal was to define the respective interests of the four powers and to reach an agreement with Turkey on the Straits question. He proposed several parallel steps: Molotov was to discuss issues raised in Berlin with Stalin, and Ribbentrop would do the same with Italy and Japan. With respect to the Turkish problem, the three European powers—Germany, Italy, and the USSR—would put pressure on Turkey to acquiesce in their demands. The next step should be to draft and discuss confidential documents, bearing in mind that the final accord would be an agreement between the signatories of the Berlin Pact and the Soviet Union. Molotov was given a draft agreement that Ribbentrop had prepared. In accordance with previous practice, Ribbentrop proposed a two-tiered agreement: one part public, the other secret. The open part, valid for a ten-year term, announced their mutual determination to avert a further widening of the war and to achieve peace as soon as possible, to respect their respective natural spheres of interests, and to consult on new questions that might arise. Germany, Italy and Japan would also affirm their recognition of the existing Soviet borders. The secret agreement would include the obligation not to join any alliance directed at any of the signatories and to assist each other in economic matters. The draft of the first secret protocol also defined the territorial objectives of the four powers. Germany, in addition to acquisitions in Europe, also laid claims to central Africa. Italy counted on territorial compensation in Europe as well as northern and northeastern Africa. Japan's interests extended over southeast Asia. The Soviet zone was to its south, in the direction of the Indian Ocean. The draft of a second secret protocol addressed the problems of the Straits, Turkey, and the aim of the three powers (Germany, Italy, and the USSR) to "liberate" Turkey from its international obligations (i.e., its agreements with Britain) and to guarantee its borders.[243]

The news that Molotov was holding talks in Berlin initially had a stunning impact on world public opinion. The British press endeavored to determine whether Molotov's trip signalled Russia's decision to join the Berlin Pact, or whether this was simply a round of preliminary talks. It also noted that the German military had put the USSR under extraordinary pressure and forced it to seek some accommodation with Berlin. The upshot was that Moscow had little alternative but to spurn the repeated attempts by Britain to reach a mutual agreement. Britain also assumed that Germany was exploiting the Soviet Union's involuntary passivity (which was not the case) to strengthen its hand in the Balkans and that Berlin aimed to distract the USSR through involvement in Near Eastern questions and pose a direct threat to India.[244] In general, the British had a very good idea of the main purpose of Molotov's trip.

Stalin has been dead for four decades, yet his version of these negotiations has proven remarkably tenacious in the former Soviet Union. According to the account that Stalin gave in 1948 (in a piece on "Falsifiers of History"), he claimed to have rejected outright Hitler's proposal to share in a division of the world. That version persisted, without exception, in all historical studies, official accounts, memoirs, and textbooks published in the USSR until 1990.

One week after Molotov returned from Berlin, the USSR proposed a treaty of friendship and mutual assistance with Bulgaria. Moscow then sent as its special emissary a general secretary in the foreign affairs commissariat, A. A. Sobolev—to no avail: Bulgaria rejected the proposal. It was no secret that the USSR had designs on the south, and the attack on Finland had served as a warning. When Molotov handed Schulenburg Moscow's counterproposals to the Ribbentrop draft, Berlin already knew that Bulgaria had declined to sign an agreement with Russia.

The Kremlin's reply to the Ribbentrop draft began with the following words: "The Soviet government is prepared to accept the draft of the Pact of Four Powers on political cooperation and economic mutual assistance." Stalin proposed five, not two, secret protocols. The first pertained to Finland. It required German troops to depart immediately from Finland, but assured that the Soviet Union would guarantee peaceful relations with Finland as well as the delivery of Finnish timber and nickel. The second protocol stipulated that within the next few months, a mutual-assistance pact be signed between the USSR and Bulgaria, including the construction of bases for Soviet land and naval forces in the Bosphorus and Dardannelles (with long-term leases). In the event Turkey agreed to support the four-power pact, its independence and territorial integrity would be guaranteed by Italy, Germany, and the USSR. The third secret protocol recognized the center of Soviet territorial dominance to be south of Baku and Batumi, in the direction of the Persian Gulf. The fourth protocol required Japan to renounce its rights to coal and oil concessions in northern Sakhalin, in exchange for an appropriate compensation. Finally, the fifth protocol (involving Germany, Italy, and the USSR) confirmed that, insofar as Bulgaria lay with in the security zone of the Soviet Union, a Soviet-Bulgarian mutual-assistance treaty was a political necessity.[245]

Moscow's counterproposals unmistakably revealed that its primary objective was to gain total dominance of the Black Sea and the Straits. And that inevitably implied direct involvement in Balkan affairs. Hence the Soviet Union's determination not to surrender control over the Balkans was now perfectly clear to both Germany and Italy. To demonstrate the Soviet Union's willingness to conclude a comprehensive agreement with Germany, it accepted the basic German requests for the delivery—by May 11, 1941—of 2.5 million tons of grain. That meant allocating 1 million tons from its own state reserves to complement the 1.5 million tons already promised. Moreover, the Soviet Union was fully obliging with respect to German demands that Germans resettled from the Baltic receive appropriate compensation. The German envoy to Moscow, Schnurre, who could not conceal his surprise and delight over the Soviet response, sent the following telegram to Berlin: "In view of the present status of the negotiations here, Molotov's statements today must be viewed as a surprising indication of good will on the part of the Soviet Government. Molotov's proposal regarding compensation for property claims in the Baltic states considerably exceeds our expectations."[246]

Stalin probably hoped to impress Hitler by the Soviet Union's readiness for immediate practical implementation of cooperation in the separation of spheres of influence; his proposals on compensation and the new economic accord, calculated for 1941 and 1942, were a kind of advance payment on cooperation between the two countries.

However, Berlin saw the Soviet territorial ambitions in the Balkans as a direct challenge to German interests and its plan to make Bulgaria into an adjunct of the Tripartite pact.[247] Molotov would later, on several occasions, ask the Germans for their response to Moscow's counterproposals, but in vain: Berlin did not give them further consideration. Significantly, however, if the two sides failed to reach agreement, the responsibility would rest with Berlin, not Moscow.

At that moment the Soviet government, with exceptional zeal and determination, made every effort to accommodate Germany's wishes in the economic sphere. On January 10, 1941 the two countries signed a new economic agreement for the period from February 11 to August 1, 1942 involving 620 to 640 million Reichsmarks on each side.[248] Simultaneously, they signed a secret accord on the compensation due Germany for the stretch of Lithuanian soil that the Soviet Union had taken from the German sphere. After lengthy negotiations the two sides settled on a sum of 31.5 million Reichsmarks. In the course of negotiations the Germans insisted that the compensation be provided in the form of nonferrous metals, which were to be delivered within the next three months. The Soviet negotiators argued that their country lacked sufficient resources to satisfy the needs of German industry in so short a period of time. The two sides eventually came to an agreement, stipulating that only one-eighth of the compensation was to be paid in non-ferrous metals within a three-month term set to expire on April 10, 1941.[249]

The original date set for German military operations was May 15, 1941. The Germans' determination to obtain nonferrous metals within a three-month period should have tripped the alarm in Moscow. But it did not.

The first months after the signing of the Nonaggression Pact and later the Economic Agreement did reveal areas of significant cooperation between Germany and the Soviet Union. Above all, that took the form of neutrality or even collaboration in acts of aggression, but it also meant closer economic cooperation, especially in areas of military and strategic importance. It was not long, however, before this shotgun marriage began to disintegrate. The economic obligations, first, were a source of continuing and rising friction, especially for the German side, which desperately needed Soviet deliveries but had great difficulty fulfilling its own obligations. Second, once the initial area of clearly defined aggression had been exhausted, the two sides grew increasingly suspicious of the other, especially after Stalin revealed his own expansionist ambitions in the Balkans. Third, Hitler came to the curious conclusion that war on a second front was necessary to win on the first one: only by shattering British hopes of Russian involvement could he finally break the will to resist. These three processes, already by July 1940, had brought Hitler to the conclusion that he must attack and defeat the Soviet Union.

6

Toward the Abyss

The German radio and press devoted considerable attention to Molotov's trip to Berlin and conveyed the impression that it satisfied every expectation. Typical were the articles in *Völkischer Beobachter* (the central organ of the Nazi party), bearing titles like "Dear Molotov" and "From Bismarck to Hitler," presumably to suggest a direct line of affinity between the latter two. Similar coverage appeared in other newspapers, such as the article "Germany and the Soviet Union" in *Allensteiner Zeitung* or the article on the Soviet army in *Niederdeutscher Beobachter*.[1]

Public Reactions to the Molotov Visit in Berlin

How did the German public perceive the real state of affairs? Although the very brevity of the visit raised some doubts, the public quickly concluded that the discussions dealt not with the question of peace but war: after all, the two sides had allegedly considered issues related to the signing of a peace treaty.[2] That thinking reflected the Germans' natural hope that the military conflict would some come to an end. These rumors, however, soon gave way to another wave of reports (this time emanating from East Prussia) that the Todt organization was constructing an "Eastern rampart" along the Soviet border,

building bomb shelters under the expansive city squares of Königsberg, and preparing the railway stations for total blackouts.[3]

The reaction to Molotov's visit was quite different in the Soviet
Union. Köstring noted in his next dispatch that the Soviet press
was curiously silent on the matter of Molotov's journey to Berlin.[4]
Moscow was still working on its reply to the Berlin proposals and
evidently decided that there was no point in prematurely raising
hopes for a further improvement in Soviet-German relations. Once
Moscow had sent its reply, it anxiously waited for Berlin's response.

Time passed, but Berlin still did not respond. On January 17,
1941 Molotov told Schulenburg of his astonishment that the German government had still not replied to the Soviet response to the
proposals tendered during his Berlin visit. He reiterated Moscow's
view that the Straits and Bulgaria were vital to Soviet security;
hence, if foreign troops were to enter Bulgarian territory or the
Straits (Molotov referred to England, but of course had Germany in
mind), this would directly threaten Soviet security interests.[5] The
Germans dismissed such comments, saying that England was hardly
in any position to seize the Straits. In the event of military conflict
in Greece, however, Berlin warned that its troops would have to
cross Bulgarian territory, but claimed that this would not infringe on
Soviet interests. It also promised, "at the appropriate time," to
approve a review of the Montreux Convention.[6] As for Soviet
counterproposals, Ribbentrop declared that the Germans were still
studying Molotov's response and consulting with Italy and Japan.[7] It
was obvious from Ribbentrop's remark that Germany had no intention of satisfying Soviet demands on Bulgaria, and planned to pursue its own military and political goals.[8]

In response to queries from Japanese Ambassador Hiroshi Oshima
regarding the progress on talks with Russia about its joining the
Berlin Pact, Ribbentrop said that the USSR was prepared to join
under certain conditions and identified the terms that Molotov had
specified. The main stumbling block was the contradictory demands
of Russia and Bulgaria. As a result, explained Ribbentrop, negotiations with Russia had basically stalled, although Germany nonetheless hoped to renew talks once the Balkan situation had been clarified.[9] Naturally, Ribbentrop did not reveal that Germany was
already laying plans for war against the Soviet Union. He did, however, observe that Stalin did not wish war, since he was well aware of
Germany's awesome military might: any German-Russian conflict

inevitably would conclude in a gigantic victory for Germany.[10] Ribbentrop emphasized that, should war break out with Russia, the main brunt of the conflict would fall on Germany. Its defeat, he added, would be tantamount to defeat for the idea of a Japanese empire as well. Nevertheless, Oshima made it clear that his country and the Soviet Union would conclude a nonaggression pact, which would free Japan to act decisively to the south.[11]

In Germany itself there were second thoughts about the present drift in Soviet-German relations; even the signing of a new Economic Agreement did not dispel distrust toward Soviet intentions.[12] Reports about Soviet-English trade talks and a possible lifting of the American embargo on weapons and other goods for the USSR provoked concern among the German public that the United States was attempting to entice the Soviet Union to join the Western democracies.[13]

The Balkans

Germany intensified pressure on Bulgaria to join the Berlin Pact, just as England and the United States were pushing it to do just the opposite.[14] The American Secretary of the Navy, William F. Knox, sent his personal emissary (William J. Donovan) to prevent Bulgaria from joining the German side, but to no avail.[15] On February 2, 1941, Germany signed a military treaty with Bulgaria that authorized the transit of German troops across Bulgarian territory. The two parties subsequently signed a further agreement on Bulgaria's posture in the event of a German conflict with Greece and Turkey: in neither case did the Bulgarian army bear an obligation to conduct offensive operations. Turkey, concluding that it could no longer count on timely, effective assistance from England and also fearing that it might be drawn into a Balkan conflict, signed a nonaggression treaty with Bulgaria on February 17, 1941. This effectively served German interests.

All these events were profoundly unsettling for Stalin. By allowing Bulgaria formally to join the Berlin Pact on March 1, Germany had flagrantly violated Soviet admonitions about its vital interest in this question: The Germans had not only ignored Soviet counterproposals for joining the Berlin Pact, but also had now openly violated its interests. A further irritant was the behavior of Bulgaria, which had spurned Soviet offers of mutual assistance even as it agreed to become Germany's ally.[16] When German troops crossed into Bulgarian territory on March 2, it provoked different responses from the general population in Bulgaria. The American emissary in Sofia, Earl, sent the following report to Washington:

> Peasants and workers met the appearance of German troops with gloomy indignation, especially since that means bringing the war closer to them. This indignation undoubtedly is increased because of Russia's condemnation of Bulgaria's actions. With the exception of a certain group of high-ranking army officers, the upper class in Bulgaria also regrets this turn of events, but believes that this is the lesser of two evils—domination by Germany instead of the Soviet Union.[17]

For its part, the Soviet Union could do nothing more than to publish an official condemnation of Germany.[18]

On the Straits question, the Soviet Union continued to seek agreement with Italy. After a rather long period of tension (including the recall of ambassadors), in the fall of 1940 relations did begin to improve. In February 1941 Molotov held a rather lengthy conversation with the Italian ambassador (Augusto Rosso) and tried to determine how Italy would react if Turkey entered the war on England's side and whether Italy understood the Soviet Union's interest in the Straits (i.e., its importance for security in the Black Sea).[19] One should recall that Hitler had carefully concealed from Mussolini his own plans for war on the USSR. Less than two weeks after signing the directives for "Barbarossa," Hitler assured Mussolini that, so long as Stalin ruled, Russia would do nothing to harm German interests or to create a crisis.[20]

The Shift in Hitler's View of the USSR

The mood, however, was quite different among those in Hitler's entourage, and the German dictator began to discuss the Soviet Union ever more frequently with his experts. In late January Hitler interrogated Schnurre about Soviet foreign policy and showed particular interest in the problem of the nickel company Petsamo.[21] Schulenburg, who had made a determined but futile attempt to return home to enlighten Berlin on the real state of Soviet-German relations, sensed great danger and complained that "we are still groping in the dark in many things."[22] At the farewell meeting with the Japanese ambassador in Berlin, Hitler emphasized repeatedly that Russia at present was not an adversary and did not represent a threat to either country. But he boasted that the 185 divisions at his disposal were a better guarantee than any treaty.[23]

On March 18 Hitler told the Turkish ambassador (H. R. Gerede) that Germany was interested in preserving Turkey's status as the overseer of the Straits—even to the point of forfeiting "Soviet friendship."[24] Hitler's aggressiveness increased with each day. On March 23 he told the Hungarian foreign minister that "Russia was only waiting to find chaos somewhere in order to establish herself," and added that "it was not possible, moreover, to live at peace for a thousand years with the gigantic, Bolshevist empire."[25] The Supreme Military Command held meetings to fix details on the campaign against Russia. On February 22 a decision was taken to declassify information that Germany had stationed 680,000 soldiers in Romania.[26] During this same period, Göring held talks with Antonescu in Vienna and expressed his concern that Germany continue to receive petroleum from both its suppliers, Romania and the Soviet Union. He also revealed his goal of increasing the production of Romanian oil from five to six million tons. As the man principally responsible for the war economy, Göring had good reason for concern if the Soviet supplies should suddenly be cut off. He also hinted strongly that this indeed could happen if the Soviet Union drew closer to England or if Germany and the USSR came into conflict over Bulgaria or Finland.[27]

The mounting tensions between Berlin and Moscow first became apparent in trivial matters. Typical was the Soviet Union's refusal to permit the conversion of German missions in Kaunas, Riga, and Tallin into general consulates.[28] More significant was the sharp reduction in Soviet deliveries of grain and raw materials in February.[29] Schnurre attributed this performance directly to the cooling in Soviet-German political relations. However, it must be noted that Germany itself had fulfilled *its* obligations only during the first year of the Economic Agreement.[30] In March, however, the USSR again increased deliveries, probably because—in the wake of its diplomatic defeat in Bulgaria—it feared making relations even worse. It was indeed at this time that the wife of the American ambassador in Moscow, L. A. Steinhardt, tearfully implored Schulenburg to tell her the truth: will there be war between Germany and the Soviet

Union?[31] Germany's Supreme Military Command, significantly, insisted that the Soviet delegation to the commission on the demarcation of the German-Soviet borders be recalled before March 25, for at that point it had already made plans to commence the concentration of army divisions along the Soviet border.[32]

As a significant index of the tension, every turn in Soviet-German relations immediately generated rumors in the German public. In late February 1941, the security service reported talk of "secret" negotiations between Russia and the United States regarding the return of territories that had belonged to Russia before 1914. It was allegedly because of these Russian demands that Germany had begun to concentrate huge numbers of military forces along the Soviet border.[33] Rumors ascribed a pro-German stance to Molotov, but concluded he was no longer strong enough to resist the Germanophobia of the Soviet government and general populace.[34] Popular imagination knew no bounds; it conjured fantastic dramas of a confrontation between the government and Molotov, who purportedly was too friendly toward Germany and who attempted to resist the Jewish influence around Stalin.[35] Many German newspapers—in Neustadt, Augsburg, Salzburg, Allenstein, Schwerin, and Dessau—interpreted the silence in the Soviet press over such issues as the Balkans, entry of German troops into Bulgaria, and the announcement of Lend-lease as a sign of serious tensions in German-Soviet relations.[36] Simultaneously, Germany was swept by rumors that a significant number of German divisions were on the verge of being sent to the Soviet border.[37]

Nevertheless, relations between the two countries were not uniformly gloomy. Schnurre reported that the transshipment of raw materials through the USSR was on schedule. Indeed, at Germany's request, the USSR agreed to provide a special train to ship rubber from Manchuria.[38] Soviet deliveries to Germany continued, augmented by a new Japanese connection, which brought additional strategic materials to Vladivosotok for transshipment to Germany. The Japanese also improved the southern Manchurian railway system, which linked directly to the Soviet Union's Siberian railroad and increased the supply of such products as soy beans.[39] At the same time, Germany preferred not to apprise Japan of its plan to attack the USSR until the very last moment. A directive from the German high command on March 5, 1941 left no ambiguity: "No hint of the Barbarossa Operation must be given to the Japanese."[40]

Notwithstanding that the USSR scrupulously met its obligation to supply raw materials to Germany, public opinion in the latter nevertheless tended to believe rumors to the contrary. Although not documentable, such rumors were probably the deliberate result of official disinformation, which was intended to prepare the populace psychologically for war with the Soviet Union. At the end of March the security services reported rumors that the USSR had stationed in Ukraine a force of 600,000 volunteers, comprised of men released from labor camps. This army's goal was to create, on the territory of the "general-governorship," a Soviet Polish republic as part of the USSR.[41] Quite naturally, Germans—especially those in East Prussia—felt a growing hatred and fear for the Soviet Union. By early April, especially after the events in Yugoslavia (described below), people began to say that conflict with the USSR was inevitable, perhaps by early summer.[42] At the same time, the German public impatiently awaited the long-promised end to the war with England and continued to speculate about the probable date for an invasion of the British Isles.

Mantsuoka in Moscow

From late 1939, for the first time in many years, the Soviet Union saw a chance for a significant, even if temporary, improvement in its relations with Japan. As noted above, the nonaggression pact of August 1939 obliged Germany to assist in this process. The Soviet-Japanese battle of Khalkhin-Gol in 1939 showed that a policy based on raw force simply did not work in dealing with the Soviet Union. Moreover, inside Japan itself, a group favoring expansion to the south had gained in influence; their goal was to seize Southeast Asian colonies belonging to European powers, not Russia. Japan set its sights on Singapore, the key strategic point of the British empire in the Indian Ocean, and did not exclude the possibility of war with the United States.

Japan's reaction to the Soviet-Finnish war did not go beyond anti-Soviet statements in the press. A number of Japanese industrialists and financiers interested in economic ties with the USSR (especially those connected with the fishing industry) put pressure on the government to improve relations with the USSR and to sign a new fishing convention to replace the one that had expired in 1939. The press published articles, moreover, expressing support for a nonaggression pact. Such was the situation prior to the German triumph in the West and the final collapse of France. These events only strengthened the Japanese faction demanding expansion southward and weakened their opponents, who demanded that priority be given to aggression against the USSR. Germany, naturally, very much preferred the "southern-expansion" faction, because this would directly attack the British Empire and distract American attention toward the Pacific Ocean. By June 1940 Japan and the USSR had resolved the question of the border between the Manchurian government and the Mongolian People's Republic. A month later the Japanese ambassador in Moscow, Togo, transmitted a proposal for a Soviet-Japanese neutrality treaty for a five-year period. It was based on the Soviet-Japanese convention on basic principles of mutual relations signed on January 20, 1925. Because of the resignation of the Japanese cabinet, however, talks were broken off in July 1940, and Togo was recalled to Tokyo. The new ambassador, Tatekawa, was instructed to prepare the ground for an improvement in relations with the USSR. A new period of temporary rapprochement followed. On February 3, 1941, a joint session of the Japanese government and military circles endorsed the "Principles of Conducting Negotiations with Japan, Italy and the Soviet Union." On March 12 the Japanese foreign minister, Yosuke Matsuoka, left for Europe. During a short stop in Moscow, he offered to sign a nonaggression pact, but found that the USSR wanted more—namely, a neutrality agreement in the event of hostilities with Germany.

This turn in Soviet-Japanese relations certainly created a dilemma for Berlin. On the one hand, because Germany was preparing to launch an attack on the USSR, it was extremely tempting to encourage a Japanese attack from the east. On the other hand, Germany also desired Japanese help to deliver the *coup de grâce* to England and to paralyze American assistance to the British Isles. In the end Berlin gave the second option higher priority. In negotiations with Matsuoka in early April, Hitler and Ribbentrop precisely formulated Germany's final objective with respect to Great Britain. "In any circumstances British hegemony would be destroyed, British influence would be excluded from Europe, and any attempt at American interference in Europe would be beaten back."[43] The objective was obviously then to destroy the British world empire. Ribbentrop declared that peace was possible only if the British replaced the present government and capitulated.[44] Matsuoka summed it up succinctly: there can be no peace based on compromise.[45]

Matsuoka informed his German allies that on the return trip to Japan he would stop in Moscow and sign either a nonaggression or neutrality treaty. At the same time, he received certain assurances that the question of the Soviet Union joining the Berlin Pact was no longer under consideration: the Soviet terms were unacceptable. Berlin explained in unequivocal terms that the honeymoon in Soviet-German relations was over. If, however, Russia should assume a hostile position toward Germany, then "the Führer will crush it."[46]

Hitler had his own views on how Soviet-German relations had developed in recent years. From October 1939 to March 1940, he held, Germany was "more or less defenseless" against the "extortion" of Russia. And Stalin had understood that fully. Although Germany still displayed civility toward Russia in the summer of 1940, the situation had changed radically. Hitler believed that the change occurred because he refused to sacrifice Finland and Bulgaria, because Berlin declined to collaborate on the Dardanelles question, and finally because Germany had given a guarantee to Romania. Stalin had attempted to counter this policy with a guarantee for Turkey in the event she were attacked by a third party. Hitler regarded the latter as an "absolute lie," since, if such a situation were to appear, Russia would exploit it to annex part of Turkish territory. Hitler interpreted Stalin's policy as a mere continuation of Russia's old tactic: encourage other states to become embroiled in military conflicts in which Russia itself had no direct interest, and see to it that the war dragged on as long as possible.[47]

At this point, Hitler came remarkably close to divining Stalin's tactics, although, as events later showed, he underestimated the potential strength of the Stalinist regime and the intellectual reserves of Stalin himself. The role of Japan in the world war was clearly set in a directive of the Supreme Military Command on March 5, 1941—two weeks prior to Matsuoka's visit to Berlin. It declared that "the *aim* of the cooperation initiated by the Tripartite Pact must be to bring Japan into active operations in the Far East as soon as possible," obviously against British colonies.[48] At the same time, as Germany waged war against the USSR, this would free Japanese forces now tied down on the borders of Mongolia and the USSR. Nevertheless, both Hitler and Ribbentrop made remarks intended to dissuade the Japanese from signing any kind of political agreement in Moscow. The German foreign min‑ ister attempted to persuade his Japanese guest that, as his country undertook to expand southward, it need not fear for the security of its rear: "If Russia ever attacks Japan, Germany shall strike back immediately."[49] Consequently, Japan's security would be vouch‑ safed by Germany; there was no need for Japan to become overly embroiled in its ties with Russia.[50] Matsuoka responded with an understanding nod, but asked for assistance in outfitting Japanese submarines. He also promised to support a plan to attack Singa‑ pore, although he had no such intention, for he had just received instructions from Tokyo to avoid making any major military com‑ mitments—of precisely that sort.

On April 8 Matsuoka arrived again in Moscow. After rather lengthy debates, the two parties signed an agreement on neutrality for a five-year period.[51] Stalin assured the Japanese minister that he was a devoted supporter of the Axis Powers and inveterate enemy of England and America.[52] According to Stalin, Russia did not join the Berlin Pact because its participants had not asked Russia to col‑ laborate. The Soviet leader added, however, that if necessary Rus‑ sia was prepared for broad cooperation with the members of the pact. That statement was most certainly intended for German ears, and the Japanese ambassador obligingly passed it on. Matsuoka assumed that the neutrality pact was dictated by Russia's fear of Germany.[53] Hitler also took an interest in the Russian's opinion about the pact with Japan. When he learned from Schulenburg that the Russians were quite satisfied with the agreement (despite certain concessions on their part), Hitler did not visibly react.[54] On several occasions Matsuoka reassured the Germans that, in the event of a German-Soviet conflict, Japan would naturally support Germany and ignore the neutrality treaty with the Soviet Union.[55] The Japanese naval attaché in Moscow repeated the same thing to his German counterpart.[56]

Those pious and disingenuous reassurances, of course, proved to be of no consequence. The treaty, indeed, alleviated the plight of the Soviet Union, especially during the first two years of the Ger‑ man-Soviet war, as Japan scrupulously observed neutrality. That did not, naturally, prevent the Soviet Union from renouncing the pact in April 1945 and later, on August 9 (after the Americans had dropped atomic bombs on Hiroshima and Nagasaki), from declaring war on Japan.

Yugoslavia

The Italian attack on Greece miscarried, which generated various complications throughout the Balkans. Therefore, in February 1941 Hitler resolved to place all the Balkan states under the German sphere of influence. His new plan obviously left no place whatsoever for a Soviet role in the Balkans. As noted earlier, Germany officially announced that it had 680,000 combat-ready troops stationed in Romania (with a high proportion as tank units), doubtlessly intended to intimidate Stalin and dissuade him from any brash steps.[57]

Germany formally observed its obligations under the nonaggression pact by forewarning the Soviet Union that Bulgaria was about to join the Berlin Pact,[58] and on March 1 sent a message that it had sent German troops to Bulgaria to parry an English threat from Greek territory. Molotov continued to insist that Bulgaria belonged to the Soviet security sphere of the Soviet Union.[59] He warned that Germany could not count on Soviet support in this matter.[60] But there was still another dimension: the Soviet Union wished to convince Germany that it had no intention of intervening in the Greek question. Thus a circular from the foreign affairs commissariat to Soviet diplomatic missions abroad emphasized that the German actions against Greece were needed to put pressure on the English colonies, to threaten the Suez Canal and to deal a blow to the supply lines to English troops in Africa. As for Yugoslavia and Turkey (not yet members of the Berlin Pact), the Soviet Union supported their neutrality and even felt sympathy for the struggle of the Greek people against the German invasion. But the sympathy did not alter policy: "We are not thinking of jeopardizing the German-Soviet treaty, which is necessary for the achievement of the most urgent goal, namely, the destruction of the English Empire."[61]

The Germans intercepted this circular, but one might well surmise that Moscow was not averse to letting it fall into German hands. After all, it suggested that the USSR and Germany could cooperate when it concerned their common goal—destruction of the British Empire—but that the USSR also expected Germany to respect its interests. The circular also clearly reflected the Soviet

counterproposals following Molotov's visit to Berlin in November
1940. But, in practical terms, the Soviet Union was powerless to
block German policy in the Balkans.

German policy in the Balkans also elicited countermeasures by
the English. Specifically, in the fall and winter of 1940–1941, England attempted to mobilize Turkey, Yugoslavia, and Greece to gener-
ate opposition to German policy and military force. The attempt
came to naught, however—notwithstanding the intense pressure put
on Ankara and Belgrade not only by Anthony Eden but also by President Franklin Roosevelt. American diplomacy was quite active at
this time. On March 7, 1941 Churchill's government decided to provide assistance to Greece, whose forces had been successfully conducting war against the Italians since the latter's attack in October
1940. In early March 1940 Churchill hoped that vigorous military
support of Greece would encourage Yugoslavia to attack the Italian
rear in Albania and also that Turkey would support England. The
British prime minister tried to convince Roosevelt that the coordinated actions of American and English ambassadors in Turkey, Russia, and Yugoslavia could prove decisive.[62] Churchill erred: Turkey
had no intention of abandoning its fence-sitting policy.

As for Yugoslavia, events were unfolding so rapidly that German
intervention became inevitable. That country had joined the Berlin
Pact on March 25, but the *coup d'état* in Belgrade (with the participation of anti-German elements) threatened to undo that alliance.
The Soviet Union, after calculating the further flow of events, concluded a friendship treaty with Belgrade on April 5, although this
agreement in fact carried no real obligations on Russia's part.[63] Germany attacked Yugoslavia the following day. As Hitler wrote to
Mussolini on April 5, he took this decision in order to offset the dispatch of English armed forces to Greece and to avert a Soviet treaty
with Yugoslavia (of which he had already received warnings from
Moscow).[64] Berlin instructed Ambassador Schulenberg in Moscow
to inform Molotov about the decision to initiate military action
against Greece and Yugoslavia. He was also to reiterate that Germany had absolutely no political or territorial interests in this
region and that its forces would be withdrawn once its objectives
there had been achieved.[65] No mention was made of the just-con-
cluded Soviet-Yugoslav treaty.

Molotov made no mention of the treaty when, in response to the
ambassador's communication, he called the expansion of the war

"extremely deplorable."[66] Nor did Weizsäcker and ambassador Dekanozov allude to the hapless treaty in their discussions two days later, although the ambassador did take a keen interest in military actions in Yugoslavia.[67]

Stalin's decision to sign a treaty with Yugoslavia came as a suprise to Hitler. In a meeting with his ambassador to Moscow in late April, he bluntly inquired "what kind of devil had possessed the Russians to conclude the Friendship Pact with Yugoslavia?" Schulenburg offered the view that the treaty represented a weird kind of declaration by Russia of its interests in the Balkans, although not specifically in Yugoslavia. Hitler, however, saw the pact as a crude attempt to intimidate Berlin.[68] Military and political circles in Berlin offered a range of radically different explanations for Soviet policy—to preserve peace, to emphasize Russian interests in the Balkans, and to encourage Yugoslavia so strongly (by concluding such an agreement) that war became inevitable.[69] In the view of Germany's temporary military attaché in Moscow (Colonel G. Krebs), the main goal of the pact was to disperse German strength in the Balkans, to provoke the involvement of other states in the Balkan war, and to leave only the Soviet Union outside the conflict. To support that thesis, he noted that the Soviet Union had not put its forces on alert—as indeed it should have, if it had any intention of supporting Yugoslavia or opposing Germany.

As for Turkey, Hitler used his meetings with its ambassador to reveal Moscow's demands with respect to the Straits—demands that Berlin had summarily rejected.[70] Hitler's disclosures, as he surely expected, had a staggering effect on the Turkish government, which hereafter would nourish hatred and distrust toward the Soviet Union. Indeed, whatever Stalin's objectives, he suffered a complete fiasco in the Balkans: Germany obtained its objectives, notwithstanding the failure of its Italian ally. All this became quite clear several days after the German invasion of Yugoslavia.

Stalin attempted to correct the Yugoslavia blunder by publicly reaffirming friendship with Germany. When Matsuoka left Moscow on April 13, Stalin and Molotov unexpectedly appeared on the platform of the Belorussian Railway Station. After wishing the Japanese envoy a good trip, Stalin approached Schulenburg, embraced him, and said: "We must remain friends and you must now do everything to that end."[71] Turning to the temporary military attaché, he said: "We will remain friends with you—in any event!"

The latter replied that he too was "convinced" of this.[72] In diplomatic circles Stalin's behavior—so unlike his usual restrained manner—was interpreted as a deliberate demonstration of friendly relations with the Germans in order to quash rumors of an impending war between Germany and the USSR, which had indeed proliferated in the wake of the Yugoslav events.[73] After quickly attempting to make up for his blunder, Stalin only revealed his profound fear of German military might.

A Soviet Attempt to Appease Hitler

A clear indication of Stalin's desire to improve Soviet-German relations was the unqualified approval given to German proposals at the commission for the demarcation of their border between Igorka and the Baltic Sea.[74] Moscow also affirmed its readiness to fulfill its obligations with respect to the delivery of goods to Germany, notwithstanding the latter's failure to meet its obligations. In April the USSR shipped Germany 208,000 tons of grain, 90,000 tons of oil, and 6,340 tons of nonferrous metals.[75] Schnurre believed that Germany could demand even more. To be sure, the deputy commissar for foreign trade (Krutikov) complained to Schnurre that the German side was not providing a sufficient supply of freight cars for its own deliveries to the Soviet Union.[76] The Germans, as earlier, continued to lag in fulfilling their commitments, especially in delivering machinery and military aircraft. But the construction of the cruiser "L" in Lenigrad proceeded according to plan, with some seventy German engineers and technicians working under the supervision of Admiral Feige.

Schnurre drew attention to the fact that one result of the rumors about an inevitable Soviet-German conflict was mounting concern in German industrial circles, which were increasingly inclined not to fulfill Soviet orders. In some cases, German firms refused to send the technical personnel to Moscow to accompany the deliveries, even though the agreements had specifically stipulated that they would do so. Schnurre assumed that the negotiations scheduled for late May or early June to achieve parity in trade would make sense only if the German side advanced new, specific conditions. Otherwise, it was better to defer the talks.[77] The point of Schnurre's comment was clear: the further development of Soviet-German economic relations would depend on a political decision about launching war on Russia.

At about this time, Moscow took still further measures to propiti-ate Germany. This included steps to improve relations with Berlin's ally, Finland. Specifically, it shut down the anti-fascist radio pro-grams from Petrozavodsk, replaced the Soviet ambassador in Helsinki, and achieved a certain improvement in Soviet-Finnish relations. The objective was to remove one possible cause of dispute with Germany.[78]

Finally, Stalin sent a letter directly to Hitler. This fact first be-came known from the memoirs of the Soviet writer, Konstantin Simonov, who learned of it from Marshal Georgii Zhukov.[79] This letter has still not been precisely dated, although Volkogonov has attributed it to spring, 1941.[80] The letter referred to the concentra-tion of troops in Poland, which gave the distinct impression of plans to launch an attack on the USSR. Hitler's reply, which was also per-sonal and confidential, asserted that the troop concentration was dictated by the need to secure them from attacks by the Royal Air Force coming from the west. He also reaffirmed the validity of the Soviet-German nonaggression pact, giving an oath "on his honor as the head of state." Zhukov added: "So far as I understand, Stalin believed this letter." This episode shows that Stalin and Hitler had a top-secret correspondence, which—except for the exchange of let-ters in 1939—has remained unpublished. One has to wonder why.

During the May Day parade in 1941, standing alongside Stalin on the platform atop the Lenin Mausoleum was the Soviet ambas-sador in Berlin, V. G. Dekanozov. The purpose was to underscore the importance of Soviet-German cooperation. It bears noting that all these episodes transpired within a two-week period and reveal the clear logic to Stalin's behavior: he wanted not only to remove any possible pretext for a German-Soviet conflict but also to demonstrate before the entire world the firm ties between the two countries.

It bears noting that, in April and early May of 1941, no one sug-gested the possibility of war at *Soviet* initiative. If conflict were to break out, all assumed that it would come from the west.

Let us first consider the views of Ambassador Schulenburg. According to Gustav Hilger (who for many years served as an aide at the embassy), Schulenburg prepared a memorandum for Hitler, which analyzed the dangers inherent in an attack on the USSR.[81] Echoes of the Schulenburg memorandum, which was probably sent directly to Ribbentrop, are audible in a note that state-secretary

Weizsäcker also prepared for the foreign minister. The Weizsäcker paper examines possible consequences of war against the USSR and comes to several important conclusions. First, he thought it highly doubtful that war against the USSR would hasten the defeat of England; on the contrary, the appearance of yet another adversary to Germany would only reinforce the British resolve to fight on. Second, even if the Germans took Moscow, they would probably risk dealing with "the well-known passive resistance of Slavs." Insofar as there was no force sufficient to replace the Stalinist system, the Germans would face the prospect that this system would survive in eastern Russia and Siberia and that it would have to renew the war in 1942. Rather than putting a quick end to the war, the result would be a protracted and exhausting conflict. Weizsäcker therefore concluded that "we would be victors over Russia only in a military sense and would, on the other hand, lose in an economic sense."[82]

Hitler received Schulenburg on April 28, the same day that Weizsäcker filed this memorandum. On the table before Hitler lay the memorandum from Moscow. The ensuing discussion seemed to represent two entirely different conceptions. Hitler attempted to extract from Schulenburg's memorandum evidence to sustain a decision that he had already taken—to attack the USSR. Schulenburg held the opposing view and reflected the thinking of conservative, professional diplomats, and politicians, who feared that a military adventure in the East could end in catastrophe. Throughout the meeting Hitler adduced arguments to justify war, and cited an alleged concentration of Soviet troops in the Baltics. Schulenburg replied that this was simply an expression of the well-known tendency of Russia to obtain a 300-percent guarantee for its security. Given Germany's manifest superiority, Schulenburg simply "could not believe that Russia would ever attack Germany." Hitler rejoined that the Yugoslav case showed how unpredictable Soviet policy could be. While conceding that England could not embroil Russia in war with Germany (as had happened in Poland, France, and elsewhere), Hitler emphasized that Soviet ambitions in Finland and the Dardanelles had not changed. Molotov had reaffirmed this during his visit to Berlin, and one had to be careful in dealing with the Soviets. Schulenburg's comment that Stalin was prepared to make new concessions (even to provide Germany with five million tons of grain the following year) made no impression whatsoever on Hitler. The latter waved his hand, saying that the inadequate transport system limited the scale of deliveries from Russia. Schulenburg replied that these difficulties could be overcome if more Russian ports were refitted for this purpose. The entire discussion lasted fifteen minutes. As Schulenburg took his leave, Hitler casually remarked that "I do not intend a war against Russia."[83]

Schulenburg was not deceived: upon his return to Moscow, he told Hilger that the Führer was inclined toward war and had deliberately lied about his intentions.[84] He repeated the same comments to Schmidt.[85] The ambassador now began to ruminate on how to forewarn the Russians of Hitler's plans. All this meant great internal struggle for the ambassador—a patriotic German who firmly believed that war against Russia would mean the destruction of Germany. Schulenburg continued to use every opportunity, in his reports to Berlin, to emphasize the peaceful intentions of the Soviet Union. For example, when he reported on May 6 that Stalin became chairman of the Council of People's Commissars, making him head of state, Schulenburg attributed this appointment to Stalin's desire to correct mistakes in foreign policy that had led to a cooling in Soviet-German relations: "I am convinced that Stalin will use his new position in order to take part personally in the maintenance and development of good relations between the Soviets and Germany."[86]

One can infer here a hint at the possibility of holding direct talks between Hitler and Stalin. A week later Schulenburg again declared that Stalin's main goal was to avert a conflict between the USSR and Germany.[87] In another telegram dated May 5, Schulenburg conveyed the opinion of Vichy's new ambassador in Moscow: it is necessary to seek close, European-wide cooperation, which must include the "great Soviet Union," with all its enormous natural resources.[88]

Nevertheless, Schulenburg did not assume that such reports could change Hitler's mind; he therefore recommended that, in the event of war, the personnel of the Soviet embassy and trade commission in Berlin be treated correctly. In reply he received a friendly admonition from Weizsäcker, who had decided not to show Schulenburg's last letter to Ribbentrop.[89] Reason is the first step to treason, and Schulenburg was proceeding down that path.

Schulenburg, a prisoner of his own conscience, nevertheless took that step. After returning to Moscow, the ambassador shared his impressions and conclusions with colleagues—in all likelihood, with the deliberate intent of having them reach the ears of Soviet intelligence organs. The main point was his confirmation of reports about the concentration of German divisions along the Soviet border. Hitler attributed this dislocation to the provocative action of the Soviet government when it signed the neutrality pact with Yugoslavia. The Turkish ambassador in Moscow also reported about Schulenburg's deep depression during the first days of May—even though the two never even held a conversation. Under-state secretary Woermann warned Schulenburg that rumors were allegedly emanating from him.[90] The ambassador categorically denied such reports,[91] but the fact remains that Hitler's comments about the concentration of German troops appear in a form very closely to those ascribed to Schulenburg.

Schulenburg finally decided on a step unprecedented in contemporary diplomatic practice: to forewarn Soviet officials about the impending attack. In any state such behavior is tantamount to high treason. All this was known previously from Hilger's account, which provided the basis for discussions in the historical literature;[92] the Soviet side until now has been lacking.[93] In 1991 Russian authorities declassified the official Soviet version of a conversation among Schulenburg and Hilger on the German side, with two Soviet officials—Dekanozov and V. P. Pavlov (chief of the section for Central European countries in the comissarat for foreign affairs). The conversation occurred on May 5, 1941, that is, shortly before Stalin became head of state. Both the German and Soviet sources provide roughly the same account of what transpired: Schulenburg clearly warned the Soviet representatives that Hitler had grave doubts about the Soviet Union in the wake of its policy in Yugoslavia and Bulgaria. Hitler had therefore decided to take "precautionary measures"—a clear allusion to the concentration of German forces along the Soviet border—despite Schulenburg's own efforts to change the Führer's mind. Rumors of an impending war between the Soviet Union and Germany were "explosive" and must be immediately quashed. Both Schulenburg and Hilger repeatedly returned to the idea that it was necessary to do something to suppress rumors of an impending war.[94] Dekanozov, however, told the Germans that he would not assume the responsibility of conveying this information to his government, since it bore an unofficial character. In fact, however, Dekanozov told Molotov about Schulenburg's warnings. At a session of the Politburo, which was immediately summoned, Stalin allegedly declared that "we shall consider that disinformation is now being passed on the level of ambassadors."[95] Schulenburg's attempt to warn Stalin had miscarried.

There is no doubt that Stalin decided to become head of state because of foreign policy considerations. It would have been impossible to propose a face-to-face meeting with Hitler if Stalin were merely head of the Bolshevik party. The rising importance of foreign-policy considerations was expressed as well in Stalin's decision to reestablish pre-revolutionary diplomatic ranks, replacing, for example, the Bolshevik neologism "political representative" (*polpred*) with the traditional term for "ambassador" (*posol*). The Soviet Union also closed its diplomatic missions in Belgium, Norway, and Yugoslavia—a sign of acquiescence to German occupation.

At the same time, Stalin made every effort to stimulate the national and patriotic feelings inside the country, emphasizing that "national goals" prevailed over all others. In a speech following the commencement ceremonies of the military academies (May 5),[96] Stalin demanded of the new officers that they improve their combat training and be prepared for war. At the same time, Stalin denied rumors of Soviet troop concentrations along the western border—a statement that might have been intended as a signal to Hitler to consider direct talks at the highest levels. But the speech also showed alarm over the possibility of war. A circular from the commissariat of foreign affairs, intercepted in Harbin by the Germans, claimed that Soviet-German negotiations (!) were proceeding normally, but that, in view of the dictatorial position taken by Germany, it was very important to ascertain the intention of other states should a Soviet-German conflict break out.[97] A later report by Schulenburg, purporting to give an account of Stalin's speech, contained clear distortions.[98] The ambassador interpreted Stalin's words to suggest a willingness to make new concessions to Germany. That judgment certainly accorded with Schulenburg's view, but hardly captured the import of the speech. Indeed, it could more easily have been read as a statement on the possibility of a military action by the Soviet Union.

As in the case of the Stalin-Hitler correspondence, the full text of Stalin's statement on May 5 has still not been published. The document, however, apparently does exist: Dmitrii Volkogonov confirms that Stalin's address was transcribed.[99] The most complete version of the speech thus far published is provided by Volkogonov himself. The speech is interesting in two important respects. The first is Stalin's explanation for the Germans' stunning victories: the German army had carefully prepared for the second world war, had outfitted their soldiers with modern equipment, had prepared politically for war (with allies), and, especially, in contrast to the first world war, had been able to fight on only one front. At the same time, Stalin declared that the German army was not invincible. It had revealed signs of arrogance, stagnation in military thought, and even its military equipment lagged behind that of the USSR. According to Volkogonov, Stalin drew a highly optimistic picture of the Red Army's condition, for he portrayed the rearming of the military—still in progress—as something already accomplished. Based on this assessment, Stalin encouraged the military to think in offensive terms: "The Red Army is a modern army, but a modern army is an offensive army."[100]

The German naval attaché in Moscow assessed military measures that could be taken by the USSR. His analysis presupposed the weakness of the Soviet military: "If the Soviet government deems preparatory measures necessary at present, these can only [be] of an exclusively defensive character."[101]

In contrast to the thinking of his diplomats in Moscow, Hitler was by now primarily preoccupied with creating a credible myth to justify the war. He tested these ideas first on his ally, the Romanian dictator General Ion Antonescu. According to Hitler, Germany had been forced to sign the treaty with Russia in 1939 because the Baltic states and Romania had followed a policy of seeking to remain outside the German sphere of interest. If these states had not joined the anti-German front, Germany would not have been forced to sign the nonaggression pact with Moscow. From the very outset ideological and national differences prevented genuine cooperation. Hitler said nothing about the partition of Poland, which assured German security to the east. Hitler then gave his version of events in the Balkans. In 1940 this area had become the focus of Russian policy, which gave rise to the threat of Soviet domination. Germany's intervention, specifically its guarantee to Romania and stationing of German troops, prevented a Soviet takeover. It was precisely at this point that the USSR came to regard Germany as its enemy. As a consequence, Soviet and British relations became more confidential and trusting. Molotov's attempts in Berlin to obtain Germany's consent to a Soviet guarantee for Bulgaria, to secure special Soviet rights in the Straits, and to portray the Finnish situation

as somehow a security threat to the USSR had all been repulsed by
Hitler. It was clear that Russia would not start a war, but was
attempting to extract the maximum advantage from the existing situation. Hitler concluded that Russia's goal was to concentrate
gigantic forces along its western border and to launch an attack on
Finland and Romania. In practical terms, that was tantamount to
an attack on Germany.

From the foregoing Hitler drew the following conclusions. First,
Stalin would never forgive Germany for spoiling his designs on the
Balkans. Second, the Soviet Union, in concentrating its forces on
the Soviet-German border, wanted to prevent Germany from maxi-
mizing its military might, and that could play a decisive role in the
war. Russia wanted Germany to lose precious time, with the hope of
gaining advantage for itself and England. Third, Stalin regarded
any display of weakness on Germany's part as a historic opportunity
to attack a state that was impeding its westward expansion into
Europe. Stalin was also tying up Japanese forces and thereby pre-
venting Tokyo from using its strength to crush the United States.
Finally, Russia was attempting to encourage England and to convince America that the USSR was its powerful continental ally in
Europe. Moscow's main goal, therefore, was to prevent an end to
the war in 1941. Hitler argued that Stalin first revealed his intentions when he signed the treaty with Yugoslavia. That agreement,
claimed Hitler, included secret provisions to supply Yugoslavia with
weapons and munitions; only Germany's swift action had thwarted
Stalin from realizing his scheme. In short, according to Hitler, Germany's task was to reinforce its eastern front, not only with infantry
and armor but also with a significant part of the Luftwaffe. The concentration of military force on both sides of the border, he said,
could lead to an explosion at any moment.[102]

That assessment did not, however, find corroboration from his
own military personnel in the Soviet Union. In a report to Berlin
on April 22, the military attaché Krebs wrote that, within the last
two weeks, the Soviet Union had begun a systematic (but still
insignificant) expansion of the Red Army by additional mobilization. He concluded that these callups could represent a real danger
only after a rather significant period of time; as yet, there were no
signs in Moscow of a general mobilization.[103] This report contrasted
sharply with those coming from other diplomatic and military
reprresentatives in Moscow, but Krebs nonetheless insisted that "as

before neither a war psychosis nor preparation for a major war is to be discerned."[104] An aide to the military attaché made a long trip between April 18 and May 2 (going from Moscow to Kiev, Odessa, Yalta, Novorossisk, Tuapse, Sochi, and back), but reported that everywhere he found complete tranquillity and not the slightest evidence of preparations for war. He had noticed only two military trains with unidentified materials near Kiev and also some groups of new recruits and reservists. There was no sign whatever of alarm among the civilian population: "Everywhere there reigned a picture of absolute peace and the greatest calm."[105]

Nevertheless, the diplomatic corps in Moscow sensed the coming conflict. Rumors of an impending Soviet-German war had been circulating among diplomats in Moscow ever since August 1940. Such speculation abated in the fall and early winter, but returned with new intensity in February 1941, constantly gaining in force thereafter. In early March the wife of the American ambassador, Steinhardt, expressed his intent to leave Moscow before war broke out. England's ambassador, who had earlier predicted an outbreak of war in September 1941, now revised his view and even gave a precise date: June 22, 1941.[106]

When Köstring, who had been ill, recovered and returned to Moscow, he demanded that wives of embassy personnel be forbidden to engage in panic buying and to export valuables from the USSR. The alarmed and irritated general asserted that it was precisely these actions that were fuelling rumors of imminent conflict. He therefore demanded that every employee at the embassy be held responsible for the conduct of their wives.[107] Such panic had no basis: "I agree fully with Krebs that there are no signs of an offensive intention on the part of the Soviet Union."[108] In his next weekly report from Moscow, Köstring also found no signs of war preparation by the USSR; the only thing to report was small groups of new recruits and reserves being sent for military training. In Köstring's opinion, if the Soviet Union were making large-scale war preparations, that would have been evident in the transportation system. He concluded that the mobilization measures corresponded only to a level of defense needed in the case of an aggressive attack from without. He added as well a hint that the Russians still hoped to resolve their differences with Germany through peaceful means.[109] A Slovak emissary in Moscow reported that Stalin was ready to satisfy German demands and to deliver the goods needed to maintain the German war economy, but would not consent to putting the Soviet Union under German domination.[110] Four days before the German invasion, Köstring reaffirmed that the country was still calm.[111]

Soviet Leadership and the War

Shortly after the peace treaty with Finland had been signed, the Central Committee held a plenary session, followed by similar sessions at the republican and oblast' (provincial) levels. The goal was to encourage communists and, through them, the general population, to believe that Soviet foreign policy was correct; it sought to acquire and sovietize new territories with a minimal expenditure in human and material resources. This was no easy task; notwithstanding the falsifications in official reports about the number of deaths and casualties, there were nonetheless many grieving families. At the time Moscow still hoped to receive compensation for Finland through a protracted war of attrition that Stalin expected to unfold between the Anglo-French coalition and Germany.

On March 15, 1940 (i.e., immediately after the end of the Soviet-Finnish War), the first secretary of the Moscow Oblast' party committee, Aleksandr Shcherbakov,[112] stated that "the Soviet Union has moved its border to the west, and the capitalist world has had to draw more closely together."[113] His words were echoed by another speaker at the same conference, the deputy chairman of the Party Control Commission, Matvei Shkiriatov.[114] To prove his claim that the Soviet banner had risen still higher, he noted that in a "short time" western Belorussia and western Ukraine had been "annexed," and that "the Red Army had really repulsed the international bourgeoisie on the Karelian peninsula."[115] In general, Soviet propaganda depicted the Soviet Union as a defensive power—which accords with Bolshevik doctrine but was, of course, contrary to the real causes of the Soviet-Finnish war of 1939–1940.

Germany's unexpectedly swift victory in the west by the spring of 1940, however, forced Stalin to reconsider what the future might bring. Before the Soviet leader loomed the prospect of remaining a noncombatant, vaguely allied to Germany, which in turn would allow the USSR to absorb territories consigned to its sphere—the Baltics and Bessarabia—and then advance on the Balkans and toward the Straits. In speeches to the party members in Leningrad (but not intended for publication), the local party chieftain, A. A. Zhdanov, candidly summarized Soviet aims amidst the general European war. *In nuce* the war offered a singular opportunity to expand the Soviet Union: "The policy of a socialist government consists of using the contradictions among imperialists, in this particular case, the military contradictions, to extend the position of socialism whenever the opportunity presents itself."[116] It would be wise to remember such candid statements when considering the problem of the German attack on the USSR. In November 1940, Zhdanov had the following to say on the subject of Soviet expansion (again in a secret speech to a closed audience):

> Comrade Stalin recommends that we know the hiding places of the international political mechanism, that we study so that we will not be louts in this respect, as Comrade Stalin puts it. . . . The role of the Bear [i.e., Russia] is to make the rounds of the forest and to demand payment for each tree as the woodcutter chops the wood. This is the sort of position that we intend to pursue henceforth. [Lively animation in the hall, thunderous ovation, laughter]. . . . We have followed this practice during the last year and, as you know, it has resulted in the expansion of the socialist territories of the Soviet Union. . . . It is clear to all of you along which lines things should progress. [Laughter][117]

Zhdanov, chairman of the Foreign Policy Committee of the Supreme Soviet, was brutally frank and unabashedly cynical in speaking to people of his own kind:

> Ours is an unusual neutrality: without fighting, we obtain some territory. [Laughter in the hall]. Strength is necessary to maintain this neutrality. . . . We should be sufficiently strong to defend the position of socialism, both diplomatically and militarily.

He then called upon his listeners "to lose not a day, not an hour in perfecting military technology, military organization, while taking into account the experience of the contemporary offensive, with all its methods and means of attack."[118] The transcript excised this part of Zhdanov's speech. Nevertheless, Zhdanov spoke exclusively of offensive actions, without a single word about defense strategy. Finally, Zhdanov's draft notes on the nonaggression pact contain curious notations about "tigers and their masters." The tigers' masters have unleashed them on the east; the beasts must be redirected back to the English, wrote Zhdanov. Less metaphorically, Zhdanov

declared that England was the principal enemy of peace and collective security, that the *Drang nach Osten* was an English fabrication.

But Zhdanov was hardly the only member of the Politburo to
underestimate the import of Nazi ideology or Hitler's vision of the
future world order. After perusing the Russian translation of *Mein
Kampf*, M. I. Kalinin[119] wrote that this book is "a valuable discov-
ery" for what he called "finance capital."[120] Whatever the merits of
this Marxist cliché, he missed the main point: Hitler's tome was a
program for the conquest of *Lebensraum* in the east. As noted earlier,
Stalin himself had toyed with the idea of closing the gap between
Communists and Nazis.

Zhdanov's comments are striking: they completely disregard the
possibility that Germany might be the potential adversary. Even
from a Marxist perspective, however, that foe might well have been
Germany. Nevertheless, until early 1941, Soviet leaders continued
to believe that England was the more likely foe . Only when Hitler
spurned the Soviet preconditions for joining the Berlin Pact and
extended German dominance to the Balkans did Moscow finally
realize the true state of affairs. That impelled Stalin to become head
of state and to make his ambivalent speech at the graduation ceremonies of the military academies on May 5, 1941. The signal was
given as well for members of the Politburo.

Soviet archival documents show the following. On May 20, 1941,
one month before the German attack, the Chairman of the Presidium
of the Supreme Soviet, Kalinin, gave a report on the international situation at a Party and Komsomol meeting of staff from the Presidium
of the Supreme Soviet. He candidly admitted that the nonaggression
pact had yielded important and immediate benefits to the USSR, yet
"was unexpected for many" and "seemed to contradict in principle
our line." But Kalinin demurred on explaining this contradiction,
saying only that the "material side" to the arrangement was well
known.[121] That last statement was a blatant lie: the secret codicils
were unknown not only to the general population but even to most
members of the Central Committee and top ranks of the government.
Kalinin's reference to Germany as an "enemy," however, was not an
indication of a shift of thinking in the Kremlin. He still directed his
greatest indignation at England and France—ironically, because they
were fighting so badly! "Their inactivity," he complained, "borders on
the criminal." He added that, "if the same thing were happening here,
it would be judged a criminal unpreparedness for war."[122]

Why indeed was Kalinin so vituperative toward England and France? Only a year earlier Moscow had supported Hitler's "peaceful initiative" and denounced his victims as "warmongers." The answer was Moscow's frustration: its strategy of reciprocal exhaustion of warring capitalist countries had failed, for it had presupposed equality of forces and therefore a long, enervating war. The analysis, based on Lenin's ideas as well as the experience of World War I, proved false. Hence Kalinin was driven to admit that Germany now pursued a war of conquest, and that many Soviet citizens responded positively to news of British success and wished to see Germany's rout.

Still, all this was not the main point of Kalinin's secret speech to an audience of party elites, to whom he sought to explain the strategy and aims of Soviet foreign policy. The fundamental criterion, he declared, was simple: "How can we use this moment to the advantage of Bolshevism?" Communists, in his opinion, must not be too keen on peace, but rather "should be interested above all in the question of what the Communist Party can extract from events that occur only once in fifty years."[123] Real Marxists, lectured Kalinin, must understand that "the fundamental idea of Marxist teaching is to extract the maximum benefit for communism during enormous conflicts within humanity." Communists should favor conflict "if there is a chance of success" and if it affords special advantages and opportunities.

Kalinin, who liked to play the role of the "nice little grandfather of the Soviet state," concluded his speech by saying that "the very best way to understand Marxism is to study military affairs, and it is even better to fight for it with weapons in hand." He admitted that war may bring suffering, but it affords a moment "when it is possible to expand communism" and "to do so with a comparatively small expenditure of means." And even if it requires "a significant effort," then communists cannot "turn away, since they represent the vanguard international brigade."[124] The main thrust of Kalinin's speech was not national defense, but expansion and "the strengthening of communism, which will perhaps be decisive for the entire subsequent historical course of events." Amidst thunderous applause he bluntly declared that "the army should think: the sooner the fight starts, the better."[125]

This speech was hardly an idiosyncratic display of individualism by the "nice little grandfather," but reflected a fundamental shift in

Stalin's political and military thinking. The theses for Kalinin's speech were prepared by F. Kretov, head of Kalinin's secretariat. Among the more striking were:

Thesis No. 9: As a result of Stalinist foreign policy, "we remained outside the war, but at the same time managed to put serious pressure on the capitalist world."[126]

Thesis No. 10: "The capitalist world is full of the greatest abominations, which can be destroyed only by the red-hot steel of a holy revolutionary war."[127]

Thesis No. 11: "It is impossible to imbibe endlessly of peace—this will turn people into banal pacifists."[128]

Thesis No. 14: "Capitalists may plan, but the communist god determines how things will turn out." In this case, the combatants "will most likely devour each other, crush each other in their mutual embrace."[129]

Interestingly, amidst all this rhetoric, one crucial detail was missing: precisely who was to be the adversary in this conflict? Stalin's apparatus may have refrained from such candor for reasons of security, but also because Stalin—even at this late hour—still hoped to strike a deal with Hitler. Given the entire history of his relations with Germany, the last seems still to be a highly probable leitmotif in his thinking.

Was Stalin Preparing a Preemptive Military Strike?

That question has been posed by those seeking to explain Hitler's own attack: was it not, as Hitler claimed, an attempt to forestall a massive Soviet offensive? This interpretation must deal with some awkward data, such as the fact that Hitler had been planning an attack for a long time and had approved Operation Barbarossa on December 18, 1940. Nevertheless, this interpretation has had its proponents. Among the most recent is Victor Suvorov (a pseudonym for V. Rozun, a former officer in the Soviet military intelligence), who has published several articles and a book on the subject.[130] Drawing exclusively upon Russian sources (primarily memoirs), Rozun argues that Stalin "used" Hitler to start war in Europe, his intent being to "break the ice" and to join the fray at the most

advantageous moment. His key point is that Stalin was prepared to
launch a preventive strike against Germany in the early summer of
1941 and had even set the date for the attack.

How tenable is this thesis?

In the second half of 1940 and in early 1941 the commanders of
various military districts were summoned along with their aides to
military headquarters to work on plans for their area. In January
1941 a strategic war game was also conducted in the presence of
Stalin and some members of the Politburo. All this transpired
before February 1941, when Germany began to shift military forces
to the Soviet-German border.[131] But what happened in the following months? Above all, one must note the changes in command at
military headquarters: on March 1 Meretskov was replaced by the
more aggressive Zhukov, who began preparing a new variant of the
operational plans. According to the Soviet historian Dmitrii Volkogonov[132] and the writer Vladimir Karpov,[133] on May 15, 1941—
after it had become obvious that Germany had amassed forces on
the Soviet border—Zhukov proposed to forestall the Germans by
attacking first.[134] This report, to put it mildly, created a sensation in
scholarly circles.

In 1992 a Soviet journal for military history (*Voenno-istoricheskii
zhurnal*) published this and other documents on the Red Army
strategic plans for the conduct of military operations against probable adversaries—against Germany in the west and against Japan in
the east. The first variant, evidently dating from September 18,
1940 and sent to Stalin and Molotov, was prepared by the deputy
chief of operations at the General Staff (Major-General A. Vasilevskii)[135] and signed by the commissar of defense (S. Timoshenko)[136]
and the chief of the General Staff (K. Meretskov).[137] The planners
began with the premise of a two-front war—against both Germany
and Japan. It directed its main force against Germany: 142 infantry
divisions, 7 motorized divisons, 16 tank divisions, 10 cavalry divisons, 15 tank brigades, and 159 air groups (with a total of 6,422
planes). The main thrust of attack was in one of two directions:
toward Lublin-Cracow-Breslau (to sever Germany from the Balkan
states) or toward the north of Brest-Litovsk (to smash the main
forces of the Wehrmacht in eastern Prussia). The final decision was
to depend on the concrete political situation. The plan foresaw the
formation of three fronts—to the northwest, west, and southwest. It
conceded, however, that the Soviet General Staff did not possess

any "documentary information on the operational plans of the likely adversaries in either the west or in the east."[138] Hence this plan represented a routine planning operation and bore a rather general character, as its formal title ("thoughts on . . .") suggests. Significantly, however, it was an offensive plan of attack.

A refined version of this plan was submitted on March 11, 1941. Prepared once again by Vasilevskii, it did not carry the signatures of his superiors (Timoshenko and Zhukov), despite initial plans to have them do so. Its main goal was to design an attack on Germany, while allowing for the possibility of war with Japan.[139] Compared to the earlier version, this plan fundamentally altered the main thrusts of the attack.

Still more concrete is the operational document of May 15, 1941, already noted above. It was written by the same Vasilevskii and addressed to the new chairman of the Council of People's Commissars—i.e., Stalin. However, it was signed by neither Zhukov nor Timoshenko. It is therefore somewhat precarious to call this "Zhukov's document," merely because it was found in Zhukov's personal archive. It proposed a preemptive strike, essentially a preventive campaign designed to shift military operations onto the adversary's home territory. One should bear in mind that that the Soviet Union was already involved in the war, at first together with Germany in the dismemberment of the Polish state, then in the local war against Finland, followed by military operations against the Baltic states, in Moldavia, and in northern Bukovina. All these operations (save that in Bukovina) were based on the secret parts of the nonaggression pact of August 1939. The plan of May 15, 1941 outlined the main offensive for Soviet armed forces in the broad theater of eastern and southeastern Europe, with timetables for their completion. It assigned divisions to smash the main forces of the German army (100 divisions) "desployed to the south of Best-Demblin and to advance by the thirtieth day to the north of Ostolenka, Narew River, Lovich, Lodz, Kreitsburg, Opel'eon, Olomutz. . . ."[140] The plan also described details of other military operations and included a map of the whole theater.

In an interview conducted in 1965 (but only recently published), Vasilevskii explains that, as a rule, the operational plans sent to Stalin were returned without any comment to indicate whether they were approved. However, he notes, "the continuing work on them testified to the fact that they had apparently received approval."[141]

On May 14, 1941 the commander of the Baltic Military District was ordered to prepare, within two weeks, a detailed plan of defense and a plan for antiaircraft defense. When the plan was submitted, it declared its main objectives as the repulsion of enemy troops, control of the air, and determination of the main thrust of the enemy attack.[142] In a preface to the Vasilevskii interview, Colonel-General Gor'kov writes that the May plan was very quickly—within nine days—discussed at a meeting with Stalin. Those present included Molotov, Timoshenko, Zhukov, N. F. Vatutin (Zhukov's first deputy), P. F. Zhigarev (chief of the Main Administration of the Air Force), as well as commanders and officers from the five border military districts.[143] V. N. Kiselev, who recently published this document, also believes that, although there is no formal proof for the plan's approval, the practical measures taken to begin a clandestine mobilization and concentration of reserves do show that the plan had been approved.

Another interpretation is also possible, however. Vasilevskii writes that in May and June of 1941 Timoshenko repeatedly appealed to Stalin to issue an immediate order for general mobilization or, at the very least, the mobilization of those troops intended for concentration along the western borders. According to Vasilevskii, Timoshenko "did not receive the authorization for this."[144] But V. N. Kiselev notes that five armies (from the Trans-Baikal, northern Caucasus, Volga, and Ural military districts) were to be placed, by July 10, along the western Dvina and Dnepr, and another three armies prepared to shift to the impending theater of military operations.[145]

According to documents from the Central Archive of the Ministry of Defense, the western military districts received a supplement of approximately 800,000 men by early June. Thus 32 infantry divisions were to be "moved" and concentrated some 20 to 80 kilometers from the border by July 1. It bears noting that Kiselev's account is very vague as to the identity of these units and whether in fact the plan was being realized. Nevertheless, on the basis of these data as well as a military order (dated June 20) to raise the fighting spirit among the troops, Kiselev comes to this conclusion: although the plan of May 15 was not approved, Stalin had in fact accepted it and had begun to implement it.[146] Stalin thus rejected the requests of his minister of defense, but did not object when Timoshenko used his authority to conscript certain age-groups for training and maneuvers. It would be silly to assume that Timoshenko took this step unless he was acting on the advice of Stalin. In other words, Stalin wanted to implement the plan, but personally to keep his own hands clean.

Still, this does not answer the question whether the troops were being moved to attack the Germans, or to intimidate them, or to demonstrate that the Soviet armed forces were on a high state of alert and battle readiness. After all, it was precisely at this time (June 14) that TASS published the famous communiqué denying rumors of an impending conflict between the USSR and Germany. This official statement was really a peculiar appeal to Hitler to resolve the differences between the two sides through peaceful means. It included this striking passage: "Germany is also, just as consistently as the USSR, observing the terms of the Soviet-German Nonaggression Pact; in view of this, according to Soviet circles, rumors of Germany's intent to sunder the pact and to attack the USSR are utterly groundless."[147] As is well known, the Germans made no response. Vasilevskii says quite clearly that implementation of the mobilization plans was realized too late—these areas of the country had already been overrun by the Wehr-macht.[148]

The main question is whether the Soviet Union planned to initiate a preventive war against Germany, as Hitler claimed and some recent analysts have asserted. Vasilevskii offers the following explanation: "The Communist Party of the Soviet Union reared and prepared our armed forces not only to repulse a sudden attack by the enemy, but also to meet him with powerful blows and broad offensive operations, and then later to destroy totally the armed forces of the aggressor."[149] Thus the offensive strategy was transposed in terms that gave the impression of a response to an enemy's attack. Vasilevskii believes that the catastrophe might have been averted if the main forces of the Red Army had been raised to a state of battle readiness and stationed along the Soviet borders. Those steps, however, carry the strong hint of a preemptive strike.

Nevertheless, all this still had one major barrier to surmount: Stalin himself, for he would have to decide whether to give the go-ahead or not. Among the problems he faced was the risk of a war simultaneously on two fronts—with Japan as well as Germany. Although the neutrality treaty with Japan (April 13, 1941) had significantly improved the strategic position of the USSR, Stalin was deeply concerned about possible allies and, most of all, feared ͬ¹ England would come to terms with Germany. The flight of ͬ Hess, Hitler's deputy in the Nazi party, to Scotland on Mͬ confirmed Stalin's worst suspicions.[150] A further problem was the unfinished state of military preparations—which the war with Finland only too clearly revealed. With all this in mind, Stalin hesitated and found it difficult to assess Germany's precise intentions. He was distrustful not only of reports from his own diplomats and spies but also of all information coming from abroad, regardless of the source, even if it was Winston Churchill.[151]

Stalin, as Molotov's negotiations in Berlin the previous November confirmed, was fully prepared to join an anti-British coalition if Hitler would accept the Soviet terms. But Vasilevskii quite deftly determined the Achilles heel of the Soviet leader: the rebuilding of the country's defense still did not give a direct answer to the main question about the likelihood of a German attack, let alone the probable dates for this.[152] Interestingly, Zhukov—who had made critical comments on his copy of the Vasilevskii interview—did not remonstrate on this key point in the text.[153]

In my judgment, the reluctance to give a direct answer to this question derives from the fact that the Stalinist scenario simply could not comprehend war with Germany. For Stalin it was only natural that the mutual interests of the two greatest continental powers demanded not only the exclusion of England from European affairs but also the liquidation and dismemberment of the British Empire. From this followed the conclusion that a military conflict between Germany and Soviet Russia only played into the hands of the British. From this followed too the skeptical attitude toward warnings from the political leaders in London and Washington, not to mention information coming from intelligence and diplomatic channels. A further reason was Stalin's self-hypnosis about the danger of a two-front war for Germany itself. It was a collosal miscalculation, which ignored the fact that German land forces were free in the west—only the Luftwaffe was still conducting serious operations in the British Isles. Hence, from Hitler's perspective in the spring of 1941, the problem of a two-front war had of course ceased to exist. Indeed, Hitler expected his usual Blitzkrieg, and once he had smashed the Soviet Army, he could refocus on the west and await England's inevitable capitulation.

Direct military conflict with Germany, moreover, would directly contradict the "Stalin doctrine"—i.e., the premise that the Soviet Union should enter the war only when the capitalist powers had fully exhausted themselves. But circumstances had undergone a radical change: one had to decide between war with Germany and an attempt to buy off Hitler, if only temporarily, until the country could be raised to full military preparedness (planned for 1942). Stalin preferred the latter course. Moreover, he probably could not imagine that Hitler would repeat the very same mistake of the first world war; Hitler, so the Kremlin dictator must have thought, had too much common sense and knowledge of the past to commit such a blunder. Stalin's vacillation perhaps also explains why the basic operational plan remained in effect for the first 15 to 20 days of the war, when the main forces were to be mobilized, concentrated, and dislocated. In practice this presumed that Germany would attack first, while the covering forces of border troops would conduct the main defensive battles. This interpretation fully conforms to the real course of events that unfolded between April and June 1941.

The Public and War

Shortly after Stalin replaced Molotov as chairman of the Council of People's Commissars, Germany was again awash with rumors of an alleged "brawl" in the Kremlin—between opponents and supports of Molotov's "pro-German" policy. There were even reports that Molotov and Stalin had murdered each other.[154] The German public also repeated stories about the concentration of their own tank divisions in East Prussia, about the continuing construction of the eastern ramparts, and about a meeting between Hitler and Molotov—which was allegedly to be held in Danzig to resolve differences, much as had been done in 1939.[155] These rumors were closely related to the signing of the Soviet-Japanese neutrality pact, which after all involved a member of the Berlin Pact. A month later the reports of a mutual concentration of forces on the German-Soviet border gave way to reports that the two sides had resolved their differences. According to these rumors, the two sides had signed a new agreement, which included the obligation of the USSR to supply grain for the next 99 years. Similar reports were disseminated by the German press in a number of towns—in Prague, Tori, Tilsit, Schwerin, and Frankfurt-am-Main.[156]

These reports curiously contain a nostalgic, wishful thinking for a long-term period of peace, if only to the east. The establishment of diplomatic relations between the USSR and the pro-fascist government in Iraq also seemed to confirm rumors of cooperation between

the Soviet Union, Germany, and Turkey in the Middle East.[157]
"Things are again going well" with Russia, reported the press and
radio in Dresden, Breslau, Augsburg, Karlsruhe, Köln, Neustetin,
and Danzig.[158] These optimistic rumors persisted for the first part
of June. The report that Moscow had broken relations with the
Greek government in exile was followed by new rumors—that of an
impending visit to Berlin by Stalin to formally sign the Berlin Pact
(a Turkish emissary was also rumored to be on the way to Berlin as
well). It was also reported that German forces were moving across
Ukrainian soil toward Iraq.[159] However, alongside these fantastic
rumors, there were also reports of a different variety, —among them
was an attack on Russia before the end of June.[160]

Moscow in Late Spring

The mood in Moscow was anything but cheerful. Reports of the
concentration of German divisions in eastern Poland, especially
after the conclusion of the Yugoslav campaign, steadily increased.
Among the recently published archival documents, one of the most
interesting is a note from the KGB assessing "security preparedness"
on the eve of the German attack.[161] Although the compilers had
the advantage of hindsight, their data make it absolutely clear: Germany was preparing military operations of a defensive and offensive
character against the USSR. The "defensive" measures included the
construction of fortifications along the Soviet-German border, the
eastern shore of the Baltic Sea, the planting of minefields, and the
expansion of production areas in military plants. But the very same
thing was transpiring on the Soviet side of the border. There was
also information about a redeployment of German divisions from
the west; this included the reassignment of tank divisions to Poland
and the appearance there of new types of bombers.[162] As early as
October 1940 Soviet agents (Germans) in the German economic
ministry and general staff reported that Germany was planning to
attack the USSR early the next year. According to NKVD information from October 1940, Germany had already amassed a third of its
army—85 divisions—against the Soviet Union.[163] Somewhat con-
fusing, however, were the later reports that some of these forces had
been redeployed to Romania, Hungary, and Slovakia. Still, all the
while the Germans continued construction work on antiaircraft stations, transport projects, and airfields.

In February 1941 and especially the following month, Germany stepped up its air reconnaissance and photography over Soviet territory, and the general staff of the Luftwaffe compiled plans for bombing the most important military targets in the USSR. In April Soviet agents in Berlin reported that Germany was conducting a "general preparation" for an attack on the USSR. They first suggested May as the likely date, but after the war against Yugoslavia, pushed this back to June 1941. Then, almost on a daily basis, they warned of an impending German attack. Similar information was also coming from channels in the Red Army. But Stalin remained skeptical of such information. General Golikov, head of military intelligence, took a similar view; even as he transmitted these reports, each time he qualified them by saying that they were exaggerated and possibly planted by the British.

First Strike?

Evidence of the intention to attack first is to be found in a directive on military propaganda and psychological preparation for war, which was discussed at a meeting of the Main Military Council on May 14. The editing of the document was the work of Timoshenko, Zhdanov (the Central Committee secretary overseeing the army), and Zaporozhets (the chief of the Main Administrtation of Political Propaganda). Interestingly, the directive was not confirmed until June 20; the Kremlin obviously did not rush in this matter. Why? I would argue that the reason lies in the fact that, despite the declaration about the need for political propaganda on an "offensive and annihilating war," the army simply was not prepared. Consequently, even if a first strike was under consideration, the Red Army was unable to carry out such an order. Of the many reasons for this, two bear emphasis: (1) Stalin's own low assessment of the Soviet army's readiness for a large-scale war; and, (2) the unclear response of England and Japan to war between the USSR and Germany.

The result was a strange gap between the content of the declaration and actual military policy. The draft of the directive spoke boldly of an "offensive foreign policy" and of "decisively eradicating centers of war on our borders."[164] It is highly likely that Zhdanov participated in compiling, not merely editing, the directive. In his own speech at a meeting of the Main Military Council on June 4, Zhdanov declared that "the wars with Poland and Finland were not

defensive wars."[165] A return to the idea of an offensive was also
implicit in Kalinin's speech the next day at the Miltitary-Political
Academy. Kalinin reiterated his basic thesis that "the most pressing
question now is whether or not we are going to fight."[166] That statement was greeted with laughter by the new corps of freshly trained
political officers: none could have any doubt that the USSR would
soon be entering the "great war."

But one man—Stalin himself—*did* have great doubts. And
for good reason: the Red Army was in no condition to wage war
on the German fighting machine. Of that Stalin had ample, and
alarming, information at his disposal. Among these secret military
documents was an analysis presented by Timoshenko at a military
conference on December 31, 1940—that is, shortly after Molotov's trip to Berlin and still a half year before the German attack.
The minister of defense drew a dismal picture of the military's lack
of preparation:

> The war with the white Finns revealed fully just how pitiful is our
> system of military preparation. . . . Our commanders and staffs did
> not really know how to organize the efforts of various categories of
> the armed forces and to organize close cooperation, but, most impor-
> tantly, they did not really know how to command. . . . The young
> commanders and Red Army soldiers learned to do everything very
> provisionally—to attack, to assault, to force rivers. . . . Military
> preparation to this very day is limping along on both legs.[167]

The army imposed strict discipline, reestablished a single-command
system, and abolished the institution of political commissars. Timoshenko also asserted that, besides an expanding command corps and
strong political and moral condition in the troops, the Red Army
now had a sufficient material base at its disposal. True, his comments do not speak to the quality of that material base.

A second secret document, also compiled by Timoshenko, was
prepared on May 17, 1941—just thirty-five days before the outbreak
of hostilities. Assessing the results of the troops' military training,
he asserted that the objectives set the previous winter for a "significant number of units and branches have not been fulfilled."[168] He
also described the readiness of the Soviet air force as "unsatisfactory."[169] A special check in the Kiev, Western, Baltic, and Odessa
military districts (conducted between May 23 and June 5, 1941)
revealed the unsatisactory level of readiness.[170]

The real condition at the moment of the German attack was evident from a judicial document regarding the annulment of sentences for top military commanders along the Western Front. A month after the attack, on July 22, 1941, the military collegium of the Supreme Court of the USSR passed judgment on General Dmitrii Grigor'evich Pavlov (commander of the Western Front), Major-General Vladimir Efimovich Klimovskii (chief of staff), Major-General Andrei Terent'evich Grigor'ev (head of communications), and Major-General Aleksandr Andreevich Korobkov (commander of the Fourth Army). It found them guilty of permitting disorganization of the country's defense and thereby making it possible for the enemy to smash through a crucial area of the front. It sentenced all four to be shot.

Sixteen years later, the same collegium just as naturally, with a different membership, annuled the verdict of 1941 and posthumously rehabilitated all the guilty. To justify that change it gave the following explanation: "By June 22, 1941, for reasons that did not depend on the condemned, a significant part of the troops of the Western special military district was in a state of reorganization and rearmament." The court noted the low level of military preparedness of the troops, a significant part of which had been recalled from reserve status. It turns out that the Western special military district consisted of a single mechanized corps. One has to wonder how this "army" could possibly have been expected to take the offensive, to force rivers and drive deeply into the enemy camp. The court records also make clear that the communications of this military district were "completely inadequate" and indeed relied chiefly on the civilian communication network. This district did not expect to complete its preparations for war until the end of 1941 or the first half of 1942.[171]

In Timoshenko's speech to the military conference cited above, the minister of defense noted the conditions for offense and cited, inter alia, the "double or triple superiority in forces in the main direction." As the military collegium makes clear, however, on the Western Front it was not the Red Army, but the Wehrmacht that had created "powerful strike forces in the most important sectors, which significantly surpassed the troops of the Western special military district." In other words, the real situation was precisely the opposite of what would have been required to wage an offensive.

Would it really have been possible to change the correlation of forces so as to allow a Soviet offensive on July 6, 1941, as Suvorov asserts? Such an attempt was in fact underway; from early June a general shift of forces from the interior of the country to the western areas had commenced.[172]

But all these measures were not consistently implemented. The situation was like an equestrian who is spurring his horse and, simultaneously pulling back on the reins. The finishing touch was a report from the NKVD chief, Lavrentii Beria,[173] on June 21, 1941, i.e., on the very eve of the German assault: "Lt.-General F. I. Golikov,[174] the head of military intelligence (where the Berzin band[175] recently reigned), complains about his Colonel Novo-branets,[176] who also lies, claiming that Hitler has concentrated 170 divisions against us on our western border. But I and my people, Iosif Vissarionovich, firmly remember your wise instruction: Hitler will not attack us in 1941!"[177]

On the basis of reliable historical materials about a preventive war in the strategy of Hitler and Stalin, what conclusions can be drawn? Hitler began to prepare the military-strategic plan in July 1940, shortly after his triumph in the west and the establishment of German control over a significant part of the European continent. At that time he did not even use the term "preventive war," for he had no need to resort to such justifications. History had seemingly opened before him the prospect of realizing his wild fantasy: the creation of a German Reich from the Atlantic to the Urals, along with the ideological annihilation of Bolshevism. His determination was reinforced after Molotov's visit to Berlin and Stalin's counter-proposals to divide up the world into spheres of influence: there could now be no doubt that the interests of Germany and the USSR had come into direct conflict in the Balkans and in Finland. As is well known, the plan to attack the USSR was finally approved on December 18, 1940; only after this point did Hitler begin to seek arguments to justify his attack on the USSR as intended to avert a sudden attack by the USSR.

For his part, Stalin preferred to exploit the European conflict to expand the territory of the USSR and its interests. His main tactic was to rely on that group of capitalist states which, at any given point, was most interested in the assistance or at least benevolent neutrality of the Soviet Union to allow the realization of its objectives. And in exchange that group would allow the USSR to realize its own plans and would offer Moscow the most tangible compensation. This tactic had indeed already yielded great benefits, with a minimum expenditure of forces on the part of Moscow. In 1939 this partner had been Germany, insofar as it needed a secure rear; Stalin's reward was Poland, the Baltics, and Bessarabia. But on three occasions Stalin had miscalculated—he had been too greedy in Lithuania and Bukovina, exposed the weakness of the Soviet army in the war with Finland, and went too far in the Balkans. All this provided Hitler with a political justification for a preventive war against the USSR, which allegedly was preparing for an attack on Germany.

Stalin had no hesitation about the acceptability of a preventive war. But the concrete situation, political expedience, and inadequate level of preparation proved decisive in determining his behavior. It was only natural for him to avoid war—given an adversary that had abundantly demonstrated its ability to conduct a modern large-scale war, given the uncertain response of London and Washington, and given the danger of an attack by Japan from the rear. But these ideas could also work in reverse and encourage a preventive strike against the German divisions concentrated along the Soviet border. However, as many sources attest, Stalin still thought of another solution—new concessions to buy off Hitler, at least for the time being.

The counsellor of the German embassy in Moscow, Hilger, sums up his impressions of that time: "Everything indicated that he [Stalin] thought that Hitler was preparing for a game of extortion in which threatening military moves would be followed by sudden demands for economic or even territorial concessions. He seems to have believed that he would be able to negotiate with Hitler over such demands when they were presented."[178] Stalin resorted to maneuvering. On the one hand, he began to redeploy troops closer to the border, but on the other demonstrated in various ways his readiness to negotiate with Hitler. But here he miscalculated: the preparations for a preventive strike were not completed, and Hitler ignored Stalin's political soundings.

The enormous might of Germany, the establishment of its domination over an enormous European territory, and the crimes perpetrated by the Nazi regime against humanity promoted the creation of an anti-Hitler coalition. The Soviet Union, which had expanded its borders with Germany's help, then received a further growth with the assistance of the Allies, which endorsed the creation of a Soviet empire at Yalta and Potsdam in 1945.

In assessing Stalin's behavior before the German attack on June 22, 1941, one is particularly struck by his obstinate desire for an alliance with Germany. The key to his position lies in his view that the Nazis were "petit-bourgeois nationalists," quite independent of capitalist traditions and hence conceivable allies.[179] In his public comments he heaped praise on the Soviet-German nonaggression pact, which he described as a turning point in world history and a sign of "friendship strengthened by blood."[180] After the war Stalin was even given to nostalgia, declaring that, "Ekh! Together with the Germans we would have been invincible."[181] In some sense, the idea of a Soviet-German alliance reappeared in the postwar period as an "alliance" between the USSR and the German Democratic Republic. The re-emergence of old attitudes informed his telegram of October 13, 1949 on the occasion of the founding of the GDR, when he declared that Russians and Germans "have the greatest potential for carrying out major actions of world-wide significance."[182]

Hitler's remains were secretly brought to Moscow, so that Stalin could personally see for himself that his adversary was truly dead.

Notes

Introduction

1. The only acceptable foreign authors were those who played by Soviet rules and adjusted their interpretations accordingly.

2. A. M. Nekrich, *1941. 22 iiunia* (Moscow, 1965); translated and published under the curious title, Vladimir Petrov, *Soviet Historians on the German Invasion. 1941, June 22* (Columbia: University of South Carolina Press, 1968).

3. "Postanovlenie TsK KPSS 'O gazete *Pravda*,' " *Pravda*, April 7, 1990.

4. "Iz istorii Velikoi Otechestvennoi Voiny," *Izvestiia TsK KPSS*, 1990, no. 1: 161.

5. Of particular importance were the publications in *Voenno-istoricheskii zhurnal* and the series *Pogranichnye voiska SSSR*.

6. Viktor Suvorov, *Icebreaker: Who Started the Second World War?* (New York: Penguin, 1990).

1. Revanchists and Revolutionaries

1. A leader of the Young Turks, Enver Pasha (1881–1922) frequently changed sides during his brief but stormy political career. He subsequently joined the anti-Bolshevik movement of basmachi in Bukhara (Central Asia); he was killed in a skirmish with the Red Army.

2. Seeckt, a Colonel General, was commander of German land forces from 1920 to 1926. He was also known as a proponent of close ties with Russia and enjoyed considerable political influence in Weimar Germany.

3. *Profile bedeutender Soldaten*, ed. Bundesarchiv and Militärarchiv, vol. 1: *General Ernst Köstring. Der militärische Mittler zwischen dem Deutschen Reich und der Sowjetunion 1921–1941*, ed. Hermann Teske (Frankfurt-am-Main: Verlag E. S. Mittler & Sohn, 1966), p. 41.

4. A. Hencke, "Die deutsch-sowjetischen Beziehungen auf militärischem Gebiet nach dem ersten Weltkrieg" (unpublished manuscript), p. 4; F. L. Carsten, *The Reichswehr and Politics, 1918 to 1933* (Oxford: Clarendon Press, 1966), p. 135.

5. Ibid., p. 67.

6. In a letter to Litvinov, the Soviet representative in Berlin, Viktor Kopp, complained that all the information from Moscow was going to Gukovskii in Revel and that he was being ignored. He testily declared that he had no intention of playing the role of court jester and asked to be recalled from Berlin. (Letter dated June 12, 1920) in Rossiiskii tsentr khraneniia i izucheniia dokumentov noveishei istorii (hereafter RTsKHIDNI), fond (f.) 5, opis' (op.) 1, delo (d.), 2137.

7. Carsten's study, *The Reichswehr and Politics*, describes Kopp's arrival in Berlin in late 1919. Kopp, whom he calls "an old friend and collaborator of Trotsky," attempted to establish contact with German arms manufacturers and induce them to invest funds in Russian enterprises, which in turn would produce military weapons for Germany. Kopp continued these negotiations in spring 1921; his partners in these discussions included firms in aviation (Albatros), submarines (Blom and Boss), and weapons and artillery (Krupp). A Politburo discussion of June 8, 1921—which alludes to Kopp's trip to Germany on a "special matter"—refers to a continuation of this special mission (RTsKhIDNI, f. 17, op. 3, d. 175, protokol 38). Kopp has been undeservedly forgotten in the historical scholarship. Born in 1880, he became the plenipotentiary of Narkomindel (People's Commissariat of Foreign Affairs) in Germany at the age of 39; he later became a member of the foreign ministry's governing board, then the ambassador (in Bolshevik acronym, *polpred*, or "political representative") in Japan (1925–1927) and Sweden (1927–1930). He died in 1930—no doubt, to his good fortune: it is hardly likely that he would have survived the terror of the 1930s. Indeed, a special commission of the Politburo had launched an investigation of denunciations (evidently from the Soviet trade mission in Berlin), alleging that he had followed his own personal advantage in making deals with German firms. Although the commission cleared him of the charges, the Politburo eventually reversed its initial decision to prosecute the author of the denunciation. It also decided to recall Kopp from his post in Germany. For

details, see the minutes of the Politburo meetings of October and November 1922 (No. 33–34) in RTsKhIDNI, f. 17, op. 3, dd. 319–320.

8. Ibid., l. 14. (Kopp to Chicherin, with copies for Lenin and Trotskii. June, 1920. Berlin).

9. Ibid., l. 15.

10. Ibid., l. 15.

11. The main shipping route for weapons from France to Poland lay on land over Switzerland and Austria. Curiously, workers in Danzig initially refused to unload arms for Poland, but finally agreed to do so—partly out of economic self-interest but also because of threats of military intervention by the French and English. On the margin of the document Kopp wrote: "Are the necessary measures taken?!" That elliptical remark may refer to attempts to put pressure on the workers through German communist organizations. Ibid., l. 16.

12. Ibid., l. 39 (Kopp to Chicherin, Sept. 27, 1920, Berlin (with a copy to Lenin).

13. Ibid., l. 29 (Kopp to Chicherin, Nov. 11, 1920, Berlin, with a copy to Lenin).

14. Ibid., l. 30.

15. Kopp evidently was alluding to the congress of the "Independent Social-Democratic Party of Germany" in October 1920, when a majority voted to joint the Comintern. In the ensuing split approximately 300,000 party members joined a reorganized "Communist Party of Germany."

16. Ibid., ll. 52–54 (Kopp to Chicherin, Berlin, Nov. 4, 1920, with a copy for the Politburo).

17. Ibid., l. 37 (Kopp to Chicherin, Berlin, Oct. 16, 1920, with a copy for Lenin).

18. Ibid., l. 38.

19. In a letter to Chicherin dated November 2, 1920, Kopp argued that Russia did not require a mere 50 to 60 million marks, but several times that amount. In that event it would be possible to exert far greater influence on German foreign policy. See ibid., ll. 54–55.

20. Ibid., l. 58 (Kopp to Chicherin, Berlin, December 2, 1920).

21. B. S. Stomoniakov (1882–1941) became the Soviet trade representative in Germany in 1921. In 1924 he was removed from this post amidst the battle around Kopp. A note in Trotskii's archive, dated July 3, 1924, refers to the episode: "Today's resolution on Stomoniakov decides his fate; we are losing a first-class, devoted official—who is better than Kopp." (Trotskii Archive, T-813, T-822). Stomoniakov subsequently held executive positions in the commissarats of foreign trade and foreign affairs. In 1934–1934 he rose to the position of deputy commissar of foreign affairs, but then fell victim to the purges.

22. Leonid Borisovich Krasin (1870–1926), a prominent diplomat and Soviet official, headed the Soviet delegation that concluded the treaty with Germany (in Brest-Litovsk) and the treaty with Estonia (in Pskov and Iur'ev). From 1921 to 1923 he was head of the People's Commissariat of Foreign Trade; he subsequently became the plenipotentiary representing the Soviet Union in Paris and London.

23. For details see the letters from Kopp and Lutovinov in ibid.

24. Hencke, "Die deutsch-sowjetischen Beziehungen," p. 6.

25. See chapter 4 for details.

26. Kopp to Chicherin, Berlin, December 22, 1922 ("absolutely confidential") in RTsKhIDNI, f. 5, op. 1, d. 2137, l. 60.

27. As Trotskii subsequently wrote: "We were completely right to raise the question of principle—can a workers' state conclude an agreement of a military-technical character (say, for example, for the joint production of munitions) with an imperialist state, which has an interest in this (because of the force of circumstances)? If the given workers' state is backward, if it lacks sufficient technical means, if it can strengthen its defensive capabilities through such an agreement, then of course it has every right and duty to make such an agreement. Lenin once posed this question in a debate with Bukharin." Trotskii Archive, T-3037.

28. That is apparent from the unpublished documents of Lenin recently published by the Russian historian, Dmitrii Volkogonov. In a memorandum to V. V. Vorovskii and dated simply "August 1918," Lenin wrote candidly about his deal with the Germans that enabled the Bolsheviks (himself included) to return to Russia in April 1917. Here are Lenin's words: "No one asked the Germans for assistance: we *concluded an agreement* on WHEN and HOW they (the Germans) were to realize their plan to march on Murman and Alekseev. Our interests coincided. We would have to have been idiots not to make use of this." Dmitrii Volkogonov, "Leninskaia krepost' v moei dushe pala poslednei," *Moskovskie novosti*, 1992, no. 29 (July 19).

29. Ebert (1871–1925) became the president in 1919.

30. Wirth (1879–1956) was chancellor in 1921–1922; together with Walter Rathenau he signed the Rapallo treaty with Russia in 1922.

31. Helm Speidel, "Reichswehr und Rote Armee. Vorbemerkungen des Herausgebers," *Vierteljahrshefte für Zeitgeschichte*, 16 (1953): 13.

32. RTsKhIDNI, f. 76, op. 3, d. 317, l. 37.

33. A. Hencke, "Der politische Einfluß des Botschafters Graf Brockdorf-Rantzau auf die Entwicklung der deutsch-sowjetischen Beziehungen. Erinnerungen seines persönlichen Referenten, Andor Hencke" (unpublished manuscript, Auswärtiges Amt, Bonn), p. 10.

34. Interestingly, Brockdorf-Rantzau was even popular in left-wing German circles. Thus when Klara Zetkin, one of the leaders of the German

Communist Party, came to Moscow to visit her son (who was working as a doctor in the Soviet capital), she often visited the "red count," as his colleagues in the German Foreign Ministry dubbed him. The ambassador also enjoyed rather strong confidential relations with G. V. Chicherin, who headed the People's Commissariat for Foreign Affairs until 1930. Ibid., p. 14.

35. RTsKhIDNI, f. 76, op. 3, d. 317, l. 37.

36. The military terms of the Versailles Peace Treaty (signed in Paris on June 8, 1919) forbade Germany to have universal military training, dissolved its general staff, and prohibited military aviation, tanks, and heavy artillery. The country's entire military forces were limited to land forces of 100,000 men.

37. Köstring, *Der militärische Mittler*, p. 47.

38. Quoted in Carsten, *The Reichswehr and Politics*, p. 140.

39. Events, however, took a different direction. But the German and Soviet hostility toward Poland did affect their relations. The situation in Poland became a particular cause of concern after J. Pilsudki's *coup d'état* in May, 1926. A half year later, Voroshilov insisted that the Soviet secret police (OGPU) make every possible effort to gather intelligence on "the processes taking place in Poland." He urged the OGPU to "make every possible sacrifice (especially material)" for this purpose. (Voroshilov to Menzhinskii and Trilisser, November 1927, No. 031/ss, in: RGASA, f. 33987, op. 1, d. 667, l. 80.)

In a conversation with the head of the German general staff (Werner von Blomberg) in November 1928, Voroshilov raised the question directly: can the Red Army count on the support of Germany in the event Poland launches a military attack? In the name of the Soviet government Voroshilov assured Blomberg that, if Poland attacked Germany, Soviet Russia would be prepared to provide every kind of assistance to Germany. (See F. L. Carsten, "Reports by Two German Officers on the Red Army," Bundesarchiv-Militärarchiv, Bestand E III, d. 116, p. 223.) Eleven years later, in 1939, Stalin and Hitler made a new agreement on the partition of Poland.

40. The Cheka was reorganized as the GPU (*Glavnoe politicheskoe upravlenie*, "Main Political Administration") in 1922, and two years later renamed the OGPU (*Ob"edinennoe glavnoe politicheskoe upravlenie*, "Unified Main Political Administration), and in 1934 reorganized as part of the NKVD (People's Commissariat of Internal Affairs).

41. At the time, Trotskii was People's Commissar for Military and Naval Affairs and chairman of the Revolutionary-Military Council.

42. Hencke, "Der politische Einfluß," pp. 28–31.

43. Rozengol'ts was subsequently the people's commissar of foreign trade; he was shot in 1938.

44. Hencke, "Der politische Einfluß," p. 34.

45. Ibid., p. 36.

46. The pacts came to an end in 1936, when German troops marched into the demilitarized Rhineland.

47. Hencke, "Der politische Einfluß," p. 40. See also the notes on Chicherin's talks with Rantzau (dated February 20, 1925) in RTsKhIDNI, f. 76, op. 3, d. 317, l. 5.

48. Spravka KRO OGPU, "Obshchestvo dlia pooshchreniia promyshlennykh predpriiatii (GEFU)," in RTsKhIDNI, f. 76, op. 3, d. 317, l. 28.

49. In addition to the OGPU, the office of intelligence in the Red Army also intercepted and read the mail of people involved in GEFU. See RTsKhIDNI, f. 76, op. 3, d. 317, l. 34.

50. Ibid.

51. A metallurgical engineer named Tille, the chief representative for the so-called "Special Group" in Moscow, was in charge of gathering this intelligence. The OGPU quoted the following extract from Tille's report to Berlin: "Notwithstanding the fact that the time will come when a flag other than today's blood-red banner shall fly over the Kremlin, until then Germany's industry should take one post after the other, thereby driving an aspen stake into the spinal column of the Bolshevik government."

52. RTsKhIDNI, f. 76, op. 3, d. 317, ll. 38–41.

53. Speidel, p. 19.

54. Thomsen was accompanied by a group of instructors: five young airforce pilots and two technicians under the command of a captain. The unit existed until 1926 (See Der politische Einfluß, p. 109). Predictably, the unit aroused OGPU suspicions of espionage.

55. "Verkhovnyi Sud Soiuza SSR. Opredelenie No. 4n-0280/57," in *Izvestiia TsK KPSS*, 1989, no. 4: 64.

56. Although the Moscow Center worked amidst strict secrecy, people like Lieth-Thomsen and Niedermayer were well-known to the intelligence agencies of the other powers. Indeed, Niedermayer was something of a public figure in Germany: for his escapades in Afghanistan, the press nicknamed him "the German Lawrence."

57. RTsKhIDNI, f. 17, op. 3, d. 391, ll. 9–10 (Protokol no. 43, dated November 10, 1923).

58. Unshlikht to Stalin, 31.12.1926 ("sovershenno sekretno"), published in Iu. L. D'iakov and T. S. Bushueva, *Fashistskii mech kovalsia v SSSR. Krasnaia armiia i Reikhsver. Tainoe sotrudnichestvo 1922–1933. Neizvestnye dokumenty* (Moscow: Sovetskaia Rossiia, 1992), pp. 71–72.

59. Berzin to Voroshilov, January 29, 1927, Moscow ("absolutely secret") in ibid., p. 80.

60. Berzin, "Doklad o sotrudnichestve RKKA i Reikhsvera" (December 24, 1928, "Sovershenno sekretno") in ibid., pp. 89–90.

61. Unshlikht sent the letter to Stalin, along with various other documents, in response to public revelations about the German-Soviet military cooperation. See Unshlikht to Litvinov, with a copy to Stalin and Voroshilov, December 31, 1926 ("top secret!") in ibid, pp. 77–79.

62. Carsten, p. 255.

63. D'iakov and Bushueva, p. 97. Stomoniakov reporting on a discussion with Dirksen, July 5, 1929 ("absolutely confidential").

64. D'iakov and Bushueva, p. 97.

65. Köstring, *Der militärische Mittler*, p. 55.

66. Ibid., pp. 49–50.

67. Ibid, p. 58.

68. RH 2/2302, p. 235 (Bericht über den Besuch des Chefs der R. L. bei der S. S.. October 3, 1929 [concerning the period between 25 and September 28, 1929]). L. Nr. 3656/29

69. RH 2/2302, pp. 33–34.

70. "Aktenvermerk über den Verlauf der Besprechung am 30.1.1930. 10 Uhr. Teilnehmer: Bersin, Alksnis, Molt, v. Niedermayer, Wichert, Lange, Hammer." Bundes- und Militärarchiv, RH (uncatalogued file), pp. 109–13.

71. RH 2/2303, p. 31.

72. F. L. Carsten, "Reports by Two German Officers on the Red Army," Bundesarchiv-Militärarchiv, Bestand E III d. 11, p. 218.

73. Ibid., p. 222.

74. See, for example, Groener's letter to Voroshilov, dated November 1, 1928, in RGASA, f. 33987, op. 1, d. 671, l. 132.

75. "Doklady Generala Gel'ma o Krasnoi Armii" in RGASA, f. 33987, op. 1, d. 681, ll. 19, 54.

76. Ibid., l. 191.

77. Carsten, "Reports," pp. 243–44.

78. RGASA, f. 33987, op. 1, d. 679, l. 157 ob.

79. RH 2/2296, p. 93. (S. G. Moscow. Berlin, February 5, 1926).

80. RH 2/2213, p. 133 ("Geheime Commandosache '1." 10.09.1926).

81. RH 2/2296, p. 55. ("Moskau, den 31. März 1926. Herrn Direktor von der Lieth.")

82. Ibid., pp. 58, 63.

83. RGASA, f. 29, op. 23, d. 119, l. 81 ("Sovershenno sekretno." October, 1926).

84. "Protokol der Besprechung des Herrn von Hammerstein mit Herrn Feldmann im Beisein von deutscher Seite der Herren Kühlenthal, v. Niedermayer, Fontane, Hofmeister und Stahr und von russischer Seite der Herrn Orlov und Rimm. Lipezk. Den 7.9.1929." RH 2/2303, pp. 23–28.

85. Some of the classified documents on the negotiations with Krupp in 1929 are to be found in D'iakov and Bushueva, "Fashistskii mech," pp. 91–95.

86. RGASA, f. 31, op. 9, d. 79, ll. 31–34 ("Spravka o vypolnenii dogov-
orov na inostrannuiu tekhnicheskuiu pomoshch' [po voennoi i grazhdanskoi
promyshlennosti], po voennym proizvodstvam]. Sovershenno sekretno.
Kopiia s kopii).

87. TsGASA, f. 31, op. 9, d. 79, l. 294–94 ob. ("Secret." March 15, 1991.
62001/29c").

88. Wirth, who played a key role in resolving the conflict, fully endorsed
the Soviet view that the trade mission—as part of the Soviet state—
enjoyed the right of extraterritoriality. See the letter from the trade mission
in Berlin to Stalin (May 17, 1924) in RGASA, f. 33988, op. 2, d. 618, l. 46.

89. *Krasnaia zvezda*, February 6, 1925.

90. RGASA, f. 4, op. 2, d. 20, l. 238.

91. D'iakov and Bushueva, "Fashistskii mech," p. 99.

92. Ibid., pp. 103–4.

93. RGASA, f. 33987, op. 1, d. 681, ll. 151–152.

94. D'iakov and Bushueva, "Fashistskii mech," p. 100.

95. Ibid.

96. RGASA, f. 33987, op. 1, d. 679, l. 46. ("Voroshilov to members of
the Military-Revolutionary Council and to the heads of the central admin-
istrations of the NKVD. Copy. Secret").

97. According to Carsten, Hammerstein was deeply impressed by the
apparent ties between the Red Army and civilian population and hoped to
apply this experience in establishing closer ties between the Reichswehr
and workers (especially those in the mass republican organizations). Such
ideas led to his sobriquet among colleagues as "The Red General." In fact,
three of his daughters became active members of the German Communist
Party, although the general himself did not share such left-wing sympa-
thies. See Carsten, "Reports," p. 326. Hammerstein was not alone in this
matter; General von Blomberg also was impressed by the example of the
Red Army and hoped to establish close ties between the Reichswehr and
"the popular masses." Carsten, ibid., p. 389.

98. RGASA, f. 33987, op. 1, d. 679, l. 222. Berzin to Voroshilov, September 25, 1929. (No. 135538). "Secret."

99. Ibid., l. 224 (dated September 29, 1929).

100. RGASA, f. 33987, op. 1, d. 679, l. 227 (September 27, 1929.
2996/s).

101. D'iakov and Bushueva, "Fashistskii mech," pp. 247–48 (Uborevich
to Voroshilov, June 18, 1926, Berlin).

102. RGASA, f. 33987, op. 1, d. 667, l. 352 (Voroshilov to Krestinskii,
with a copy to Litvinov. March, 1928. No. 02115/ss).

103. Ibid., l. 352 ob.

104. RGASA, f. 33987, op. 1, d. 667, l. 115 (Voroshilov to Chicherin.
December, 1927. "Completely secret").

105. RGASA, f. 33987, op. 1, d. 667, ll. 128–129 (Voroshilov to Ubore-vich, December 1927. No. 069/ss).

106. D'iakov and Bushueva, "Fashistskii mech," pp. 261–262 (Eideman to Voroshilov, February 11, 1927 "Completely secret").

107. D'iakov and Bushuev, "Fashistskii mech," p. 258.

108. Ibid., p. 258.

109. Ibid., p. 259. July 13, 1930.

110. Ibid., p. 272 (Belov to Voroshilov, October 7, 1930, Germany).

111. Ibid., pp. 263–64 (Berzin to Voroshilov. 1928. Absolutely secret).

112. Ibid., p. 265 (Voroshilov to Politburo [Comrade Stalin]. March, 1929. "Absolutely secret").

113. Ibid., pp. 274–278 (Berzin to Voroshilov. November 6, 1931. Absolutely confidential).

114. RGASA, f. 4, op. 2, d. 411, ll. 7, 10.

115. Ibid., f. 33987, op. 1, d. 667, l. 129.

116. Carsten, "Reports," p. 241.

117. RGASA, f. 33987, op. 1, d. 667, l. 9 (No. 04/ss).

118. Hencke, p. 73.

119. RTsKhIDNI, f. 76, op. 3, d. 317, l. 2 (Chicherin to Brodovskii, no. 46. "Highly secret." July 29, 1924).

120. Ibid., f. 76, op. 3, d. 317, l. 4 ("Secret. [To be communicated] only in person. Copy. 30.7.[1924] F. Dzerzhinskii. This letter is to be destroyed immediately after it has been read.") PAGE 45, NOTE 126.

121. Ibid., f. 76, op. 3, d. 317, l. 4.

122. Ibid., f. 76, op. 3, d. 317, ll. 5–6 ("From a conversation between Chicherin and the German ambassador," February 20, 1925).

123. Ibid., f. 76, op. 3, d. 317, l. 9 (Memorandum from Dzerzhinskii to Trilisser and Iagoda, July 6, 1925).

124. Ibid., f. 76, op. 3, d. 317, l. 11 (Artuzov to Dzerzhinskii. July 14, 1925. "Personal").

125. According to the OGPU, there were seven German organizations: "The Union of Germans in the Volga," "Union of Germans in Southern Russia," "Union of Germans in the Caucasus," "Union of Germans in Northern Russia," "Association of Siberian Germans," and the "Corpora-tion of Former Students in the German Schools of Moscow and Leningrad." See "Germanskaia kontr-revoliutsionnaia rabota v SSSR" in Ibid., f. 76, op. 3, d. 317, ll. 12–13.

126. Ibid., f. 76, op. 3, d. 317, l. 13. These publications included: *Zarubezhnyi nemets, Nemetskaia zhizn' v SSSR, Ezhemesiachnik nemtsev Povolzh'ia,* and *Nemetskii kolonist.*

127. RTsKhIDNI, f. 76, op. 3, d. 317, l. 13.

128. Ibid. l. 14.

129. Ibid. l. 17.

130. Ibid. l. 17.
131. Ibid. l. 18.
132. Ibid. l. 20.
133. Ibid. l.20.
134. Ibid. l. 20.
135. Ibid. ("Circular Letter of the OGPU, No. 7/37. Per the Counter-Intelligence Section. Absolutely Secret . . . Moscow 1924").
136. Ibid. l. 43.
137. Ibid. l. 44.
138. Ibid. l. 44 ob.
139. Ibid. l. 44 ob.
140. Köstring, *Der militärische Mittler*, pp. 70–71.
141. Ibid., 78.
142. Hencke,"Der politische Einfluß," p. 78.
143. Ibid., p. 78.
144. Ibid., p. 77. The attache was Captain Kinzel (later a general and head of the general staff of Army Group Bush at the end of World War II). In 1945 he conducted negotiations for capitulation with Field Marshal Montgomery and later committed suicide.
145. Hencke, "Der politische Einfluß," p. 80.
146. Ibid., p. 81.
147. Köstring, *Der militärische Mittler*, p. 66.
148. Ibid., p. 69.

2. German Military Installations in the USSR

1. The German aircraft company Junkers, which was located in Dessau, was established by Professor G. Junkers in 1919; its existence finally came to an end in 1945.
2. RTsKhIDNI, f. 17, op. 3, d. 486.
3. In particular, the GPU asserted that "airplanes were in part built from old and unsuitable materials, or from materials obviously and deliberately chosen for their poor quality." Ibid., l. 23.
4. Among the allegations were that the firm had failed to build the "workers' town" for white-collar personnel and workers at the plant, took repressive measures against workers who joined the trade union, and systematically engaged in contraband. The most substantive accusations, however, were delivered in a hypothetical form: "There is information that the firm 'Junkers' [manufactures] particularly powerful gases and poisons for purposes of wreaking [havoc]." The following accusation lacks proof altogether: "The Junkers plant was to have contributed to the flight

of three German student-terrorists by providing them with an airplane."
Ibid., ll. 23–24.

5. Ibid., l. 24.

6. Ibid., l. 27.

7. Ibid., l. 27 (Protokol No. 46: 27 January 1925).

8. D'iakov and Bushueva, "Fashistskii mech," pp. 141–44. ("Report from Brio, director of GAZ No. 1. Onufriev to Stalin et al. March 11, 1926. Moscow. Absolutely confidential"), 144–47 ("Conclusion of the chairman of Glavmetall, Mezhlauk and board member Gudniak, addressed to the chairman of the All-Union Council of National Economy, Dzerzhinskii. April 29, 1926. Absolutely confidential").

9. RGASA, f. 4, op. 2, d. 90, l. 122.

10. Ibid., f. 4, op. 2,d. 90, l. 122 ob.

11. Ibid., l. 123.

12. Ibid., f. 4, op. 2, d. 4, l. 14 (Chicherin to Rykov. Absolutely confidential. June 11, 1926. Copy). Information about this had been received still earlier by the Foreign Section (Inostrannyi otdel) of the OGPU in Copenhagen (ibid., l. 17).

13. Ibid., l. 15. Schlieben, according to Chicherin, was especially insistent about the need for an amicable resolution of a dispute involving 12 bombers, which the firm had already built, but which the Soviet side refused to accept on the grounds that they did not meet the agreed-upon technical specifications.

14. RGASA, f. 4, op. 2, d. 204, ll. 4, 6 (the trade mission refers here to a review of the 1922 contract).

15. Ibid., l. 22 (Report from the head of the Soviet air force to the deputy chairman of the Military-Revolutionary Council. Secret. September 17, 1926).

16. The commission included representatives from the air force, Main Committee on Concessions and Aviatrest. Ibid., l. 22 ob.

17. Ibid., l. 33–33 ob. "Unshlikht (Deputy chairman of the Military-Revolutionary Council) to the Politburo commission of Comrade Rykov, November 11, 1926. Absolutely confidential, no. 1633/ss."

18. Ibid., l. 48–48 ob. ("Deputy chairman of the Military-Revolutionary Council Unshlikht to Commissar of Commerce, Comrade Mikoian. Secret. March, 1927.")

19. Bundesarchiv-Militärarchiv, RH 2/2214 (Protokolle über Vereinbarungen zwischen der Russischen Luftwaffe und dem Vertreter der Sondergruppe in Moskau über die Einrichtung einer Fliegerschule und eines Geratelagers in Lipezk), pp. 1–5.

20. D'iakov and Bushueva, pp. 167–169 ("Minutes of Soviet-German negotiations on the question of aviation, March 24, 1926").

21. Bundesarchiv-Militärarchiv, RH 2/2294, pp. 17–18. Lieth-Vorowsko-go 48. n 17. Moskau, 30.5.1926 (An den stellvertretenden Herrn Volks-kommissar für Heeres- und Marine-Angelegenheiten Herrn Unschlicht.

22. Hencke, "Der politische Einfluß," p. 109.

23. Bundesarchiv-Militärarchiv, RH 2/2218, Nr. 35 (331/228), pp. 146–48.

24. D'iakov and Bushueva, "Fashitskii mech," p. 173.

25. Ibid., pp. 169–70.

26. Hencke, "Der politische Einfluß," p. 110.

27. Bundesarchiv-Militärarchiv, RH 2/2213, p. 139.

28. D'iakov and Bushueva, "Fashitskii mech," p. 73.

29. Ibid., p. 141.

30. Bundesarchiv-Militärarchiv, RH 2/2304. Abschrift: Programm der Arbeiten und Versuchen Ost 1, 1926/27, p. 1.

31. Köstring, *Der militärische Mittler*, p. 48. Stuka is the popular, short form for Sturzkampfflugzeug.

32. Ibid., p. 49.

33. D'iakov and Bushueva, "Fashitskii mech," pp. 173–74. Köstring (German military attaché) to A. I. Egorov (Chief of Staff of the Red Army), July 22, 1933. Moscow.

34. To cite some examples: the aviation industry (Glavaviaprom) had nineteen plants; the war-chemicals industry (Vokhimtrest) had seven plants; the "All-Union Trust of Organic Production" (VTOP) had two plants; the All-Union Trust of Synthetic Fibers (VIV) had five plants; the Main Administration for Ship-Building Industry (GUSP) had eight plants; the Cartridge-Ammunition Trust had two plants; Artillery-Shell Trust had two plants; the Special-Vehicle (tank) Trust had three plants, the Main Military-Medical Administration (GVMU) had eighteen plants. For details see RTsKhIDNI, f. 76, op. 3, d. 948, ll. 104–5.

35. RGASA, f. 4, op. 2, d. 103.

36. Ibid., d. 26, ll. 68–71, 73–74 (Memorandum on the Russian-German Company "Bersol." P. P. Butkov. October 26, 1924). See also the note from the OGPU's Counter-intelligence Office on GEFU in RTsKhIDNI, f. 76, op. 3, d. 317, ll. 28–29.

37. RGASA, f. 4, op. 2, d. 59, ll. 124–125 (Minutes of Meeting No. 8 of the Revolutionary Military Council February 1, 1926. "Absolutely confidential"). Ia. M. Fishman remained at this pot until June 15, 1937. RTsKhIDNI, f. 17, op. 3, d. 987, l. 57 (Politburo protocol no. 49).

38. Ibid., f. 4, op. 2, d. 203, l. 1 (May 24, 19026, No. 6050, s.s.)

39. Ibid., d. 59, l. 105 (No. 2032 s.s.).

40. These included a cartridge plant in Tula, a steel plant in Zlatoust, a

gunpowder plant in Kazan, a pipe-manufacturing factory in Leningrad, an explosives plant in Bogorodsk, and a gunpowder plant in Oxtinsk. RGASA, f. 4, op.2, d. 26, l. 74.

41. D'iakov and Bushueva, "Fashistskii mech," p. 74.

42. Ibid., p. 74.

43. Ibid., p. 76.

44. RGASA, f. 4, op. 2, d. 288, ll. 1, 2, 3 ob., 4–4 ob., 6.

45. Ibid., l. 1–1 ob. (Conclusion on the report of Comrade Gal'perin, July 1, 1927).

46. Ibid., l. 2.

47. Ibid., f. 31, op.9, d. 79, ll. 30–31 (Memorandum on foreign technical assistance in the military-chemical sector).

48. Ibid., l. 30 ob.

49. Köstring, Der militärische Mittler, p. 49.

50. RGASA, f. 33987, op. 1, d. 671, l. 223 (Voroshilov to Menzhinskii, December 21, 1928, No. 0542/ss).

51. Ibid., l. 234.

52. E. L. Carsten, Reports, pp. 220–21.

53. Bundesarchiv-Militärarchiv, RH 12–4/54, pp. 229–30 (Geheime Kommandosache, May 7, 1931).

54. Ibid., RH 12–4/55, p. 25 (1) (2) (Provisional program at Tomka, 1932).

55. Ibid., RH 12–4/55, p. 45 ("Geheime Kommandosache. Auszug aus Besprechung zwischen Herrn Oberst Fischer und Herren Bersin und Fischman. Den 13.4.1932. Anwesend Oberst Roestring, Herr Schüttel").

56. Ibid., RH 12–4/55, pp. 9–10. (Was Prw N 829/33. g. Kdos. Was Prw YI. Betr: Versuche To. Berlin, den 27.5.1933).

57. Ibid., RH 12–4/55, p.68 ("Geheime Kommandosache. Deutsche Botschaft Moskau. Der Militärattasche N 143/33, Moscow, den 22.5.1933").

58. Ibid., RH 12 -4/55, p. 64. ("Deutsche Botschaft Moskau. Der Militärattasche. N. 142/33. Moskau, den 16.5.1933").

59. Ibid., pp. 65–66.

60. Ibid., RH 12 -4/55. Wa Prw N 829/33, p. 11.

61. Ibid., RH 12 -4/55, p. 62. Gesamtbild der Abwicklung der Station To. 1933.

62. Ibid.

63. For details see D'iakov and Bushueva, "Fashitskii mech," pp. 177–182 ("The Basic Agreement between Viko-Moskva and Red Army-Moscow on the organization of a tanks school").

64. E. L. Carsten, "Reports," p. 223.

65. D'iakov and Bushueva, "Fashsitskii mech," p. 186.

66. Köstring, Der militärische Mittler, p. 49.

67. D'iakov and Bushueva, "Fashitskii mech," p. 186 (Griaznov to Voroshilov on the Work of 'TEKO.' March 14, 1932.
68. Ibid.

3. Crossroads

1. The 13th plenum of the Comintern (December 1933) claimed that the revolutionary upsurge had already commenced in Germany. See *XIII plenum IKKI*, p. 591.

2. For details on the Comintern and Soviet foreign policy, see Thomas Weingartner, *Stalin und der Aufstieg Hitlers* (Berlin: Walter de Gruyter & Co., 1970).

3. D'iakov and Bushueva, "Fashistskii mech," p. 283 (Levandovskii to Voroshilov. July 19, 1933. Berlin).

4. Ibid., p. 280 (Levandovskii to Voroshilov, February 28, 1933. Berlin).

5. Ibid., p. 284.

6. Ibid., pp. 288–289 (Levichev, April 25, 1933, letter from Germany).

7. Ibid., p. ;290 (Levichev to Voroshilov, May 12, 1933).

8. Ibid., p. 288 (document of a group of commanders undergoing training [in Germany], compiled by the Soviet military attaché in Germany, V. N. Levichev). April 1933.

9. Ibid., p. 309. Report from Hartmann to Berlin, March 27, 1933.

10. Ibid., p. 310 (April 1, 1933).

11. Gustav Hilger and Alfred G. Meyer, *The Incompatible Allies* (New York: MacMillan, 1953), p. 256.

12. D'iakov and Bushueva, "Fashistskii mech," p. 314 (excerpts from a report on the [German] visit to the USSR, May 8–28, 1933).

13. Ibid., p. 315.

14. Ibid., pp. 311–12 (Krestinskii's diary, April 3, 1933).

15. Ibid., p. 313 (Dirksen to Hitler, April 1933; copy obtained by Soviet intelligence).

16. Ibid., p. 339 (Krestinskii's diary, October 28 and November 1, 1933).

17. Ibid., p. 341 (report of the Soviet diplomatic mission in Germany, December 31, 1933. Classified).

18. Karl-Heinz Niklaus, *Die Sowjetunion und Hitlers Machtergreifung* (Bonn, 1966), pp. 120–21.

19. Herbert von Dirksen, *Moskau, Tokio, London* (Stuttgart, 1950), p. 128.

20. *Documents on German Foreign Policy* [hereafter *DGFP*), Series C, 2: 40.

21. Ibid., 2: 83.

22. RTsKhIDNI, f. 17, op. 120, d. 107, l. 86 (Khinchuk to Kaganovich).

23. Ibid., l. 87.

24. *Vneshniaia politika SSSR*, 16: 743.

25. See *Istoriia Kommunisticheskoi partii Sovetskogo Soiuza* (Moscow, 1959), p. 453.

26. *DGFP*, Series C, 2: 338–39 (Nadolny to the German Foreign Ministry. Moscow, January 11, 1934); 2: 352–53 (Nadolny to German Foreign Ministry. Moscow, January 13, 1934).

27. *DGFP*, 2: 333–34 (Nadolny to Foreign Ministry. Moscow. January 10, 1934).

28. Stalin, *Sochineniia*, 13: 293.

29. Ibid. (Emphasis mine—A.N.).

30. Ibid.

31. Dimitrov (1882–1949), a Bulgarian communist, had been arrested by German authorities and accused of collaborating in the Reichstag fire of February 27, 1933. He was acquitted, however, by the court in Leipzig. For details on Dimitrov's role in the Leipzig trial, see his own account in *Pered fashistskim sudom* (Moscow: Partizdat, 1936). In late February, 1934 Dimitrov came to Moscow, where he was soon elected as a member of the Political Commission of the Comintern and designated chief of its Central-European Secretariat, which he headed from 1935 to 1943 (when the Comintern was formally dissolved).

32. Typical is the following document from the Comintern's archive: "To the General Secretary of the IKKI [Comintern], Comrade Dimitrov, G. M. The Personnel Section of the IKKI asks that comrade Volkov, Aleksandr Vasil'evich, be confirmed as senior advisor in the Personnel Section, with a salary of 900 rubles per month. *Comrade Volkov has been given a security check by the appropriate organs.*" RTsKhIDNI, f. 495, op. 18, d. 1286, l. 257 (dated July 7, 1939). Emphasis mine—A.N.

33. W. G. Krivitsky, *In Stalin's Secret Service* (New York: Harper and Brothers Publishers, 1939), p. 74.

34. In a secret letter to the secretaries of the national communist parties in the various Soviet republics and to the secretaries of the oblast party committees, Stalin called for physical violence even against those who had already been convicted and sentenced. See the Politburo protocol (No. 43) of November 11, 1936 in RTsKhIDNI, f. 17, op. 3, d. 981, l. 58.

35. B. M. Leibzon and K. K. Shirinia, *Povorot v politike Kominterna* (Moscow, 1975), p. 93.

36. Ibid., p. 91.

37. In a letter to the Central Committee (July 2, 1934) Dimitrov posed the question whether "it is correct to consider social democrats everywhere and under all circumstances the main social bulwark of the bourgeoisie." Stalin replied in a scornful, ironic tone: "Not, of course, in Persia. In the main capitalist countries—yes indeed!" Dimitrov also asked whether "it is correct to consider all left social-democratic groups under all conditions to

be the main danger." Stalin's answer was typical of his political thinking: "Objectively, yes." See F. I. Firsov, "Stalin i Komintern," *Voprosy istorii KPSS*, 1989, no. 9: 12.

38. The author heard about this conversation from a member of the editorial staff for *Diplomaticheskii slovar'*; they had heard the account from Surits himself. It is not known whether Surits ever recorded this conversation himself.

39. Krivitsky, p. 183.

40. Gustav Hilger, *The Incompatible Allies* (New York: MacMillan, 1953), pp. 267–68.

41. Ibid. Hitler had a different view: a former communist could still become a good Nazi, but not vice versa. As the experience of East Germany subsequently showed, however, Hitler was wrong: after the collapse of the Third Reich, many Nazis joined the Communist Party of Germany and the Socialist Unity-Party of Germany (Sozialistische Einheitspartei Deutschlands).

42. *DGFP*, Series C, 1: 14 (Dirksen to State Secretary Bülow. Moscow, January 31, 1933).

43. Ibid., 1: 71–72 (Foreign Minister to the embassy in the Soviet Union. Cipher letter. Berlin, February 22, 1933).

44. Ibid., 1: 190n.

45. Ibid., 1: 190 (Dirksen to Foreign Ministry. Moscow, March 20, 1933).

46. The Archive of Foreign Policy (in the Soviet Ministry of Foreign Affairs) contains an enormous number of verbal protests to the German foreign ministry; these include complaints about the maltreatment of *Izvestiia* correspondents Liia Kait and Hartmann and *Pravda* correspondents Cherniak and Izakson. See Arkhiv vneshnei politiki (hereafter AVP), f. 82, op. 18, ll. 409, 416–19, 424–27.

47. *DGFP*, Series C, 1: 289–90 (Dirksen to the Foreign Ministry. Moscow, April 14, 1933).

48. *DGFP*, 1: 189 (Dirksen to the Foreign Ministry. Moscow, March 20, 1933).

49. K. Radek, "Reviziia Versal'skogo dogovora," *Pravda*, May 10, 1933.

50. *DGFP*, 1: 450 (Dirksen memorandum of May 16, 1933, reporting on his conversation with Litvinov of the same date).

51. Ibid.

52. *DGFP*, 1: 389 (Dirksen to the Foreign Ministry. Moscow, May 5, 1933).

53. Gustav Hilger, *The Incompatible Allies* (New York: Macmillan, 1953), p. 256.

54. *DGFP*, 1: 717 (Dirksen to the Foreign Ministry. Moscow, August 4, 1933).

55. Foreign Office, 371, N 24845, p. 47 (N. Butler to O. Sargeant. Washington, D.C., September 13, 1940).

56. *DGFP*, Series C, 2: 41 (Von Neurath, Memorandum by the Foreign Minister. Berlin, October 24, 1933).

57. Ibid., p. 40.

58. The farewell dinner held in Dirksen's honor and hosted by the deputy commissar of foreign affairs (Krestinskii) was attended by Enukidze, Anastas Mikoian, many other commissars, and also high-ranking military officers (including Tukhachevskii and Egorov). See ibid., 2: 76–77 (Dirksen to State-Secretary Bülow. Moscow, November 3, 1933).

59. Ibid., 83.

60. *Vneshniaia politika SSSR*, 16: 714.

61. Ibid., 16: 743.

62. Ibid.

63. See *Istoriia Kommunisticheskoi Partii Sovetskogo Soiuza* (Moscow, 1959), p. 453.

64. *DGFP*, Series C, 1: 875 (Memorandum by von Tippelskirch, Dept. IV. Berlin, September 29, 1933).

65. Ibid., 2: 338–39 (Nadolny to the Foreign Ministry. Moscow, January 11, 1934), 352–53 (Nadolny to the Foreign Ministry. Moscow, January 13, 1934).

66. Ibid., 2: 122–23 (Directives to Ambassador Nadolny on the occasion of his being sent as Ambassador to Moscow. Berlin, November 13, 1933).

67. Ibid., 2: 297 (unsigned note. Moscow, January 1, 1934).

68. Interestingly enough, Stalin adopted precisely this model after World War II, when he annexed Polish territory and provided compensation in the form of German land.

69. Ibid., 2: 297–98. But not everyone in Moscow shared this assessment of Hitler's plans. The chief of the General Staff, Marshal Aleksandr I. Egorov, dismissed the importance of *Mein Kampf* in his conversations with the German military attaché Köstring: "Hitler wrote that in the bitterness of his Landberger prison cell. We do not therefore take this seriously!" Köstring, *Der militärische Mittler*, p. 85.

70. *DGFP*, 2: 338–39 (Nadolny to the Foreign Ministry. Moscow, January 11, 1934).

71. Ibid., 2: 352–53 (Nadolny to the Foreign Ministry. Moscow, January 11, 1934).

72. Ibid., 2: 376–78 (Military Attaché to the Reichswehr Ministry and the Foreign Ministry. Moscow, January 17, 1934).

73. Ibid., 2: 476 (State-Secretary Bernhard von Bülow to Nadolny. Berlin, February 12, 1934).

74. Ibid., 2: 731–33 (Foreign Minister von Neurath to the German embassy in Moscow. Berlin, April 9, 1934), 862–63 (Unsigned memorandum. Berlin, May 31, 1934).

75. Ibid., 2: 866.

76. Ibid., 2: 647–48 (Memorandum from the director of Dept. IV (Meyer). Berlin, March 20, 1934).

77. Ibid., 3: 111–12 (Chargé d'affaires to the Foreign Ministry. Moscow, July 2, 1934).

78. Decree of the Presidium of the Supreme Soviet: "On the resettlement of Germans living in the area of the Volga." Cited in Gugo Vormsbekher, "Nemtsy v SSSR," *Znamia*, 1988, no. 11: 193.

79. V. Shishkin, "Sovetskie nemtsy; u istokov tragedii," *Nauka v Sibiri*, 1992, August, no. 28: 5. Shishkin cites a coded telegram from the Central Committee to "all Central Committees of national communist parties, krai committees and oblast committees, to R. I. Eikhe (secretary of the West-Siberian krai committee).

80. Ibid.

81. Ibid.

82. Ibid. ("Resolution of the Bureau of the West-Siberian Krai Committee 'on measures in the struggle with counter-revolutionary elements among the German population.'" Novosibirsk, November 13, 1934. Secret)

83. Ibid. (Information from the German Raion Committee to the West-Siberian Krai Committee "on conducting work in the German Raion against fascist [Hitlerite] 'aid.'" Gol'dshtadt, December 4, 1934).

84. Shishkin, p. 6 (report of the krai court to the West-Siberian Krai Committee "on the work of the krai court with respect to the krai committee's directive of November 13, 1934 on Germans").

85. Ibid. (report to the West-Siberian Krai Committee, dated December 19, 1934).

86. Ibid. (report from Ia. P. Gailit, commander of forces in the Siberian military district, to the deputy chief of the special unit of the West-Siberian Krai Committee. December 23, 1934).

87. V. Shishkin, p. 6 (report from the chief of the NKVD Administration of State Security to R. I. Eikhe (secretary of the Krai Committee) 'on the results of the operational work in German colonies in Western Siberia.' Novosibirsk, December 25, 1934. "Absolutely confidential.")

88. Ibid. (Report from Eikhe to the Central Committee "on implementing the directive of the Central Committee of November 5, 1934 for a struggle with counter-revolutionary fascist elements in German colonies." Novosibirsk, February 1935).

89. Ibid.

90. AVP RF, f. 82, op. 18, d. 61(2), ll. 56–59.

91. Krivitsky, p. 10.

92. *DGFP*, 3: 455 (Schulenburg to the Foreign Ministry. Moscow, October 3, 1934).

93. Ibid., 3: 522 (Schulenburg to Foreign Ministry. Moscow, October 22, 1934).

94. B. M. Leibzon and K. K. Shirinia, pp. 96–97.

95. See, for example, *DGFP*, 3: 461–62 (Schulenburg to the Foreign Ministry. Moscow, October 7, 1934).

96. Rossiiskii gosudarstvennyi arkhiv ekonomiki (RGAE), f. 413, op. 13, d. 2478, l. 15.

97. *Pravda*, March 31, 1935; *Izvestiia*, April 1, 1935; *Krasnaia zvezda*, April 1, 1935.

98. "Nakanune voiny," *Izvestiia TsK KPSS*, 1990, no. 1: 161.

99. Ibid., pp. 170–71 (an entry from M. M. Litvinov's diary, regarding a conversation with the German ambassador in Germany, W. von Schulenburg. No earlier than April 4, 1935. "Secret").

100. *DGFP* 4: 7 (State Secretary to the German embassy in Moscow. Berlin, April 2, 1935).

101. Ibid.,, 4: 1–2 (Schulenburg to the Foreign Ministry. Moscow, April 16, 1935).

102. Ibid., 4: 18–20 (Military attaché to the Reichswehr Ministry and the Foreign Ministry. Moscow, April 5, 1935).

103. See *Izvestiia TsK KPSS*, 1990, no. 1: 171–72 (report from A. I. Gekker, chief of the foreign section in the defense commissariat, to the chief of military intelligence, Berezin (April 4, 1935) does not quote the attaché on this last point.

104. *DGFP*, 4: 778–79 (Schulenburg to State-Secretary Bülow. Moscow, October 28, 1935).

105. *Vneshniaia politika SSSR*, 18: 249.

106. Ibid., p. 250.

107. Ibid.

108. RGAE, f. 413, op. 13, d. 1009, ll. 29–30.

109. AVP, f. 82, op. 19, papka 65, d. 24, ll. 301–4.

110. Ibid., l. 305.

111. *DGFP*, 4: 453–54 (Schacht to the Foreign Ministry. Berlin, July 15, 1935).

112. Ibid., 4: 778–79 (Schulenburg to State-Secretary Bülow, October 28, 1935).

113. Ibid., 4: 897 (Twardowski, "Memorandum." Berlin, December 10, 1935), 931–33 (no. 472: Roediger, "Memorandum." Berlin, December 21, 1935).

114. Ibid., 4: 813 (Schulenburg to ministerial director Köpke. Moscow, November 11, 1935)

115. Köstring, *Der militärische Mittler*, p. 160.

116. *DGFP*, 4: 783 (Memorandum by an official of Department II, Bräutigam. Berlin, November 1, 1935).

117. Ibid., 4:783–84 (Minutes of an official of Dept. II. Berlin, November 1, 1935).

118. Ibid., 4: 1033 (Russian Committee of German Industry to the Foreign Ministry. January 24, 1936).

119. Ibid., p. 933.

120. Ibid., 4: 897–99 (memorandum from Twardowski, deputy director of Department VI. Berlin, December 10, 1935).

121. Ibid., 4: 985–87 (Schulenburg to the Foreign Ministry. Moscow, January 11, 1936).

122. Köstring, *Der militärische Mittler*, pp. 165–66.

123. Ibid., p. 126.

124. Ibid., p. 134.

125. Eduard Karlovich Fridrikhson (1879–1937?) was born in Latvia (Donzangen of Kurland province) and participated in the civil war. From 1921 he worked in the People's Commissariat of Foreign Trade; he may also have been the GPU's representative in Germany. During the Great Terror he was recalled (together with Kandelaki) to Moscow, arrested, and (apparently) shot. Some biographical information about him is to be found in RGAE, f. 413, op. 8, d. 3873.

126. *DGFP*, 5: 571–73 (Herbert L. W. Goering to Schulenburg. Berlin-Dahlem, May 20, 1936).

127. Ibid., 5: 571.

128. Auswärtiges Amt. Handel-Politsch. Wiehl Akten. Rußland, January 1935-September 1939. Vermerk. S. 452530. Berlin, May 13, 1936 (signed by Herbert L. W. Goering).

129. *DGFP*, 5: 572.

130. Ibid., 5: 581 (Schulenburg to Herbert Goering. May 25, 1936).

131. Ibid., 5: 512 (memorandum by an official of Department II [Hencke]. Berlin, May 6, 1936).

132. 5: 965 (memorandum from the head of the Economic Policy Division, Schnurre. Berlin, September 12. 1936).

133. Ibid., 5: 1070 (Herbert Goering, "Note for Herr Swiekowsky").

134. Ibid., 6: 252–53 (Foreign Ministry to the German Embassy in the USSR, January 6, 1937).

135. Ibid., 6: 687 (Schacht to the Foreign Minister. Berlin, April 24, 1937).

136. Ibid., 6: 692–93 (Foreign minister Neurath to Prussian Minister-President Goering. Berlin, April 27, 1937).

137. Ibid., 5: 574 (Memorandum by the Foreign Minister, Neurath. Berlin, May 22, 1936).

138. *Stalin und Hitler. Pakt gegen Europa*, ed. F. W. Brügel (Vienna, 1973), p. 38.

139. The son of A. L. Parvus, Evgenii Gnedin worked for the commissariat of foreign affairs in Moscow and in Berlin. In the early 1930s he was also chief of the foreign section of the newspaper *Izvestiia*. On the eve of his arrest in July 1939, he was head of the Press Section in the foreign affairs commissariat. After spending seventeen years in Soviet prisons and camps, Gnedin returned to Moscow and devoted all his energies to writing. His works include memoirs, countless articles, and also an interesting volume on Soviet-German relations.

140. E. Gnedin, *Iz istorii otnoshenii mezhdu SSSR i fashistskoi Germaniei. Khronika-press* (New York, 1977), p. 37.

141. Krivitsky, p. 15.

142. Ibid.

143. *DGFP*, 6: 379–80 (Reichsbank President Schacht to Foreign Minister Neurath. Berlin, February 6, 1937).

144. Krivitsky, p. 21.

145. Ibid., p. 21.

146. Foreign Office, N. 371, File 203466. 1936. Soviet Union N 4771g. (Collier to Chilston, January 29, 1936).

147. *Manchester Guardian*, February 7, 1936.

148. Radek supported accusations against the other defendants at the trial and saved his own life; but not for long—he died in prison in 1940.

149. Köstring was also accused of espionage in the case of Tukhachevskii and other high Soviet officers. An investigation of the "military conspiracy" of 1937, conducted two decades later, came to the conclusion that all the information sent from Köstring to Berlin came from "the official information and reports of German officers who had come to the USSR to participate in military maneuvers of the Red Army." See "Delo o tak nazyvaemoi antisovetskoi trotskistskoi voennoi organizatsii v Krasnoi armii," *TsK KPSS*, 1990, no. 4: 63 (Verkhovnyi sud SSSR. Opredelenie No. 4n-0280/57).

150. *DGFP*, 6: 274–77, 298, 611 et passim.

151. Ibid., 6: 514–15 (No. 253: Schulenburg, "Memorandum." Berlin, March 6, 1937).

152. Ibid., 6: 403–4 (Neurath to Reichsbank president, Schacht. Berlin, February 11, 1937).

153. *Vneshniaia politika SSSR*, 20: 164 (no. 98); see also *DGFP*, 6: 664n. (no. 322).

154. *DGFP*, 6: 669–71 (Schulenburg to Counsellor Bismarck. Moscow, April 19, 1937).

155. Ibid., 6: 174–75. According to Krivitskii, when Kandelaki returned from Berlin (in the company of an NKVD operative), he carried "the draft

of an agreement with the Nazi government." He was received by Stalin himself; he evidently assumed that he had at last attained his goal. Krivitsky, p. 21. There is no other confirmation of this report.

156. Ibid., 6: 234–35 (telegram from Surits to the foreign affairs commissariat. Berlin, May 9, 1937).

157. Ibid., 6: 204 (Surits to Litvinov. Berlin, April 27, 1937).

158. Ibid., 6: 429–30 (conversation of Iur'ev with State-Secretary Ernst Weizsäcker. Berlin, July 30, 1937).

159. In 1937 the pact was joined by Italy, in 1939 by Hungary and Manchuria, and in 1941 by Bulgaria, Denmark, Romania, Slovakia, Finland, Croatia and the Chinese government in Nanking.

160. A resolution of the Supreme Court in 1957 officially confirmed all this: "From the materials it is clear that all these people, at the first interrogation, categorically denied engaging in any kind of criminal activity. Only later did they make confessions about belonging to a counter-revolutionary military conspiracy. As an investigation has established, these confessions were false. They were obtained from the accused by illegal methods of investigation: deception, blackmail and measures of physical coercion." For details see "Delo o tak nazyvaemoi antisovetskoi trotskistskoi voennoi organizatsii v Krasnoi armii," *Izvestiia TsK KPSS*, 1989, no. 4: 42–73. A laboratory analysis, for example, found blood on the protocols of Tukhachevskii's interrogation.

161. Ibid., p. 61.

162. Ibid.

163. Stalin's fulminations against the Reichswehr merit fuller quotation: "I think that these people are marionettes and toys in the hands of the Reichswehr. The Reichswehr wants that we have a plot here, and these gentlemen have taken up the conspiracy. The Reichswehr wants these gentlemen systematically to deliver military secrets, and these gentlemen delivered the secrets. The Reichswehr wants that the existing government be removed, destroyed, and they tried to do this, but failed. The Reichswehr wants that, in event of war, all be prepared, that the army go over to wrecking so that the army not be prepared for defense. This is what the Reichswehr wanted, and this is what they did." Ibid., 53–54.

4. Partners

1. During a meeting with Mussolini in Rome on January 12, 1939, Prime Minister Neville Chamberlain endeavored to clarify Hitler's immediate plans. Mussolini shook his head when Chamberlain asked whether one should anticipate a sudden German attack on the west. For his part, Chamberlain remarked that, were a German attack to be aimed eastward,

it would not necessarily involve the West. *Documents of British Foreign Policy, 1919–1939.* (Third Series), 3: 525.

2. Ministerstvo inostrannykh del SSSR. *God krizisa, 1938–1939. Dokumenty i materialy* (Moscow: Gospolitizdat, 1990), p. 323 (Maiskii to Litvinov, March 24, 1939).

3. Ibid., pp. 386–87 (Proposal, transmitted by Litvinov to the British ambassador in Moscow, W. Seeds. April 17, 1939).

4. Zhdanov (1896–1948) was a secretary of the Central Committee and Leningrad oblast committee from 1934 and a Politburo member from 1939 until his death in 1948.

5. RTsKhIDNI, f. 7, op. 1, d. 895, l. 18 (undated).

6. I. V. Stalin, *Sochineniia,* 7 (Moscow, 1949), p. 24.

7. In this respect, he did not err. On November 19, 1937 the British foreign minister, Sir Edward Halifax, met with Hitler in Berlin. During the conversation he noted Hitler's achievements in making Germany a "bastion against Bolshevism." He also informed the Führer that Great Britain did not oppose changes in Europe, but desired that they occur through a "peaceful evolution." Halifax noted that it would be possible to reach agreement in other spheres. See Ministerstvo inostrannykh del SSSR, *Dokumenty i materialy kanuna vtoroi mirovoi voiny,* 1 (Moscow, 1948): 16 (conversation of Hitler and Halifax). Ten days prior to the Anschluss, the British ambassador in Berlin, Henderson, confirmed to Hitler that Lord Halifax had already agreed that changes in Europe were "fully possible" (ibid., p. 55). However, Hitler had his own schedule: he wanted to deal his blows before the western states were prepared for war.

8. In early 1939, the British military attaché in Berlin, referring to the opinion of his other colleagues, wrote that the odds were 10 to 1 that Germany would attack in the west rather than in the east. *DGFP,* 3: 551.

9. I. V. Stalin, *Voprosy leninizma* (M. 1939), p. 569.

10. In Stalin's judgment, Anglo-French policy is to "let all the participants of war to become mired in war, to encourage them to this on the sly, to let them weaken and exhaust each other, and then when they are sufficiently weak, to intervene with fresh forces and, of course, to intervene 'in the interests of peace', and to dictate their own terms to the combatants. So cheap and so nice!" Ibid., pp. 570–71.

11. Ibid., p. 571.

12. Köstring, *Der militärische Mittler,* p. 225.

13. *Nazi-Soviet Relations, 1939–1941. Documents from the Archives of the German Foreign Office* (Washington, 1948), p. 76.

14. *Akten zur deutschen auswärtigen Politik 1918–1945* (hereafter ADAP), Serie D, 6: 322. Curiously, the Soviet variant of this conversation omits these words, as well as some other details of the conversation. The Soviet document was first published in 1990 in *God krizisa,* 1: 389.

15. Ibid., pp. 386–87 ("Proposal by M. M. Litvinov to the British ambassador in the USSR, U. Seeds. Moscow, April 17, 1939).

16. Z. Sheinis, *Maksim Maksimovich Litvinov: revoliutsioner, diplomat, chelovek* (Moscow, 1989), 363–64.

17. *DGFP*, 7: 204 (No. 192: unsigned memorandum about Hitler's speech to the commanders-in-chief on August 22, 1939).

18. *Sto sorok besed s Molotovym. Iz dnevnika F. Chueva* (Moscow, 1991), p. 274 (notation from November 23, 1971). Molotov added that in the commissariat "Jews comprised the majority in the leadership and among the ambassadors. That was wrong, of course. Latvians and Jews were there; and each one had many other [fellow nationals] dragging along behind. In addition, they regarded me condescendingly when I came and derided the measures that I began to pursue."

19. *SSSR—Germaniia 1939*, pp. 12–13.

20. *ADAP*, 6: 346 (Tippelskirch to Weizsäcker, May 4, 1939).

21. Ibid., pp. 13–14 (memorandum by Schnurre).

22. Ibid., p. 15 (Schulenburg to Weizsäcker, June 5, 1939).

23. Ibid., p. 16.

24. Auswärtiges Amt, Deutsche Botschaft. Tgb. Nr. A/1173/39.178668–72 ("Aufzeichnung." Moscow, June 7, 1939).

25. V. M. Molotov, "O mezhdunarodnom polozhenii i vneshnei politike SSSR. Doklad na 3-i sessii Verkhovnogo Soveta SSSR, 31 maia 1939," *Izvestiia*, June 1, 1939.

26. On June 8, Germany signed a nonaggression agreement with Estonia and Latvia, which aroused considerable alarm in Moscow over Germany's real intentions. According to a report from the British ambassador in Tallin, a prominent Estonian official declared that his country accepted German assistance to avert a Soviet attack, but that it refused to accept a Soviet guarantee against German aggression. *DGFP*, 6: 326 (July 11, 1939).

27. *ADAP*, 6: 607–8 (No. 529: Wermann's notes about his conversation with Draganov).

28. To speed up talks, the British sent a high-ranking diplomat, William Strang, as its plenipotentiary to Moscow. His authority, however, was purely consultative. The day after the announcement of Strang's trip to Moscow, the British ambassador in Berlin told Göring that, if Hitler would enter negotiations with England, he would receive "a not unfriendly reply." Göring, in turn, reiterated the German demands: Danzig, the Polish Corridor, return of the former colonies, and resolution of economic issues. *DGFP*, 6: 12–15 (No. 9: Henderson to Halifax, June 9, 1939).

29. This question is examined in detail in my book, *Politika angliiskogo imperializma v Evrope (oktiabr' 1938—sentiabr' 1939)* (Moscow: Iz-vo Akademii nauk, 1955). Although this book suffers from the serious defi-

ciencies of Soviet historiography in the Stalinist era, it contains extensive material on the history of Anglo-German relations on the eve of
World War II.

30. *Documents on British Foreign Policy*, 5: 646 (no. 589).

31. In accordance with the secret agreement with Germany, Soviet
troops at that point were on the eve of invading Poland.

32. ADAP, Serie D, 6: 673–74 (Schulenburg to the Foreign Ministry.
Moscow, June 29, 1939).

33. A. A. Zhdanov, "Angliiskoe i frantsuzskoe pravitel'stva ne khotiat
ravnogo dogovora v SSSR," *Pravda*, June 29, 1939.

34. GDFP, Serie D, 6: 813 (Weizsäcker to the German embassy in the
USSR. June 20, 1939).

35. Köstring, *Der militärische Mittler*, p. 136.

36. *SSSR-Germaniia 1939. Dokumenty i materialy o sovetsko-germanskikh
otnosheniiakh v aprele-sentiabre 1939 g.* (New York, 1983), p. 23.

37. Ibid., p. 24.

38. DGFP, 7: 19 (memorandum by Schnurre. Berlin, August 10, 1939).

39. Ibid., 7: 27 (Schulenburg to the Foreign Ministry. Moscow, August
11, 1939).

40. Ibid., 7: 49 (record of the conversation between Hitler and Ciano, in
the presence of von Ribbentrop. Obersalzberg, August 12, 1939).

41. Ibid., 7: 54–56 (record of the conversation between Hitler and Ciano,
in von Ribbentrop's presence. Obersalzberg, August 13, 1939).

42. Ibid., 7: 59 (Schnurre to the German embassy in Moscow. Berlin,
August 14, 1939).

43. Ibid., 7: 68–69 (Weizsäcker to the German embassy in Moscow.
Berlin, August 15, 1939).

44. Ibid., 7: 77 (Schulenburg to the Foreign Ministry. Moscow, August 16,
1939); 7: 87–90 (no. 79: Schulenburg to the Foreign Ministry, same date).

45. Ibid., 7: 90.

46. Ibid., 7: 114–16 (Schulenburg to the Foreign Ministry. Moscow,
August 18, 1939).

47. Ibid., 7: 555.

48. Ibid., 7: 121–123 (Ribbentrop to Schulenburg. Berlin, 18 Aug. 1939).

49. *Pravda*, August 21, 1939.

50. Indeed, this was an historic turning point for Hitler himself. In his
subsequent speeches, comments, and letters, the Nazi dictator felt obliged
to justify his decision to enter into direct contact with the Bolsheviks he so
passionately despised.

51. Ibid., 7: 156–67 (Ribbentrop to Schulenburg. Berlin, August 20,
1939).

52. Ibid., 7: 168 (Schulenburg to the Foreign Ministry. Moscow, August
21, 1939).

53. Ibid., 7: 282 (Hitler to Mussolini. August 25, 1939).

54. Ibid., 7: 204.

55. Ibid., 7: 206 (unsigned memorandum on Hitler's second speech of August 22).

56. Auswärtiges Amt. Politisches Archiv. Büro des Staatssekretärs. R29723.e.o.Pol.V 8433 (coded telegram, dated August 22, 1939). (24000)

57. *Izvestiia*, August 24, 1939.

58. *God krizisa*, 3: 335.

59. *ADAP*, Serie D, 7: 206–7 (no. 229: secret additional protocol, signed by Ribbentrop and Molotov). The Soviet Union did not publish this supplementary document until 1990. See Ministerstvo inostrannykh del SSSR, *God krizisa, 1938–1939. Dokumenty i materialy*, 2 (Moscow: Politizdat, 1990), 319–21.

60. Ibid.

61. Stalin asked, however, that Ribbentrop be careful not to give the Japanese the impression that the initiative for this emanated from Moscow. *DGFP*, 7: 225 (Memorandum by Hencke on a conversation on the night of August 23–24 between von Ribbentrop, Stalin and Molotov [Moscow, August 24, 1939]).

62. Ibid., Series D, 7: 228.

63. Auswärtiges Amt. Politisches Archiv. S.69664 (October 19, 1939).

64. Ibid. S.69671.

65. *DGFP*, 7: 229.

66. Ibid., 7: 227–28.

67. Ibid., 10: 10–11 (memorandum by Ribbentrop. Baumschule, June 24, 1940).

68. Köstring, *Der militärische Mittler*, p. 142.

69. *Pravda*, August 24, 1939.

70. *Izvestiia*, August 23, 1940.

71. *God krizisa*, 2: 328 (notes from a conversation between the deputy commissar of foreign affairs, S. A. Lozovskii, with the Chinese ambassador in Moscow. August 26, 1939)

72. *DGFP*, 7: 250 (unsigned memorandum by Ribbentrop).

73. Ibid., 7: 296 (Weizsäcker to the German embassy in Moscow [Berlin, August 25, 1939]).

74. Ibid., 7: 317 (Ribbentrop to the German embassy in Moscow [Berlin, August 25, 1939]).

75. Ibid., 7: 280 (unsigned memorandum on Hitler's statement to the British ambassador on August 25, 1939).

76. Ibid., 7: 425 (memorandum by Dr. Schmidt on a conversation between Ribbentrop and the Russian chargé d'affaires, Ivanov, on August 29, 1939 [Berlin, August 29, 1939]).

77. See *Trial of the Major War Criminals before the International Military Tribunal* (Nuremberg, 1947), 10: 271, 514–15; 39: 107. For details of the political crisis in late August, see my *Politika angliiskogo imperializma v Evrope* (Moscow: izd-vo Akademii nauk, 1955), 402–37.

78. *DGFP*, 7: 438n.

79. Ibid., 7: 409 (Köstring and Schulenburg to the Foreign Ministry. Moscow, August 29, 1939).

80. Ibid., 7: 439–40 (Schulenburg to the Foreign Ministry. Moscow, August 30, 1939).

81. *Izvestiia*, September 1, 1939 [emphasis mine].

82. Ibid.

83. *Pravda*, September 2, 1939.

84. *DGFP*, 7: 540–41 (Ribbentrop to the German embassy in Moscow [Berlin, September 3, 1939]). Ribbentrop emphasized that "in our estimation this would be not only a relief for us, but also be in [conformity with] the sense of the Moscow agreements, and in the Soviet interest as well" (p. 541).

85. *ADAP*, Serie D, 8: 3–4 (Schulenburg to the Foreign Ministry. Moscow, September 5, 1939).

86. Auswärtiges Amt. Botschaft Moskau. Abschrift. Pol.V. Geheime Staatspolizei. Berlin August 30, 1939. 69761.

87. Ibid. Abschrift Pol.V 2060 g. Geheime Staatspolizei. Berlin, September 7, 1939. 69705.

88. Ibid. Berlin, September 14, 1939. 69707.

89. *DGFP*, 8: 34–35 (Schulenburg to the Foreign Ministry. Moscow, September 10, 1939).

90. *Pravda*, September 14, 1939; *Izvestiia*, September 15, 1939.

91. *DGFP*, 8: 60–61 (Schulenburg to the Foreign Ministry. Moscow, September 14, 1939).

92. Ibid., 8: 69 (Ribbentrop to the German Embassy in USSR. Berlin, September 15, 1939).

93. Ibid., 8: 95–97 (memorandum by Hilder, an official at the German embassy in Moscow. September 18, 1939).

94. *Izvestiia*, September 18, 1939.

95. Ibid.

96. *Izvestiia*, September 19, 1939.

97. Partiinyi arkhiv Moskovskogo komiteta i Moskovskogo gorodskogo komiteta KPSS, f. 69, op. 1, d. 1038 (korobka L-37), l. 37 (stenogram of a plenary session of the RK, September 9, 1939).

98. Ibid., l. 42.

99. Ibid., f. 3, op. 24, d. 204 (korobka 355), l. 120.

100. *DGFP*, Series D, 8: 77 (Schulenburg to the Foreign Ministry. Moscow, September 16, 1939).

101. Ibid.

102. Ibid., 8: 92 (Schulenburg to the Foreign Ministry. September 18, 1939).

103. Ibid., 8: 103 (Ribbentrop to the German embassy in the USSR. Berlin, September 19, 1939).

104. Auswärtiges Amt. Politisches Archiv. Botschaft Moskau. Geheim. Protocoll. Moscow, September 21, 1939. S.146372.

105. DGFP, 8: 105 (Schulenburg to the Foreign Ministry. Moscow, September 20, 1930). The reason for the démarche was the report of the aide to the Soviet military attaché, who saw the German operational map, which consigned L'vov to the German sphere of interests.

106. Olaf Groeler, *Selbstmörderische Allianz. Deutsch-russische Militärbeziehungen, 1920–1941* (Berlin: Vision Verlag, 1992), p. 120.

107. Köstring, *Der militärische Mittler*, p. 144.

108. Auswärtiges Amt, Politisches Archiv. Deutsche Botschaft, S. 69743–44.

109. Ibid. Der Militär- und Luftattaché. Moscow, September 24, 1939 (S. 69713).

110. Groehler, pp. 12–13, 122–23.

111. See G. F. Krivosheev, *Poteri vooruzhennykh sil SSSR v voinakh, boevykh deistviiakh i voennykh konfliktakh. Statisticheskoe issledovanie* (Moscow: Voennoe izdatel'stvo, 1993), p. 87.

112. Ibid., p. 86.

113. Adam B. Ulam, *Stalin: The Man and His Era* (Boston: Beacon Press, 1989), pp. 515–16.

114. DGFP, 8: 105 (Schulenburg to the Foreign Ministry. Moscow, September 20, 1939).

115. Ibid., 8: 130 (Schulenburg to the Foreign Ministry. Moscow, September 25, 1939).

116. ADAP, 8: 127–128.

117. Ibid., 8: 128.

118. Ibid., 8: 129.

119. Ibid.

120. Ibid., 8: 129–30.

121. *Izvestiia*, December 25, 1939.

122. ADAP, Series D, 12(2): 889–90.

123. DGFP, Series D, 8: 886 (memorandum by an official in the Foreign Minister's secretariat. Rome, March 10, 1940).

124. C. Attlee, *As It Happened* (London, 1954), p. 111.

125. For details of Germany's "peace offensive" after the annihilation of Poland, see A. M. Nekrich, *Vneshniaia politika Anglii v gody vtoroi mirovoi voiny, 1939–1941 gg.* (Moscow: Akademiia nauk, 1963), pp. 186–208.

126. Arnold and Veronica Toynbee, eds., *The Initial Triumph of the Axis* (London, 1958), p. 97.

127. *DGFP*, Series D, 8: 167 (declaration of September 28, 1939 by the Soviet and German governments).

128. Auswärtiges Amt. Deutsche Botschaft. Moscow, September 30, 1939 969701); October 2, 1939 (69669, 69700).

129. Ibid. (Notes by A. Metzger. Moscow, September 22, 1939. 69736–38).

130. Gosudarstvennyi arkhiv Novosibirsk oblasti, f. 4, op. 3, d. 296, l. 179 (Radio guidelines sent to the secretaries of local party committees on September 17, 1939).

131. Ibid., f. 4, op. 3, d. 49, ll. 229–33 (report from the Tomsk city committee) and ll. 156–72 (information sent from the Stalinsk [Novokuznetsk] city committee for September 19, 1939).

132. Ibid., f. 4, op. 3, d. 302, l. 429.

133. Ibid., d. 302, l. 338 (reports to the propaganda and agitation office of the Novosibirsk oblast' committee).

134. *Izvestiia*, November 1, 1939.

135. In fact, of course, Stalin simply wanted to foist responsibility for the Poles onto Hitler.

136. RGASA, f. 9, op.40, d. 63, ll. 62–64.

137. Ibid., ll. 29–33.

138. Ibid., f. 25880, op. 4, l. 288 (see also the report from the head of the military section of the Central Committee, U. Chubukov, dated October 9, 1939).

139. Ibid., f.9, op.40, d. 63, ll. 212–15.

140. "Komintern i sovetsko-germanskii dogovor o nenapadenii. Analiticheskii material, podgotovlennyi Institutom Marksizma-Leninizma pri TsK KPSS, sovmestno s Mezhdunarodnym otdelom TsK KPSS," *Izvestiia TsK KPSS*, 1989, no. 4: 210.

141. Stalin made this statement on September 7, 1939—that is, prior to the time when the Red Army invaded Poland.

142. Ibid., p. 207.

143. Ibid., p. 210.

144. Ibid., p. 211. See F. I. Firsov, "Arkhivy Kominterna i vneshniaia politika SSSR v 1939–1941 gg.," *Novaia i noveishaia istoriia*, 1992, no. 6: 26.

145. "Komintern i sovetsko-germanskii dogovor," p. 214.

146. P. J. Goebbels, *The Goebbels Diaries, 1939–1941* (New York: Penguin Books, 1982), p. 42.

147. *DGFP*, 8: 187 (memorandum by Schmidt on conversations between Hitler and Ciano on October 1, 1939).

148. Ibid., 8: 208–12.

149. Ibid., 8: 887–88.
150. Ibid., 8: 891 ("What Program do you have for your stay in Rome, Comrade Ribbentrop?")
151. Heinz Boberach, ed., *Meldungen aus dem Reich*, Die geheimen Lageberichte des Sicherheitsdienstes des SS 1938–1945, 7 vols. (Herrsching: Pawlag Verlag, 1984), 3: 700 (January 28, 1940).
152. Ibid., 3: 524 (December 4, 1939).
153. Ibid., 3: 701.
154. Ibid., 3: 711 (January 31, 1940).

5. Conquests and Conflicts

1. Bundesarchiv-Militärarchiv, RH 2/2932, pp. 112–17 (Köstring memorandum of October 1, 1939).
2. *DGFP*, 8: 174–75 (German envoy Frohwein in Estonia to the Foreign Ministry. Tallinn, 29 Sept. 1939).
3. *Izvestiia*, April 7, 1962.
4. TsGAOR Estonskoi SSR, f. 84, op. 1, d. 1046, l. 32.
5. Ibid., p. 149.
6. Winston Churchill, *The Second World War*, 1 (London, 1949) : 667.
7. *DGFP*, 8: 207 (Ribbentrop to the German embassy in the USSR. Berlin, October 4, 1939).
8. Ibid., 8: 198–99 (German envoy in Latvia, Kotze, to the German Foreign Ministry. Riga, October 3, 1939), 212–13 (Schulenburg to the German Foreign Ministry. Moscow, October 5, 1939).
9. Ibid., 8: 214 (Ribbentrop to the German embassy in the USSR. Berlin, October 5, 1939).
10. "Kommentarii Ministerstva oborony SSSR. Smena rukovodstva Narkomata oborony SSSR v sviazi s urokami sovetsko-finliandskoi voiny 1939–194 gg.," *Izvestiia TsK KPSS*, 1990, no.1: 211.
11. V. Kholodkovskii, "Eta zimniaia voina," *Leninskaia pravda* (Petrozavodsk), January 4, 1990. The late historian Kholodkovskii was the best Russian specialist on the history of Finland and Soviet-Finnish relations.
12. *Izvestiia*, November 1, 1939.
13. RTsKhIDNI, f. 77, op. 1, d. 889, ll. 1–6. The document also announced that the Finns had been liberated from the power and oppression of "the bourgeoisie and its stooges."
14. Ibid., ll. 19–25.
15. Ibid., d. 891, ll. 1–2. In fact, Zhdanov also edited and corrected all the major documents dealing with the new areas of western Belorussia as well.
16. "Kommentarii Ministerstva oborony SSSR. Smena rukovodstva Narkomata oborony SSSR v sviazi s urokami sovetsko-finliandskoi voiny 1939–1940," *Izvestiia TsK KPSS*, 1990, no. 1: 212.

17. "Poteri," p. 96.

18. Ibid., p. 103.

19. Auswärtiges Amt. Politisches Archiv. W 1Y 3375 S.452678–680 (note, signed by Schmidt. Berlin September 2, 1939).

20. Ibid. Ha.-Pol. Wiehl. Akten 33/4 concerning Russia (Oct. 1939-Feb. 1940). Bd. 13: E041519.

21. Ibid. W 4110, 452734–738 ("Concerning the Moscow Negotiations").

22. Ibid. (Encoded telegram. Berlin, April 3, 1940).

23. A. I. Shakhurin, Kryl'ia pobedy (3rd ed.; Moscow, 1990), pp. 99–102.

24. Ibid., pp. 118–19.

25. DGFP, Series D, 8: 740 (Ribbentrop to the German embassy in the USSR. Berlin, February 3, 1940).

26. Ibid., 8: 755–57 (Memorandum from Ritter and Tippelskirch at the German embassy to the Foreign Ministry. Moscow, February 9, 1940).

27. Ibid., 8: 816 (memorandum by Schnurre, chairman of the Economic Delegation in the Soviet Union. Berlin, February 26, 1940). This sum included deliveries set by the August 19, 1939 agreement as well as other goods shipped to Czechoslovakia (under prior commitments).

28. Ibid., 8: 817.

29. RGAE, f. 413, op. 13, d. 2767, l. 69 (memorandum entitled "The Significance of Economic Cooperation between the Soviet Union and Germany").

30. Ibid., l. 165.

31. Ibid., f. 413, op. 13, d. 2778, l. 73.

32. Bundesarchiv-Militärarchiv RW 4/Y, 328 (Note from the head of the transportation system, October 4, 1939).

33. DGFP, Series D, 8: 921 (Ribbentrop to the German embassy in the USSR. Berlin, March 14, 1940).

34. RGAE, f. 413, op. 13, d. 2856, ll. 78–79.

35. Ibid., l. 5.

36. Ibid., d. 2856, l. 55.

37. Ibid.

38. Ibid., f. 413, op. 13, d. 2778, l. 76.

39. Ibid., d. 2778, l. 55.

40. Ibid., l. 56.

41. DGFP, Series D, 8: 369 (Schnurre and Schulenburg to the Foreign Ministry. Moscow, November 1, 1939).

42. RGAE, f. 413, op. 13, d. 2856, ll. 5–6.

43. Ibid., ll. 5–6.

44. DGFP, Series D, 8: 589 (memorandum from German ambassador Ritter, "The Conference in the Kremlin on December 31, 1939").

45. Boberach, Meldungen aus dem Reich, 4: 1208 (June 3, 1940).

46. Ibid., 4: 1234–35 (June 6, 1940).

47. Ibid., 4: 1241 (June 10, 1941).

48. *DGFP*, Series D, 8: 923–24 (memorandum by ambassador Ritter. Berlin, March 15, 1940).

49. RGAE, f. 413, op. 13, d. 3033, ll. 2–5.

50. Ibid., d. 2477, ll. 40–77 ("Information bulletin of "Mashinoimport").

51. F. Friedensberg, "Die sowjetischen Kriegslieferungen an das Hitlerreich," *Vierteljahrheft zur Wirtschaftsforschung*, 4 (1962) : 331–68.

52. RGAE, f. 413, op. 13, d. 2852, ll. 8, 17, 24, 34, 47, 79 et passim.

53. Copy located in ibid., f. 413, d. 2407, l. 151.

54. Ibid., d. 2478, l. 78.

55. Ibid., l. 79.

56. *DGFP*, Series D, 8: 825 (memorandum by an official in the Foreign Minister's secretariat. Berlin, March 1, 1940).

57. Ibid., 8: 876 (Hitler to Mussolini. Berlin, March 8, 1940).

58. Ibid., 8: 887 (memorandum by an official of Ribbentrop's secretariat. Rome, March 10, 1940).

59. Bundesarchiv-Militärarchiv, RM 11/35, p. 4 (Telegram from Schulenburg. Moscow, October 5, 1939. "Secret").

60. Ibid., pp. 81–84 (Roeder to the Aussenminister. Berlin, October 12, 1939).

61. Ibid., p. 254 (Berlin, October 18, 1939).

62. Ibid., p. 24 (Baumbach. Coded telegram from Moscow, October 22, 1939).

63. Ibid., p. 32 (Wagner - M Att. Berlin, November 7, 1939).

64. Ibid., p. 36 (coded telephone conversation from Moscow, October 10, 1939); p. 52 (Naval attache B.Nr. 401/39 gKdos. Moscow, November 15, 1939).

65. Ibid, p. 102 ("for Mr. State-Secretary personally" and "for the Supreme Command of the Navy." Moscow, December 9, 1939).

66. Ibid., p. 106 (coded telegram from the naval attaché in Moscow, December 12, 1939).

67. Ibid., p. 126 (coded telegram from the naval attaché in Moscow, 11.12.1939).

68. Ibid., p. 112 (report from the naval attaché to the chief naval command, December 13, 1939).

69. Bundesarchiv—Militärarchiv RM 11/396, p.2 (memorandum from the Chief Naval Command to the Foreign Ministry. Berlin, August 29, 1940). A year later, when the Germans left its secret refueling and supply station on Soviet territory, the German Foreign Ministry deleted the reference to the base in a note from the German naval command expressing its gratitude. (ibid., p. 4: appended to B. Nr. 376/40).

70. Ibid, p. 10.

71. Ibid., p. 20 (memorandum from the German naval attaché, September 24, 1940).

72. Ibid., p. 28 (memorandum from the German naval attaché to the chief naval command, September 30, 1940).

73. Ibid., pp. 27–28 (report from the naval attaché to the Chief Naval Command, October 14, 1940).

74. *New York Times*, October 15, 1992. This text has been slightly edited for felicity and consistency (*Trans.*).

75. Alexandre Cretzianu, *The Lost Opportunity* (London, 1957), p. 137.

76. For details on the Balkan conflict in 1939–41, see A. M. Nekrich, *Vneshniaia politika Anglii v gody vtoroi mirovoi voiny, 1939–1941 gg.* (Moscow, 1963).

77. *Foreign Relations of the United States : Diplomatic Papers* [hereafter FRUS], 1 (Washington, D.C.) (Bullitt to the Secretary of State, January 26, 1940).

78. *Les évenements survenue en France de 1933 à 1945* (Paris,), 6: 1951.

79. Ibid., 5: 1142.

80. *DGFP*, 8: 885 (memorandum by an official, Schmidt, in the secretariat of the German Foreign Minister. Rome, March 10, 1940).

81. Firsov, p. 28.

82. *DGFP*, 8: 631–33 (chief of the German High Command, Keitel, to the Foreign Minister. Berlin, January 8, 1940).

83. Ibid., 8: 709–11 (unsigned memorandum from the German embassy in Moscow. January 25, 1940).

84. Ibid., 8: 89 (Hitler to Mussolini. Berlin, March 8, 1940).

85. Ibid., 8: 900 (memorandum by Schmidt, an official in the secretariat of the Foreign Minister. Rome, March 11, 1940).

86. Kemenov (b. 1908), an art historian, was a proponent of "socialist realism." In 1938–1940 he had served as director of the Tret'iakov Art Gallery in Moscow, but was then appointed chairman of VOKS, a post he held until 1948. He was later a deputy minister of culture in the USSR, a Soviet representative at UNESCO and president of the Academy of Arts of the USSR.

87. GA RF, f. 5283, op. 5, d. 754, l. 50 (Deutsche Botschaft. "Verbalnote an das Volkskommissariat für Auswäritge Angelegenheiten." Moscow, October 21, 1940).

88. Walter Schmidt, "Russische Jahre. Erlebtes aus 40 Jahren deutsch-sowjetischer Beziehungen" (manuscript in the Auswärtiges Amt, Bonn. January 1988), p. 39.

89. Ibid., p. 40.

90. GA RF, f. 5283, op. 5, d. 750, ll. 6–8 (conversation with the consultant on cultural question in the German Foreign Ministry, Dr. Kleist, in VOKS, on January 27, 1940).

91. Ibid., d. 748, l. 191.

92. Ibid., d. 746, ll. 111–12.

93. Ibid., l. 112.

94. Those participating included Aleksandr M. Aleksandrov (chief of the bureau for central Europe in the commissariat) and Bitiaev (his deputy), together with Vladimir S. Kemenov (chairman of VOKS, later vice-president of the Academy of Arts) and G. Kheifets (his deputy).

95. GA RF, f. 5283, op. 5, d. 750, l. 11.

96. Kobulov later became a colonel-general and deputy ministry of state security; he was executed together with Beria in 1953.

97. GA RF, f. 5283, op. 5, d. 750, l. 16 (note on a conversation with Schotte, a secretary of the Central Bureau for Eastern Europe. Berlin, April 25, 1940.

98. Dekanozov was the last ambassador in Berlin before the outbreak of war; he was also a deputy commissar of internal affairs. He was executed in connection with the Beria case in 1953.

99. A. Lozovskii (1878–1952) was shot as part of the Anti-fascist Jewish committee.

100. Arkadii A. Sobolev (1903–1964) was general secretary of the NKVD (1939–1942).

101. GA RF, f. 5283, op. 5, d. 750, ll. 1–2 (minutes of the meeting, August 27, 1940).

102. Ibid., f. 5283, op. 5, d. 750, ll. 3–5 (Kemenov to Molotov, draft).

103. Boberach, *Meldungen aus dem Reich*. B.5, N 122 (September 9, 1940).

104. Ibid.

105. GA RF, f. 5283, op. 5, d. 749, l. 6.

106. Ibid., d. 755, l. 243–243 ob. (Rudomino, director of the Central State Library of Foreign Literature, to VOKS, first Western office. February 13, 1941).

107. Colin Ross (1885–1947) was born in Vienna. He was a mining engineer by training, but became a journalist following the success of his first book, *Im Bann des Eisens*, in 1911. He traveled and wrote extensively. He served in World War I and afterward resumed his journeys and writing. In 1922 he visited the Soviet Union, which he described in the book *Der Weg nach Osten*, which—contrary to the widespread opinion that the Bolshevik government would inevitably collapse—predicted that it would be long-lived. His most important book was *Die Welt auf dem Waage*, which was published in 1928.

108. GA RF, f. 5283, op. 5, d. 749, l. 10.

109. Ibid., p. 20. The following telegram was sent to the Leningrad bureau, Kul'tsviaz' : "On the 17th is arriving [in Leningrad] the German journalist Ross. Organize a program of cultural shows. [From] VOKS. Kheifets." An analogous telegram was sent to Kiev.

110. Ibid., l. 3.

111. Ibid.

112. Ibid., ll. 4–5.

113. Ibid., d. 746, l. 198.

114. Pal'gunov (1898–1971) was head of the press section in the NKVD from 1940 to 1943.

115. GA RF, ll. 49–50.

116. Ibid., d. 746, l. 239.

117. Ibid., l. 240.

118. Ibid., d. 758, l. 17 (Kheifets to Pavlov, the chief of the office on central Europe at the foreign affairs' commissariat. March 3, 1941).

119. GA RF, f. 5283, op. 5, d. 759, l. 18.

120. Schmidt, p. 49.

121. *DGFP*, Series D, 9: 40–41 (Ribbentrop to the German embassy in the USSR. Berlin, March 28, 1940).

122. Ibid., 8: 53–54 (Schulenburg to the Foreign Ministry. Moscow, March 30, 1940).

123. Firsov, p. 18.

124. *DGFP*, Series 4, 9: 134–36 (Schulenburg to State-Secretary Weizsäcker. Moscow, April 11, 1940).

125. Ibid., 9: 81–82 (Schulenburg to the Foreign Ministry. Moscow, April 6, 1940).

126. Ibid., 9: 59–61 (memorandum by Dr. Gramsch, an official in the Four-Year Plan. Berlin, April 1, 1940).

127. Ibid., 9: 82–83 (Schulenburg to the Foreign Ministry. Moscow, April 6, 1940).

128. J.R.M. Butler, *Grand Strategy*, 2 (London 1957) : 119–20.

129. *DGFP*, Series D, vol. 9, no. 104 (Schulenburg to the Foreign Ministry. Moscow, April 13, 1940).

130. Ibid., 9: 173 (Ribbentrop to the German embassy in the USSR. Berlin, April 15, 1940).

131. Ibid., 9: 106 (Schulenburg to the Foreign Ministry. Moscow, April 9, 1940).

132. Ibid., 9: 108.

133. Ibid., 9: 157–58 (Minutes by Ambassador Ritter. Berlin, April 13, 1940).

134. Ibid., 9: 222–24 (State-secretary Weizsäcker to the Germany embassy in the USSR. Berlin, April 23, 1940).

135. *Vneshniaia politika SSSR*, 4 (M. 1946), 459–60, 474–75.

136. *DGFP*, 9: 248–49.

137. Ibid., 9: 505.

138. Ibid., series D, 9: 317 (Ritter to the embassy in the USSR).

139. *Vneshniaia politika SSSR*, 4: 505–6.

140. *DGFP*, Series D, 9: 454 (Schnurre to the German embassy in the USSR. Berlin, May 28, 1940. Draft of telegram).

141. Ibid., 9: 293–94 (Ribbentrop to the German ambassador. Berlin, May 28, 1940 [draft telegram]).

142. Ibid., 9: 316 (Schulenburg to the Foreign Ministry. Moscow, May 10, 1940).

143. Paul Reynaud, *La France a sauvé l'Europe*, 2: 94.

144. Ibid., 9: 331–32 (Ritter to the German embassy in the USSR. Berlin, May 12, 1940).

145. *DGFP*, Series D, 9: 412–14 (memorandum by ambassador Ritter. Berlin, May 22, 1940).

146. Ibid., 9: 470–71 (Schulenburg to the Foreign Ministry. Moscow, May 29, 1940).

147. Ibid.

148. Walter Ansel, *Hitler Confronts England* (Durham, 1960), p. 71.

149. Ibid, pp. 107–8.

150. Boberach, *Meldungen aus dem Reich* 4:1276 (June 20, 1940).

151. Ibid. 5:1334 (July 4, 1940).

152. *DGFP*, Series D, 9: 595–96 (circular of state-secretary Weizsäcker. Berlin, June 17, 1940).

153. Ibid. (Schulenburg to the Foreign Ministry. Moscow, June 18, 1940).

154. Ibid., 9: 636 (memorandum by an official of the Political Division IM [Heyden-Rynsch]. Berlin, June 20, 1940).

155. *DGFP*, Series D, 10: 11–12 (Schulenburg to the Foreign Ministry. Moscow, June 24, 1940).

156. Ibid., 9: 661–62 (Schulenburg to the Foreign Ministry. Moscow, June 22, 1940).

157. Ibid., 10: 3–4 (Schulenburg to the Foreign Ministry. Moscow, June 23, 1940).

158. Ibid., 9: 26 (Schulenburg to the Foreign Ministry. Moscow, June 26, 1940).

159. Ibid., 10: 12 (Ribbentrop to the German embassy in the USSR. Sonderzug, June 25, 1940).

160. Ibid., 9: 58–59 (Adolf Hitler to King Carol II of Romania. Führer's headquarters, June 29, 1940).

161. Boberach, *Meldungen aus dem Reich* 5: 1358 (July 8, 1940).

162. Ibid. 5: 1336 (July 4, 1940).

163. Ibid. 5: 1376 (July 15, 1940).

164. Ibid. 5: 1369 (July 18, 1940).

165. Ibid. 5: 1479–80 (August 19, 1940).

166. Ibid. 5: 1381.

167. Ibid., 5: 1383.

168. Ibid. 5: 1395 (July 18, 1940).

169. Ibid., 5: 1396.

170. Ibid., 5: 1402 (July 22, 1940).

171. Ibid., 5: 1415–16 (July 25, 1940).

172. Ibid. 5: 1456–67 (August 8, 1940).

173. Ibid., 5: 1482 (August 19, 1940).

174. Ibid., 5: 1580–81 125 (19 Sept. 1940), 1605 (26 Sept. 1948), 1620 (30 Sept. 1940), S. 1620.

175. DGFP, 10: 270–71 (memorandum from Schnurre, an official of the Economic Policy Department. Berlin, July 22, 1940).

176. Ibid., 11: 221–223 (memorandum by an official in the Economic Policy Department [Schnurre]. Berlin, September 28, 1940).

177. Ibid., 10: 497 ("Note concerning the Problem of Yugoslavia." Berlin, August 16, 1940).

178. Ibid., 10: 115 (State secretary and deputy to the commissioner for the Four-Year Plan (Körner) to Ribbentrop. Berlin, July 3, 1940); 10: 401–3 (Commissioner of the Four-Year-Plan, Göring, to the Reich Commissar, August 2, 1940).

179. Ibid., 10: 584 (Ribbentrop to Romanian Foreign Minister Mano-ilescu. Vienna, August 30, 1940).

180. Ibid., 10: 156, n. 2.

181. Ibid., 238 (Schulenburg to the Foreign Ministry. Moscow, July 17, 1940).

182. Ibid., 10: 132 (minister in Hungary [Erdmannsdorff] to the Foreign Ministry. Budapest, July 5, 1940). The Hungarian emissary to Berlin told Weizsäcker that Soviet-Hungarian relations were "even better than correct" (ibid., n.1).

183. Ibid, 10: 341 (unsigned memorandum about the conversation between Hitler and the Bulgarian Minister-President, Filov. July 27, 1940).

184. Ibid., 10: 487 (Ribbentrop to the German embassy in Italy. Berlin, August 16, 1940).

185. Ibid., 10: 61 (von Papen to the Foreign Ministry. Ankara, June 29, 1940).

186. Ibid., 10: 77–78 (Ribbentrop to von Papen. From the "Special Train," July 1, 1940).

187. Ibid., 10: 107 (von Papen to the Foreign Ministry. Ankara, July 3, 1940).

188. Ibid., 10: 231 (Von Papen to the Foreign Ministry. Ankara, July 16, 1940).

189. Ibid., 10: 196, n.4 (Schulenburg to state-secretary Weizsäcker. Moscow, July 11, 1940).

190. Ibid., 10: 280–81 (memorandum from the director of the Political Division VII [Melchers]. Berlin, July 23, 1940).

191. Ibid., 10: 416–19 (German ambassador in Italy, Mackensen, to the Foreign Ministry. Rome, August 6, 1940).

192. W. S. Churchill, *The Second World War*, 2 (London 1949) : 119–20.

193. "Russia and the West," *Economist*, July 27, 1940, p. 113.

194. J.R.M. Butler, ed., *Grand Strategy*, 7 vols. (London, 1956–76), 2: 211–12.

195. Franz Halder, *The Halder Diaries*, 2 vols. (Boulder : Westview Press, 1976), 1: 487. (Hereafter cited as Halder.)

196. Ibid., 1: 503 (July 7, 1940).

197. Ibid., 1: 506.

198. For details see Nekrich, *Vneshniaia politika Anglii, 1939–1941*, pp. 285–324.

199. Churchill, 2: 229.

200. Halder, 1: 518 (July 22, 1940).

201. *DGFP*, 10: 207–8 (Schulenburg to the Foreign Ministry. Moscow, July 13, 1940).

202. Halder, 1: 518 (July 22, 1940).

203. Between July 10 and October 31, 1940, the Luftwaffe lost 1,103 airplanes, the Royal Air Force only 642 fighters. In the period between April and September 1940, the English production of airplanes (mostly fighters) increased from 256 to 467 a month. M. M. Postan, *British War Production* (London, 1952), p. 116.

204. *Hitlers Weisungen für die Kriegführung* (Munich, 1965), p. 81.

205. Ribbentrop proposed full collaboration and satisfaction of any desire (a hint that the Duke could reclaim the crown) if the Duke and his wife would assist in restoring peace between Germany and England. *DGFP*, Series D, 10: 378 (Ribbentrop to the legation in Portugal. Special Train, Fuschl, July 31, 1940).

206. *Izvestiia*, August 2, 1940.

207. See, for instance, Ribbentrop's stern protest to the Soviet ambassador (Shkvartsev) over a trivial incident involving the publication of an article in a Riga newspaper (*Januakas Zinas*) entitled "German Communist Against Diktat at Compiegne." *DGFP*, Series D, 10: 425–26 (memorandum by Ribbentrop. Berlin, August 6, 1940).

208. Ibid., 10: 428–29 (State-secretary Weizsäcker to the German embassy in the USSR. Berlin, August 6, 1940).

209. Ibid., 11: 8–10 (Ribbentrop to the Germany embassy in the USSR. Berlin, September 6, 1940). See also ibid., 10: 23–24 (Berlin, September 6, 1940).

210. Ibid., 11: 23–24 (Schulenburg to the Foreign Ministry. Moscow, September 5, 1940).

211. Ibid., 11: 73–74 (Schulenburg to the Foreign Ministry. Moscow, September 14, 1940).

212. Ibid., 11: 116–22 (record of a conversation between Ribbentrop and Mussolini in Rome, September 19, 1940).

213. Ibid., 11: 78 (German embassy in Washington to the Foreign Ministry, September 24, 1940).

214. Ibid., 11: 249 (record of a conversation between Hitler and Mussolini at the Brenner, October 4, 1940).

215. Ibid., 11: 188 (Ribbentrop to the German embassy in the USSR. Berlin, September 26, 1940). The pact, valid for a ten-year term, acknowledged Germany's and Italy's right to establish a new order in Europe and Japan's hegemony to do the same in "Greater East Asia." The agreement stipulated economic, political and military assistance in the event that any one of the signatories were attacked by a new power not currently engaged in the European or Sino-Japanese conflict. Ibid., 11: 204–5 (Tripartite Pact, September 27, 1940).

216. Ibid., 11: 195–96 (charge d'affairs in the Soviet Union to the Foreign Ministry. Moscow, September 27, 1940).

217. Ibid., 11: 206 (Ott to Matsuoka. Tokyo, September 27, 1940).

218. Ibid., 11: 268, n.2 (memorandum of State-Secretary Weizsäcker. Berlin, October 9, 1940).

219. Pravda, September 30, 1940.

220. Ibid., October 5, 1940.

221. Meldungen aus dem Reich, 5: 1632–33 (October 3, 1940).

222. Ibid., 5: 1654 (October 10, 1940).

223. Köstring, Der militärische Mittler, p. 280.

224. DGFP, 11: 248 (record of talks between Hitler and Mussolini at the Brenner, October 4, 1940).

225. Ibid., 11: 632 (record of a conversation between Hitler and Count Teleki in Berlin, November 26, 1940).

226. Köstring, Der militärische Mittler, p. 282.

227. Ibid., p. 284.

228. Ibid., p. 285.

229. Ibid., p. 286.

230. DGFP, 11: 291–97 (Ribbentrop to Stalin. Berlin, October 13, 1940).

231. Ibid., 10: 296–97.

232. Ibid., 11: 291.

233. "Perepiska V. M. Molotova so I. V. Stalinym. Noiabr' 1940g.," Voenno-istoricheskii zhurnal, 1992, no. 9: 18–23.

234. Ibid., p. 20.

235. Ibid., p. 18 (telegram from V. M. Molotov to I. V. Stalin. November 12, 1940).

236. Ibid., p. 18 (Stalin to Molotov. November 12, 1940).

237. Ibid., 11: 549 (record of the talks between Hitler and Molotov on November 12, 1940).

238. Ibid., 11: 550–62 (record of the conversation between Hitler and Molotov on November 13, 1940).

239. "Perepiska Molotova so Stalinym," p. 13 (telegram from Molotov to Stalin, November 13, 1940).

240. Ibid., p. 20.

241. Ibid., p. 21 (telegram from Molotov to Stalin, November 14, 1940).

242. Ibid., p. 20 (telegram from Stalin to Molotov, November 13, 1940).

243. DGFP, Series D, 11: 562–70 (record of the final talks between Ribbentrop and Molotov. Berlin, November 13, 1940).

244. Bundesarchive-Militärarchiv, RM 7/667, p. 73 (Seekriegsleitung, Politisches Übersicht, November 12, 1940).

245. DGFP, Series D, 11: 714–15 (Schulenburg to the Foreign Ministry. Moscow, November 26, 1940).

246. Ibid., 11: 724 (Schnurre to the Foreign Ministry. Moscow, November 28, 1940).

247. Hitler tried to persuade the Bulgarian foreign minister to join the Axis powers on the grounds that this would force Russia to abandon its designs. Failure to do so would invite Soviet intervention and pressure : "As long as the Russians knew that Bulgaria was not a member of the Tripartite Pact, Russia would try to blackmail Bulgaria in every conceivable way." Ibid., 11: 770 (conversation between Hitler and the Bulgarian foreign minister, Draganov, on December 3, 1940).

248. Ibid., 11: 1066–68 (Economic Agreement of January 10, 1941).

249. Ibid., 11: 1068–69.

6. Toward the Abyss

1.Boberach, Meldungen aus dem Reich, 6: 1774–1775.

2. Ibid., 6: 1787.

3. Ibid., 6: 1868.

4. Köstring, Der militärische Mittler, p. 289 (report dated December 4, 1940).

5. DGFP, Series D, 11: 1124–25 (Schulenburg to the Foreign Ministry. Moscow, January 17, 1941).

6. This convention regulating the Straits was signed on July 21, 1936 by Great Britain, Australia, Bulgaria, Greece, Romania, the USSR, Turkey, France, Yugoslavia and Japan. It took effect November 9, 1936. It permitted the unimpeded transit of trade vessels through the Straits both in wartime and peacetime; military vessels and their presence in the Black Sea were governed by special rules. In the event Turkey became a combatant, the decision on the transit of military vessels of other powers through the Straits was to be determined by Turkey alone.

7. Ibid., 11: 1155–56 (Ribbentrop to state-secretary Weizsäcker. Fuschl, January 21, 1941).

8. Ibid., 11: 1172 (Schulenburg to the Foreign Ministry. Moscow, January 23, 1941).

9. Ibid., Series D, 12: 150 (record of the conversation between Ribbentrop and Ambassador Oshima at Fuschl on February 23, 1941).

10. Ibid., 142.

11. Ibid., p. 150.

12. Boberach, *Meldungen aus dem Reich*, 6: 1895 (January 13, 1941), 1907 (January 16, 1941).

13. Ibide., 1954–55 (January 30, 1941).

14. *FRUS 1941*, 1: 272 (memorandum from Sumner Welles. Washington, January 1 1941).

15. AVP (Istoriko-diplomaticheskii arkhiv Ministerstva inostrannykh del SSSR), f. 296, d.3 (Bulgarian ambassador, Naumov, to the Bulgarian Foreign Ministry. Washington, February 11, 1941).

16. *DGFP (D)*, 12: 195 (Schulenburg to the Foreign Ministry. Moscow, March 1, 1941). See also ibid., 213–16 (Schulenburg to the Foreign Ministry. Moscow, March 3, 1941).

17. *FRUS 1941*, 1: 296 (Earl to the Secretary of State. Sofia, March 4, 1941).

18. *Vneshniaia politika SSSR*, 4: 544–45.

19. *DGFP(D)*, 12: 5–8 (Waizsäcker, memorandum of February, 1 1941).

20. Ibid., 11: 933 (Hitler to Mussolini. December, 3 1940).

21. Ibid., 12: 4–5 (Schnurre to Schulenburg. Berlin, February 1, 1941).

22. Ibid., n.3 (from Schulenberg's reply of February 6, 1941).

23. Ibid., 12: 10 (memorandum by an official [Schmidt] in the foreign minister's secretariat. Berlin, February 3, 1941).

24. Ibid., 12: 312 (memorandum by Schmidt. Berlin, March 18, 1941).

25. Ibid., 12: 331–32 (memorandum by Schmidt. Munich, March 23, 1941).

26. Ibid., 12: 127 (Ambassador Ritter to the Germany embassy in the USSR. Berlin, February 22, 1941).

27. Ibid., 12: 221–22 (memorandum by Schmidt, in the foreign minister's secretariat. Berlin, March 8, 1941).

28. Ibid., 12: 243–44 (Schulenburg to the Foreign Ministry. Moscow, March 8, 1941).

29. Ibid., 12: 282–83 (deputy-director of the Economic Policy Department, Clodius, to the German embassy in the USSR. Berlin, March 12, 1941).

30. Ibid., 12: 474 (memorandum by Schnurre. Berlin, April 5, 1941).

31. Ibid., 12: 285 (Schulenburg to the Foreign Ministry. Moscow, March 12, 1941).

32. Ibid., 12:181) (memorandum by Woermann, director of the Political Department. Berlin, March 18, 1941).

33. Boberach, *Meldungen aus dem Reich*, 6: 2038–39 (February 24, 1941).

34. Ibid., 6: 2111 (March 17, 1941).

35. Ibid., 6: 2150–51 (March 20, 1941).

36. Ibid., 6: 2137 (March 25, 1941).

37. Ibid., 6: 2137 (March 25, 1941).

38. *DGFP*, 12: 475.

39. Ibid., 12: 329 (memorandum by the director of the Economic Policy Department. Berlin, March 21, 1941).

40. Ibid., 12: 220.

41. Boberach, *Meldungen us dem Reich*, 6: 2158 (March 27, 1941).

42. Ibid., p. 2178 (April 3, 1941), 2193 (April 10, 1941).

43. *DGFP*, 12: 388–89 (memorandum by Schmidt on the discussions of Hitler and Matsuoka. Berlin, April 1, 1941).

44. Ibid., 12: 473 (memorandum by Schmidt on the conversation between Ribbentrop and Matsuoka in Berlin on April 5, 1941. Berlin, April 7, 1941).

45. Ibid.

46. Ibid., 12: 379 (memorandum on the conversation between Ribbentrop and Matsuoka on March 27, 1941. Berlin, March 31, 1941).

47. Ibid., 12: 360 (memoranduym by Schmidt of the conversation between Hitler and Ciano. Vienna, March 25, 1941).

48. Ibid., 12: 219–20 (directive of the Supreme Military Command. March 5, 1941).

49. Ibid., 12: 413 (record of the talks between Ribbentrop and Matsuoka in Berlin on March 29, 1940).

50. Ibid.

51. *Vneshniaia politika SSSR*, 4: 549. The essence of the pact was contained in articles 1 and 2, which obliged the signatories to respect the territorial integrity and inviolability of each other and to remain neutral in the event the other were attacked by a third party. The two sides also issued a declaration reaffirming the territorial integrity of the Manchurian Government and the Mongolian People's Republic. Finally, Matsuoka promised to assist in terminating the activity of the Japanese concession in northern Sakhalin.

52. *DGFP*, 12: 537 (Schulenburg to the Foreign Ministry. Moscow, April 13, 1941).

53. Ibid., 12: 724–25 (German ambassador in Japan. Tokyo, May 6, 1941).

54. Ibid., 12: 666–67 (memorandum by Schulenburg on his conversation with Hitler on April 28, 1941).

55. Ibid., 12: 725, 809 (German ambassador in Japan to the Foreign Ministry. Tokyo, May 6 and May 14, 1941).

56. Bundesarchiv-Militärarchiv, RM 12/34, p. 199 (Moscow April 13, 1941).

57. DGFP, 12: 126–27 (Ambassador Ritter to the German embassy in the USSR. Berlin, February 22, 1941).

58. Ibid., 12: 182 (Ribbentrop to the German embassy in the USSR. Fuschl, February 27, 1941).

59. Ibid., 12: 195 (Schulenburg to the Foreign Ministry. Moscow, March 1, 1941).

60. Ibid., 12: 215 (Schulenburg to the Foreign Ministry. Moscow, March 3, 1941).

61. Ibid., 12: 250–51 (consulate in Harbin to the Foreign Ministry. Harbin, March 9, 1941).

62. Winston Churchill, The Second World War, 3 (London, 1950): 97.

63. The sides agreed to refrain from an attack, to respect the other's independence, territorial integrity and sovereignty. In the event of an attack by a third party, the other party agreed to pursue a friendly policy toward the victim of aggression.

64. DGFP, 12: 476 (Hitler to Mussolini. Berlin, April 5, 1941).

65. Ibid., 12: 480 (Ribbentrop to Schulenburg. Berlin, April 6, 1941).

66. Ibid., 12: 484 (Schulenburg to the Foreign Ministry. Moscow, April 6, 1941).

67. Ibid., 12: 490 (memorandum by Weizsäcker. Berlin, April 8, 1941).

68. Ibid., 12: 667 (Schulenburg's memorandum on his conversation with Hitler on April 28, 1941).

69. Köstring, 296 (Col. G. Krebs to Gen. G. Matzky. Moscow, April 9, 1941). Krebs was serving as the temporary replacement for the ailing Köstring.

70. Ibid., 4: 310 (memorandum by an official of the Foreign Ministry's secretariate, Schmidt. Berlin, March 18, 1941).

71. Ibid., 12: 537.

72. Köstring, 301 (Krebs to Matzky. Moscow, April 15, 1941).

73. DGFP, 12: 564 (charge d'affairs in Moscow to the Foreign Ministry. Moscow, April 16, 1941).

74. Ibid., 12: 560–61 (charge d'affairs to the Foreign Ministry. April 15, 1941).

75. Ibid., 12: 826 (memorandum by Schnurre. Berlin, May 15, 1941).

76. Ibid., 12: 602 (Foreign Ministry to the Supreme Military Command and to the Ministry of Transportation. April 21, 1941).

77. Ibid., 12: 827 (May 15, 1941).

78. Ibid., 12: 635–36 (charge d'affairs to the Foreign Ministry. Moscow, April 25, 1941).

79. Voenno-istoricheskii zhurnal, 1987, no. 9: 50–51.

80. Dmitrii Volkogonov, "22 iiunia 1941 g.," Znamia, 1992, no. 6: 7.

81. Gustav Hilger and Alfred G. Meyer, *The Incompatible Allies; a Memoir-History of German-Soviet Relations, 1918–1941* (New York: Macmillan, 1953), p. 328.

82. *DGFP*, 12: 661–62 (memorandum dated April 28, 1941).

83. Ibid., 12: 667–69.

84. Ibid., 12: 669, n. 6.

85. Walter Schmidt, "Russische Jahre," p. 98.

86. Ibid., 12: 730 (Schulenburg to the Foreign Ministry. Moscow, May 12, 1941).

87. Ibid., 12: 793 (Schulenburg to the Foreign Ministry. Moscow, May 12, 1941).

88. Ibid., 12: 734 (Schulenburg to Weizsäcker. Moscow, May 7, 1941).

89. Ibid., 12: 750.

90. Ibid., 12: 751 (Woermann to Schulenburg. Berlin, May 10, 1941).

91. Ibid., 12: 789–90 (Schulenburg to Woermann. Moscow, May 12, 1941).

92. Hilger and Meyer, *Incompatible Allies*, p. 330.

93. See my earlier comments about this in *1941. Juni 22.*, pp. 134–35.

94. "Dnevnik polpreda v Germanii t. Dekanozova," *Voenno-istoricheskii zhurnal*, 1991, no. 6: 22–23 (notes on the talks with Schulenburg on May 5, 1941).

95. This quotation comes from A. Mikoian, during an interview with the historian G. Kumanev. It is cited in an overview of Soviet diplomatic correspondence for 1940–1941 compiled by V. A. Vaiushin and S. A. Gorlov, "Fashistskaia agressiia: ochem soobshchali diplomaty," *Voenno-istoricheskii zhurnal*, 1991, no. 6: 20.

96. The same day that Schulenburg and Hilger met the Soviet representatives and the day preceding his own elevation to head of state.

97. *DGFP*, 12: 793 (consul at Harbin to the Foreign Ministry. May 13, 1941).

98. Ibid., 12: 964–965 (Schulenburg to the Foreign Ministry. Moscow, June 4, 1941).

99. Volkogonov reports that after the war, when plans were made to published volumes 14 and 15 of Stalin's collected works, the staff had a text prepared by an official in the defense ministry, K. Semenov. See Volkogonov, p. 4.

100. Volkogonov, p. 4.

101. *DGFP*, 12: 982 (memorandum by the head of Political Division I M. Berlin, June 7, 1941).

102. Ibid., 12: 996–1004 (record of a conversation between Hitler and Antonescu in Munich on June 11, 1941, in the presence of several top-ranking military officers).

103. Köstring, *Der militärische Mittler*, p. 301 (Krebs to Matzky. Moscow, April 22, 1941).

104. Ibid., p. 304.

105. Bundesarchiv-Militärchiv. RM 12/II/34, p.205 (report of May 3, 1941).

106. Ibid., RM 12/II/34, p. 216 (naval attaché in Moscow. April 24, 1941).

107. DGFP, 12: 304–7 (Köstring to Matzky. Moscow, May 14, 1941), 307–8 (enclosure to memorandum for the charge d'affairs, April 24, 1941).

108. Ibid., 12: 310 (Köstring to Matzky, May 21, 1941).

109. Ibid., 12: 311–12 (Köstring to Matzky. Moscow, May 28, 1941).

110. Bundesarchiv-Militärchiv. RMII/34, p. 238 (report from the German naval attaché in Moscow, May 21, 1941).

111. Ibid., RM/II/34, p. 320 (Köstring to Matzky. Moscow, June 18, 1941).

112. Shcherbakov (1901–1945), a member of the Central Commitee from 1939, became a candidate member of the Politburo in 1941. During World War II he was the head of the Soviet Information Bureau, later head of the Chief Political Administration of the Soviet army.

113. RTsKhIDNI, f. 17, op. 22, d. 1773, ch. 1, l. 16 (transcription of the eighth Moscow Oblast' and VII city conference, March 15, 1940).

114. Shkiriatov (1883–1954) first entered the apparatus of the Party Control Commission in 1939; the same year he became deputy chairman, acceding to the post of chairman in 1952.

115. Note that Shkiriatov unabashedly used the word "annex" (prisoedinit'), not the customary euphemistic "unite with" (vossoedinit'sia). RTsKhIDNI, f. 17, op. 22, d. 1773, ch. 3, l. 147 (March 17, 1940).

116. Ibid., f. 77, op. 1, d. 913, l. 62.

117. Ibid., d. 913, l. 65.

118. Ibid., ll. 65–66.

119. Kalinin (1875–1946), a member of the Politburo since 1926, was chairman of the presidium of the Supreme Soviet.

120. RTsKhIDNI, f. 78, op. 8. d. 140 (Kalinin's marginalia on the text of the Russian edition, entitled *Moia bor'ba*).

121. RTsKhIDNI, f. 78, op. 1, d. 84, ll. 6–7.

122. Ibid.

123. Ibid., l. 21.

124. Ibid., l. 20. Stalin would revive this language in 1949.

125. Ibid., l. 20.

126. Ibid., l. 35.

127. Ibid.

128. Ibid., l. 36.

129. Ibid.

130. Viktor Suvorov, *Icebreaker: Who Started the Second World War?* (London: Hamish Hamilton, 1990).

131. This has been abundantly described in Soviet and western historiography during the last two decades; a mere citation of titles would occupy more than a page.

132. Dmitrii Volkogonov, *Triumpf i tragediia*, 2/1 (Moscow, 1989): 136.

133. Vladimir Karpov, "Zhukov," *Kommunist vooruzhennykh sil*, 1990, No. 5: 67–68.

134. Both Volkogonov and Karpov cite a document in Zhukov's personal dossier in the archive of the Ministry of Defense.

135. Vasil'evskii (1895–1977) later attained the rank of marshal, then chief of staff (1943) and minister of the armed forces (1949–53).

136. Timoshenko (1895–1970) had achieved the rank of marshal and served as defense minister in 1940–41.

137. Meretskov (1897–1968), who served as chief of staff until March 1941, subsequently became a marshal of the USSR (1944).

138. "Soobrazheniia ob osnovakh strategicheskogo razvertyvaniia Vooruzhennykh sil Sovetskogo Soiuza na Zapade i na Vostoke na 1940 i 1941 gody," *Voenno-istoricheskii zhurnal*, 1992, no. 1: 24–27.

139. "Utochnennyi plan strategicheskogo razvertyvaniia Vooruzhennykh sil Sovetskogo Soiuza na Zapade i na Vostoke," *Voenno-istoricheskii zhurnal*, 1992, no. 2: 18–22.

140. Ibid., p. 17.

141. A. M. Vasilevskii, "Nakanune voiny," *Novaia i noveishaia istoriia*, 1992, no. 6: 8.

142. "Gotovil li SSSR preventivnyi udar?," *Voenno-istoricheskii zhurnal*, 1992, no. 1: 4–5.

143. *Novaia i noveishaia istoriia*, 1992, no. 6: 4–5.

144. Ibid., p. 10.

145. V. N. Kiselev, "Upriamye fakty nachala voiny," *Voenno-istoricheskii zhurnal*, 1992, no. 2: 14.

146. Ibid., p. 15.

147. *Izvestiia*, June 14, 1941.

148. Vasilevskii, "Nakanune voiny," p. 10.

149. Ibid., p. 7.

150. A. M. Nekrich, *Vneshniaia politika Anglii* (Moscow: Izdatel'stvo Akademii nauk SSSR, 1963), pp. 490–98, 508, 518.

151. For details see my book *1941. 22 iiunia* (Moscow, 1965). This volume has since appeared in English, although in a bizarre form: Vladimir Petrov, ed.,*Soviet Historians on the German Invasion. 1941, June 22* (Columbia: University of South Carolina Press, 1968).

152. Vasilevskii, "Nakanune voiny," p. 7.

153. Ibid., p. 6.

154. Boberach, *Meldungen aus dem Reich*, 7: 3374 (May 8, 1941).

155. Ibid., 7: 2286–87 (May 12, 1941).

156. Ibid., 7: 2313 (May 19, 1941).

157. Ibid., 7: 2331 (May 22, 1941).

158. Ibid., 7: 2341 (May 26, 1941).

159. Ibid., 7: 2380 (June 9, 1941).

160. Ibid., 7: 2394 (June 12, 1941).

161. *Izvestiia TsK KPSS*, 1990, no.4: 198–218.

162. Ibid., p. 200.

163. Ibid.

164. *Voenno-istoricheskii zhurnal*, 1992, no. 2: 15.

165. Ibid.

166. RTsKhIDNI, f. 78, op. 1, d. 846, l. 2.

167. *Voenno-istoricheskii zhurnal*, 1992, no. 1: 22.

168. Volkogonov, "22 iiunia 1941 g.," *Znamia*, 1992, no.6: 5.

169. Ibid.

170. Ibid., p. 6.

171. *Voenno-istoricheskii zhurnal*, 1992, no. 4–5: 20–21. The court separately reviewed the case of the head of artillery in this front, Lieutenant-General Nikolai Aleksandrovich Klich, who was sentenced to execution on September 7, 1941. (ibid., pp. 21–22).

172. Nekrich, *1941, iiun' 22*, p. 140.

173. Lavrentii Pavlovich Beria was a Politburo member, head of the NKVD and marshal of the Soviet Union; he was arrested shortly after Stalin's death and executed in December 1953.

174. Filipp Ivanovich Golikov (1900–1980) became head of the Main Intelligence Administration shortly before the outbreak of the war. He became a marshal of the USSR in 1961. A portion of my interview with Golikov appeared in *1941, 22 iiunia*; the full text is in *Forsake Fear. Memoirs of an Historian* (Boston: Unwin Hyman, 1991).

175. Ian Karlovich Berzin (1889–1938) was appointed head of the Main Intelligence Administration in 1937, but executed the following year.

176. V. A. Novobranets, the head of the information bureau of military intelligence, had come into conflict with Golikov, who (in Novobranets's opinion) sought to please Stalin and constantly downplayed intelligence reports on the number of German divisions poised along the Soviet border. Novobranets was dismissed from his post after changing the numbers of a document that Golikov had signed and that was to be sent to Stalin. Novobranets's memoirs circulated in Moscow in the 1960s, and have been previously cited in the works of General P. G. Grigorenko as well as the present author.

177. *Znamia*, 1990, no. 6: 165.

178. Hilger and Meyer, *Incompatible Allies*, p. 330.

179. *Izvestiia TsK KPSS*, 1990, no.4: 202–3.

180. *Izvestiia*, December 25, 1939.

181. S. Allilueva, *Only One Year* (New York: Harper and Row, 1970), p. 392.

182. *Vneshniaia politika SSSR. 1949* (Moscow, 1953), p. 28.

Bibliography

Archives

Arkhiv vneshnei politiki Rossiiskoi federatsii (Moscow)
Auswärtiges Amt (Bonn)
Bundesarchiv-Militärarchiv (Freiburg-im-Breisgau)
Foreign Office (London)
Gosudarstvennyi arkhiv Novosibirskoi oblasti (Novosibirsk)
Gosudarstvennyi arkhiv Rossiiskoi Federatsii (Moscow)
Partiinyi arkhiv Moskovskogo komiteta i Moskovskogo gorodskogo
  komiteta KPSS (Moscow)
Rossiiskii gosudarstvennyi arkhiv Sovetskoi armii (Moscow)
Rossiiskii gosudarstvennyi arkhiv ekonomiki (Moscow)
Rossiiskii tsentr khraneniia i izucheniia dokumentov noveishei istorii
  (Moscow)
Trotsky Archive (Harvard University, Cambridge, Mass.)
Tsentral'nyi gosudarstvennyi arkhiv oktiabr'skoi revoliutsii Estonskoi SSR
  (Tallin)

Newspapers and Journals

Izvestiia
Izvestiia TsK KPSS
Krasnaia zvezda
Pravda
Voenno-istoricheskii zhurnal

Works Cited

Akten zur deutschen auswärtigen Politik 1918–1945. 42 vols. Baden-Baden, 1950–1988.

Allilueva, S. *Only One Year.* New York: Harper and Row, 1970.

Ansel, Walter. *Hitler Confronts England.* Durham: Duke University Press, 1960.

Aptekar', P.A. "Opravdanny li zhertvy? O poteriakh v sovetsko-finliandskoi voine," *Voenno-istoricheskii zhurnal,* 1992, no. 2:43–44.

Attlee, C. *As It Happened.* London, 1954.

Boberach, Heinz, ed. *Meldungen aus dem Reich. Die geheimen Lageberichte des Sicherheitsdienstes des SS 1938–1945.* 7 vols. Herrsching: Pawlag Verlag, 1984.

Butler, J.R.M. *Grand Strategy,* 2 (London 1957): 119–20.

Carsten, F. L. *The Reichswehr and Politics, 1918 to 1933.* Oxford: Clarendon Press, 1966.

Carsten, F. L. "Reports by Two German Officers on the Red Army," Bundesarchiv-Militärarchiv (Bestand E III, d. 116).

Chuev, F. *Sto sorok besed s Molotovym. Iz dnevnika F. Chueva.* Moscow, 1991.

Churchill, Winston. *The Second World War,* 1 (London, 1949): 667.

Cretzianu, Alexandre. *The Lost Opportunity.* London, 1957.

D'iakov, Iu. L. and T. S. Bushueva. *Fashistskii mech kovalsia v SSSR. Krasnaia armiia i Reikhsver. Tainoe sotrudnichestvo 1922–1933. Neizvestnye dokumenty.* Moscow: Sovetskaia Rossiia, 1992.

Dirksen, Herbert von. *Moskau, Tokio, London.* Stuttgart, 1950.

Dnevnik polpreda v Germanii t. Dekanozova," *Voenno-istoricheskii zhurnal,* 1991, no. 6: 22–23.

Documents on German Foreign Policy, 1918–1945, from the Archives of the German Foreign Ministry. Series C (16 vols) and Series D (1–14 vols). Washington: U.S. Government Printing Office, 1949–1983.

Dongarov, A.G. "Pred"iavlialsia li Finliandii ul'timatum?" *Voenno-istoricheskii zhurnal,* 1990, no. 3: 43–45.

Firsov, F. I. "Stalin i Komintern," *Voprosy istorii KPSS,* 1989, no. 9: 12.

Firsov, F.I. "Arkhivy Kominterna i vneshniaia politika SSSR v 1939–1941 gg.," *Novaia i noveishaia istoriia,* 1992, no. 6: 12–35.

Foreign Relations of the United States. Diplomatic Papers. 1940, vol. 1 (Washington,). 1941: vol. 1. (Washington, 1948).

Friedensberg, F. "Die sowjetischen Kriegslieferungen an das Hitlerreich," *Viertelsjahrheft zur Wirtschaftsforschung,* 4 (1962): 331–68.

Gnedin, E. *Iz istorii otnoshenii mezhdu SSSR i fashistskoi Germaniei. Khronika-press.* New York, 1977.

Goebbels, P. F. *The Goebbels Diaries, 1939–1941.* New York: Penguin, 1982.

"Gotovil li SSSR preventivnyi udar?," *Voenno-istoricheskii zhurnal,* 1992, no. 1: 7–15.

Great Britain, Foreign Office. *Documents of British Foreign Policy, 1919–1939.* Third Series (10 vols.). London, 1946-in progress.

Groeler, Olaf. *Selbstmörderische Allianz. Deutsch-russische Militärbeziehungen, 1920–1941.* Berlin: Vision Verlag, 1992.

Halder, Franz. *The Halder Diaries.* 2 vols. Boulder: Westview Press, 1976.

Hencke, A. "Der politische Einfluß des Botschafters Graf Brockdorf-Rantzau auf die Entwicklung der deutsch-sowjetischen Beziehungen. Erinnerungen seines persönlichen Referenten, Andor Hencke." Unpublished manuscript, Auswärtiges Amt, Bonn.

Hencke, A. "Die deutsch-sowjetischen Beziehungen auf militärischem Gebiet nach dem ersten Weltkrieg." Unpublished manuscript, Auswärtiges Amt, Bonn.

Hilger, Gustav and Alfred G. Meyer. *The Incompatible Allies.* New York: MacMillan, 1953.

Hilger, Gustav. *The Incompatible Allies.* New York: MacMillan, 1953.

Hitlers Weisungen für die Kriegführung. Munich, 1965.

Istoriia Kommunisticheskoi partii Sovetskogo Soiuza. Moscow, 1959.

"Iz arkhivov partii," *Izvestiia TsK KPSS,* 1990, no. 2: 194–17. 1990, no. 1: 173–217; no. 3: 203–23; no. 4: 219–23

"Iz istorii Velikoi Otechestvennoi Voiny," *Izvestiia TsK KPSS,* 1990, no. 1.

"Iz otklikov na stat'iu M.N. Tukhachevskogo," *Izvestiia TsK KPSS,* 1990, no. 1: 170–72.

Karpov, Vladimir. "Zhukov," *Kommunist vooruzhennykh sil,* 1990, No. 5: 67–68.

Kiselev, V. N. "Upriamye fakty nachala voiny," *Voenno-istoricheskii zhurnal,* 1992, no. 2: 14–15.

"Komintern i sovetsko-germanskii dogovor o nenapadenii," *Izvestiia TsK KPSS,* 1989, no. 12: 202–15.

"Kommentarii Ministerstva oborony SSSR. Smena rukovodstva Narkomata oborony SSSR v sviazi s urokami sovetsko-finliandskoi voiny 1939–1940 gg.," *Izvestiia TsK KPSS,* 1990, no. 1: 211.

Köstring, Ernst. *General Ernst Köstring. Der militärische Mittler zwischen dem Deutschen Reich und der Sowjetunion 1921–1941,* ed. Hermann Teske *Profile bedeutender Soldaten,* ed. Bundesarchiv and Militärarchiv, vol. 1: (Frankfurt-am-Main: Verlag E. S. Mittler & Sohn, n. d.), p. 41.

Krivitsky, W. G. *In Stalin's Secret Service.* New York: Harper and Brothers Publishers, 1939. Reprint: Frederick, Maryland, 1985.

Krivosheev, G. F. *Poteri vooruzhennykh sil SSSR v voinakh, boevykh deistvi-*

iakh i voennykh konfliktakh. Statisticheskoe issledovanie. Moscow: Voennoe izdatel'stvo, 1993.

Krummacher, F.A. and G. Lange. "Planiroval li Stalin voinu protiv Germanii?" *Voenno-istoricheskii zhurnal*, 1992, no. 6: 26–40.

Kuznetsov, N.G. "Nashi otnosheniia s Zhukovym stali poistinne dramaticheskimi," *Voenno-istoricheskii zhurnal*, 1992, no. 2: 74–82. G.M. Shtern

Lebedev, V.A. "O masshtabakh represii v krasnoi armii v predvorennye gody," *Voenno-istoricheskii zhurnal*, 1993, no. 1: 56–63.

Leibzon, B. M. and K. K. Shirinia. *Povorot v politike Kominterna.* Moscow, 1975.

Les evenements survenue en France de 1933 à 1945 7 vols. Paris, 1947–51.

Manchester Guardian, 7 February 1936.

Ministerstvo inostrannykh del SSSR. *God krizisa, 1938–1939. Dokumenty i materialy.* Moscow: Gospolitizdat, 1990.

"Nakanune voiny (1940–1941)," *Izvestiia TsK KPSS*, 1990, no. 2: 180–93; no. 4: 198–218; no. 3: 192–202.

Nazi-Soviet Relations, 1939–1941. Documents from the Archives of the German Foreign Office. Washington, 1948.

Nekrich, A. M. *1941. 22 iiunia.* Moscow, 1965. Translated in full in: Vladimir Petrov, *Soviet Historians and the German Invasion. 1941, June 22* (South Carolina University Press, 1968).

Nekrich, A. M. *Forsake Fear. Memoirs of an Historian.* Boston: Unwin Hyman, 1991.

Nekrich, A. M. *Politika angliiskogo imperializma v Evrope (oktiabr' 1938—sentiabr' 1939).* Moscow: Akademii nauk, 1955.

New York Times, 15 October 1992.

Niclauss, Karl-Heinz. *Die Sowjetunion und Hitlers Machtergreifung.* Bonn, 1966.

Novaia i noveishaia istoriia, 1992, no. 6: 4–5.

Perepiska V. M. Molotova so I. V. Stalinym. Noiabr' 1940g.," *Voenno-istoricheskii zhurnal*, 1992, no. 9: 18–23.

Postanovlenie TsK KPSS 'O gazete *Pravda*,' " *Pravda*, April 7, 1990.

Reynaud, Paul. *La France a sauvé l'Europe.* 2 vols. Paris, 1947.

Russia and the West," *Economist*, July 27, 1940, pp. 113–14.

Schmidt, Walter. "Russische Jahre. Erlebtes aus 40 Jahren deutsch-sowjetischer Beziehungen." Manuscript. Auswärtiges Amt, Bonn.

Shakhurin, A. I. *Kryl'ia pobedy.* 3rd ed. Moscow, 1990.

Sheinis, Z. *Maksim Maksimovich Litvinov: revoliutsioner, diplomat, chelovek.* Moscow, 1989.

Shishkin, V. "Sovetskie nemtsy; u istokov tragedii," *Nauka v Sibiri*, 1992, August, no. 28:.

Simonov, K. M. "Zametki k biografii," *Voenno-istoricheskii zhurnal*, 1987, no. 6: 45–56, no. 7: 45–56, no. 9: 48–56, no. 12: 56–63, no. 12: 40–45.

"Soobrazheniia ob osnovakh strategicheskogo razvertyvaniia Vooruzhen-
nykh sil Sovetskogo Soiuza na Zapade i na Vostoke na 1940 i 1941
gody," *Voenno-istoricheskii zhurnal*, 1992, no. 1: 24–27.
Speidel, Helm. "Reichswehr und Rote Armee," *Vierteljahrshefte für Zeit-
geschichte*, 16 (1953): 10–45.
Stalin, I. V. *Sochineniia*. 13 Vols. Moscow, 1949–51.
Stalin, I. V. *Voprosy leninizma*. Moscow, 1939.
Suvorov, Viktor. *Icebreaker: Who Started the Second World War?* London:
Hamish Hamilton, 1990.
Trial of the Major War Criminals before the International Military Tribunal.
Nürnberg, 1947.
Ulam, Adam B. *Stalin: The Man and His Era*. Boston: Beacon Press,
1989.
"Upriamye fakty nachala voiny," *Voenno-istoricheskii zhurnal*, 1992, no. 2:
14–23.
"Utochnennyi plan strategicheskogo razvertyvaniia Vooruzhennykh sil
Sovetskogo Soiuza na Zapade i na Vostoke," *Voenno-istoricheskii zhurnal*,
1992, no. 2: 18–22.
"V komissiiakh TsK KPSS," *Izvestiia TsK KPSS*, 1989, no. 7: 28–38.
V. Kholodkovskii, "Eta zimniaia voina," *Leninskaia pravda* (Petrozavodsk),
4 January 1990.
Vaiushin, V. A. and S. A. Gorlov, "Fashistskaia agressiia: o chem soob-
shchali diplomaty," *Voenno-istoricheskii zhurnal*, 1991, no. 6: 20.
Vasilevskii, A. M. "Nakanune 22 iiunia 1941 g.," *Novaia i noveishaia
istoriia*, 1992, no. 6: 3–11.
"Verkhovnyi Sud Soiuza SSR. Opredelenie No. 4n-0280/57," in *Izvestiia
TsK KPSS*, 1990, no. 4: 64.
Vneshniaia politika Sovetskogo Soiuza. 8 vols. Moscow, 1945-in progress.
Vneshniaia politika SSSR, vols 16, 18, 20
Vneshniaia politika SSSR. 1949. Moscow, 1953.
"Voennye razvedchiki dokladyvali," *Voenno-istoricheskii zhurnal*, 1992, no.
2: 36–42.
Volkogonov, Dmitrii. "22 iiunia 1941 goda," *Znamia*, 1992, no. 6: 3–15.
Volkogonov, Dmitrii. "Leninskaia krepost' v moei dushe pala poslednei,"
Moskovskie novosti, 1992, no. 29 (19 July).
Volkogonov, Dmitrii. *Triumf i tragediia*. 2 vols. Moscow, 1989.
Vormsbekher, Gugo. "Nemtsy v SSSR," *Znamia*, 1988, no. 11: 193–203.
Weingartner, Thomas. *Stalin und der Aufstieg Hitlers*. Berlin: Walter de
Gruyter & Co., 1970.
XIII plenum IKKI. Tezisy i postanovleniia. Moscow: Partizdat, 1934.
"Zakliuchitel'naia rech' narodnogo komissara oborony SSSR S.K.Timo-
shenko na voennom soveshchanii 31 dekabria 1940 g.," *Voenno-istorich-
eskii zhurnal*, 1992, no. 1: 16–29.

Other Books by the Same Author

"June 22, 1941." Soviet Historians and the German Invasion. Columbia:
  University of South Carolina Press, 1968.
The Punished Peoples. New York: W. W. Norton, 1979.
Utopia in Power. The History of the Soviet Union from 1917 to the Present.
  (Co-authored with Mikhail Heller). New York: Summit Books, 1985.
Forsake Fear. Memoirs of an Historian. Boston: Hyman, 1991.

Index